Naci Yorulmaz trained in economics (BA) and economic history (MA) at the University of Marmara, Turkey. He completed his PhD at the University of Birmingham in 2011. Prior to his doctoral studies, Dr Yorulmaz has also studied economics and economic history at the University of Heidelberg, Tübingen and Freie University Berlin in Germany. Dr Yorulmaz carried out his post-doctoral research at the University of Washington, Seattle and at Stanford University. His research interests include economic history, business history and political economy in general, the political economy of the international arms trade and defense industry in particular.

ARMING THE SULTAN

German Arms Trade and Personal Diplomacy in the Ottoman Empire Before World War I

NACI YORULMAZ

I.B.TAURIS
LONDON • NEW YORK • OXFORD • NEW DELHI • SYDNEY

I.B. TAURIS
Bloomsbury Publishing Plc
50 Bedford Square, London, WC1B 3DP, UK
1385 Broadway, New York, NY 10018, USA
29 Earlsfort Terrace, Dublin 2, Ireland

BLOOMSBURY, I.B. TAURIS and the I.B. Tauris logo are
trademarks of Bloomsbury Publishing Plc

First published in Great Britain 2014
Paperback edition published 2021

Copyright © Naci Yorulmaz, 2014

Naci Yorulmaz has asserted his right under the Copyright,
Designs and Patents Act, 1988, to be identified as Author of this work.

For legal purposes the Acknowledgements on p. xvii constitute
an extension of this copyright page.

All rights reserved. No part of this publication may be reproduced or
transmitted in any form or by any means, electronic or mechanical,
including photocopying, recording, or any information storage or retrieval
system, without prior permission in writing from the publishers.

Bloomsbury Publishing Plc does not have any control over, or responsibility for,
any third-party websites referred to or in this book. All internet addresses given
in this book were correct at the time of going to press. The author and publisher
regret any inconvenience caused if addresses have changed or sites have
ceased to exist, but can accept no responsibility for any such changes.

A catalogue record for this book is available from the British Library.

A catalog record for this book is available from the Library of Congress.

ISBN: HB: 978-1-7807-6633-1
PB: 978-0-7556-4229-8
ePDF: 978-0-8577-2518-9
eBook: 978-0-8577-3668-0

Series: Library of Ottoman Studies 43

Typeset by OKS Prepress Services, Chennai, India

To find out more about our authors and books visit
www.bloomsbury.com and sign up for our newsletters.

To my father and mother for their endless support and encouragement. To my wife for her patience and support. To my children İbrahim Esad, Tarık Yahya and Yusuf Tuna for being my true inspiration.

CONTENTS

List of Tables and Figures viii
List of Maps and Images xi
List of Abbreviations xii
Notes on Usage xv
Acknowledgements xvii

Introduction 1
1. The German Expansionist Wave and the Political Economy of German Style of War Business in the Ottoman Empire (1880–98) 15
2. German Military Advisers: Businessmen in Uniform 68
3. Arms Orders and Contracts: The First Fruits of Personal Diplomacy 97
4. Kaiser Wilhelm II and the Political Economy of Personal Diplomacy (1898–1914) 133
5. Sultan Abdülhamid II and his Bureaucrats (1876–1909) 177
6. The Power Shift and its Consequences (1908–14) 230
Conclusion 252

Notes 262
Bibliography 325
Index 342

LIST OF TABLES AND FIGURES

Table 1.1: Allocation of the Deutsche Bank Loan in 1888
(in Ottoman Lira)   39

Table 1.2: German Colonial Expansion, 1884–96
(in Square Miles)   48

Table 1.3: Steel Production by Major Producers,
1886–1910 (in 1000 Tons)   50

Table 1.4: Pig-iron Production by Major Producers,
1887–1911 (in 1000 Tons)   51

Table 1.5: Germany's Foreign Trade, 1860–1913
(in British Pounds)   52

Table 1.6: Five Principal Manufactured Goods in Germany
and their Percentage Exports in 1913   53

Table 1.7: The Length and Opening Dates of the
Railways Laid by Anatolian Railway Company   61

Table 1.8: Tithe Paid (in Ottoman *Kuruş*)   61

Table 1.9: Ottoman Trade with Germany, 1880–97
(in Marks)   64

Table 1.10: War Materials Exports from Germany to
the Ottoman Empire 1888–98 (in Marks)   65

List of Tables and Figures

Table 1.11: Export from Germany to the Ottoman
Empire (selected items; in Marks) — 65

Table 1.12: The Bondholders of the Ottoman Converted
Debt, 1881–98 (in Thousands of Ottoman Lira) — 67

Table 2.1: Sales of Krupp: Military Products 1875–1891
(in Marks) — 69

Table 2.2: Sales of Krupp: Non-Military Products
1875–91 (in Marks) — 70

Table 2.3: Mauser's Total Sales (1874–1914) — 72

Table 2.4: First Appointed German Military Mission
(Kähler Mission) in 1882 and its Staff's Annual Salary — 78

Table 2.5: Salary of the Ottoman Officers (1902) — 79

Table 3.1: Rifle Production in *Tüfenkhâne-i 'Âmire* in 1881 — 98

Table 3.2: Ottoman Artillery Orders from the Krupp
Company (1861–75) — 99

Table 3.3: Ottoman Warships and the Krupp Orders
(1883) — 101

Table 3.4: Krupp Guns and their Prices (Ordered in 1885) — 104

Table 3.5: Krupp Guns and their Prices (Ordered in 1886) — 104

Table 3.6: Ottoman Artillery (Guns and Mortars) ordered
from the Krupp Company — 106

Table 3.7: Names and their Encrypted Codes (in November
1886) — 112

Table 3.8: Mauser Rifles in the Ottoman Army
(1886–1908) — 128

Table 3.9a: Places to Which the Purchased Mauser Rifles
Were Sent (M/90:7.65) — 129

Table 3.9b: Places to Which the Purchased Mauser Rifles
were sent (M/93:7.65)   130

Table 3.9c: Places, to Which the Purchased Cartridges
Were Sent (M/90–93:7.65)   130

Table 4.1: Ottoman Trade with Germany, 1895–1912
(in Marks)   147

Table 4.2: Financial Participation of Foreign Financiers
in the Baghdad Railway (1903)   152

Table 4.3: The Bondholders of the Ottoman Converted
Debt, 1898–1913 (in %)   157

Table 5.1: The Technical Comparison of the World's
Major Contenders/Gun Producers (1889)   227

Figure 1.1: Population Growth in Europe: 1820–1915
(000 at mid-year)   49

Figure 1.2: Ottoman Trade with Germany 1878–96
(in marks)   63

Figure 2.1: Information Flow via Some of the GMAs
and the Government   75

Figure 2.2: Goltz Pasha's Special Information Net   88

Figure 2.3: Change in Total Active *Nizâmiye*-Troops   94

Figure 3.1: Mauser's Entrance into the Ottoman Market
1886/87   113

Figure 4.1: Ottoman Trade with Germany, 1878–1913
(in Marks)   148

Figure 5.1: The Information Flow towards the German
Arms Companies   199

LIST OF MAPS AND IMAGES

Map 4.1: Haydarpaşa–İzmit Railway with its Projected Extensions in Asia Minor up to the Persian Gulf, dated 4 February 1885   149

Image 2.1: Photo Sent by Gazi Mustafa Kemal Pasha (Atatürk) to Kamphövener Pasha   77

Image 4.1: The Wreath Laid by Kaiser Wilhelm II on the Tomb of Sultan Saladin (in 1898)   141

Image 5.1: *Türkenbau* in Oberndorf am Neckar built in 1887   221

Image 5.2: Turkish Young Volunteers in *Türkenbau* in Oberndorf am Neckar   222

Image 5.3: Playing Cards in the Pavilion Rosenberg/ Oberndorf am Neckar (*c*.1893)   223

Image 6.1: The Sale of German Warships, Karagöz and Kaiser Wilhelm II   246

LIST OF ABBREVIATIONS

GAFs	German Armament Firms
GCMAs	German Civil and Military Advisers
GMAs	German Military Advisers
HA, Krupp: FAH	Historisches Archiv-Krupp – Familie Archive Essen
HA, Krupp: WA	Historisches Archiv-Krupp – Werk Archiv Essen
LA, Schleswig-Holstein	Landesarchiv Schleswig-Holstein
MA, Freiburg	Military Archive, Freiburg
NA, London	National Archives, London
NA, London: ADM	Admiralty Office: National Archives, London
NA, London: FO	Foreign Office: National Archives, London
NA, London: GFM	German Foreign Ministry Microfilm: National Archives, London
NA, London: WO	War Office: National Archives, London
NARA	National Archives, College Park, Maryland
OL	Ottoman Lira
PA.AA	Politisches Archiv des Auswärtigen Amtes

LIST OF ABBREVIATIONS

SA, Oberndorf	Stadt-und Zeitungsarchiv Oberndorf/ Neckar-Germany
WWI	World War I

*** *** ***

A.MKT.MHM.	Sadâret Mektûb-i Kalem-i Mühimme Odası
BOA	Başbakanlık Osmanlı Arşivi
DH. MKT.	Dahiliye Nezâreti Mektûbi Kalemi
HR. SYS.	Hariciye Nezâreti Siyasî
HR.татар.	Hariciye Evrâkı
İ. ASK.	İrâde – 'Askeri
İ. DH.	İrâde – Dahiliye
İ. HR	İrâde – Hariciye
İ. MMS	İrâde – Meclîs-i Mahsûsa
MV.	Meclîs-i Vükelâ Mazbatası
Y. A. HUS.	Yıldız Perâkende Sadâret Hususi Mâ'rûzât Evrâkı
Y. A. RES.	Yıldız Perâkende Sadaret Resmi Mâ'rûzât Evrâkı
Y. EE.	Yıldız Esas ve Sadrazam Kâmil Paşa Evrâkı
Y. MRZ. D.	Yıldız Mâ'rûzât Defteri
Y. MTV.	Yıldız Mütenevvi Mâ'rûzât
Y. PRK. ASK.	Yıldız Perâkende 'Askeri Mâ'rûzât Evrâkı
Y. PRK. AZJ.	Yıldız Perâkende Arzuhaller ve Jurnaller
Y. PRK. BŞK.	Yıldız Perâkende Başkitâbet Dâiresi
Y. PRK. EŞA.	Yıldız Perâkende Elçilik ve Şehbenderlik Mâ'rûzâtı
Y. PRK. HH.	Yıldız Perâkende Hazine-i Hâssa Nezâreti Evrâkı

ARMING THE SULTAN

Y. PRK. HR.	Yıldız Perâkende Hariciye Nezâreti Mâ'rûzâtı
Y. PRK. KOM	Yıldız Perâkende Komisyonlar Mâ'rûzâtı
Y. PRK. ML.	Yıldız Perâkende Maliye Nezâreti Mâ'rûzâtı
Y. PRK. MM.	Yıldız Perâkende Mâbeyn Müşîriyeti
Y. PRK. MYD.	Yaverân ve Maiyet-i Seniye Erkân-ı Harbiye Dâiresi
Y. PRK. NMH.	Yıldız Perâkende Nâme-i Hümâyûnlar
Y. PRK. OMZ.	Yıldız Perâkende Orman, Ma'âdin, Ziraat Nezâreti Mâ'rûzâtı
Y. PRK. PT.	Yıldız Perâkende Posta ve Telgraf Nezâreti Mâ'rûzâtı
Y. PRK. SGE.	Yıldız Perâkende Mâbeyn Erkânı ve Saray Görevlileri
Y. PRK. SRN.	Yıldız Perâkende Ser-kurenâlık Evrâkı
Y. PRK. TKM.	Yıldız Perâkende Mâbeyn Mütercimliği
Y. PRK. UM.	Yıldız Perâkende Umum Vilâyetler Tahrîrâtı
Y. PRK. ZB.	Yıldız Perâkende Zabtiye Nezâreti Mâ'rûzâtı

NOTES ON USAGE

(1) In this study, the modern Turkish spelling system has been used for Ottoman–Turkish words, according to the transliterations given in the Redhouse Turkish/Ottoman–English Dictionary (İstanbul 1999).

(2) Aside from the following exceptions, the Latin letters of the Ottoman/Turkish are pronounced almost the same as in English. The exceptions and their sounds are as follows:

Ş/ş	sh
Ç/ç	ch
İ/i	i
I/ı	like the *io* in *pension*
Ö/ö	like the German ö
Ü/ü	like the German ü

(3) Turkish place names have been spelled in the modern Turkish way, e.g.
- İstanbul, not Constantinople/Istanbul;
- Haydarpaşa, not Haidarpascha/Haidarpasha;
- Eskişehir, not Eskischehir;
- İzmir, not Smyrna.

(4) The following rates have been used for the currency conversions.

	1 Ottoman Lira (c.1892)	1 Silver Kuruş (c.1892)
Pound	0,9033	0,008804
Franc	22,7841	0,222067
Mark	18,4551	0,179874

Source: McCarthy, Justin, *The Arab World, Turkey and the Balkans (1878-1914): A Handbook of Historical Statistic* (Boston, MA, 1982), p.155.

(5) Dates in Hijri Calendar were converted into Gregorian dates by using the converter at the following website: www.ttk.gov.tr/*Tarih Çevirme Kılavuzu*. The Ottoman documents used in this dissertation are listed in the footnote as follows:

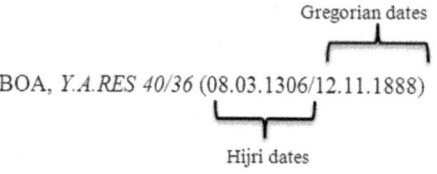

BOA, Y.A.RES 40/36 (08.03.1306/12.11.1888)

with Gregorian dates indicated and Hijri dates indicated.

ACKNOWLEDGEMENTS

The publication of this book could not have been possible without the support of numerous academic institutions and individuals from various parts of the world. Firstly I must express my sincere thanks to all who helped me throughout this process, but my special thanks are to Rhoads Murphey for his guidance, friendship and unfailing encouragement during and after my doctoral research at the University of Birmingham, where this book first took shape as a dissertation.

I must also express my sincere gratitude to Professors Ahmet Tabakoğlu, Sabri Orman, Erol Özvar, Gülfettin Çelik, Fahri Solak and R. Deniz Özbay of University of Marmara, İstanbul, for their constant friendship, support and guidance. I am especially indebted to Ahmet Tabakoğlu, who was the first person to direct me into postgraduate studies in Economic History of the Ottoman Empire. Erol Özvar has always encouraged and supported my academic endeavours even since my earlier days of undergraduate studies. I also wish to acknowledge Inayatullah Baloch, Wolfgang-Peter Zingel of the University of Heidelberg, and Nikolaus Wolf, Holm Sundhaussen of Freie Universität Berlin for their friendship and assistance during and after my study in Germany.

I should also like to extend my gratitude to Reşat Kasaba, the Director of the Henry M. Jackson School of International Studies at the University of Washington, where I was a Postdoctoral Visiting Scholar. I also owe a special thanks to the wonderful staffs of the Center for

Latin American Studies at Stanford University, where I conducted a comparative research on Germany's state-backed arms sales operations in the Ottoman Empire and the Latin American countries (1880–1914). My sincere thanks are to Professor Rodolfo, Elizabeth, Angela, Laura and Molly for their invaluable friendship, help and for providing the facilities of *Bolivar House* that extremely facilitated my postdoctoral research and stay in Stanford: *Muchas Gracias*.

Since this book is heavily based upon archival documents, I would like to acknowledge the staffs of the following archives in Turkey, Germany, England and the United States for their generous assistance, kind hospitality and the permission to use and display some images and records from their collections: The Prime Minister Ottoman Archives-State Archive (İstanbul/Turkey), British National Archives (London-Kew Gardens/UK), *Politisches Archiv des Auswärtigen Amtes* (Berlin/Germany), *Bundesarchiv* (Berlin/Germany), *Bundesarchiv-Militärarchiv* (Freiburg/Germany); *Stadt- und Zeitungsarchiv Oberndorf* (Oberndorf am Neckar/Germany), *Historisches Archiv Krupp* (Essen/Germany), *Landesarchiv Schleswig-Holstein* (Schleswig/Germany), The National Archives and Records Administration (College Park, MD/USA); The Hoover Institution Library and Archives at Stanford University (Stanford, CA/USA). Among them however my special thanks are to the director of the *Stadt-und Zeitungsarchiv Oberndorf*, Andreas Kussmann-Hochhalter, who was very helpful and generous with the archival materials including the books and newspapers housed there as well as with his time and understanding. Manuela Fellner-Feldhaus of the *Historisches Archiv Krupp/Essen* provided me also with kind assistance and was also very helpful and amiable during my research in *Villa Hügel* in Essen/Germany. Gerhard Keiper of Politisches Archiv des Auswärtigen Amtes in Berlin was also very friendly and helpful.

I am also grateful to my publisher I.B.Tauris Publishers, an imprint of Bloomsbury Publishing, and especially I would like to thank to Rory Gormley, Yasmin Garcha and Tomasz Hoskins for enabling me to publish this paperback edition. I am also thankful to Allison Walker, Kevin Randall, Sarah Hutchinson and Elizabeth Angell for their feedback, editing and proofreading. Finally, my deepest thanks are to my family and parents. Without their constant support and encouragement, this book would not have been possible.

INTRODUCTION

'We need to make the country economically dependent on us in order to be able to control it politically later.'

Friedrich Naumann[1]

On the eve of World War I, German armament firms (hereafter GAFs) gradually achieved a monopoly position in the Ottoman arms market. The main determinants of their success cannot be ascribed to the market theory of supply and demand, but lie instead in a range of manipulative instruments built on foundations that were formed through close personal relations. Germany's success in the Ottoman arms trade was, basically, a dependent function of a mutual political/economic interest within the two Empires, and the decisions made by their absolute rulers, one of whom (the Kaiser) needed markets and raw materials for his nation's industrial development, and the other of whom (the Sultan) needed a strategic European partner as a bulwark against possible external aggression.

From the perspective of the Sultan, who was forced to give up two-fifths of his Empire's territory and one-fifth of its population following the Treaty of Berlin in 1878, Germany seemed to be the only European power that had neither a colonial nor a political interest in Ottoman territory. For Germany – under the leadership of Bismarck and then Kaiser Wilhelm II – the Ottoman Empire was primarily of interest for her strategic importance. In the context of Germany's desire to become a World Power (*Weltmacht*), only the Ottoman Empire could offer the strategic route that placed Germany 'in a position to attack two of Britain's vulnerable points: India and Egypt'.[2] In addition, it possessed abundant and rich resources of raw materials and provided a virgin market for Germany's industrial products.

The application of military diplomacy by means of a rapprochement strategy, which was strengthened by lucrative armaments contracts, proved to be one of the most useful and effective tools through which the Sultan initiated and maintained a close relationship with Germany. In this respect, two wars and their multifarious consequences helped to shape and support the Sultan's rapprochement policy: The Franco–Prussian War in 1870–1, and the Ottoman–Russian War in 1877–8. The Ottoman army's severe defeat by Russia in 1877–8 paved the way for a modernization project in the military field, where Germany had proven her superiority through the victory over France in 1870–1. So these two wars and the political and economic changes they wrought provide the first solid explanation justifying the Sultan's inclination towards Germany in general and towards the GAFs in particular. Without neglecting the importance of political preferences and strategic considerations, this study emphasizes the impact of the personal intervention of the following personalities in the war business in a form of personal diplomacy: German Chancellor Otto von Bismarck (1815–98); Kaiser Wilhelm II (1859–1941); the German military advisers, especially Colmar Freiherr von der Goltz Pasha (1843–1916) (hereafter Goltz Pasha); Sultan Abdülhamid II (1842–1918); and Ottoman civil and military officials.

The GAFs, especially the Krupp (artillery) and Mauser (rifle) companies, obtained a monopoly in the Ottoman arms market in the late nineteenth century and held this status for decades. The question naturally arises: how did the GAFs manage to achieve and retain this status in a highly competitive market, where maintaining such a position for a relatively long period should have been difficult? In order to simplify and illuminate the frame of the German success in the Ottoman arms market this book terms the concept of *German Style of War Business*, which refers to the distinctive importance of personal diplomacy applied to arms sales negotiations through the creation of an influence network or influence networks based on close personal relationships. In addition to that, moreover, this term also refers to the implementation of several manipulative tactics, such as bribery, political blackmail, corruption and industrial espionage, in the arms trade marketplace. Because of the distinctive nature of the methods the Germans used to manipulate the Ottomans' armament purchasing processes, throughout this study Germany's success is analysed with reference to this term.

From the outset onwards, as an obvious distinguishing feature of the German Style of War Business, the German state apparatus, openly and strongly supported the GAFs' business endeavours in the Ottoman market. Bismarck, who did not initially support German involvement in Ottoman railway construction, gave full patronage to the arms makers' efforts in the Ottoman arms market. Kaiser Wilhelm II, who was a personal friend of both the Krupp family and Sultan Abdülhamid, strongly believed the arms trade was an inseparable part of bilateral relations between the Ottoman Empire and Germany.

While the governments of other countries and their representatives in Istanbul did not initially involve themselves directly in the arms trade, the German government aggressively intervened in the competitive Ottoman market to manipulate the purchasing process in favour of the GAFs, for the sake of Germany's expansionist foreign economic policy. The trading strategy, supported by state power, used from the outset was described by Adolf Marschall von Bieberstein (Germany's former foreign secretary and ambassador in Istanbul between 1897–1912, hereafter Marschall), as the German method [*Deutsche Methode*], which was applied both to military and non-military interests. In light of its success, the *Deutsche Methode* was subsequently affirmed in the speech and acts of various German statesmen.[3] The German method also began to be recognized by some contemporary newspapers. In one magazine, the German method was perceptively described as follows: 'Germany has begun to create "Her India" in China and "Her Egypt" in Mesopotamia, and she uses gentler and finer means to attain this end than those employed by England and France.'[4]

In contrast to the colonial approach and attitudes that other European countries employed, the German government used a peaceful, amicable, 'gentler, and finer' language. Great Britain, for instance, strongly suggested the re-introduction of the parliamentary system suspended by Sultan Abdülhamid II in 1878 and sharply criticized the Sultan's domestic policy towards the non-Muslim subjects in an imperious manner. Bismarck, on the other hand, expressed his admiration for the Sultan's decision to dissolve the parliament and advised the *Turkification* of the Empire as a precondition for 'regaining the former glory that the Empire had', which might have encouraged Abdülhamid to continue pursuing his policy agenda. Without any doubt, statements of this kind helped to establish and strengthen trust between the two Empires, and eased the way for the German firms, which enjoyed the benefits of the Sultan's trust in Germany.

Another significant feature of the German Style of War Business was the collaboration between German banks, arms makers and civil and military diplomats for the purpose of securing the Ottoman market for German-made armaments. The German loans to the Sublime Port were mostly conditioned on awarding the German arms industry with armament contracts. Consequently arms sales began to provide the German bankers with profitable means. Basically, one of the functions of German diplomacy at this juncture was to support and promote both the financial activities of the banks and the arms exports in the Ottoman market. The financial guarantees of German banks strengthened the arms purchasing power of the Ottoman Empire.

The German military advisers, particularly Goltz Pasha, and the German embassy were involved directly in the negotiations during the armament purchasing process and became a part of the war business using *sui generis* business follow-up techniques. The arms sales became a very critical determinant of Germany's economic foreign policy towards the Ottoman Empire. Behind this policy, moreover, there were three successive waves that shaped the German-Ottoman relationship until World War I:

INTRODUCTION 5

(1) The first wave (1881–98): From the year of Bismarck's meeting with the Ottoman delegation in Berlin until Kaiser Wilhelm II's second visit to the Ottoman Empire, famously known as the *Orientreise* in 1898.

(2) The second wave with a subsequent 'drawback' (1898–1909): From the Kaiser's *Orientreise* until the Young Turks' Revolution in 1908, which was followed by a short drawback between the proclamation of the re-establishment of the Constitution of 1876, on 24 July 1908, and Sultan Abdülhamid II's dethronement on 27 April 1909.

(3) The third and last wave (1909–14): From the dethronement of Sultan Abdülhamid until the Ottoman participation in World War I on the side of Germany, this ultimately brought about the end of the Empire.

The first wave of Germany's expansionism towards the Ottoman Empire was initiated by the dispatch of German civil and military advisers to the Ottoman Empire at Abdülhamid's request during Bismarck's chancellorship. Bismarck's foreign policy towards the Ottoman Empire has been widely discussed by scholars under the shadow of his famous speech of 1876, in which Bismarck gave his opinion that the so-called 'Eastern Question' was 'not worth the bones of a single Pomeranian grenadier'.[5] However a comprehensive report of 1881 submitted to Sultan Abdülhamid II by his private secretary Reşid Bey, who was sent together with Ali Nizami Pasha, to Berlin to negotiate a possible alliance between the Ottoman Empire and Germany and to submit an official request for civil and military advisers from Germany, clearly exposes how Bismarck's Ottoman policy had changed dramatically in five years.

Furthermore, the three most important factors that fundamentally shaped bilateral relations during the first wave were the dispatch of German Military Advisers (GMAs) to Ottoman service in 1882; the *İrâde* (Sultan's Order) granting the Deutsche Bank exclusive rights to the Anatolian Railways project in October 1888; and the Kaiser's first visit to the Sultan in 1889. It was during this period that – thanks to the obvious support of the GMAs – the Krupp Company restarted its lucrative business with the Ottoman Empire, which had not placed any orders with Krupp since 1875. Krupp ended up holding the monopoly position as the artillery supplier to the Ottoman Army. During this period, the GAFs utilized their ties with the GMAs and the Ottoman bureaucrats in a most effective way. Perhaps the best example of this co-operation was Mauser's entrance into the Ottoman arms market as a rifle supplier in 1886–7. Through the intervention and support of German civil and military diplomacy, the owner and co-founder of the Mauser Rifle Company, Paul Mauser (1838–1914), signed the company's first and most profitable contract with the Ottoman government, under the shadow of the Sultan's 'personal trust'. Following that first contract (for 500,000 rifles and 50,000 carbines) the company achieved the monopoly position in supplying Ottoman infantry rifles, a rank it held for decades.

While during the first wave of the German expansionism towards the Ottoman Empire Chancellor Bismarck and Kaiser Wilhelm II were dominant actors in ruling and shaping Germany's foreign policy, the second and third waves were primarily shaped by the Kaiser, who dismissed Bismarck in 1890 and became 'his own chancellor'. Through his second visit to the Ottoman Empire in October 1898 the Kaiser publicly declared his intensified interest in the Ottoman Empire. Additionally, the second *Orientreise* gave him an opportunity to publicize and demonstrate his desire to be the unique architect of his Empire's foreign policy. Through the speeches he delivered in the major cities he visited during his journey (İstanbul, Haifa, Jaffa, Jerusalem and Damascus), Kaiser Wilhelm II openly declared his neutral position on some critical issues – especially the Crete and Armenian questions – about which the other European powers had put pressure on the Sultan. Following the Kaiser's *Orientreise* the second German expansionist wave started in 1898. Through the second *Orientreise*, Kaiser Wilhelm II's appearance on the international stage as a personal friend of the Sultan, who had been isolated by other European governments, fundamentally affected Ottoman–German relations.

INTRODUCTION

The Kaiser's influential speeches on controversial issues and his friendly actions during this trip, along with the Sultan's generous display of hospitality and presentation of special gifts to the Kaiser, had a deep impact on the economic and political relations of the two Empires. In particular, the Kaiser's speech in Damascus during his second *Orientreise* in 1898 expressed Germany's public support for Sultan Abdülhamid in precisely the terms the Sultan would have desired. However, German companies exploited the personal trust that underlay this declared friendship by using it as a stepping-stone for their business interests in the Ottoman market. The GAFs were the most prominent group of firms to take advantage of the Kaiser's support for their Ottoman businesses. But German financial and commercial interests in the Ottoman market, which had predominantly emerged during the first expansionist wave, were deepened and secured in general over the course of the second and third waves.

The power shift from the Sultan to the Young Turks in 1908 and the Sultan's subsequent dethronement by a military revolution in 1909 was a test of the German Style of War Business. Since the German style was mostly based on personal relations and the related persons' administrative power, this power shift was initially regarded as a blow for the German strategy. The subsequence period between July 1908 and April 1909 might be regarded therefore as a 'drawback' which eventually triggered the final and the destructive third wave.

During all three expansionist waves, the GMA were the key instruments working for the sake of Germany's peaceful penetration strategy in general and for the profit of the GAFs in particular. Therefore, this book calls them Businessmen in Uniform. Archival documents make it clear that the GMAs worked together with the GAFs in perfect cohesion, and lobbied ardently for their fatherland's armaments industry through their reports to the Ottoman government and also using their personal 'friendship' with some influential military and civil officers. Whenever any decisive opposition to an order for German-made war materials arose, the GMAs intervened and supported their fellow countrymen's interests.

They submitted several reports to the Ottoman government in which they praised German-made war materials and criticized those of Germany's competitors. A German artillery officer, Ristow Pasha, included an order for Krupp guns in a suggestion for reform; a cavalry officer, Hobe, advised purchasing stallions from Germany; Kamphövener Pasha, an infantry officer, also wrote several reform suggestions pointing out the superiority of Mauser rifles over the other options, especially Austrian Mannlicher rifles. But Goltz Pasha was the officer who most deserved the title of 'Businessman in Uniform'.

Because of his position in the Ottoman Army, Goltz Pasha was privy to various reliable sources of confidential information about the products that various competing companies submitted to the Ottoman arsenal. He then secretly shared this specific technical information with some GAFs, an act that amounted to industrial espionage. As it is articulated in this book, German foreign policy makers regarded armament exports as one of the principal elements of a strategy for successful economic–political penetration of the countries where German strategic interests were at stake. For this purpose, the German military mission in general and Goltz Pasha in particular were touchstones of Bismarck's well-planned expansionist strategy towards the Ottoman Empire. Goltz Pasha, in particular, proved himself an able lobbyist and marketing agent for the German arms makers. Thanks to the influential personal network Goltz Pasha created during his service, the German arms makers could penetrate the circle of Ottoman decision makers and subsequently were able to continue their close association with the Ottoman governments both during and after the reign of Abdülhamid II, until World War I.

Both the arms makers' and the military advisers' personal ties with Ottoman bureaucrats, especially officials at the Yıldız Palace, from which the Sultan ruled the Empire throughout his entire reign between 1876 and 1909, were the effective means behind the successful war business of German arms companies. However, this study will particularly focus on the two key domestic factors that facilitated the Germanization of the Ottoman arms market: Sultan Abdülhamid II and some of the military and civil bureaucrats.

Sultan Abdülhamid's personal attitude, which was logically intertwined with his political inclination towards Germany, was a vital factor in Ottoman dealings with GAFs in comparison with other nations' armament firms. In addition, because of the arms trade's magnitude, value and importance, governmental approval and the Sultan's *İrâde* were indispensable obligations during the ordering process, which meant that the Sultan's personal approach and inclinations played a crucial role. The Sultan's personal trust in Germany was well known, and he also tried to position his Empire's arms market as a political arena in which the European Great Powers would fight with each other.

In addition to the Sultan's role, however, Ottoman military and civil bureaucrats also had the power to manipulate the arms purchasing process. Their personal ties with either the arms makers themselves or their agents in Istanbul, and also with the German military advisers, provided them with an effective sphere of influence. So, over time the German agents and bureaucrats began to describe certain Ottoman bureaucrats or officers who worked in favour of Germany and the GAFs with terms like the following: 'more German than Turkish'; 'a loyal friend'; 'a reliable informant'; '[an officer] who used his whole influence in order to make Germany unique supplier for the Ottoman arms orders.'

My focus here is not on the personalities of the Sultan or the Kaiser per se, or on the Ottoman Empire's bureaucratic structure – instead, the point of this discussion is the importance of the pro-German stance adopted by the Sultan and his bureaucrats and its resulting influence on the arms trade. The major aim of this study is to identify and analyse the main determinants of the arms trade between the Ottoman Empire and Germany for the period between 1876 and 1914, mostly focusing on the impact of personal diplomacy. Being focused on the bilateral relations with a specific interest in the arms trade, however, this book is not a general study of German–Ottoman relations. Germany's endeavours in the Ottoman Empire during the period under review have been called a perfect example of 'the border between capitalism and imperialism',[6] and as Luxemburg asserted, the Ottoman Empire 'became the most important field of operations of German imperialism'.[7] However, this book, as a document-based case study, is largely confined to a treatment of the impact of personal contacts on Germany's successful war business in the Ottoman market and does not enter any theoretical debate. Based on extensive multinational archival research, this study aims to achieve the following basic objectives:

- To explore the direct or indirect contribution of the following non-commercial influences on the German Style of War Business in the Ottoman market: Chancellor Bismarck, Kaiser Wilhelm II and the GMAs employed in the Ottoman Army – especially Goltz Pasha.
- To indicate the correlation between the arms trade and foreign policy in the case of German–Ottoman relations during the period under review.
- To investigate the impact of personal relations on Germany's successful arms trade with the Ottoman arms market.
- To demonstrate the effectiveness of the GMAs in furthering Germany's political and economic ambitions in the Ottoman Empire.
- To reveal the importance of the arms trade in the shaping of Ottoman–German relations.
- To assess the impact of the changing foreign policies of the Ottoman Empire on the diversification of its trading partners.
- To evaluate the archival documents in order to illuminate the motivation of both arms trade-dependent friendship and friendship-dependent arms trade.

With regard to late nineteenth century Ottoman–German relations, the literature mostly focuses on the construction of the Baghdad Railway and on Kaiser Wilhelm II's second *Orientreise* in 1898. The arms trade, which actually started well before Kaiser Wilhelm's second *Orientreise*, and its multidimensional consequences, have been largely neglected. Most of the works that deal with the arms trade dimension, however, are based on English and/or German archival material, generally ignoring the Ottoman archival sources. There is one study which deals extensively with the Ottoman–German arms trade for the period under observation: a doctoral dissertation written by Fahri Türk. Türk's study pays considerable attention to the German arms makers' trade activities in the Ottoman Empire for the period 1871–1914.[8] In his dissertation, however, Türk uses only documents from German archives: Politisches Archiv des Auswärtigen Amtes in Berlin, (hereafter PA.AA.) and the Historisches Archiv Krupp in Essen (hereafter HA, Krupp). In spite of the availability of the Ottoman archives during the time when his doctoral dissertation was prepared, Türk cites limited access to the Başbakanlık Osmanlı Arşivi (The Prime Ministry Ottoman Archives: BOA) as a reason for not using Ottoman documents. Despite some serious miscalculations regarding the cost of Krupp's military materials delivered to the Ottoman Empire[9] and confusion about the events pertaining to the reigns of Sultan Abdülhamid II (r.1876–1909) and Abdülaziz (r.1861–76), his study is worthy of mention.[10]

Jonathan Grant's well-researched study of the global arms trade from 1860–1914 devotes some treatment to the German armament firms' sales to the Ottoman Empire. His discussion of Germany's increasing influence and its relation to the arms trade is compatible with the present study's findings.[11] However, Grant's failure to include either Ottoman or German sources when analysing the German war business in the Ottoman market is a major shortcoming. Grant bases his conclusions about the German arms trade on documents from the British National Archives in London alone.

Apart from these studies dealing directly with the arms trade, there is an enormous literature on Ottoman–German relations in both economic and political matters. However, this literature refers mostly to the limited topic of German involvement in the Ottoman military modernization process and the activities of the German military advisers, which are also covered in this study. Griffiths' doctoral dissertation (1966) about the reorganization of the Ottoman

Army between 1880 and 1897, and McGarity's doctoral thesis (1968) are among the first studies to deal with foreign influence on the Ottoman Army during the period under consideration.[12] Wallach's well-known and widely quoted work, published in 1976, also deals with the Ottoman military organizational reform process led by German instructors.[13] Wallach's study is notable for its extensive use of original documents from the German Foreign Office. Akmeşe's book and Yasamee's article, based on research with Goltz Pasha's papers in the Military Archive Freiburg (MA, Freiburg), clarify Goltz Pasha's extensive influence on the Ottoman Army and Ottoman military officers.[14]

Additional studies by Jastrow, Earle, Blaisdell, Önsoy, Bode, Ortaylı, Kössler, Rathmann, Schöllgen, Schölch, Trumpener, McMurray, Franzke, Jerusalimski, Kampen, Gencer, Soy and McMeekin are also relevant to the scope of this study.[15] However, these studies deal more generally with the diplomatic and historical background of Ottoman–German relations in a broader sense, focusing on the Baghdad Railway construction as the key element of the bilateral relations; they pay only superficial attention to the GAFs' business activities in the Ottoman market. Almost all of them mention Krupp, Mauser and other prominent German companies, and they point out the contribution of German military advisers – especially Goltz Pasha – but only a few provide authentic documents relating to the German war business in the Ottoman market.

The extremely rich and descriptive collection of documents at the Ottoman Archives in İstanbul has not been systematically used in these previous studies. The insufficient interest in scholarly circles led me to explore this topic by conducting research in the Ottoman archives. Therefore, in addition to the sources used in the abovementioned studies, this book makes extensive use of the BOA's resources and draws on crucial material from them, especially to illustrate how the Sultan and his bureaucrats, as well as the German advisers employed in the Ottoman service, were involved in the arms trade negotiation process. In addition, the Ottoman archives provide invaluable information on the operational details of the Ottoman–German arms trade: the cost of the arms purchasing; the negotiations; contract proposals; the Sultan's *İrâde*s regarding arms purchasing orders; the reports of the Ministry Council; the offers made by various suppliers; etc. The collection of the Yıldız Evrakı, which provided most of the documents used in this book, is a fundamental source on the period of the reign of Abdülhamid II.[16]

The Stadt-und Zeitungsarchiv Oberndorf/Neckar in Oberndorf on the Neckar (hereafter SA, Oberndorf), where the Mauser rifle factory was located, provided me with a wealth of documents that shed light on the German Style of War Business in a broader sense. The letters of Goltz Pasha, Paul Mauser, Ragıb Bey (the Sultan's private secretary) and the Huber Brothers (August and Joseph Huber), agents of the Krupp and Mauser companies, were the most important materials in the archive for my research topic. Aside from Wolfgang Seel's articles, which mention a few of the archival documents (referring not to the SA, Oberndorf, but rather to the private collection of Walter Schmid, the ex-Director of the Waffenmuseum Oberndorf), this study is the first use of the documents relating to the Mauser Company's Ottoman business discovered in the SA Oberndorf.[17]

Moreover, during my reading I noticed that a majority of the researchers who referred to the documents of the PA.AA. in Berlin tended to use only the machine-written documents, while neglecting the handwritten documents due to palaeographic difficulties. As a result, I tried to transcribe these documents and consequently found crucial information on both the importance of the arms trade for Germany's expansionist foreign policy, and the significance of the Kaiser's and Goltz Pasha's direct intervention in the arms trade process.

Documents in the National Archives in London (hereafter NA, London) and also the National Archives in the Washington D.C. Area at College Park, Maryland (hereafter NARA-Microfilm, College Park) highlighted how the British and American armament firms lost the trust they had previously enjoyed from the Sultan. The impact of Britain's political choices and the consequences of Germany's increasingly influential position in the Ottoman Empire could be observed in the Foreign Office documents found in The NA, London. These documents suggest that the reason American and British firms lost their earlier strong position in the Ottoman market, especially in the field of small arms, was not related to the quality of their products. On the contrary, the main factor proved to be both governments' strong political pressure on the Ottoman government concerning particularly the Armenian Question and its political consequences.

During my research I also visited several libraries in Berlin, London, and İstanbul. The Staatsbibliothek in Berlin was the most important and useful library for this project, and the Special Collections of the University of Birmingham (Main Library); the British Library in London; and the Library of the Türkiye Diyanet Vakfı İslam Araştırmaları Merkezi (ISAM Library) in İstanbul also provided access to some rare sources, such as unpublished dissertations, memoirs, newspapers and the like.

CHAPTER 1

THE GERMAN EXPANSIONIST WAVE AND THE POLITICAL ECONOMY OF GERMAN STYLE OF WAR BUSINESS IN THE OTTOMAN EMPIRE (1880-98)

'... and Caesar crossed the Rubicon'

Bismarck and His Ottoman Policy: Towards the First Expansionist Wave

'The new Alexander will have to come from Germany or at least be German-inspired.'
Paul Dehn[1]

'The war of the future will be the economic war, the struggle for existence on the largest scale.'
Otto von Bismarck[2]

Kaiser Wilhelm II's accession to the throne, in 1888, was widely regarded as a turning point for German economic and political influence in the Ottoman Empire. It has been argued that, prior to his accession, the German ruling élites stood almost completely in accord with Bismarck's vision for diplomacy, which might be described as a policy of non-involvement in Ottoman affairs. In the years following the unification of Germany, Bismarck's authority in all points of domestic and foreign policy became so overwhelming that a great majority of the population viewed him as the real ruler of the newly founded German Empire. Just before the outbreak of the Russo–Turkish War (1877–8), Bismarck gave a famous speech concerning his Eastern policy to the German parliament on 5 December 1876. Bismarck indicated that the policy Germany pursued should be dictated solely by its own interest. The following well-known quotation from Bismarck' speech shows how he phrased his opinion concerning the Eastern question: 'We will not permit ourselves to be influenced by any proposal whatsoever to pursue any other policy. I do not therefore advise any active participation on the part of Germany, as I do not see for Germany any interest which would warrant our sacrificing – excuse the harshness of the expression – the bones of a single Pomeranian grenadier.'[3]

According to *The New York Times*' comment, Bismarck's dismissal of the Ottoman Empire might have stemmed from his realization that 'Turkish intrigue was a dangerous business for European powers'.[4] Kaiser Wilhelm II also mentioned Bismarck's 'unfavourable opinion' of the Ottoman Empire and 'the men in high position there [Abdülhamid II and his bureaucrats], and of conditions in that land'.[5]

While some historians accept Bismarck's claim of disinterest in the Ottoman Empire 'at face value', Ismail Kemal Bey, the former Ottoman Governor-General of Tripoli and Beirut, argued that 'to extend German influence in the East became an essential part of the Bismarckian policy'.[6] Although his above cited speech has been widely presented as the framework of Bismarck's Balkan policy, the Eastern Question was, according to Bismarck's formulation, a 'question of Turkey'.[7] Furthermore Marschall also portrayed Bismarck's speech as a situation-specific statement. In one of his correspondences with Prince Bülow, he wrote, 'when he [Bismarck] addressed the speech, he diagnosed the real existing state and at the same time in the East he secured the role of the honest broker'.[8] Regarding Bismarck's well-known remarks and the interpretations thereof, Ismail Kemal Bey wrote: 'No historical utterance has been more often quoted than the celebrated remark of Bismarck that the "Eastern Question was not worth the bones of a Pomeranian grenadier". But, although so often quoted, no historical utterance has ever been the cause of so much ambiguous comment, or has been more constantly misunderstood and misinterpreted.'[9] In his memoir, Ismail Kemal Bey made the following illuminating comment about Bismarck's pretended disinterestedness in the Ottoman affairs:

> Bismarck ... continued to push his views concerning Turkey. In spite of his pretended disinterestedness, when it was decided to send German officers and officials to Turkey to help organise her army and the civil and financial administration, in answer to those who had doubts as to whether such arrangements might be agreeable to the other Powers, he replied that, when Prussia was on the best terms with Russia, the Turkish artillery was organised by Prussian officers. Insisting as he did upon keeping a hand on Turkey, and, above all, on Asia Minor, he considered that Germany would reap much advantage by sending her officers and functionaries to those countries.[10]

The first step taken by the Sultan was to invite civil and military advisers from Germany, on 14 May 1880. This invitation, which Yasamee calls 'both original and in some ways surprising',[11] opened the door to German political, economic, and military penetration of the Ottoman Empire. However, as Griffiths pointed out, because of British protests and some other diplomatic problems that had emerged subsequent to the chaos in the Balkans, Bismarck had to postpone the fulfilment of Abdülhamid's initial request.[12] Although it was widely believed that Bismarck did not favour sending military advisers to the Ottoman Empire and postponed their dispatch as a result, he actually supported the assignment of

German civil and military advisers to the Ottoman Empire.[13] According to Reşid Bey's report, Bismarck's reservations were not about the sending of civil and military advisers but were about the Ottomans' request to enter the Triple Alliance.[14] As the Prince of Hohenlohe-Schillingsfürst (hereafter Prince Hohenlohe) also stated, Bismarck wanted to send the mission to the Ottoman Empire, while the Crown Prince Frederick III (1831–88) was doubtful about doing so. Having said that, however, Bismarck thought that the Austrian approval was needed in order to agree to the Ottoman request to enter the Triple Alliance. According to Ismail Kemal Bey, Bismarck realized that through sending military advisers to the Ottoman Empire, Germany 'would have at her command a number of officials who knew and had studied these regions, and these at some time or another might be able to render great service'.[15]

On 14 July 1880, following his initial request, Sultan Abdülhamid II sent the draft terms of appointment for the prospective German military and civil advisers who would enter in the Ottoman service.[16] Nevertheless, the 12 articles of draft terms did not assuage Crown Prince Frederick's doubts. As Prince Hohenlohe recorded, the Crown Prince asked whether the dispatch of military officers and civil instructors to the Ottoman Empire should be postponed, because Bismarck thought that the officers might be used to help the Porte resist other European powers.[17] After mentioning his point of view, the Crown Prince had bidden Prince Hohenlohe to communicate his doubts to the Chancellor Bismarck. Prince Hohenlohe sent the following report to the Crown Prince on 16 July 1880 in which he wrote:

> Your Imperial and Royal Highness was on my last visit to Potsdam graciously pleased to entrust to me communications to the Chancellor, which I hastened to convey, and concerning which I take the liberty of most humbly reporting. As to the doubts of your Imperial and Royal Highness in regard to the sending of officers and civil servants to Turkey, the Chancellor has come to the conclusion that he cannot share them. He considers the measure in various respects advantageous.[18]

In fact, Bismarck was not ambivalent about sending the civil and military advisers to the Ottoman Empire; on the contrary he was well aware of the potential for mutual benefits of the presence of the Germans in the Ottoman service. According to Prince Hohenlohe, Bismarck emphasized that 'it might be useful to Germany to have the Turks as friends in as far as this might be to their [the Ottoman Empire] advantage'. During his conversation with Hohenlohe, Bismarck also pointed out clearly the importance of increasing the influence of Germany in Istanbul. In his report, Hohenlohe summarized Bismarck's argument that sending civil and military advisers to the Ottoman Empire would be multiply advantageous. Bismarck was of the opinion that the duties to be discharged by the advisers would be very instructive and would give them opportunities to show the extent of their capacity. Additionally, the Germans employed in the Ottoman Empire had some undeclared and unrecorded duties. During his conversation with Prince Hohenlohe, Bismarck put emphasis on that possible advantage and said: 'It will furnish us with a number of reliable informants whom we could obtain in no other way.'[19]

Actually, Bismarck had made the same point in one of the official reports submitted by German ambassador on July 1880. At the end of the report, Bismarck had added that the Germans in the Ottoman service would provide the German government 'with influence and informants'.[20] In fact, as future events proved, Bismarck's assumption, which was based on well-calculated political observations, was correct. Bismarck's vision of obtaining reliable information regarding the political, economic, and military state of the Ottoman Empire through the advisers was fulfilled indeed. The German civil and military missions, thanks to their intimate relation with Ottoman officials and officers, provided a large quantity of important information, especially concerning the military contracts arranged by some high-ranking Ottoman officers.[21] Prince Hohenlohe gave the following details:

> [Bismarck said that] ... the consequences the arrangement may have for the Turks and its acceptability to the European Powers

need not concern us. It is not our policy, [Bismarck] says, to further either Turkish or European interests. A European interest is, to his mind, a fiction useful to all who want to use others, and can find persons who believe in the phrase. It might be useful to us to have the Turks as friends in as far as this might be to our advantage. The Turkish artillery had been trained by Prussian officers at a time when we were living on terms of the utmost cordiality with Russia, and we had thus acquired influence and useful connections in Turkey. If Chauvinism, Panslavism, and the anti-German elements in Russia should attack us, the attitude and the military efficiency of Turkey would not be indifferent to us. She could never be dangerous to us, but under certain circumstances her enemies might be ours.[22]

However, the German government did not take any immediate action, and thus appeared reluctant to approve the request.[23] In December 1881, more than one year, after Prince Hohenlohe conducted this interview with Bismarck, Abdülhamid II sent a special delegation to Berlin in order to accelerate the process and also to show his persistence.[24] The head of the delegation was a member of the Sultan's military household, Ali Nizami Pasha, who was accompanied by Reşid Bey, Sultan Abdülhamid's private secretary (*Kâtib-i husûsî-i hazret-i şehriyârî*).[25] One of Reşid Bey's contemporaries, Ali Ekrem Bolayır, emphasized Reşid Bey's important position in the palace, stating that he had a very bright influence on the sultan's administrative affairs.[26] The main agenda of the mission was to negotiate a possible alliance with the German Empire and to request civil and military assistance.[27] On 10 December 1881, the mission started with the decoration of the Emperor Wilhelm I with the *Nişan-ı imtiyaz* (the high order of distinction), which had never before been conferred on a foreign sovereign.[28] Afterwards, Ali Nizami Pasha and Reşid Bey were hosted for dinner by the Kaiser and Chancellor Bismarck, followed by several meetings during which they negotiated to obtain a commitment for military and civil assistance from Germany.[29] Bismarck received Ali Nizami Pasha two times, on

15 and 17 December, and two days after Ali Nizami's second audience, on 19 December, Bismarck received Reşid Bey.[30]

As a matter of fact, the Ottoman delegation was going to Berlin to convince Bismarck and insist on him dispatching the advisers to Istanbul, but in actual fact, Bismarck did not need to be persuaded, since he was well aware of the future benefit of this 'tool' and had already decided to let them enter the Ottoman service.[31] Yet, on the occasion of this visit, Bismarck had found the best opportunity to share his thoughts about the British, Russian, and French governments and their territorial and political interest in the Ottoman Empire. Through these personal meetings and conversations, in which personal diplomacy had been perfectly applied by the chancellor, he successfully confirmed his non-interventionist approach towards Ottoman internal affairs in a way that the Sultan would like. Meanwhile he also ventured to give some very sharp advice on one of the most critical and bitter issues of Sultan Abdülhamid's reign: namely the precarious balance between the Muslim and non-Muslim subjects of the Empire.

As Reşid Bey's notes illuminatingly shown, Bismarck seemed to have been well prepared for this meeting and elevated the minorities subject to one of the basic elements of Germany's foreign policy agenda-setting in terms of German–Ottoman relations. Bismarck did make highly inflammatory remarks regarding the minorities of a multi-ethnic and multi-religious Empire, the non-Muslim subjects of the Ottoman Empire. From that point of view, the following paragraph provides a remarkable and also illuminating sample of Bismarck's advice for the administration of the minority subjects within the Empire. Through a political metaphor emphasizing the use of coercive government power to administer the Christian subjects, Bismarck also advised an organized and systematic policy to eliminate the possible threat of any foreign intervention:

> For those reasons, you should not disregard any precautionary measures even for an instant. Namely, in the sultan's Glorious Lands [*memalik-i şâhâne*], there is a need for you to proclaim that Christian subjects are under the His protectorate to

counter the claims by external powers that they are protectors of those subjects. However, at the same time the sultan should rule based on the principle of govern with the lion's claw covered by a silken glove (this expression is the direct translation from Excellency Bismarck's statement, which was repeated during the conversation by His Excellency two or three times).[32]

Reşid Bey seemed to be astonished to hear such a statement, and felt himself to be obliged to express how many times Bismarck repeated it. Bismarck's overly provocative and straightforward expression, which was carefully noted down by Reşid Bey, was for the sultan to pursue something akin to assimilation (*Türkler ile mezc olarak*) of the non-Muslim subjects through a government 'with the lion's claw covered by a silken glove' (*harirden ma'mul eldiven ile mestur arslan pençesiyle idare-i hükümet*). The 'honest broker' Europe continued giving provocative advice about diminishing of 'the influence and significance of [the Empire's] Christian subjects':

> Thus, if one acts cautiously in this way, in a short time the influence and significance of the Christian subjects, namely the subjects other than Turks, would diminish [*zail*] or possibly they might even entirely merge [*mezc*] with Turks and shortly afterwards be transformed [*qalb*] in the Turks. As a result of that, because the State will become a solely Turkish State, consequently, its [the State's] power will increase, and it will with minimal effort regain its reputation, its glory, and its greatness existed several centuries previously and will acquire these attributes multiplied several times.[33]

Interestingly, the man who made all these provocative and seemingly impulsive statements had once given the following advice to Lord Beaconsfield – 'Do not quarrel with Russia. Let her take Constantinople, while you take Egypt – France will not prove inexorable. Besides, one might give her Syria or Tunis.'[34] However, in 1881, a completely different Bismarck came onto the scene. At this point, Bismarck was giving practical advice to Ottoman bureaucrats, explaining to them how they could increase the prosperity of the Ottoman Empire and proposing methods to achieve that aim. He expressed the significance of increasing the volume of the Empire's foreign trade and its agricultural output, and also suggested the construction of new roads and building railway. He then continued:

> At the same time, you should not hold back from showing effort day and night, without resting, for the improvement of your country and for expanding the zone of its prosperities and contentment. You should strike to advance the level of education and increase trade and agricultural productivity. You should attend to the necessary terms for enriching the country. You should open new roads and passes and should build rail lines throughout the country. You should also manage your forest and mining resources in the most advantageous and suitable manner.[35]

Moreover, Bismarck's statement to Ali Nizami Pasha about the dissolution of the Ottoman parliament in 1878 was just what Abdülhamid might have hoped to hear: 'You acted very well with the dissolution of the parliament. Because, it would do more harm than good to a state, unless it does not consist of a single nation [*millet-i vahide*].'[36] In every respect, this conversation can be seen as a general declaration of German interest in the Ottoman Empire from the economic, political and military points of view, and as a declaration of the end of Bismarck's 'disinterested policy' vis-à-vis the Ottoman Empire. The advice offered in this conversation might have a triggering effect on the process of peaceful penetration of German economic and political influence into the Ottoman Empire. Bismarck was not unaware that the Ottoman Empire could not afford to materialize all the investment proposals or to achieve all of the modernization tasks that he mentioned with its resources alone. In fact Bismarck, who had pursued an 'open door' policy in his foreign trade with the Far East,[37] was probably trying to open the Ottoman market to German investors, traders and industrialists. For that reason Bismarck's remarks can be interpreted as an indirect declaration of the German economic interest in the Ottoman market. Bismarck stated that: 'So long as domestic employees and companies exist that are able to achieve those goals you should prefer them. Otherwise, you can apply to well-intended and honest, and competent sources of foreign expertise among other nations with whom you are friends and allies.'[38]

In every respect, this report reveals two essential points: First, contrary to extensively accepted beliefs, Bismarck was not unwilling to dispatch the German advisers to the Ottoman Empire. Second, although Bismarck pretended not to involve Germany into the internal affairs of the Ottoman Empire, he did not hesitate to give the Sultan overly provocative advice on how the Sultan should govern and assimilate the Empire's non-Muslim subjects, who were, according to Bismarck, disloyal to the Ottoman government and 'seek their benefit at the expense of harm to the Turks'. Finally, based on Bismarck's remarks extracted from this document, it can be argued that this conversation proved to be an official declaration of Germany's support for the Sultan as Caliph in pan-Islamic terms and interest in the Ottoman Empire from the economic, political and military points of view. Although Kaiser Wilhelm II sought to portray himself as the sole architect of Germany's Ottoman policy, a policy that provided German industrialists and businessmen with a variety of advantages, I argue that he was instead just an eager promoter and perhaps an aggressive facilitator of the expansionist strategy initially formulated and put into effect by Bismarck.

Bismarck was a gifted strategist who undoubtedly understood the multidimensional advantages of having advisers stationed in the Ottoman Empire, and it was he who approved the dispatch of Goltz Pasha and the other civil and military advisers to İstanbul. Goltz Pasha entered Ottoman service in 1883, was entrusted with the task of heading the GMAs in 1885, and remained in his position for 12 years. The German advisers became the triggering forces behind the first wave. Consequently, Bismarck agreed to dispatch to İstanbul military and civil advisers. In this way, Abdülhamid's step-by-step insistence on obtaining German assistance ultimately resulted in an agreement signed in May 1882. As a British diplomat noted in an annual report for the Ottoman Empire in 1907, Sultan Abdülhamid's struggle for the invitation and employment of German officers in the Ottoman army was a conceived, planned and formulated step, which dramatically changed the Empire's relationship with Germany in the following years.[39] In the meantime, moreover, Abdülhamid's remarkable 'importunities' as Lord Ampthill, the British ambassador in Berlin, described it,[40] gave Bismarck the opportunity to test and to fulfil the assumption and expectation that he had shared with Prince Hohenlohe on 16 July 1880.[41]

Thanks to these civil and military advisers, Germany, unlike Britain or France, became a steadfast Ottoman ally, the one who instructed the Ottoman military forces until World War I, and enjoyed access to the highest levels of Ottoman civil and military circles. In terms of producing a new alliance system or new international block, which ultimately ended with the war, this visit, along with its political, economic and military outcomes, proved to be a watershed in late nineteenth- and early twentieth-century European history. Placing a civil and military mission in the Ottoman service provided Germany the perfect basis upon which to build multifaceted influence. When Bismarck approved the first German advisers in response to the Sultan's insistent invitation, the first dominoes began to fall, and they were going precisely the right way as far as Germany's point of view was concerned. By the time the last of them fell, the Ottoman Empire found itself entering World War I as one of Germany's brothers-in-arms (*Waffenbrüderschaft*).

After their arrival, German arms makers started to co-operate closely with them. Their influential position in the Ottoman army made them an indispensable resource of critical information for the German arms industry. The advisers acted as if they were the intermediaries between the arms makers and the Ottoman army. In this respect, they served as the connection between the demand side and supply side of the arms trade. Thus the armaments industry became the first harvester of the seed Bismarck had planted.

Bismarck's endeavour successfully aimed to exploit the economic strength and military reputation German had gained during the Franco–Prussian War (1870–1) on behalf of an expansionist economic foreign policy. Rather than pursuing a strategy of direct colonization by imperial military power, Bismarck saw the potential to penetrate overseas countries peacefully, through the export of German-made products and dispatching civil and military advisers. According to the well-known German colonialist, Dr Carl Peters, who was named President of the Society for German Colonisation and who received the first patent for a charter of colonial protection (*kolonialen Schuztbrief*) from Bismarck for the colonization of German East Africa on 27 February 1885,[42] overseas colonization was another important determinant of the German Empire's economic expansion policy.[43] However, for Bismarck, the colonies were important more as a potential *Absatzmarkt* (market) for German-made products, than purely as an imperialistic venture.[44] Wehler contends that in Bismarck's overseas-centred foreign policy, there was 'a remarkable continuity of both the ideas and the methods of free-trade commercial expansionism'.[45]

At the beginning, Bismarck did not want to join the European colonization race, and as a late-comer, he avoided disturbing the European balance of power. As a verbal declaration of his neutral position to the European concert, Bismarck once said: 'In Serbia I am an Austrian, in Bulgaria I am a Russian, in Egypt I am English.'[46] At the same time, he was aware of the recently united empire's fragile geopolitical position. The establishment and maintenance of peaceful relations with neighbouring states, especially France, therefore became a *sine qua non* of Germany's prosperity. For that reason, he was unwilling to spend the Empire's restricted resources on a colonial adventure. As Kaiser Wilhelm II wrote in his memoir, 'the political interest of Bismarck was, in fact, concentrated essentially upon continental Europe'.[47] Wehler points out that Bismarck was quite sincere when he assured the French ambassador De Courcel in September 1884 that 'the aim of German policy' was the expansion of free trade, and not 'the territorial expansion of German colonial possessions'.[48] A letter from Bismarck to Bucher demonstrates that

Bismarck had predicted the character of the future wars that would be the consequence of economic growth:[49]

> Up to the year 1866 we pursued a Prussia–German policy. From 1866 to 1870 we pursued a German–European policy. Since then we have pursued a world policy... The war of the future will be the economic war, the struggle for existence on the largest scale. May my successor always bear this in mind and always take care that Germany will be prepared when this battle has to be fought.[50]

In his mind, perhaps, Bismarck prioritized the needs of his country's industrializing economy, which were to develop markets to absorb surplus inland production and serve as a source of raw materials for growing industry.[51] In Germany, especially after the Franco–Prussian War, one of the prominent industries with a production surplus was the armaments sector. Additionally, German policy makers were aware of the export potential of the arms trade. As Sampson notes, 'by the early years of the century the arms trade had become the most international industry in the world, with a web of inter-connections between the continents'.[52] Hirst also noticed the transnational character of the arms trade. In his 1916 book, he emphasized the spirit of the war business as follows:

> Swords, like guns, torpedoes, or battleships, were made for profit. Turks, Spaniards, and Englishmen have fallen often enough by homemade weapons. The armaments tree has now grown until its leafy ramifications throw shadows over all the world. There is a market in the most barbarous countries for the most refined machinery of destruction. Thus, though the preparations for war are national, the trade is international. The most fashionable firms, Krupp, Creusot, Vickers, Armstrong, etc., sell very largely to foreign governments. They also co-operate from time to time for the purpose of stimulating the demand or raising prices.[53]

It could be said that arms production and export, which was dependent on the progress of the iron and steel industries, constituted one of the most significant components of the commercial expansionist strategy that Bismarck left to his successors as a vision for and an integral part of the *Weltmacht* policy. At the same time, the armaments industry was one of the key sectors triggering innovation of and paving the way to economic expansion.[54] In fact, as will be discussed below, after Wilhelm II forced Bismarck to resign in 1890, he continued to apply his expansionist foreign policy, but with a more aggressive approach. However, Bismarck was also conscious of the importance of increased armaments for his country's security. He was well aware of the fact that the quantity and quality of armaments that a state possesses might be regarded a symbol of both its international status and its strength. On 6 February 1888, Bismarck delivered a speech on the military bill, in which he claimed that an increase in armaments production and the armed forces was the best guarantee of peace. In his speech, Bismarck asserted, 'that sounds paradoxical, but it is true. With the powerful machine which we are making of the German army no aggression will be attempted.'[55] That was, in fact, what the German arms makers desired to hear. As Bismarck noted, this powerful reinforcement would have had a quieting effect on the German nation, and would have lessened – at least to some degree – the nervousness of German public opinion, the stock market and the press.[56] In his speech, he clarified the necessity for armaments in an enthusiastic way:

> We are situated in the middle of Europe. We have at least three fronts of attack... God has placed us in a situation in which we are prevented by our neighbours from sinking into any sort of indolence or stagnation. He has set at our side the most war-like and the most restless of nations, the French; and he has permitted warlike inclinations, which in former centuries existed in no such degree, to grow strong in Russia. Thus we get a certain amount of spurring on both sides, and are forced into exertions which otherwise perhaps we should not make.

The pikes in [the] European carp-pond prevent us from becoming carps, by letting us feel their prickles on both our flanks; they constrain us to exertions which perhaps we should not voluntarily make; they constrain us Germans also to a harmony among ourselves that is repugnant to our inmost nature: but for them, our tendency would rather be to separate.[57]

Based on his strong belief in a united and militarily prepared nation, he encouraged his fellow countrymen to discover new markets and new sources of materials, which were vitally important to the rising economy and the country's industrial potential. In this way, the country gradually became more dependent on the success of informal and formal expansion,[58] which could provide access to raw materials and new markets. His armaments policy and his colonial approach lay on the same line. Bismarck would not consider any significant costly step 'as long as the finances of the Reich have not been consolidated'. However, Bismarck was of the opinion that 'the state cannot administer colonies directly; it can do no more than give support to trading companies'.[59] Kaiser Wilhelm II claimed, moreover, that Bismarck did not intend to use 'the colonies as commercial objects, or objects for swapping purposes, other than to make them useful to the fatherland or utilise them as sources of raw materials'.[60]

Bismarck's approach towards the arms trade as an influential tool for his foreign economic policy can be best illustrated by examining his personal relationship with the arms makers and his official support for their international business. Bismarck, as an advocate and supporter of an economic expansionist policy, established a close relationship with the German arms makers. Among them, the Krupp Company had a particularly special place in Bismarck's formulation of foreign economic policy that deserves to be mentioned in the first instance. As an admirer of the idea of 'internationalism of profit',[61] the Krupp Company might be called 'a natural ally' of Bismarck's expansionist foreign economic policy. Therefore, it is hardly surprising that most of Krupp's demands conformed closely to the Bismarckian economic foreign policy. For instance, in 1865 Krupp was in serious difficulties and needed a loan of several million marks, which the banks refused to provide. So Krupp went to Bismarck – in Menne's words, 'his patron Bismarck'[62] – to persuade him to extend support and, eventually, to place an order. According to Menne, during the interview with Bismarck, Krupp pretended 'that he might have to permit foreign interests [the French banking firm of *Seillière*] to acquire control of his firm'. But the real state of affairs was otherwise. Menne provides more detail of this interview, quoting from Krupp's own writing:

> [Bismarck] was very upset over the matter and agreed to discuss it with the King and the Minister of War, but he stated that it would be hard to secure a decision without the approval of the Minister of Commerce. I treated the matter as a trifle and rubbed in the fact that if I availed myself of the offers of capital freely made to me in France, I might lose my future liberty of action, and the works pass under partial foreign control. I did not omit to say that I could sell out for 10 million, any day.[63]

The possibility of French influence on a well-known German industrial giant set Bismarck into action, and he discussed the issue with Kaiser Wilhelm I (1797–1888) on Krupp's behalf. After some deliberation, Wilhelm I placed a huge order for coastal defence and naval guns with a payment on account of 3,787,000 marks for Krupp's work.[64] This took place in 1866, which was a depressing year for German industry overall, including Krupp. According to Menne, Krupp also applied to the government for a grant of more than six million marks on a later occasion mentioned below.[65] At Bismarck's urging, the company also obtained a credit in the millions from the state, in order to equip Prussia for a possible war against France.[66] Wilhelm I, even though he was still Prince Regent [*Prinzregent*], hinted that he would support Krupp against other German arms producers.[67] The military and ruling elites, both were the Krupp Company's open supporters. Epkenhans, considering the above-mentioned examples, asserts: 'The best-known and most notorious case of military–industrial relations in Imperial Germany remains the relationship between the military and the firm of Krupp in Essen'.[68]

In 1874, Krupp was in another difficult financial situation – there was a danger of it causing the company's inevitable demise (*der unvermeidliche Untergang*).[69] The firm was in urgent need of funds and Alfred Krupp (1812–87) asked Bismarck, confidentially, if the Prussian State Bank (could) advance him six million marks. According to Manchester, 'in the past the government had always been accommodating. Now he was rudely told that he would have to take out a private mortgage on his raw materials with the Seehandlung Bankinstitut.'[70] In order to rescue the firm from the threat of collapse, a syndicate under the leadership of the Prussian State Bank (Seehandlung Bankinstitut) was formed soon after to issue and guarantee a loan of 10 million thalers at five per cent interest.[71] As Riesser pointed out, this transaction deserves special mention because it was the first time in Germany that 'the loan took the form of fractional bonds secured by blanket mortgage and provided for common representation of the holders of these bonds, which after that [became] the common form of such obligations'.[72]

Through such means, Bismarck and Wilhelm I demonstrated their support for the Krupp Company during its difficult days. According to an article from *The New York Times* dated 1 November 1887, Krupp tried to take advantages of being close to these authorities, asking for official support for winning international business and to persuade Alfred (Krupp) to lend his assistance: 'Herr Krupp... is prolonging his stay with the Chancellor. It is understood that among other things which have induced him to visit Prince Bismarck at the present time is certain business with reference to Turkey, whose Government, I am informed is indebted to Herr Krupp to the extent of a million sterling.'[73]

In addition to both his domestic and international support for the Krupp Company, the Mauser Company of Oberndorf and the Ludwig Loewe Company of Berlin had also benefited from Bismarck's official support for their very first business in the Ottoman arms market. The contract signed in February 1887 was for 500,000 rifles and 100 million cartridges and was, as discussed more fully later on, a contract that entirely changed Mauser's fortunes, and contributed to the economic and social development of the city of Oberndorf, where

Mauser was located.[74] Ahmed Tevfik Pasha (1845–1936), the Ottoman ambassador in Berlin, noted that before the agreement between the Mauser Company and the Ottoman Empire was signed in 1887, he had frequently turned to Bismarck to procure information and advice about the Mauser products. According to Tevfik Pasha, Bismarck praised Mauser's rifles and vigorously recommended the company.[75]

In addition, Bismarck appeared on the diplomatic stage to support German arms makers, for instance by persuading the Ottoman government to place a contract with the Pulverfabrik Rottweil-Hamburg (hereafter the Rottweiler) in 1887.[76] The following statement, from an archival document signed by Bismarck himself on 19 April 1887, demonstrates his obvious interest and intervention in the war business, as a facilitator – or more accurately, patron – of German armamants companies' activities both domestic and abroad.[77] Throughout the letter, Bismarck, the neighbour and the close personal friend of the Rottweiler founders and directors Max and Carl Duttenhofer,[78] endeavoured to obtain an order from the Sultan, was discussing some technical features of the Rottweiler gun powder, of course in a very complimentary way:

> Rottweiler gun powder is the best for the Mauser rifle, for it possesses three significant traits: Bullet's power of transit, enhancement of accuracy of bullet's trajectory, and safe firing system, which prevents premature explosion of cartridge and removes the causes and effects bringing about the destruction of the rifle. For those reasons, this gunpowder is appropriate for the Mauser system rifles currently in the hands of our soldiers.[79]

It might be interesting to note that one of the production premises of Duttenhofers' company had been built on one of Bismarck's estates.[80] According to Stern, the annual profit this estate yielded rose from 10,900 marks to nearly double that by the late 1880s.[81] Otto P. Pflanze, a well-known biographer of Bismarck, adds that the Chancellor's precondition for the leasing was that the needed fuel (*Sprengstoff*) had to be acquired in Sachsenwald.[82] Vagts claims further that Bismarck kept 'within bounds the State factory inspectors' demands for unduly strict safety measures just to protect the powder factory'.[83] In his diary which covered 25 years of official and private intercourse with Bismarck, Moritz Busch gives detailed information about Bismarck's income from the Rottweiler lease:

> Afterwards, at tea, we were joined by the Prince, who spoke on a variety of subjects, and particularly of his estates and their relatively poor returns. Apart from the mills, Varzin brought him in nothing. It was hardly possible to dispose of the grain, as the railway tariffs for foreign corn were too low. It was just the same with timber, which realised very little, owing to competition, and even the neighbourhood of Hamburg to the Sachsenwald was of little use to him at present.[84]

After mentioning these poor returns, the Chancellor mentioned the estate on the banks of the Elbe, where Duttenhofer had established one if its powder factories. Busch continued:

> He then spoke about the powder factory which a Würtemberger had established on a piece of ground belonging to him on the banks of the Elbe, describing it and the manner in which it was worked. He said that the Würtemberger paid him an annual rent of 12,000 marks, and that after a certain number of years the factory would become his, the Prince's, property. The lessee was doing a very good business during the present war, as he was earning 150 per cent [profit per annum].[85]

Although there is no document-based proof of Busch's claim that after a certain numbers of years the factory would in fact become Bismarck's property, his letter sent to İstanbul in favour of the Rottweiler gun powder still provides important proof of his intervention in the war business. Additionally, Isidor Löwe wrote that Bismarck's support facilitated the placement of the first Ottoman order with Mauser.[86] A British report dispatched to Lord Salisbury provides some illuminating details of the German

Chancellor's involvement in the process. According to the report, the English Martini-Henry contract to supply 400,000 rifles to the Porte was nearly completed until Prince Bismarck interceded:

> When the arrangement for this supply was nearly concluded, a letter was received from Prince Bismarck himself, in which he toughly recommended the Sultan, if he was going to rearm his troops, to do it with repeating rifles. The consequence was that an order was given to a German firm [Mauser] for 300,000 repeating rifles.[87]

The anonymous author of the report offered to send the letter to Salisbury, if he wished. Then he addressed a question to Lord Salisbury: 'Do you think it worthwhile to inquire of Sir W[illiam] White [The British ambassador in İstanbul, hereafter White] whether this is the case?' Salisbury's answer was clear: 'Yes I think so. Merely for information, for outcome we can do nothing.'[88] Subsequently a telegram was sent to White, asking him to investigate the accuracy of this 'rumour' and to report on the matter. On 30 January 1887, White responded that a commission had been appointed to decide between the Mauser rifle and the Henry-Martini rifle, adding that the Sultan strongly favoured the German firm. White noted that he would have to remain neutral in this matter given that two British firms were competing. Afterwards, he added that there was no evidence of an English order having been nearly completed. However, in response to an order to investigate the letter from Prince Bismarck, he confirmed the letter existed and added the following details: 'In this interval, a reference was made to Berlin as to whether the rifle offered was the same as the one in use in the German army, a satisfactory reply was received which may have led to the report of a letter from [Prince] Bismarck.'[89] White concluded his telegram by mentioning the German officers' influence on the Ottoman Army and on Ottoman arms purchasing decisions, and declared that the German military mission strongly supported the German position. Goltz Pasha and Kamphövener Pasha were both present at the practical comparison test, after which the final decision was made in favour of the Mauser rifles.[90] These two German officers had taken a position in favour of Mauser.[91] Moreover, the Sultan's inclination towards the German firms was real. In this way, Mauser had obtained the huge order.

However, White asserted that the Ottoman government had not chosen the German rifles because of the diplomatic intervention of the German ambassador. White emphasized the importance of the Sultan's personal intervention and noted, 'the German Mauser Rifle contract was given and obtained by H.I.M. [His Imperial Majesty]'s personal intervention – but how was this obtained – the public believe it was solely through the diplomatic intervention of the German Embassy – but I am assured £200,000 were spent as *Baksheesh* [bribery] in the parties immediately concerned at the Palace [and] elsewhere.'[92] However, it appears that this statement, which seems to exaggerate the amount of bribery involved, was an attempt at self-defence aimed against criticism of White's failure during the arms trade negotiations. Referring to a document dated 12 May 1888, Colin L. Smith notes that because of his lack of attention to British commercial and financial interests in the Ottoman market, White was bitterly attacked by a British ammunitions maker from Birmingham, Mr Kynoch. According to Smith, 'Mr Kynoc[h] complained to the Foreign Office that White failed personally and domestically as an unfavourable comparison between him and the German ambassador who eagerly fostered his country's financial interests at the Porte and the Palace.'[93]

Mauser's entrance into the Ottoman arms market made losers not only of the British firms; reliable American firms, which 'were well known to [the] Turkish Government,[94] lost their market share in the Ottoman business as well. On 27 January 1887, the Department of State in Washington sent a message to the US Legacy at İstanbul, with instructions from the Secretary of State, Thomas F. Bayard, to Pendleton King, the first secretary in the American Legation (1886–90): "Union Metallic Cartridge Company and Winchester Repeating Arms Company are reputable American Houses well known to Turkish Government. You will lend all proper countenance to secure for them full opportunity to lender bids and obtain contracts on equal footing with any other competitors."'[95]

The motive behind Bayard's telegram was the same as that underlying Salisbury's correspondence: the rumour of an officially biased decision in favour of German armaments companies, supported by Bismarck. Bayard actually sent three telegrams concerning this issue. The first is quoted above, the second was written, as Bayard said, 'in plain English', and the third, dated 29 January 1887, which dealt with the issue in detail and pointed out the Sublime Porte's possible favour for 'other companies', used 'blunter' language:

> Representations having been made to me that the agent, in Constantinople, of certain American houses of established repute, engaged in the manufacture of military supplies, encountered in the presentation of bids obstacles which, it is said, are not interposed in the case of competing contractors of other nationalities [...] Any obvious bar to open competition in disfavour of our producers and on behalf of those of another country, would suggest a discrimination which the Turkish Government cannot be supposed to intend.[96]

The Ottoman Empire's foreign policy under Sultan Abdülhamid can be summed up by the mantra 'trust Germany and distrust others', including the USA. Therefore, Bayard's suspicion of 'an obvious bar' was well-founded, but not provable. From all appearances, this contract was an international race, which the German firm having the strong and open support of Bismarck and the German government, won. The foreign offices of the countries whose companies strove to procure the contract – Germany, Britain and the USA – were officially involved in the Ottoman war business. Significantly, neither Bayard nor Salisbury sent any letters of recommendation directly or indirectly to the Ottoman government, whereas Bismarck, who had won the Sultan's trust through his meeting with Reşid Bey in December 1881, did.[97] The diplomatically weak intervention of the British and American embassies was not as influential as Bismarck's personal involvement.[98] Subsequently, William White and Pendleton King, and later Solomon Hirsch, justified their hands-off approach to the war business as a consequence of their role: the position of an ambassador must be neutral.[99] In terms of the war business, the ambassadors' perspective could have been an Achilles' heel for their countries, and Germany was well aware of that.

In this regard it is illuminating to cite a statement made by Mauser's business partner Isidor Loewe of Ludwig Loewe & Company of Berlin, who had accompanied Paul Mauser during his stay in İstanbul and took part in the negotiations with the Porte. As an eyewitness, Isidor Loewe also pointed out the importance of Prince Bismarck's intervention as a key component of the Mauser bid's success. 'At the end of the year 1886,' wrote Loewe,

> I went with Mr Mauser and Mr Alfred v. Kaulla to Constantinople in order to apply for an order for rifles and ammunition in common with the Mauser arms factory... And we succeeded through the very energetic and tireless support of the former Chancellor [Prince Bismarck] and through the self-sacrificing support of General Baron von der Goltz Pasha to obtain an order of 500,000 rifles and 100 million cartridges... This order is the basis of the great prosperity that the Mauser arms factory had.[100]

Behind Bismarck's official and personal support there was a well-calculated strategy, which demonstrates that Bismarck knew that international arms sales could be used as a significant symbol of support and a declaration of friendly relations that could create influence in the recipient countries. Brazilian case also could be named here as an illuminating supportive example. According to Mitchell, the German rulers 'did intervene more often and more aggressively to help Krupp than any other German company operating in Brazil [...] German arms dealers in Brazil did manage to edge out their competition more successfully than did merchants of any other commodity.'[101] As a consequence, international sales operations of the German arms makers benefited from Bismarck's official support, a support that Bismarck withheld from some other German international enterprises. When Alfred Kaulla and Georg von Siemens appealed to the German Foreign Office to request official support for their enterprise in the railway construction in the Ottoman Empire, namely, the Anatolian Railway Concession (La Société du Chemin de Fer Ottomane d'Anatolie) Bismarck declared his position through a note signed on 2 September 1888 saying that the German government would be remaining neutral on this matter.[102] Nonetheless, Bismarck, who let them return empty-handed, took an official stand in favour of the German armament companies, especially the Krupp and Mauser companies, and backed them in their Ottoman business.

This double standard practised by Bismarck shows he was aware of the functional differences between the two projects, which reveals the backbone of the peaceful penetration strategy. While a railway construction, as the future Bagdad Railway Project proved, had the potential to raise an international voice against German existence as a newcomer in the region, the armament firms and its sales to a foreign nation could not been regarded initially as a serious threat to their political interests and presence. In addition, Bismarck might have thought that competing in a field where the other countries' companies were more sophisticated and more experienced would not be strategically and economically beneficial to Germany. Germany, the country that defeated France using German-made war materials, could get the best opportunity to sell military products, the quality of which had been proved in the battlefield, to a country that employed the German military advisers.

However, as some countries experienced, neglecting the political implication and significance of the international arms trade, especially in terms of penetration of the country's ruling military elites, were costly strategic mistakes. As the consular correspondences, especially in the 1880s, indicate Germany's competitors did not pay enough attention to their armament firms' marketing efforts in the Ottoman market, and mainly focused on, in addition to some domestic political questions, railway construction or other commodity trades, as a result of which they lost their former political and military influence in the region. It seems clear that Germany discovered the importance of arms sales as a multidimensional instrument of doing economic foreign policy in an earlier time. As the official correspondence between the Foreign Offices and the embassies located in İstanbul clearly show, other arms supplier countries did not realise the critical meaning of the international arms trade as much as the Germans did. Moreover, through creating military, political and economic waves, the arms trade paved the road for peaceful German economic and financial penetration of the Ottoman Empire.

Since the Ottoman Empire could not finance expensive military contracts, for instance the above-mentioned Mauser contract, the cost of which was estimated at around two million OL (nearly 37 million marks) with its resources alone the Ottoman Empire had to apply to the German financial markets. Two German banks declared their willingness to act as guarantors for the payment.[103] As a consequence of this application, German capital began to appear in the Ottoman financial market and subsequently, in 1888, the Ottoman government signed a loan agreement with the Deutsche Bank for 21 million marks (1,135,000 OL).[104] As Bode asserted, this agreement was the first shock to the monopoly position of the French-dominated Banque Ottomane in the Ottoman financial market.[105] As the following table clearly demonstrates, the arms purchase was the foremost motive behind this loan application. On 12 November 1888, Ottoman bureaucrats prepared the following payment table based on the Deutsche Bank loan and its allocations: Table 1.1 clearly shows that more than half of the borrowed money (54 per cent) was reserved for war materials purchased from the

Table 1.1 Allocation of the Deutsche Bank Loan in 1888 (in Ottoman Lira)

Miscellaneous Expenses*	Ministry of War**	Mauser Rifles	Krupp Guns	Germania Shipyard	Total
283,201.24	238,897.58	299,664.42	213,236.75	100,000	1,135,000
25%	21%	26%	19%	9%	100 %
46%			54%		100 %

*Weekly wages of Military Officers and other important military expenses.
**Allocated for arrears of weekly wages of the Military Officers.
Source: BOA, Y.A.RES 40/36 (08.03.1306/12.11.1888).

German armament firms (Mauser, Krupp and the Germania Works in Kiel). Furthermore, as the German ambassador correctly foresaw, the involvement of German banks in Ottoman financial affairs would lead to long-term opportunities. In a report dated 3 July 1889, sent to Berlin, the German embassy in İstanbul predicted that within a few years 'a golden age might well dawn for creditors of the Turkish State'.[106] This loan marked the start of the process by which German capital interests began to dominate the Ottoman market, while others, especially the British capital and financial groups, began gradually to lose their hold.[107] In addition to Bismarck's patronage and the German military mission's advocacy, the German banks' financial support strengthened the German arms makers' position in the Ottoman market. As a result of this triple strength, German monopoly success in the Ottoman arms market became inevitable.

The timing of the contract signed between the Ottoman government and the Mauser Company was also remarkable. It took place at a time when Russian–Austrian tensions over the 'Eastern Question' had reached their zenith, so rearming the Ottoman Army with the new German-made weapons served at the same time as a political message to Russia.[108] According to Kössler, Bismarck, through his open support for the Ottoman Empire, intended to warn Russia that Germany was able to counter any Russian threat by building closer relations with the Sultan, sending military advisers and providing weapons.[109] As Smith states, during the autumn and winter of 1887, Russo–German relations became increasingly strained.[110] Furthermore, in August 1887, Bismarck encouraged the Sublime Porte to take immediate military action against Prince Ferdinand of Bulgaria following his announced annexation of East Rumelia. Tevfik Pasha, the Ottoman ambassador in Berlin, reported that Bismarck told him:

> If the Ottoman Government sends troops to Eastern Rumelia in a short period of time, the Government could guarantee its right over [Eastern Rumelia]. And also through warding off [*def'i*] Prince Ferdinand from Bulgaria, the Government could

assure the public order [there]. If not, Russia would be compelled to occupy [Bulgaria].[111]

Although the Sublime Porte intensified its armaments policy considering this critical moment, Sultan Abdülhamid did not want to enter a war and so he did not send his army to Eastern Rumelia.[112] Abdülhamid was, as Yasamee notes, adamant that he would not take military action against the Bulgarians, nor any other measure 'which might lead to the use of force'. Yasamee gives the following quotation from a *İrâde* issued on the Bulgarian question:

> If, in accordance with the advice of [Russia, Germany, and France] recourse is had to violent measures... there is no knowing how the Imperial troops despatched to Eastern Rumelia will be received by the Bulgarians. If they are met with armed force, blood will flow and the efforts which we have made over two years to avoid such a state of affairs will go to waste.[113]

In this manner, supplying weapons and appointing military advisers to the foreign armies became one of the fundamental elements of Germany's economic foreign policy. Moreover, as Krupp director Carl Menshausen wrote to the Under-Secretary of German Foreign Affairs, Freiherrn von Richthofen, a war materials order obtained from a foreign state was a reflection of the political power/influence situation (*eine politische Machtfrage*) or an outcome of a political commercial transaction (*Ergebnis eines politischen Handelsgeschäftes*).[114] This statement was an attempt to explain why German arms makers so persistently demanded the special support of the German embassies abroad (*der besonderen H{i}lfe der Kaiserlichen Vertretungen*). However, Kössler suggests that Bismarck's intervention had a political as well as an economic basis, since Bismarck was aware of the importance of the arms trade as a political instrument that German ambassadors abroad could use as a political negotiation tool. Kössler notes that 'on 14 January 1887 Bismarck issued a directive to the German ambassadors concerning the eco-political aspect of Germany's Ottoman arms business, stating that the German diplomats should leverage their influence and support the German companies in obtaining [the armaments] orders in question'.[115]

Moreover, when considering Bismarck's point of view on the Ottoman question and the link between the arms trade and its finance, the prominent German banking house of Bleichröder must also be taken into account.[116] Until 1895, the House of Bleichröder was the only German bank in the syndicate which represented the German delegate in the Ottoman Public Debt Administration, and was one of the three members of the Tobacco Regie.[117] This key institution had a clear impact on Bismarck's approach to building Germany's foreign trade policy. According to Stern, 'the House of Bleichröder was selected as having the right to name the German delegate in the Ottoman Public Debt Administration' and this selection was made with 'the blessing of the German Foreign Office'.[118] Indeed, Gerson von Bleichröder (1822–93), the Chancellor's banker, or – as Europe knew him – Bismarck's secret agent in foreign affairs, was one of the leading characters in Bismarck's economic expansion strategy towards the Ottoman Empire.[119] Illich suggests that 'the expansion of German influence abroad must be seen within the context of Bleichröder's participation in Ottoman affairs'.[120] Stern argues that the foreign governments and bankers needed Bleichröder's support, and he needed their business, noting that Bleichröder 'negotiated with the foreign governments; he formed alliances with or against other bankers or syndicates in other countries'.[121]

Stern also confirmed that Bismarck was well aware that German capital investment abroad was a source of power, influence and prestige for Germany.[122] A principal field was Ottoman railway construction, where most German capital was invested. However, another critical subject was the modernization of the Ottoman army, which needed new weapons and also some structural changes; it also required foreign loans. For that reason, foreign capital became indispensable for the Ottoman government. So procuring foreign loans and obtaining arms contracts from abroad became a new type of penetration of the supplier country, especially for Bismarck's, and later Wilhelm II's, Germany.

His influence on the German arms trade in the Ottoman market was obvious. In foreign markets – in this case, the Ottoman Empire – German arms makers colluded with the holders of German capital. Bismarck's closeness to Bleichröder played a crucial role in his interest in German capital investment abroad. Furthermore, the exports of war materials made an extraordinary contribution to Germany's total foreign trade. The increasing share of the arms trade started as early as the 1880.[123] The years after 1880 became a turning point for German interests in the Ottoman Empire. As Epkenhans points out, between 1888 and 1893 German exports to the Ottoman Empire rose by 350 per cent and the arms trade was the most significant part of the picture.[124] Germany's export growth coincided with her increasing political influence in the Ottoman Empire. As *The {London} Times* noted in 1881, while the Ottoman special mission was still in Berlin, 'Germany has now in Constantinople that commanding political influence which England once possessed'.[125] Moreover, Lord Ampthill, the British ambassador in Berlin, reported that German–Ottoman relations had reached 'a state of real intimacy which has never before existed'.[126]

The crucial part of the German war business had begun and flourished during the Bismarckian era. The influential military missions, under Kähler and later Goltz Pasha, were sent to the Ottoman Empire during his chancellorship. It was during these years that the major steps in the Ottoman military modernization process were taken. In the end, as the *Fortnightly Review* noted, 'the good German officers were happy in the belief that they were regenerating Turkey, and in the receipt of handsome pay; the Turks imagine that they were gaining the friendship of Bismarck. All the parties were pleased and contented.'[127] However, the Kaiser's impact on the German arms makers' business abroad was even more impressive than Bismarck's. His expansionist activities, including his two *Orientreise*, which will be detailed below, went hand in hand with the German arms makers' successful business. For that reason, it is essential to focus on Kaiser Wilhelm II's intervention in the war business, which was based on his aggressive expansionist foreign policy and also affected by his personality.

Kaiser Wilhelm II and the Origin of His Ottoman Policy

The foundation of Germany's peaceful penetration strategy toward the Ottoman Empire was laid by Bismarck, but it was strengthened and aggressively broadened by Kaiser Wilhelm II, who made a concerted effort to extend German economic and political influence in the Ottoman Empire. Like Abdülhamid II in Ottoman foreign and domestic policy, the German Emperor, Wilhelm II – especially after he dismissed Bismarck from his post as Imperial Chancellor in the second year of his reign, in 1890 – became the most potent and active figure in the Empire's domestic and foreign affairs. Smith asserted in a 1915 article that, even before Bismarck's dismissal from office, 'the old prince prophesied that, the young emperor would someday be his own chancellor'.[128] Smith further argued that Kaiser Wilhelm's chancellors had been vice-chancellors and his secretaries of state for foreign affairs had been under-secretaries.[129] Interestingly, but unsurprisingly, both Abdülhamid II and Wilhelm II were described by some contemporaries as their own foreign ministers.[130] Kaiser Wilhelm II gathered the power of the decision-making process, both in foreign and internal policy, under his own authority, as Abdülhamid II did likewise in his Empire.

According to some commentators, Wilhelm II's personality had a significant impact on his political choices and decision-making processes. An analysis of his character is not the main aim of this chapter, but nevertheless, since the Kaiser's personality played a crucial role in the shaping of Germany's eastward expansion policy, it is important to consider his personality.[131] Thomas A. Kohut, for instance, in his book *Wilhelm II and the Germans: A Study of Leadership*, pays a good deal of attention to the Kaiser's personality and its impact on his concept of rule. The subtitles of the book's chapters themselves highlight the context of the book. The first chapter is called 'The politicization of personality' and the second is 'The personalization of politics'. 'German politics' Kohut contends, 'influenced Wilhelm II's psychological development and came to be incorporated in his psyche. Of course every human being is shaped by the political and social forces of the day. In Wilhelm's case, the influence of those forces was not small but extensive.'[132] Passant also links Kaiser Wilhelm's personality and his foreign policy, arguing the Kaiser's character, which he describes as 'vain, romantic, versatile, self-willed, rash in utterance, alternating between excessive self-confidence and nervous depression', exercised a powerful influence on events.[133] McMeekin also argues that the Kaiser's first trip to Istanbul in 1889 particularly highlighted his 'reckless sense of statecraft, born of his restless, unbalanced character'.[134]

Prince Bülow (1849–1929) who accompanied Kaiser Wilhelm during his second *Orientreise*, expressed the view that 'Wilhelm II was not mentally deficient, but he was certainly superficial, hyper-sensitive to impressions, lacking in self-criticism and self-control, and hence, frequently at the mercy of rapidly-changing influences'.[135] Ellis Barker, one of Wilhelm's contemporaries, discussed the impact of his personality on German foreign policy, saying that 'the net result of Kaiser Wilhelm's unceasing activity during the 17 years of his reign seemed to be that Germany lost ground and prestige in foreign politics'.[136] According to *The Outlook*, Prince Bismarck's fall was the result of, and evidence of, the Kaiser's intention to become his own Foreign Minister.[137] Trumpener also describes the changed foreign politics after Bismarck's forced retirement as 'increasingly erratic and fumbling'.[138]

As can be seen, almost all of the writers quoted above were of the opinion that Kaiser Wilhelm II tried to shape his Empire's foreign policy in line with his own political vision and preferences. On the other hand, it is crucial to note that the ground on which the Kaiser built his political plans was prepared by Bismarck's economic expansionist approach. As much as some of the Kaiser's speeches sounded like expressions of a solely colonial expansionist desire, the major motivation behind his acts and deeds, in terms of foreign economic policy, might be seen instead as the pursuit of economic benefits for German firms. Based on his Empire's growing and varying industrial production capacity, particularly in the iron and steel industries, and its accumulation of capital, he encouraged companies and financiers to invest abroad, where they could find more market possibilities.

For Kaiser Wilhelm II, like Bismarck before him, the Ottoman Empire appeared as an open field where Germany's export-oriented economic expansionist agenda might successfully be put into practice. In practice, Kaiser Wilhelm II followed the path Bismarck had laid for German foreign diplomacy. As Hans Delbrück justly asserted, 'everything that he [Kaiser Wilhelm II] undertook and strove after has its origins, is present in embryo, in the policy of Bismarck'.[139] As a part of his desire to become 'a world-emperor', the Kaiser tended to use every possible circumstance to sustain his Empire's foreign reputation as a *Weltmacht*.[140] A December 1897 note from the American embassy in İstanbul demonstrates that Kaiser Wilhelm successfully applied this desire in his Ottoman policy. In his report, dealing with German influence in the Ottoman Empire, James B. Angell, wrote:

> For the last two or three years the German Emperor has lost no opportunity to add to his prestige in Turkey. He [the Kaiser] apparently took pains to give no offense to the Sultan by any adverse criticisms in the time of the great disorders here. He has furnished some of his most accomplished officers to instruct and to guide the Turkish army.[141]

However, Wilhelm's Ottoman approach was consistent with the application of Carl Peters' general expansionist formulation.[142] In his economic and political expansion policy, Wilhelm II, seemed to conform to the leadership role envisaged by Peters: 'These purely commercial questions' asserted Peters,

> certainly play a key role in politics, or so it was supposed. From a macro point of view, the head of state of a nation is no different than a managing director of a business company [*Geschäftsführer*]. Even to just survive on this unpleasant planet, we have to eat and drink. So in other words, it is the first and foremost responsibility of the leader of the 'herd' to provide his herd with food and drink.[143]

In the mind of the *Geschäftsführer* of the German Empire, Kaiser Wilhelm II, the Ottoman Empire was a region that could provide vital natural resources and a virgin market for the German *Volks*. When Germany reached that stage of development, the foreign markets became a vital element to her prosperity.[144] Chancellor Caprivi noted, in December 1891, that Germany 'must export either goods or men'.[145] His statement was an earlier expression of the idea Friedrich Ratzel later formulated as the necessity of *Lebensraum*.[146] In contrast to Bismarck's policy of balance in Europe, Kaiser Wilhelm II opened the way for a Franco–Russian alliance against the German Empire, which crystallized between 1892 and 1894. On 18 January, 1896, on the occasion of the 25th anniversary of the unification and establishment of the German Empire, the Kaiser made a dinner speech (*Tischrede*) in the *Königlichen Schloβ* in which he emphasized Germany's ambition to become a colonial empire:

> What our fathers hoped for, what the German youth dreamingly sang about and longed for, was their wishes for the two Kaisers together with the princes, to gain back and re-establish the German Reich. We may gratefully enjoy the benefits, and we should be happy on this particular day. With this, however, comes on us the serious duty to also retain what our ancestors and leaders have gained back for us. The German Reich has become a World Reich.[147]

After these provocative introductory remarks, the Kaiser told those in attendance that their duty was to help him to strengthen the Great German Empire (*dieses größere Deutsche Reich*), one that included all Germans scattered across the globe.[148] On 20 October 1896, ten months after the Kaiser's speech, *The {London} Times* published an article showing the amount of land acquired by Germany in the space of 12 years, from 1884–96.

As Table 1.2 clearly indicates Germany, which had almost no territories under her control in 1884, became – on the eve of World War I – a colonial power that ruled over an area of more than one million square miles. However, this great expansion in overseas

Table 1.2 German Colonial Expansion, 1884–96 (in Square Miles)

	1884	1896
Africa	0	920,920
The Pacific	0	102,150
Total	0	1,023,070

Source: *The {London} Times*, 20 October 1896.

territory did not provide enough income for a rapidly growing population that exceeded 60 million people by 1914. Another prominent colonialist, Friedrich Naumann, formulated the necessity for an expansionist strategy based on the fundamental economic requirements of 'bread and jobs' (*Brot und Arbeit*), citing the fact that 'the national agriculture could not provide enough production to sustain the whole population'.[149] Earle's following conclusion of the German need for new sphere of influence is very illuminating: 'as the German worker was dependent upon imported grain, so the German manufacturer was dependent upon imported raw materials'.[150] In a contemporary article, the gravity of the issue was described as a 'black necessity' that shaped German expansionist policy.[151] As the article explained, 'hence German statesmen, to find room for their surplus population and to extend German trade and provide for the mill and factory workers at home, must try to expand the German colonial empire'.[152] As Feis pointed out, 'by the end of the century the industrial organisation of a unified Germany had taken massive form. Its foreign commerce was rivalling that of the British. Its highly concentrated banking system was finding the means not only to finance the impulsion of industry at home, but also implant offshoots abroad.'[153] Germany was no longer the relatively poor country it had been at the beginning of the nineteenth century. In the year 1820, in the territory that came to lie within the frontiers of the German Empire by 1914,[154] there lived only 24,905,000 people, but by the year 1871, when the Empire was established, the population had reached 39,456,000. In 1888, Wilhelm II became the Kaiser of some 46,538,000 people. By 1898, at the time of his second *Orientreise* in İstanbul, the Kaiser led more than 52 million people.[155]

The rapid growth in Germany's population, as Figure 1.1 shows below, especially from the 1870s, triggered fears of economic shortages in some crucial areas. Therefore Naumann's concept of *Brot und Arbeit* became more vital to German *Lebensinteresse*;[156] or at least this fact was used as an agitating issue by the supporters of colonialist and expansionist foreign policy. So it was likely that the young Kaiser Wilhelm II, as *der führende Kopf der Herde*, felt himself obliged to take into account the growing population, the vast industrial progress, and the production surplus in formulating his foreign policy. The growing shortage of raw materials forced him to act to become a strong participant in the *Weltmarkt*, which carried, as Naumann dictated, an essential interest (*Lebensinteresse*) for the whole German people, but also a special interest for industrial entrepreneurs, traders and workers.[157] This challenge was well summarized by Howe in 1919, when he emphasized Germany's dependency on the outside world for raw materials: 'Any interruption of the source of supply [of raw materials] would weaken or destroy her [Germany's] life.'[158]

It also became clear in Wilhelm II's Germany that the domestic market was too small to absorb the surplus of industrial production,

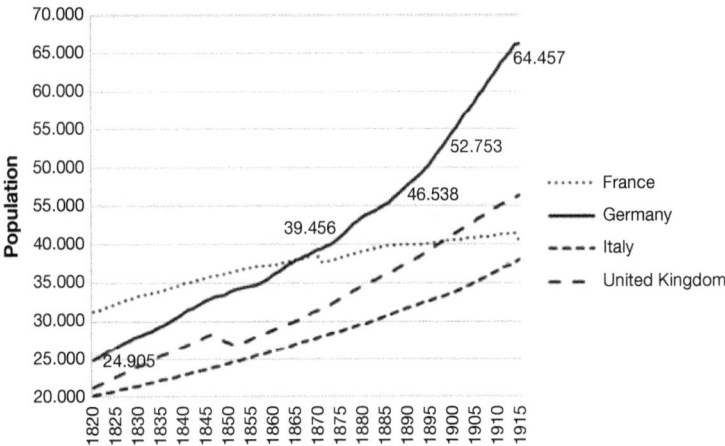

Figure 1.1 Population Growth in Europe: 1820–1915 (000 at Mid-year)
Source: Angus Maddison, 'Historical Statistics of the World Economy: 1–2008 AD'.

especially some of the output of the iron and steel industries, which had become the most important component of German economic growth. In order to be able to provide the necessary resources for the growing industrial demand upon which 'the life of the nation seemed to depend[ed]' Germany needed new markets and new sources.[159] From railway construction to arms making, the iron and steel industries played a crucial role in Germany's economic progress and the expansionist strategy based on it. A key motivation behind the aggressive expansionist policy was to increase their capacity. The following comparison table (Table 1.3) illustrates the vast growth in the sector between 1886 and 1910, and provide some figures that highlight Germany's ability to 'contend' in the very competitive *Weltmarkt*.

As seen in the table, by 1910 Germany had outdistanced Britain and her continental rivals.[160] Through a rapid increase in steel production, Germany had become the second largest steel producer in the world, after the USA. Passant asserts that the German iron masters and metal manufacturers learned much from their British rivals: he writes that 'they paid careful attention to the problem of the location of their plants, and they appreciated the importance of concentration in their industry'.[161] As the next table (Table 1.4) clearly demonstrates, Germany's pig-iron output outdistanced Britain's in less than three decades.

Table 1.3   Steel Production by Major Producers, 1886–1910 (in 1000 Tons)

	1886	1910	Growth (%)
USA	2,604.4	26,512.4	910.3
Germany	954.6	13,698.6	1,335.0
Great Britain	2,403.2	6,106.8	154.1
France	427.6	3,390.3	692.9
Russia	241.8	2,350.0	871.2
Belgium	164.0	1,449.5	783.6

Source: Karl Helfferich, *Germany's Economic Progress and National Wealth 1888–1913* (Berlin, 1913), p. 64.

Germany, which had produced only four million tons of pig-iron in 1887, achieved within 14 years an output of 15,574,000 tons, which made it the world's second-largest pig-iron producer in 1911. For export-oriented economic expansion strategists, iron and steel became the leading industry. The statistics quoted prove that in the key industries (additionally in mining, manufacture, agriculture and commerce) Germany's progress was 'stupendous'.[162] Among the outputs, railway and war materials were the most prominent 'German-made' productions of these industries; they were extensively exported. In fact, foreign markets were of vital significance for the sustainability of German industrial growth, which Naumann termed a *Lebensinteresse*.[163] As Ripley's calculation indicates in 1880–8, Germany's total exports had more than doubled. Especially, through the protective economic system, argues Ripley, Germany became one of the great manufacturing nations of Europe, namely the second to England.[164]

In the context of the *Lebensinteresse*, 'travel to the East' became a journey of hope to find a new *Lebensraum* that would overcome the shortages and risks in the event of inadequate demand for the new manufactured goods. Germany's dependence on other countries for so much of its raw materials and some semi-finished goods put it in a precarious position.[165] The import requirements of Germany's growing industry and increasing population were enormous. As Earle noted, the Ottoman Empire was rich in certain important raw

Table 1.4 Pig-iron Production by Major Producers, 1887–1911 (in 1000 Tons)

	1887	1911	Growth (%)
USA	6,520	24,028	268.5
Germany	4,024	15,574	287.6
Great Britain and Ireland	7,681	10,033	30.06
France	1,568	4,441	181.3
Russia	612	3,588	486.3
Belgium	758	2,106	178.8

Source: Karl Helfferich, *Germany's Economic Progress and National Wealth 1888–1913* (Berlin, 1913), p. 124.

materials, such as minerals, fuels and lubricants, as well as in textile production. Earle described the chrome, antimony, manganese, copper, emery, meerschaum, oil, cotton and silk that constituted the Ottoman Empire's great natural wealth as 'a lure to European traders and investors'.[166]

Due to expansionist motivations and the vast development of its industrial production, Germany increased her foreign trade dramatically. Germany imported raw materials and foodstuffs and exported a great variety of manufactured goods; finished industrial products held an increasingly important place in export growth. The table below indicates the dramatic increase in Germany's total foreign trade between 1860 and 1913.

This remarkable increase in German foreign trade (from £124 million in 1860 to some £1,050 million in 1913) went hand in hand with the political expansionist strategy. In fact, German policy makers found a point of intersection between foreign policy motives and economic priorities. The iron and steel industry and the export of its production, especially war materials and railway, was the first of five principal groups of German manufactured goods, and became a very useful foreign policy instrument. Table 1.6 shows the five most important sectors of German manufactured goods and their percentage of total exports in 1913.

Table 1.5 Germany's Foreign Trade, 1860–1913 (in British Pounds)

Years	Export	Import
1860	70,000,000	54,750,000
1872	124,600,000	173,250,000
1880	148,850,000	142,200,000
1890	170,500,000	213,650,000
1900	237,650,000	302,150,000
1910	373,735,000	446,705,000
1913	504,825,000	538,515,000

The values given in the table excluded re-exports and precious metals.
Source: Ernest James Passant, *A Short History of Germany 1815–1945* (Cambridge, 1959), p. 112.

Through export relations, German bureaucrats abroad became more able to penetrate government decision-making processes and to lobby on behalf of German commercial interests. The Ottoman Empire, which was not self-sufficient in arms production or railway construction, was more vulnerable in this context. In contrast to other suppliers who invested in the Ottoman market, the Germans penetrated that market through a well-prepared strategic package in which economic motives were perfectly harmonized with the political approach. For that reason, the economic activities of German companies, particularly arms makers, and their success in the Ottoman market, cannot be considered only from a commercially-focused point of view. On the contrary, in the mind of Kaiser Wilhelm II, the business actors were the commercial representatives of his *Weltmacht* policy, in tandem with the experienced diplomatic personnel of the German Foreign Office – *Auswärtiges Amt*. For German foreign policy, economic strength – along with all its instruments, such as capital, industry and trade – ranked highly among the determinant factors of the expansion policy. According to the German ambassador to İstanbul, Marschall, German capital, industry and trade – as instruments of expansionist power – were protected by the German government, and they created political interests in the countries where they established themselves.[167]

The German war business in the Ottoman market serves as an excellent case for observing the existence of the link between

Table 1.6 Five Principal Manufactured Goods in Germany and their Percentage of Exports in 1913

Manufactured goods	Per cent (%)
Iron products	15.8
Machinery	11.2
Textiles*	12.7
Chemicals and dyes	9.4
Leather and leather articles	5.4

*Not including clothes.
Source: H. G. Moulton, 'Economic and Trade Position of Germany', in *Annals of the American Academy of Political and Social Science* 114, (1924), p. 2.

economic growth and expansionist foreign policy. The relationship was also clearly formulated by Prince Bülow, who argued that German foreign policy should follow the expansion of economic strength. In one of his speeches, he noted that 'as the German production [*deutsche Arbeit*] conquered [*erobert*] further her dominant position on the world market, our foreign policy should follow the consequences of our current economic strength [*wirtschaftlichen Kräfte*]'.[168] German economic growth had a driving effect on expansionist and aggressive foreign policy. It was these ideas and circumstances that encouraged Kaiser Wilhelm II to pay two visits to the Ottoman Empire during Abdülhamid II's reign.[169] These visits had both political and economic motivations, and they resulted in multidimensional consequences.

Kaiser Wilhelm II's First *Orientreise* in 1889 and its Consequences

Kaiser Wilhelm II visited Abdülhamid II in İstanbul in 1889, one year after his accession.[170] The German Emperor and Empress remained there for five days, from 2–6 November, visiting all the principal sights.[171] As widely stated, the visit was planned as an addition to a family visit to Greece, where Kaiser Wilhelm's sister Sophie was married to Crown Prince Constantine. However according to one document – a telegram Abdülhamid II sent to the Kaiser on 4 September 1889 – the Sultan invited the Kaiser to İstanbul as his guest.[172] This telegram reveals the Kaiser had expressed his intention to visit İstanbul as early as September of the same year. Referring to his good relations with the Kaiser's father and his predecessors, Abdülhamid prefaced his expectations of future bilateral relations. In reply, the Kaiser expressed his gratitude upon the acceptance of his intention to visit İstanbul.[173] According to McMurray, Wilhelm's intention was 'to take a first-hand look at the Ottoman Empire's offerings'.[174]

Because Wilhelm II was the first European monarch to visit İstanbul,[175] the Ottoman press showed very keen interest in the young Kaiser's visit.[176] One of the most important newspapers,

Sabah, welcomed the Kaiser and Kaiserin on its front page, publishing a welcome notice in German and in Turkish under the pictures of the German royal couple.[177] *Tercümân-ı Hakikât* published a translation of the German national anthem along with the original German as a sign of Ottoman sympathy for the German Empire.[178] *The Levant Herald and Eastern Express* published a special edition on 3 November 1889 with details about the Kaiser's arrival and his first day in the city.[179] The pavilion in Yilidz Palace where the Kasier and the Kaiserin were accommodated was furnished 'with every possible luxury'.[180] Regarding the dinner they had with the Sultan, Vice-Admiral Paul Hoffmann noted in his diary that 'the dinner was very elaborate, the table was a magnificently arranged, we ate off nothing but gold'.[181] As cited by Röhl, Kaiser Wilhelm had brought a large rococo clock decorated with figures costing 1,800 marks and two nine-branched candelabra worth 1,100 marks as a present for the Sultan; however, according to Röhl 'these costly gifts were far outdone by the Sultan's presents to his guest'.[182]

When the Kaiser visited İstanbul, Bismarck was still Chancellor, and in fact did not favour the Emperor's visit. However, his opposition was based mainly on Germany's geopolitical position. As Kaiser Wilhelm narrated in his memoir, published in 1922, Bismarck, on his return from İstanbul in 1889, had inquired about the Kaiser's impressions. 'In doing this,' said the Kaiser,

> it struck me that Prince Bismarck spoke quite disdainfully of Turkey, of the men in high position there, and of conditions in that land. I thought I might inspire him in part with essentially more favourable opinions, but my efforts were of little avail. Upon asking the Prince the reason why he held such an unfavourable opinion, he answered that Count Herbert [von Bismarck (1849–1904)] had reported very disapprovingly [*abfällig*] on Turkey. Prince Bismarck and Count Herbert were never favourably inclined toward Turkey and they never agreed with me in my Turkish policy the old policy of Frederick the Great.[183]

Apparently, the statement the Kaiser made demonstrates a diversion from the tone of Bismarck's remarks in conversation with Reşid Bey in December 1881. The Kaiser's statement might have been motivated by his desire to be regarded as the unique architect of German Ottoman policy, which had offered profitable opportunities for German industrialists and capitalists for decades. According to McMeekin, 'the Kaiser was anxious to make a name for himself and emerge from shadow of Germany's long-serving Chancellor [...] The state visit to Constantinople accomplished both tricks at once.'[184] In fact, the fundamental differences between the Kaiser's approach to improving German–Ottoman relations and Bismarck's approach were only in their tone and in the style. Bismarck preferred a stealthy approach, whereas Kaiser Wilhelm II followed an ostentatious path.[185] The general motivation behind their tactics was the same: achieving the success of the German expansionist policy. In this regard, it is important to recall that Bismarck – in spite of his 'pretended disinterestedness' – and the Kaiser were the creators of the first wave of the German expansionist strategy towards the Ottoman Empire. As stated above, Bismarck's principal contribution to this wave was his decision to send civil and military advisers to assist the Ottoman Empire. The effectiveness and strength of this policy were fortified by Kaiser Wilhelm's first visit to İstanbul in 1889.

Although Bismarck opposed the public impression of a politically oriented visit to the Sultan, the Kaiser's first visit accelerated and strengthened the expansionist wave of German penetration of the Ottoman Empire. However, in a letter sent to the German ambassador in Rome, Bismarck recounted how he struggled to convince the other European states, particularly Russia, that the purpose of the Kaiser's visit was solely a simple 'sightseeing desire'.[186] Rumours of the Ottoman entrance into the Triple Alliance perturbed the other European powers greatly, and Bismarck was anxious to convince them that the Ottoman Empire would stay out of the Triple Alliance.

On 4 November, Count Herbert von Bismarck, Bismarck's oldest son, visited the British ambassador in Istanbul, Sir William White. According to an Ottoman document, it was a rather lengthy visit (*uzunca bir ziyâret*).[187] Count Herbert's obvious purpose was to eliminate the rumours about the purpose of the Kaiser's visit. Count Herbert is said to have assured White that 'political questions were hardly touched upon between the two Sovereigns'.[188] However, the short visit of the Kaiser created an obvious rapprochement. 'All accounts,' White reported to London, 'concur in stating that the relations between their Imperial Majesties and the Sultan were throughout of a very cordial character and led to the foundation of intimate relations such as exist between allied Sovereigns.'[189] However, according to an Ottoman document White expressed his thoughts about the Kaiser's visit in the following words: 'The visit of His Majesty the Kaiser of the German Empire entailed your [the Sultan's] humble servant's gratitude and gladness.'[190] Nevertheless, Bismarck was of the opinion that the establishment of friendly relations between the two leaders must not necessarily lead to a formal political and military alliance. Therefore on 15 October 1889, he felt himself obliged to deny Germany had any political interest in the Black Sea and Mediterranean region:

> Germany does not have any political interests in either the Black Sea or the Mediterranean, and thus attributing political motives to our majesties' visit to İstanbul is out of the question. Admittance of the Porte to the triple alliance is not possible; we could not place the German nation with the burden of waging a war against Russia for the future of Baghdad.[191]

As Smith clearly stressed, the keystone of Bismarck's entire foreign policy, from the unification of Germany to his dismissal from the Imperial Chancellorship in 1890, was the maintenance of friendly relations with Russia: 'As long as Russia was friendly, no dangerous coalition could be formed against united Germany.'[192] *The Levant Herald and Eastern Express* quoted a comment from *The Berlin Post* noting that the Kaiser's visit to İstanbul aimed 'neither at the inception nor at the conclusion of any political combinations, but it remains nevertheless an event of high importance because it will contribute to consolidate the international position of Turkey'.[193] As a matter of fact, the short visit became an important and influential step that changed the parameters of German and Ottoman foreign policy and determined the character of bilateral ties for many years.[194] Marriott's discussion of the Kaiser's intentions provides an enlightening frame for the Kaiser's first visit to İstanbul: 'It was precisely seven hundred years as the German colony of Constantinople reminded their sovereign, since a German emperor had first set foot in the imperial city. But Frederick Barbarossa had come sword in hand; the Emperor William came as the apostle of peace; as the harbinger of economic penetration; almost, as was observed at the time, in the guise of a commercial traveller.'[195]

Despite the brevity of the Kaiser's first visit, from a long-term perspective its political and economic impact was crucial. The outcomes of the Kaiser's visit and the German influence in the Ottoman Empire were remarkably foreseen in an article published in *Sabah* on 12 November 1889, which predicted that the 20 years following the visit would see a clash of German and French interests in the Ottoman Empire.[196] While the Kaiser was in İstanbul, he received 'a prime piece of real estate in Therapia'.[197] This served as the German ambassador's summer residence, which was described by Pendleton King, the first secretary in the American Legation at İstanbul, as 'a beautifully situated palace'.[198]

One remarkable and symbolic consequence of the visit was the permission extended by the Sultan for the construction of a German church in Jerusalem.[199] The foundation stone of this church, the Church of the Redeemer (*Erlöserkirche*), the first German Protestant Church in Jerusalem, was laid in 1893, and Kaiser Wilhelm II was himself present at the consecration during his second *Orientreise* in 1898.[200] After this visit, the closeness between Kaiser Wilhelm II and Abdülhamid II had clearly increased.[201] On 4 November 1889, Kaiser Wilhelm II was decorated with an *Osmaniye Nişânı*.[202] Furthermore he received an honorary title of 'Ottoman Artillery Commander' (*Grand maitre Honoraire Artillerie Ottomane*), which was basically a title created for him, in recognition of his contribution to the artillery purchasing process with the German firm Krupp.[203] In short, as he wrote in a telegram to Prince Bismarck, the Kaiser seemed to be generally very pleased with the Sultan's hospitality. *The Times* reported that on the Kaiser's return voyage, on 7 November, Bismarck received the following telegram from the Kaiser: 'After a stay which seems like a dream and which the magnificent hospitality of the Grand Seignior [Abdülhamid II] rendered paradisiacal, I am now passing the Dardanelles in beautiful weather.'[204] The Kaiser sent several telegrams to Bismarck during his trip. For instance, upon his arrival he wrote to Bismarck: 'At this moment I have arrived to İstanbul. The weather is very nice and the beauty of the landscape cannot be described.'[205]

Apart from these symbolic expressions of alliance and the other benefits for Germany, the impact of the visit is revealed in foreign trade statistics. The most important development towards improving trade relations between Germany and the Ottoman Empire occurred when the Sultan granted the Deutsche Bank exclusive rights over the Anatolian Railways project on 6 October 1888 (before the visit occurred, but after several exchanges between the Kaiser and the Sultan).[206] This concession, extended to the German group (Deutsche Bank, Württembergische Vereinsbank, and Deutsche Vereinsbank), represented a confirmation of the change in Germany's attitude towards the Ottoman Empire, as well as the changed orientation of the foreign policy of the Ottoman Empire in terms of European relations. Shaw asserts that one of Sultan's motives was to divert political and imperial rivalries into economic ones.[207] In fact, in 1888, the only railway in Asia Minor (the İzmir–Aydın, İzmir–Kasaba, Mersin–Adana and Bosporus–İzmit lines) were completely or, as Woods said, at least practically, in the hands of English capitalists.[208] As the German *chargé d'affairs* at İstanbul pointed out, since Abdülhamid was distrustful of British and French finance, German financial undertakings in his Empire might be welcomed.[209] The interest of British capital in the Anatolian Railway Company disappeared when the German syndicate bought out the British shareholding.[210] Subsequently the company became, as Jastrow described it, 'a purely German enterprise'.[211]

Sultan Abdülhamid granted the Germans (headed by the Deutsche Bank) the right to buy the existing railway from Haydarpaşa to İzmit and to build a new line from İzmit to Ankara in October 1888. The

Sultan guaranteed the Ankara line minimum annual revenue of 15,000 francs per kilometre.[212] The concession was to last for 99 years and the construction was to take three years.[213] The construction of the first railway line (İzmit–Ankara) started in 1889 and it was completed by 31 December 1892; naturally, the Sultan and his government appreciated the 'rapid completion of the Ankara section'.[214] A couple of months after the opening of that line, on 15 February 1893, Abdülhamid issued a new *İrâde* authorizing the construction of another line from Eskişehir to Konya, which in turn was opened in 1896.[215]

Woods suggested that German diplomacy influenced the Porte to forcibly dispossess the British company, with the consequence that the line was handed over to a German syndicate financed by the Deutsche Bank.[216] The building of the railway was financed by the sale of Ottoman bonds, which were issued to the Anatolian Railway Company and guaranteed on a kilometric basis. Government income sources, like agricultural taxes, were held in reserve for payment of these guarantees, through which the company was assured 'a certain amount of gross revenue per kilometre of track laid and in use'.[217] As the British embassy reported in 1899, the Anatolian Railway (1,023 kilometres with a kilometric guarantee of 15,000 francs a year) became the most important of the railways built in the Ottoman Empire.[218] Table 1.7 shows the opening dates of the German-made railway lines. It also can be read as an indicator of the German-origin Anatolian Railway Company's increasing share of Ottoman railway construction.

The economic contribution of the German-built railways to the region's economic outcomes was published in the company's periodical reports (*Statistiques du Service des Recettes*). According to a report published on 25 February 1893, for instance, the tithes collected had increased by around 41 per cent in three years. The following table, also published in the report, shows the increase in the amount of the tithe collected by the government from the cities through which the Anatolian Railway Company operated, namely Ankara, İzmit and Kütahya. The company was able to assert that the Ottoman Treasury had not been substantially burdened as a consequence of the kilometric guarantee.[219]

Table 1.7 The Length and Opening Dates of the Railways Laid by the Anatolian Railway Company

Lines	Kilometres	Opening Date
İzmit–Arifiye	41	June 1890
Arifiye–Eskişehir	182	June 1892
Eskişehir–Ankara	263	December 1892
Eskişehir–Alayurt–Kütahya	77	December 1894
Alayurt–Afyon	94	August 1895
Afyon–Konya	274	July 1896
Total	931	

Source: Manfred Pohl, *Philipp Holzmann: Geschichte eines Bauunternehmens 1849–1999* (München, 1999), p. 100.

Contrary to the company's assertion, while the guarantee system reduced the German investors' entrepreneurial risk, it was 'uneconomic' for the Ottoman Empire.[220] Quataert suggests that the financial performance of the Anatolian Railway Company was poor, and asserts that 'the railroad's major contribution, as the government had intended, lay not in economic development but in added military strength'. He writes:

> For these strategic and economic benefits, the Ottoman Empire paid a high price. The subsidy paid to the company from 1893 to 1909 totalled 3,500,000 Turkish pounds, which exceeded the total agricultural tax revenues from Ankara province during those years. Put another way, it equalled one-half of all revenues collected in Anatolia during a typical year in the mid-1890s.[221]

Table 1.8 Tithe Paid (in Ottoman *Kuruş*)

	1890–1	1891–2	1892–3
Ankara	2,100,791	3,645,554	4,948,470
İzmit	3,321,612	4,471,783	3,923,136
Kütahya	7,599,371	10,834,047	11,471,869

Source: *Statistiques du Service des Recettes*, 1893: 57.

Although the Anatolian Railway's impact on Ottoman domestic economic outcomes was described as 'limited', its contribution to the total bilateral trade was remarkable. The following graph clearly illustrates that the years 1888–9 were a turning point for bilateral trade relations between Germany and the Ottoman Empire. Once Deutsche Bank was granted the exclusive rights to the Anatolian Railways project, the locomotives and wagons for Anatolian Railways were provided almost entirely by German firms: the rails, for example, came from Krupp, which started producing railway materials in 1864,[222] and from Krauss & Company; the locomotives were ordered from J. A. Maffei, the Hannoversche Maschienenbau-Actien Gesellschaft, and Maschienenfabrik Esslingen.[223] The imported materials were transported by the Deutsche Levante Linie, which was established on 6 September 1889, one year after the privileged rights for the Anatolian Railway were granted.[224] The Deutsche Levante Linie also increased its number of ships (1890: 4 ships; 1898: 15 ships) and sailings (1891: 24; 1898: 61).[225]

The railway became a profitable enterprise for German investors. According to his memoirs,[226] the Sultan believed that the Germans deserved to reap the benefit: 'Ultimately, it is just that the Germans have good profits, because after all they also run risks. But it's still up to us to receive the lion's share of the profits.'[227] In parallel to the increase in the volume of maritime traffic between Germany and the Ottoman Empire, the bilateral trade volume also increased dramatically, as seen below.

The following figure (Figure 1.2) clearly indicates that the period immediately following 1888 was remarkable for the explosion of German involvement in the Ottoman market, and economic influence in the Ottoman Empire increased significantly. Grant described 1889, the year of the Kaiser's visit to İstanbul, as 'a banner one for German arms sales to the Ottomans'.[228] After the Kaiser's first visit 1889 till 1910, Germany's share in the Ottoman Empire's trade volume increased from 6 per cent to 21 per cent.[229] Renewed customs and trade regulations, which came into effect on 26 August 1890, also positively affected the quantity of the total foreign trade.[230] As the table below indicates, Ottoman exports to Germany

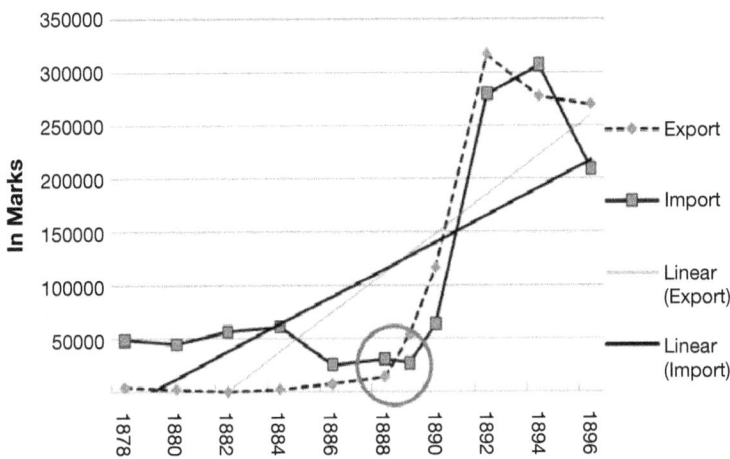

Figure 1.2 Ottoman Trade with Germany 1878–96 (in Marks)
Source: Andreas Birken, *Die Wirtschaftsbeziehungen zwischen Europa und dem Vorderen Orient im ausgehenden 19. Jahrhundert* (Wiesbaden, 1980), p. 176.

rose from a value of 1,910,000 marks to 25,900,000 marks between the years 1880 and 1896, while German exports to the Ottoman Empire rose exponentially from 6,710,000 marks in 1880 to 28 million marks in 1896.

As a result of the Kaiser's first visit to İstanbul, the German military industrial establishment strengthened its position, winning massive new orders from the Ottoman government. Between the years 1885 and 1898, Germany gained a dominant position in both Ottoman military and naval orders. In June 1885 the Ottoman Empire ordered from the Krupp Company 500 guns in various calibres, the Mauser's name entered the Ottoman military market in 1886–7 and has never left the Ottoman market as well as the memory of the Turks ever since then. The Kaiser's visit had a clear impact on the sustainability of this status. In fact, the Germans began to appear strongly in the Ottoman naval market, while the French disappeared after 1886, a shift Grant described as 'the beginning of German hegemony in the Ottoman naval market'. Grant points out that the Ottoman Navy had no German-built ships in 1877, but between 1886 and 1892 the German firms

Table 1.9 Ottoman Trade with Germany, 1880–97 (in Marks)

Year	Ottoman Export	Ottoman Import	Year	Ottoman Export	Ottoman Import
1880	1,910,000	6,710,000	1889	7,090,000	29,900,000
1881	1,620,000	8,060,000	1890	9,610,000	34,100,000
1882	1,290,000	6,020,000	1891	13,900,000	37,000,000
1883	2,250,000	7,020,000	1892	27,900,000	39,700,000
1884	2,710,000	8,260,000	1893	16,600,000	40,900,000
1885	3,610,000	7,900,000	1894	18,800,000	34,400,000
1886	2,190,000	9,150,000	1895	22,000,000	39,000,000
1887	3,210,000	12,000,000	1896	25,900,000	28,000,000
1888	2,360,000	11,700,000	1897	30,500,000	30,900,000

Source: Birken, *Die Wirtschaftsbeziehungen zwischen Europa und dem Vorderen Orient*, p. 176.

Schichau (five boats in 1886) and Germania Works/Kiel (eight boats in 1887–92) produced 13 torpedo boats.[231] Additionally, as stated earlier, Mauser/Loewe entered the Ottoman market at the end of 1886 when the Ottoman Army decided to rearm its infantry with new faster-firing rifles. The order was placed with Mauser in the first month of 1887. The following tables highlight the importance of war materials in the total volume of Ottoman–German foreign trade.

The German arms trade's contribution to the German economy via participation in the Ottoman market might have made it more profitable than other business ventures. As Table 1.11 indicates, compared with the railway construction materials, war materials made up more than half of the total trade volume. The tables above demonstrate the significance of the arms trade within foreign trade between the Ottoman Empire and Germany. The war business, working together with the German military mission, led to the most prominent change in trade relations. The main gains of the German war industry during the period 1880–98, including the year of the Kaiser's first visit to İstanbul, were as follows:

Table 1.10 War Materials Exports from Germany to the Ottoman Empire 1888–98 (in Marks)

Year	Rifles	Cartridges	Munitions*	Powder	Total
1888	2,269,839				2,269,839
1889	5,812,265	611,480			6,423,745
1890	6,341,111	2,515,648			8,856,759
1891	1,690,595	3,556,181		613,312	5,860,088
1892	8,703,228	1,392,125			10,095,413
1893	8,992,022	4,064,450			13,056,472
1894	2,447,800	3,463,940	69,190		5,980,930
1895	7,258,086	3,005,547	1,974,782		12,238,415
1896	2,762,744	1,605,113		56,854	4,367,857
1897		1,362,889	226,403		1,646,146
1898**	61,050	481,000	1,217,300	160,000	1,919,350

*Geschütze mit Munition.
**First quarter of the year 1898.
Source: Reichsministerium des Innern, *Deutsches Handels-Archiv; Zeitschrift für Handel und Gewerbe*, vol. 2 (Berlin, 1898), p. 512.

Table 1.11 Export from Germany to the Ottoman Empire (Selected Items; in Marks)

	1895	1896	1897
1) War Materials	12,238,415	4,367,857	1,646,146
2) Eskisehir-Konya (Railroad)	5,374,023	2,979,947	344,295
3) Selanik-Dereağaç (Railroad)	214,400	–	–
4) Kasaba-Afyon-Karahisar (Railroad)	–	187,200	370,400
Total (1 + 2 + 3 + 4)	17,826,838	7,535,004	2,360,841
War Materials/Total (%)	68.6	57.9	69.7

Source: Reichsministerium des Innern, *Deutsches Handels-Archiv; Zeitschrift für Handel und Gewerbe*, vol. 2 (Berlin, 1898), p. 512.

1) Mauser rifles aggressively moved into the Ottoman war business with the support of the Chancellor and the German military mission, particularly Goltz Pasha.
2) Krupp secured a monopoly position over artillery supplies in the Ottoman market.

3) German shipyards, especially the Germania Work and Schichau, gained prominence as alternative suppliers for the Ottomans' naval modernization during this period, despite the long-standing predominance of British and French shipyards in the Ottoman naval market.
4) The new railway opened fruitful marketing opportunities for the German iron and steel industry, which was also involved in the armaments industry (1888–98).

Arms sales and railway construction were naturally related to the growing financial interests of the German capitalists in the Ottoman market. As the financial sources of the Ottoman economy were not adequate to cover the cost of the ordered rifles, artilleries, ironclads, and torpedo boats, the German financial market and institutions became the new source of capital for the Ottoman government. Between 1888 and 1914 the German share of capital investment grew most remarkably, from about one per cent to 27 per cent of the total.[232] As Barth points out, from the late 1880s, the German capital group headed by Deutsche Bank became the major railway entrepreneur in the Ottoman Empire.[233] Table 1.12 shows the fluctuation in the nationality of the bondholders in the Ottoman converted debt in which the German capital interest increased.[234]

The armaments imported from Germany increased the Ottomans' dependence on German finance. Thus, in addition to their position in the arms market, the Germans acquired a noteworthy position in the Ottoman capital market. As seen in Table 1.12 between 1881 and 1898 the German share in Ottoman bonds increased dramatically (+7.42 per cent) whereas the British share decreased sharply (−18.10 per cent). The impact of German military sales played a very crucial role in this dramatic growth. Between 1885 and 1898 the German armament firms were awarded with several lucrative contracts financed by foreign, mostly German, capital.[235] Apart from railway construction abroad, international arms sales became the new lucrative source of borrowing.

Table 1.12   The Bondholders of the Ottoman Converted Debt, 1881–98 (in Thousands of Ottoman Lira)

	1881		1898		
	Value in OL*	%	Value in OL*	%	Change in %
France	36,716	39.98	35,000	44.87	+4.89
Britain	26,618	28.99	8,500	10.89	−18.10
Ottoman Empire	7,281	7.93	5,000	6.41	−1.52
Belgium	6,612	7.20	14,000	17.94	+10.74
Netherlands	6,974	7.59	3,500	4.48	−3.11
Germany	4,320	4.75	9,500	12.17	+7.42
Italy	2,407	2.62	1,000	1.28	−1.34
Austria-Hungary	0,886	0.96	1,500	1.92	+0.96
Total	91,818	100	78,000	100	

*In Ottoman Lira.
Source: Charles Morawitz, *Die Türkei im Spiegel ihrer Finanzen* (Berlin, 1903), p. 258.

In summing up this period, it can be said that the form of the supply-demand relationship for war materials, which can be seen in the tables herein, offers clear proof of the emergence of mutual trust between the two governments. This mutual trust, which was won by personal endeavour, was the principal foundation of the German influence in the Ottoman Empire. Furthermore, Bismarck's critical conversation with Reşid Bey and the subsequent dispatch of German military advisers to İstanbul and the Kaiser's first visit to Istanbul can be seen as the key moments that produced the first wave of the German expansionist strategy towards the Ottoman Empire.

CHAPTER 2

GERMAN MILITARY ADVISERS: BUSINESSMEN IN UNIFORM

'In the wake of Prussian soldiers went German traders and German financiers.'

Sir John A. Marriott, 1917[1]

A Vital Link for the Export-Dependent Armaments Industry

Dependency on the foreign market was a prominent feature of the German armament firms during the period under consideration. The bulk of the war materials that Krupp and Mauser produced were being exported. The strong links established with German bureaucrats for the domestic market were used as a springboard for foreign markets, where the profitability of sales was decidedly higher. Over the course of time, the German armament firms, especially the Krupp Company, turned a domestic monopoly into an unassailable monopoly power position in particular foreign markets, a process for which the support of both the German and corresponding foreign government was indispensable. In fact, achieving a monopoly in the domestic market was almost a precondition for gaining the same monopoly position in a foreign market.

The share of international market sales in the companies' total sales of produced materials (military or non-military production) gives a clear picture of their dependence on German foreign policy and political relations with the importing countries. As a result, German representatives abroad, namely the German civil and military advisers and also the ambassadors, who put the German expansionist policy into effect, became decisive instruments in gaining monopoly power in foreign markets. The successful marketing strategies employed by Krupp and the other state-supported armaments firms were followed by orders for war materials obtained from abroad; the German Foreign Office considered such orders to be political achievements and reinforcements of 'national prestige'.[2]

The following tables provide statistical evidence for the importance of the foreign market for the German arms industry. Table 2.1 shows that, in the case of Krupp, which *The New York Times* called the world's largest gun foundry in 1884,[3] the export of war materials was the firm's main operation. The reputations of Krupp,

Table 2.1 Sales of Krupp: Military Products 1875–91 (in Marks)

Years	Domestic Sales	Per cent (%)	Foreign Sales	Per cent (%)
1875–7	3,992,495	20.2	15,765,405	79.0
1876–7	2,278,300	9.9	20,631,645	90.1
1877–8	7,531,075	27.6	19,737,190	72.4
1878–9	5,673,630	30.8	12,773,235	69.2
1879–80	1,100,765	15.8	5,853,705	84.2
1880–1	1,566,220	15.1	8,779,395	84.9
1881–2	1,878,320	16.4	9,585,840	83.6
1882–3	1,176,075	9.5	11,238,610	90.5
1883–4	1,986,715	19.9	7,983,865	80.1
1884–5	2,320,850	12.4	16,420,525	87.6
1885–6	3,841,505	15.4	21,128,235	84.6
1886–7	2,856,195	15.0	16,168,405	85.0
1887–8	2,430,095	12.1	17,676,690	87.9
1888–9	4,275,385	22.4	14,804,625	77.6
1889–90	2,759,550	18.4	12,267,580	81.6
1890–1	2,114,275	13.6	13,442,760	86.4

Source: Willi A. Boelcke, *Krupp und die Hohenzollern in Dokumenten. Krupp-Korrespondenz mit Kaisern, Kabinettschefs und Ministern 1850–1918* (Frankfurt am Main, 1970).

Mauser and other prominent armament firms were fundamentally based on their foreign sales. As Grant has noted, armament firms found exports essential for their viability.[4] Epkenhans also points out that, in the foreign market, the armament companies 'could try to make as much profit as possible so long as their prices were not undercut by other competitors'.[5]

Table 2.1 shows that exports were of vital importance for the Krupp factories' industrial and financial existence from the outset. A document from the Krupp archives indicates that 77 per cent of the war materials produced in the Krupp factories between 1878–9 and 1891–2 were sold to foreign countries, whereas only 23 per cent was procured by the Prussian government.[6] The intense exportation of the manufactured goods was not restricted to war materials. As Table 2.2 indicates, the bulk of non-military production was also purchased by foreign countries.

Table 2.2 Sales of Krupp: Non-Military Products 1875–91 (in Marks)

Years	Domestic Sales	Per cent (%)	Foreign Sales	Per cent (%)
1875–6	8,713,740	39.9	13,106,695	60.1
1876–7	8,238,840	44.9	10,130,220	55.1
1877–8	9,343,320	45.0	11,438,795	55.0
1878–9	11,296,145	56.5	8,688,170	43.5
1879–80	10,518,085	45.6	12,564,790	54.4
1880–1	10,846,390	35.9	19,400,675	64.1
1881–2	14,201,310	40.6	20,737,410	59.4
1882–3	16,313,670	48.5	17,298,635	50.5
1883–4	12,991,600	48.9	13,550,070	51.1
1884–5	12,213,495	51.3	11,604,670	48.7
1885–6	12,023,920	53.8	10,324,480	46.2
1886–7	10,084,085	43.5	13,072,770	56.5
1887–8	13,739,630	50.2	13,624,420	49.8
1888–9	17,761,975	61.7	11,048,480	38.3
1889–90	22,976,390	63.2	13,402,485	36.0
1890–1	24,968,025	62.0	15,329,660	38.0

Source: Boelcke, *Krupp und die Hohenzollern in Dokumenten*.

Although these tables indicate only the figures for the Krupp Company, the general composition of the export dependency and the importance of the foreign market were, by and large, similar for all the armaments firms, particularly the Mauser Company. According to the statistics given in Table 2.3 below, in the period 1874–1914, Mauser sold 88 per cent of its manufactured rifles to foreign countries. 'It must be observed,' says Wolf 'that without orders from abroad, the Mauser factory would not have achieved such great importance.'[7]

The economic importance of arms exports and their contribution to the German economy was also clarified by Paul Mauser himself. In a letter to the Prussian Minister of War in February 1908, he indicated that 'within the last 19 years his company produced 1,650,000 Mauser Rifles worth 96.5 million marks and with the exception of the 290,000 rifles Model-98 delivered for the German Army (15,373,000 marks) all the others were delivered to foreign countries that paid with foreign currency'.[8]

Germany's international arms sales operation became almost a joint business of the State apparatus; the representatives of German foreign policy and the German arms makers worked in perfect cohesion. For the makers of foreign policy, armament exports became one of the main ways to achieve a successful penetration of the countries where Germany had political, military, strategic, or economic interests to defend. This outlook shaped the responsibilities of the German military advisers (GMAs) in the Ottoman Army. While there were no defined, predetermined areas of responsibility for the arms trade, several archival documents suggest that all GMAs were somehow involved in the war business and were responsible for the continuing success of German prestige; that prestige was principally represented by German arms makers, as Kaiser Wilhelm II and Bülow once said.[9] Accordingly, building close relationships with the armaments firms' agents and supporting their interests in the Ottoman Empire became one of the GMAs' foremost diplomatic duties.

Over time, however, as will be detailed below, the GMAs also became reliable informants who furnished the German government with critical and specific information that could not have been obtained from other sources.[10] They also worked ardently as lobbyists

Table 2.3 Mauser's Total Sales (1874–1914)

Period	Domestic Sales (Pieces)	Domestic Sales (in Marks)	International Sales (Pieces)	International Sales (in Marks)	Total (Pieces)	Total (in Marks)
1874–1890	125,000	6,339,300	359,853	21,260,430	484,852	27,599,730
1890–1904	65,000		1,165,212		1,230,212	
1904–1906	134,000	10,732,000*	96,800	75,810,600*	1,463,012*	86,542,600*
1907–1914	179,950	8,318,095	215,037	13,091,305	394,987	21,409,403
Total	503,950	25,389,395	1,835,901	110,162,338	2,342,851	135,551,733

*For the period 1890–1906: Robert Ball, *Mauser Military Rifles of the World* (Iola, WI, 2006), p. 226.
Source: Hellmut Wolf, *Die wirtschaftliche Entwicklung der Stadt Oberndorf a. Neckar mit besonderer Berücksichtigung der Mauserwerke und der Schwarzwälder Boten* (Tübingen, 1933), p. 51.

for the German armaments firms (GAFs) with the Ottoman government. Because of their positions as either advisers or inspectors in the Ottoman Army, the GMAs had every opportunity to obtain confidential information, which in some cases led the armaments companies to revise their marketing strategies. As a consequence, the GMAs became an indispensable part and an effective instrument of the marketing strategy of the German war business. In particular, the need for the newest and most reliable information about the market and their competitors encouraged the GAFs to establish good and close relations with the GMAs and to hold regular and detailed consultations with them. These links were an obvious form of life insurance for the GAFs' export-oriented marketing strategy and, at the same time, for Germany's export-oriented expansionist foreign policy. The accurate, timely and relevant information the GMAs provided to the GAFs strengthened their position in the negotiation process; the GAFs also became more successful in their marketing strategy. These results show that the GMAs' most important contribution to the GAFs was the gathering of confidential information; indeed, such information became the lifeblood of the German war business. The topics of the information the GMAs gathered included:[11]

- The marketing strategies of competing countries and companies.
- Detailed information about the technical features and quality of rival products supplied to the Ottoman inspection commission.
- Competitors' marketing strategies and their personal connections with the Ottoman government.
- Any modernization or rearming decisions by the Ottoman government.
- The process by which contracts were obtained, both by German and other firms.
- Ministerial discussions regarding possible new war materials orders.
- Identification of influential personalities and their characters.

Since the Sultan was the final arbiter of the Ottoman arms-purchasing process, the flow of information from the Sultan to the

GAFs was of vital importance. In this context, the GMAs played a crucial role in ensuring and maintaining access to critical information. Based on the above summary, Figure 2.1 is a simplified model explaining of the flow of information to the GAFs through the GMAs.

Because of their position, the GMAs were in the midst of all stages of negotiations in the arms trade. By working together with the firms' agents to obtain important military orders from the Ottoman Empire, they facilitated signing of contracts for the sake of the GAFs. There were clear signs of collaboration between civil and military diplomacy in the arms trade, and if there was a great victory, as Krupp stated, it was because of these joint efforts.[12] In 1900, Krupp mentioned the impact of diplomatic interference on the success of Germany's war business in the Ottoman Empire.[13] This chapter deals with the contribution of the GMAs and their relation with the German arms makers.

Trojan Horse for the German Arms Industry: The German Military Mission in the Ottoman Empire (1882–5)

German military diplomacy played an essential role in Germany's diplomatic efforts during the peaceful penetration of the Ottoman Empire – namely, during Bismarck's Chancellorship and Wilhelm II's early reign. Victory in the Franco–Prussian War (1870–1) had given the German Army an international reputation and provided an invaluable instrument for exports of German-made war materials. After that military victory, Germany acquired more influential wins in the fields of economics and politics, in what Bismarck explicitly termed an 'economic war'. But the very nature of this 'economic war' meant military personnel and military diplomacy were among the principal means to achieve success. 'The war of the future', said Bismarck, 'will be the economic war, the struggle for existence on the largest scale'.[14] Bismarck's vision of that future foresaw mass-production plants in the iron and steel industry, one of the most profitable products of which was war materials. Thus, as the case of the Ottoman Empire proved, the members of the German military

German Military Advisers: Businessmen in Uniform

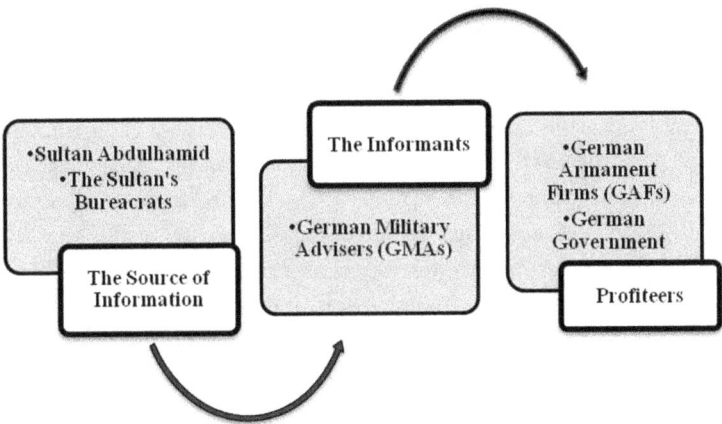

Figure 2.1   Information Flow via Some of the GMAs to GAFs and the Government

mission worked primarily for the sake of German industrial victory. Because of their role in the business of war, they deserve to be called the vanguards of the 'German industrial army' in the economic war.

German military diplomacy in the late Ottoman Empire, which was established mainly through the hard work of Goltz Pasha (1843–1916) under German official patronage, provided a profitable link between the Ottoman military decision maker(s) and the German arms companies. As shown in Figure 2.1 above, the German military advisers were able to obtain important information either directly from Sultan Abdülhamid or indirectly from Ottoman officials and officers. In addition to their efforts to modernize the Ottoman Army, the GMAs also served as the most reliable sources for the GAFs, for whom new information was of vital importance. In this manner, the German military mission became an indispensable part of the German Style of War Business, in which military diplomacy and war business fed off each other. Their methods and the tools for gathering information were the most prominent features of the German Style of War Business.

As stated in the previous chapter, on 14 July 1880, Abdülhamid II notified Bismarck of his request with a draft version of the terms of appointment for the prospective German military and civil advisers. The draft terms of the contract specified the officers' salary scales and the duration of their service.[15] However, it was not a matter that could be arranged in a rushed manner. Although Bismarck enthusiastically supported the plan to dispatch the advisers to the Ottoman Empire, the final contract was not signed until 1882. The agreements concerning the advisers' status in the Ottoman and German armies were finalized on 29 April 1882 and only after that was the mission ready for departure to İstanbul.[16] The Ottoman government's initial request was for eight military officers, in addition to the civil advisers. However, only four officers were employed in the Ottoman service.[17] The group was headed by Staff Officer Otto Kähler (who served from 1882–5 and entered Ottoman service as a Major-General).[18] Another prominent figure was Kamphövener Pasha, who served in the Ottoman Army for 27 years between 1882 and 1909 as an infantry colonel. Despite his extended period of service, his contribution to both sides was not as productive as might have been expected from someone serving such a long term. As Sultan Abdülhamid's first secretary, Tahsin Pasha, wrote in his memoir, Kamphövener Pasha's position was more performative than functional. Krupp's representative, Menshausen, defined him as 'not intelligent but discreet'.[19] However, he was promoted to the rank of Marshall in 1895.[20] Although he was not as influential as Goltz was, his name and his service was, as the notes written by Mustafa Kemal Pasha (Ataturk) indicates, remembered by the founder generation of the Turkish Republic.

Another member of the group was Ristow Pasha, an artillery officer; he entered the Ottoman army in 1882 as a colonel and stayed in Ottoman service for nine years till his death in İstanbul in 1891. According to Henry Woods, a British naval officer in the Ottoman service, Ristow Pasha 'found so little to do that he spent much of his time in *Janni Bier Halle* in Pera, and attained the distinction of being known as *Berah Pasha*'.[21] The fourth member of the group, Hobe (served between 1882 and 1894), was a cavalry officer, and his rank was raised to colonel when he entered Ottoman service in 1882.[22]

German Military Advisers: Businessmen in Uniform 77

Image 2.1 Photo Sent by Gazi Mustafa Kemal Pasha (Atatürk) to Kamphövener Pasha
The notes written by Gazi Mustafa Kemal Pasha in Ottoman Turkish: 'Türkiye Reis-i Cumhuri Gazi Mustafa Kemal Paşa tarafından Türkiye Devleti Mütekaid Müşiri ve Prusya Hükümeti Feriki Kamphövener Paşaya.' (Ankara, 03.12.1340/12 February 1924).
Source: Nachlass Kamphövener, *Landesarchiv Schleswig-Holstein* Abt. 399.26 Nr.8.

The contract between the Ottoman government – represented by Gazi Osman Pasha, the Minister of War, and Said Pasha, the Minister of Foreign Affairs – and Otto von Kähler, as the head of the German Military Mission, was finalized on 30 May 1882.[23] Kähler served in the German army as a lieutenant-colonel, while the other three officers were ranked as majors for their service to Germany. On entering Ottoman service, each of them was promoted to one rank higher.[24] Based on the first article of the contract, Kähler entered the Ottoman Army promoted to the rank of Major-General (*Mirlivâ*) for which the *İrâde* was issued on 14 June 1882.[25] His salary, which was paid in gold at the end of each month, was 30,000 francs annually.[26] The other benefits mentioned in the contract (Article IV) were: a liberal pension, a travelling allowance, and incident and death benefits.[27] The names, ranks and salaries of these officers are listed in Table 2.4 below:

The most important difference between the first draft of the contract made by the Ottoman government in July 1880, and the final one completed in 1882, was the issue of salary.[28] The Sublime Porte initially proposed a salary of 20,000 francs for each officer.[29] It seems that this topic was the subject of some of the most crucial negotiations. As Wallach indicates, citing a document sent to the Foreign Office by the German Military Cabinet, the latter insisted that the Ottoman government should pay the German officers at least 30,000 francs annually.[30] In the end, the officers received the amount sought by the German Military Cabinet. Apparently their salary was considerably higher than those of the officers who were of the same rank in their own country.[31] As seen in Table 2.4, three officers – all except Kähler – received salaries of 23,000 francs (1,010 OL), whereas Kähler received 30,000 francs (1,316 OL); in addition, they were given the right to other benefits like rations

Table 2.4 First Appointed German Military Mission (Kähler Mission) in 1882 and its Staff's Annual Salary

Name	Appointment	Salary in Francs	Salary in OL*	Duration of the first Contract
Kähler (Major-General)	Chief of the Group	30,000	1,316	3 years
Kamphövener (Colonel)	Infantry	23,000	1,010	3 years
Ristow (Colonel)	Artillery	23,000	1,010	3 years
Von Hobe (Colonel)	Cavalry	23,000	1,010	3 years

*Conversion of the Ottoman currency (about 1892): (1 OL = 22.78 francs) and (1 OL = 18.45 marks) See McCarthy, Justin, *The Arab World, Turkey and the Balkans (1878–1914): A Handbook of Historical Statistic* (Boston, MA, 1982), p. 155.
Source: Kemal Beydilli, 'II. Abdulhamid Devrinde Gelen İlk Alman Askeri Heyeti Hakkında' *İstanbul Üniversitesi Edebiyat Fakültesi Tarih Dergisi* 32, (1979), p. 494.

(*ta'yin*).³² As a result, not counting their rent (which was paid by the Sultan's Privy Purse), the annual cost of these four officers reached a total of 1,188,000 francs (52,151 OL).³³ The big difference between the salaries paid to Ottoman officers and the Germans became a point of contention; unsurprisingly, the Ottoman officers were aware of and, naturally, displeased with this apparent inequality.³⁴ Table 2.5 highlights the dimension of the pay gap.

In spite of this obvious difference, the German officers demanded salary increases when the Sultan decided to renew their contracts.³⁵ Before they entered the Ottoman service all had been in financial difficulties, so they did not want to pass up this opportunity. As Cram says, 'none of them showed desire to return home'.³⁶ Each of the German officers prepared several studies and recommendations concerning their appointments and submitted reports to the Sultan within their first six months.³⁷ Ristow, for instance, submitted a report at the end of September 1882 regarding the current state of the Ottoman field artillery and made some recommendations about the fortification of the Straits.³⁸ Kamphövener's proposal, which suggested establishing a school for the infantry, was welcomed by the High Commission.³⁹ On 14 February 1883, Hobe Pasha submitted a *lâyiha* in which he suggested several changes to improve the Imperial stables, as might be expected of a cavalry officer.⁴⁰ However, the submitted reports merely ascertained the facts, which had been unknown to these officers.

In addition, Kähler Pasha also offered a comprehensive programme.⁴¹ Griffiths asserts that Kähler Pasha, as the head of

Table 2.5 Salary of the Ottoman Officers (1902)

Rank	Annual Salary (in OL)
Marshal/General	960
Lieutenant-General	720
Major-General	480
Colonel	240
Lieutenant-Colonel	150
Major	120

Source: Calculation based on data given by Morawitz, *Die Türkei im Spiegel*, p. 140.

the adviser group, gave in his report 'a very comprehensive picture of the gaps which existed in the Ottoman military organisation at that time'.[42] According to Griffiths, Kähler Pasha identified three essential obstructions that blocked the Ottomans' military progress: 'lack of money, poor organisation of the general administration and the corruptibility of the administrators'.[43] These three problems, however, were generally known and much discussed, and the Sultan was well aware of them.[44] Such circumstances in the Ottoman Army were the principal reasons why the Sultan had sought foreign assistance in the first place. An anonymous British military observer – most probably the British military attaché at İstanbul, Colonel Herbert Chermside (1850–1929) – made disparaging remarks to *The {London} Times* for 13 September 1882 in which he criticized Ottoman officials, describing them as the obstacle to desired reforms:

> All the organisation which had then been prepared for several years collapsed at once, simply because the existing officials could not take the trouble to use it. We see now, even in time of peace, that the paper organisation is not being carried out, and there is every reason to suppose that the same carelessness would occur in time of war. In fact, the Turkish army is at present neither on a peace nor a war footing [...][45]

In the meantime, Kähler Pasha's report and recommendations were addressed by the High Inspection Commission of the Army (*Teftîş-i Umûm-i 'Askeri Komisyon-u 'Alisi*), which was established in May 1880 under the presidency of Gazi Ahmed Muhtar Pasha.[46] The resulting discussion was submitted to the Sultan as a report. Sultan Abdülhamid showed a keen interest in the submitted proposals, and intended, it seemed, immediate action. However, the proposed reforms would have been too expensive, and the cost of such a plan was the first fundamental obstacle to be overcome. Kähler's report to the German ambassador demonstrates that, according to Sultan Abdülhamid, lack of money was the most critical issue. Some prominent military figures, like Gazi Ahmed Muhtar Pasha, who was according to the British Colonel Chermside, 'the best man the

[Ottoman] Turks had'[47] shared the same viewpoint.[48] In a report Josef Maria von Radowitz (Radowitz) the German ambassador in İstanbul from 1882 to 1892, described the empire's financial state as the Sultan's main concern.[49]

During the years the GMAs were employed with generous salaries in the Ottoman Army, the Ottoman government faced financial bankruptcy and the economy was in deep crisis. The war indemnity that the Ottoman Empire had to pay to Russia as a result of defeat in 1877–8 'threatened catastrophe'.[50] As a result of this state of affairs, the Ottoman Empire lost its credibility in European capital markets.[51] Sultan Abdülhamid was aware of his difficult financial situation. As he noted in one statement, 'the army which the 1877–8 War had decimated could not yet be rebuilt. The Treasury was empty. Military supplies and even the pay of officials could be met only with great difficulty. In the *vilâyet*s (provinces) there were members of the Gendarmerie who could not be paid for 20 or 30 months.'[52]

Based on this awareness, Sultan Abdülhamid's hope was that the employment of Germans in Ottoman service would establish a closer relationship with Germany and attract the support of German capitalists and industrialists, who would then be willing to invest in the Ottoman market by extending loans on reasonable terms.[53] The Sultan hoped that the critical financial and political problems the empire faced could be eliminated through German friendship. The Sultan believed that the military mission might be one of the most effective ways to achieve this goal.[54] As a result, he acted as if he were keenly interested in modernizing the army. Modernization of the army would naturally involve issuing many commercial contracts to buy rifles, guns and other military materials from abroad, for which a strong financial base was an indispensible condition. Perhaps the Sultan expected that the German arms companies would stimulate the country's capitalists to support the Ottoman government, enabling it to purchase the war materials it needed from German firms. From Sultan Abdülhamid's perspective, his empire's pressing need was not for a 'paper reform [which] would have done more harm than good',[55] but instead an honest source of money that would make the projected reform possible. 'Want of money' said *The {London} Times* writer, 'prevents the proper training of the men during peace and keeps them in a state of semi-starvation'.[56] He was not wrong.

Based on this outlook, Sultan Abdülhamid wished to attract the interest of German capitalists to his empire. Both the modernization of the army and the process of railway construction could offer great opportunities to German financial investors looking for long-term investments. During several conversations, Abdülhamid expressed his real intentions in a very indirect manner and sent a letter to Kaiser Wilhelm II concerning Kähler Pasha's potentially important role in the development of bilateral relations.[57] The Sultan might have expected the German military mission to act as a mediator between him and Berlin. Colonel Herbert Chermside, the British military attaché, was also aware that 'in Germany, both for political and military reasons it [wa]s wished to retain [the Military Mission] in Turkish employment'.[58] However, neither Kähler Pasha nor the other three members of the mission apparently had the ability to swiftly interpret Abdülhamid's ulterior motives, which were shaped by many different dynamics, including political, military, and economic elements. Perhaps that is the reason why none of them are credited with making particularly noteworthy contributions to the interests of both Germany and the Ottoman Empire during their service in the Ottoman Army.[59] The exception was the latecomer among the German advisers: Goltz Pasha. Chermside also noticed Goltz's exceptional talents. In the memorandum quoted above, he wrote that 'increase of pay, rank, and service of decorations has been bestowed lavishly, but with one exception the officers have been mainly titular. The exception is Goltz Pasha, the able Prussian military writer...'[60]

Colmar Freiherr von der Goltz Pasha (1843–1916): A Hero for Everyone

'Büyük Goltz Paşa, ölüm seni bizden zamansız aldı. Pek sevdiğin bu millet, sana ikinci vatan olan bu topraklar, seni daha mesut ve zaferli günlerin arasında görmek isterdi.'

Enver Paşa, 1916[61]

Garbın en kahraman soyundan gelerek 'Şarkın en cengaver bir soyu arasında hizmetle ömrünü geçiren büyük kumandan...'
Türk Yurdu, 1916[62]

A good deal of research has been undertaken on the subject of the influence of the German military missions, especially the one headed by Goltz Pasha (1843–1916), within the Ottoman Empire and especially in its army.[63] Although these works do not provide sufficient document-based proof with regards to Goltz Pasha's contributions to German military industry during his service in the Ottoman Army, a broad consensus has emerged in the scholarly literature that Goltz Pasha and the German missions played a crucial role in the Ottomans' arms purchasing process. However, to demonstrate Goltz Pasha's tangible contribution to Germany's multidimensional success in the Ottoman Empire, it is necessary to conduct an analysis with the help of authentic documents. The sources discussed here shed light on Goltz Pasha's general influence in the Ottoman Empire, and in particular, his manipulative role in the war business. This discussion is based mainly on Goltz's own letters, reports, *lâyihas,* and telegrams from the years 1886 to 1896, most of which have not been evaluated previously.

Goltz Pasha was regarded as one of Germany's greatest strategists and military thinkers, and also as one of the most distinguished military writers of his time.[64] In 1908, *The New York Times* described him as 'without exception the highest military authority in Germany'.[65] His Europe-wide reputation was well known within Ottoman military circles.[66] Before he entered Ottoman service in 1883, he had been serving in the German Army as a major.[67] In his first two years in the Ottoman Army (1883–5) he was subordinate to Kähler Pasha, and was assigned as an adviser to the Military Academy with an annual salary of 26,000 francs.[68] When Kähler Pasha died of a carbuncle on 3 November 1885, Goltz Pasha became head of the German mission and promoted to the rank of colonel.[69] His rank was raised to general in 1886, and he stayed in Ottoman service until 1 November 1895,[70] when he returned to (and later became commanding general of) the First Army Corps in Königsberg.[71] In the years leading up to the outbreak of World War I, the Sublime Porte requested Goltz Pasha to visit and inspect the Ottoman Army;[72] between 1909 and 1914 he received four such invitations.[73]

When Kähler Pasha was struggling with organizational and also personal obstacles, Goltz Pasha, a well-known military thinker and strategist who had been recommended by Kähler Pasha himself as a personal friend,[74] came to İstanbul on 15 June 1883.[75] He received an audience with Abdülhamid II two days later.[76] Afterwards he wrote to his wife and mentioned his initial impression of the Sultan: 'One gets the feeling very quickly that [he] is in the presence of a highly intelligent person.'[77] Goltz's responsibility at the beginning of his contract was the reorganization of the Ottoman military schools, under the title: *General-Inspecteur des Militär-Bildungswesens*.[78] After a couple of days, in a document dated 20 June 1883, his contract was prepared, and he started planning his programme for reforming the Ottoman military school.[79] By 24 July 1883 he had prepared a *lâyiha* and submitted it to the Sultan, who forwarded it to a military commission. According to the commission, Goltz Pasha advocated that first, there should be an increase in the military content of the courses taught in the schools; second, the timetable of the courses should be revised; and finally, the nutrition standards of the food served to the cadets should be improved.[80]

At the end of his service in 1895, Goltz Pasha's departure left an obvious gap in the lobbying effort on behalf of the German armament firms in the Ottoman Empire. The only person able to fill the gap was apparently Marschall von Bieberstein, one of the Germany's most capable diplomats and the former de facto German Foreign Minister, who was appointed German ambassador to the Ottoman Empire in 1897. Goltz Pasha had worked as if he were an ambassador as well as a military adviser. However, as some of Goltz Pasha's letters to the Krupp Company and to Alfred von Kiderlen-Wächter (later the Secretary of Foreign Affairs, hereafter Kiderlen) in 1891 indicate, he was not pleased with Radowitz's lack of commitment to supporting the German arms makers' business endeavours in the Ottoman market. In 1891, for instance, when the Sultan seemed ready to place an order with French firms, Goltz Pasha, who saw the arms trade as an effective instrument for German foreign policy, suggested that Menshausen make a diplomatic push on the Ottoman government.[81] His advice was clear: if you want to obtain the contract or prevent the Ottomans from ordering French guns you must persuade Berlin to act. 'This is the right time for a diplomatic intervention,' wrote Goltz Pasha, before commenting on Radowitz's reservations:

> Several conversations with the Ambassador have, however, convinced me that the same could hardly be expected from his side. Although he [Radowitz] said in his last conversation 'Let us see,' I still believe that he will only take positive action upon certain encouragements from Berlin. So I can only urge to stir up things there in Berlin.[82]

The important information Goltz Pasha submitted to the German Foreign Office created a domino effect, which culminated when the Kaiser himself intervened in the war business in a significant way: he threatened the Sultan with severance of political and economic relations.[83] Goltz's letter served Germany's political, military and economic interests in the Ottoman Empire. He was well aware that as a military adviser his sphere of influence was limited; even so, he sought to interfere in political issues, which obviously annoyed Ambassador Radowitz. A letter written by a member of the German military mission – most probably Goltz Pasha – drew attention to the conflict of authority in İstanbul between the German ambassador and the members of the military mission.[84] According to the writer, 'Radowitz, who was jealous [*eifersüchtig*] of his position as well has his reputation/prestige [*Ansehen*], gave the Sultan always to understand that even if he had the intention to use one of us to entrust his policy towards Germany, that [Radowitz] was there for that purpose and that the Kaiser did not wish for anything to go through [the German military mission]'.[85] After stressing these points, the writer added: 'Several of us, who were at the court of the Sultan as part of their position, had won the trust of the man who was otherwise unapproachable and became closer to him and established a personal contact. Those have been intentionally alienated from the Sultan by the ambassador so that they do not communicate anything political with him [the Sultan].'[86] In 1892, after ten years' service as the ambassador in İstanbul, Radowitz was appointed to Spain.

Goltz Pasha's work in the Ottoman Army harmonized with the strategy anticipated by Bismarck. Sending the military mission to the Ottoman Empire furnished the German government with a number of 'reliable informants whom they could obtain in no other way'.[87] Goltz Pasha realised almost everything that Bismarck envisaged in terms of the benefits of despatching the German officers to Ottoman service. In recognition of this, when Goltz Pasha was presented in Berlin during his Ottoman service, he was received by Bismarck and asked about the military, economic and political state of the Ottoman Empire.[88] Within a relatively short time, the German mission headed by Goltz Pasha demonstrated the usefulness of such a tool.

Military missions abroad subsequently became an essential instrument for achieving a strategy of peaceful penetration. When Goltz entered Ottoman service, one of his classmates from the Prussian Kriegsakademie, Emil Körner, was sent to Chile in 1885 on the recommendations of the Chief Staff of Prussian Army, Helmuth von Moltke (1800–1901), who had also served the Ottoman Army for four years (1835–9), and Kaiser Wilhelm I.[89] The military missions abroad gave Germany the opportunity to place 'national military power into the framework of the international politics of the day'.[90]

As his actions showed, Goltz did not want to remain just an ordinary member of a military mission whose responsibilities were limited to military education, modernization of the Ottoman recruitment system, and so forth. He quickly became aware that Sultan Abdülhamid's military reform project was not as substantive as it was supposed to be. According to him, the Sultan's intention was merely to give the impression that the Ottoman military would be organized by the German reformers. Based on this thought, Goltz Pasha wrote a letter, using what the commentators have described as 'gallows humour' (*Galgenhumorstimmung*): 'Basically, we [German military advisers] are nothing other than His Majesty's court jesters. My most serious competitor here is a court dwarf, who is a ventriloquist and can walk on his hands at the same time that he does somersaults. All of that I cannot do.'[91] Goltz Pasha's overwhelming desire was to be a 'German politician in uniform'.[92]

Goltz Pasha desired to expand his sphere of influence from that of a simple military adviser to that of a consultant in various fields including the military procurement process and also on Ottoman internal and foreign policies, which were essentially shaped by Abdülhamid's own priorities.[93] Accordingly, he intervened in the negotiations on the Baghdad railway; he was a keen supporter of the project because he understood all too well the railway military as well as its commercial importance. According to Harrison, Goltz Pasha underlined the railway's strategic importance for the Ottoman Empire and to Germany.[94]

Goltz Pasha became increasingly influential because Sultan Abdülhamid provided him with opportunities to express his thoughts about these critical issues when he was received in audiences at Yıldız Palace. In March 1887, before his departure to Berlin, Goltz was received by the Sultan, who ordered him to discuss some foreign political issues of the Ottoman Empire, including Ottoman relations with Russia and Britain, with Bismarck.[95] In addition to these exceptional roles, in 1889 Goltz Pasha was attached directly to the Imperial Military Household, whereas all other German officers were subject to the *Serasker*.[96] This change gave Goltz the unique right to address his reports directly to the Sultan. While there is no documentary proof, it seems that Abdülhamid might have been aware of Goltz Pasha's critical position as an informant for the German Foreign Office and the GAFs.

Over time, Goltz Pasha established close relations with the Sultan's 'first circle men' at Yıldız Palace, and based on these relationships he built an information network. He obtained crucial information either from his 'very confidential sources' located at the Yıldız Palace, like one of the Sultan's key secretaries, Ragıb Bey, who was given the code name 'Robert' in some documents,[97] or directly from the Sultan, who occasionally accorded him an audience at the Yıldız Palace. In addition to these Palace sources, Goltz Pasha, as a person admired by the young Ottoman officers, could also gain crucial information and inside observations from his cadets in the Military Academy.

As is shown by the case of Pertev Pasha (later Demirhan), a well-known admirer of Goltz Pasha and later his biographer, Goltz was able to receive detailed information and intelligence from his former cadets even after he left for Germany.[98] The information gained and the critical observations made on different personalities and institutions were supplied by Goltz Pasha to the GAFs and also to the German Foreign Office. As Figure 2.2 below indicates, the audiences to which Goltz Pasha provided information included Kaiser Wilhelm II, the Foreign Office (Kiderlen), F. A. Krupp and his firm's management, and Paul Mauser and his company's management. Goltz Pasha's reports and letters were long and detailed. Additionally, as the authors of *Denkwürdigkeiten* asserted, Goltz Pasha prepared nearly 4,000 pages of instructions for the purpose of a military manual, which suggests that preparing reports, letters, *lâyiha*s and books might have occupied most of Goltz's time.[99] 'The

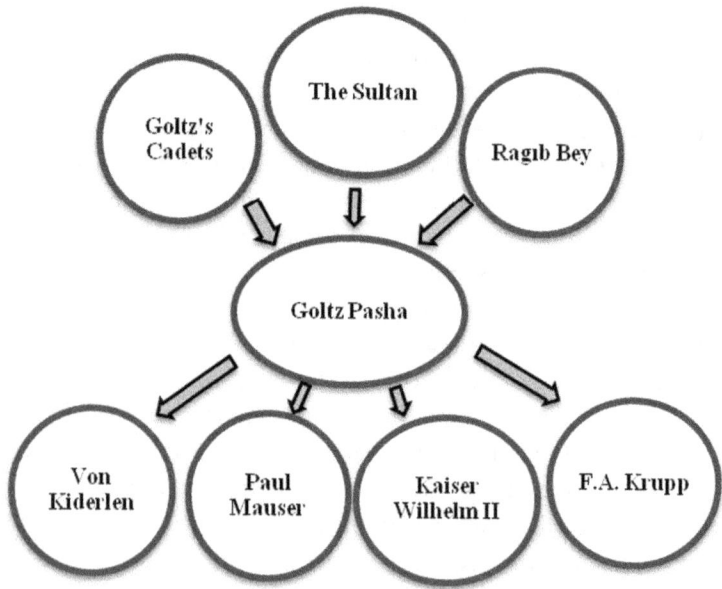

Figure 2.2   Goltz Pasha's Special Information Net

honest Germans,' noted the *New York Times* in 1885, 'sent in long, painstaking reports on every imaginable subject connected with financial, military, or government matters.'[100] As previously mentioned, Goltz was a key node in the information flow between Ottoman sources and Germany. Thanks to his privileged position in the Ottoman Army, he was able to gain access to important information and share it with the GAFs. The following figure depicts the path of information based on Goltz Pasha's correspondence or reports discovered in several archives. Most of these messages related directly to armaments orders, but some of the writings contain information concerning the recent political circumstances at the Sublime Porte.

The factor that facilitated this information flow was Goltz Pasha's personal relationship with both sides, namely with the Ottoman officers and officials, and with the German authorities and arms firms. At the beginning of his service, he realised the impact of personal relations in finalizing almost all issues in the Ottoman Empire. In particular, he noticed that the allocation of supplies for the Ottoman Army was not decided objectively, but rather through personal influence.[101] According to Colonel Chermside, his interest in supplies of military materials by German firms was one of the main reasons for the accusation of intrigue against Goltz Pasha.[102]

After his first three years of service in the Ottoman Army, Goltz Pasha intended to terminate his contract in 1886; to this end on 28 January 1886, he submitted to the Sultan notice of his intention to retire from the task of the *Mekâtib-i 'Askeriye Müfettiş-i Umûmisi*, offering the explanation that the cadets and the soldiers did not follow his orders.[103] At the time his contract was due to end, in May 1886, he did not want to extend it for another three years. However, the Sultan insistently tried to persuade him to remain in Ottoman service. According to the Austrian Military Attaché, Ritter von Manéga, Abdülhamid's secretary, Ragıb Bey, met Goltz Pasha almost every day in an effort to change his mind.[104] Abdülhamid also appealed to Kaiser Wilhelm I to pressure Goltz Pasha that he should renew his contract.[105] The Sultan's request was basically compatible with the German government's expansion strategy, and Goltz Pasha proved to be also one of the most capable persons for accomplishing this mission. To serve his fatherland, Goltz must stay in the Ottomans' service. The Kaiser decided the most desirable [*aller erwünschteste*] of all solutions was for Goltz Pasha to remain.[106] Apparently, Goltz's lengthy stay in the Ottoman service – it lasted until 1 October 1889 – was the result of an order given by Kaiser Wilhelm I on 19 July 1886.[107] In other words, he had no choice but to stay in İstanbul. However, he did not disclose this fact during his negotiations with the Sultan.[108] Feigning reluctance about his continued service in the Ottoman Army, Goltz Pasha stipulated some conditions for staying. Abdülhamid II accepted them, and on 22 July 1886, Goltz Pasha signed a new contract with the Ottoman government.[109] The German Kaiser, the Sultan, the German arms companies, and Goltz Pasha himself were pleased with this outcome.

Significantly, the Austrian–Hungarian Empire also wanted to see Goltz Pasha serving in the Ottoman Army.[110] Goltz's extended contract was welcomed by Germany's Austro–Hungarian ally. In this regard, the Austrian government had directly communicated to the German Chancellor Bismarck that Goltz Pasha's presence in İstanbul was of great importance for them.[111] It appears that Goltz was 'an irreplaceable person'[112] not only for the Ottoman Empire and Germany, but also for the Austrians. During a conversation with the German ambassador in Vienna, the Austrian Foreign Minister, Count Gustav Kálnoky, declared his gratitude to the Kaiser for his order to extend Goltz's contract. As the German ambassador remarked, Goltz's presence in the Ottoman service was doubly desirable (*doppelt wünschenswert*), according to the Austrian Foreign Ministry. Count Kálnoky's argument was based on concern about the looming possibility of good relations between the Ottoman Empire and Russia, which implied at the same time a friendship with France, who supplied the guns for the Ottomans' Mediterranean coastal defences.

In September 1886, Goltz also saw that a Russian–Ottoman alliance was not in the least improbable.[113] As a matter of fact, at that time a draft version of a defensive alliance proposal between the Ottoman Empire, Russia, and France was being prepared by the Ottoman government.[114] Meanwhile, the Ottomans' disinclination to fortify the Bosporus defences was, according to Count Kálnoky, proof in favour of his argument. However, the foreign minister was of the opinion that Goltz Pasha's presence in İstanbul could prevent these threatening developments.[115] Kálnoky was right. Goltz Pasha encouraged the Sultan to undertake a defensive armament in case of a possible Russian attack. But Kálnoky perhaps did not foresee that Goltz Pasha was not only in a position to prevent a possible Russian approach towards the Golden Horn, but was also able, at the same time, to lobby for the German rifle companies in the Ottoman market, at the expense of the Austrian firm Mannlicher. As a matter of fact, one of Goltz Pasha's most obvious influences in the Ottoman Empire occurred as a result of his intervention in the Mauser transactions, which were finalized at the expense of Austrian, American and British rifle suppliers.[116] Goltz Pasha, whose efforts on behalf of German industry effectively excluded the Austrians, also tried to strengthen the political relations of his own country's ally with the Ottoman Empire after the extension of his contract in the Ottoman service. In June 1887, when he returned to İstanbul from a European tour during which he was received by the Austrian Emperor and met the Austrian military and civil elite in Vienna, he praised the Austrian Army and the country itself in the following words: 'Austria is stronger than the other European states think; she is even stronger than her own estimation.'[117]

Before turning to Goltz Pasha's contribution to Mauser's entrance into the Ottoman market, it is essential to point out his influence on the new Recruitment Law of 1886–7, which paved the way for an increase in the size of the Ottoman Army and consequently an increase in the demand for war materials. Thanks to the new contract, Goltz Pasha widened his sphere of influence. In particular, through his appointment to lead the special Military Reform Commission, Goltz Pasha won exceptional authorization to submit directly to the Sultan any relevant proposals.[118] This gave him the opportunity to convince the Sultan to support the Germanization of the Ottoman Army and its equipment. Among the first achievements of Goltz Pasha's face-to-face communication with the Sultan was the Sultan's approval for a modification of the existing conscription system, which had been in use since 1869.[119] Goltz Pasha had wanted to make this change for a long time and 'after much hesitation and negotiation' the new law was approved by the Sultan on 25 November 1886.[120] Based on a draft submitted by Goltz Pasha in 1886, the new Recruiting Law extended the obligation of military service to all able-bodied Muslim males aged 20 and over, and the term of military service remained at 20 years. Griffiths pointed out that despite the fact that the term of service was not changed, the time to be spent in each category was rearranged: three years in the active forces, or *Nizâmiye*; six years in the active reserve, *İhtiyât*; nine years in the reserve, *Redîf*; and two years in the territorial force, *Müstahfız*.[121] Accordingly, the total peacetime ranks of the Ottoman Army would be raised to 850,000.[122]

As Akmeşe has pointed out, Goltz Pasha believed that conscription was the best way to achieve 'the full amalgamation of military and civilian life'.[123] The new geography-based distribution of armies was another of the fundamentally important tools for realising the idea of 'militarization of society' that Goltz Pasha advocated.[124] Thus, the commission made another crucial reform on the distribution of the military forces according to districts in 1887. As Griffiths asserts with the new district-based division system spelled out in the new regulation the commission had 'slavishly followed' the European system.[125] In 1891, Goltz proudly wrote that such an equally powerful reform of the Ottoman military system had not been carried out since the reign of Sultan Mahmud II.[126]

In the meantime, the mobilization plan of the forces recommended by the commission dictated a new strategy for the construction of new railway and communication systems, which would be mainly provided by German firms over the course of time.[127] The utilization of the railways, in particular the Baghdad railway, for military purposes was one of the most significant parts of Goltz Pasha's plan for the modernization of the Ottoman military system. From this point of view, Goltz Pasha's presence in Ottoman service became almost an indispensable force for the development of German interests in the Ottoman Empire.

Although Goltz Pasha had suggested an increase of troops in 1886–7, in February 1890 he submitted to the Sultan another *layiha* recommending a reduction (*tenkihât*) of active (*Nizâmiye*) troops.[128] Goltz Pasha prepared this *layiha* in response to an 1889 *İrâde* from the Sultan ordering a study of ways to reduce the active forces for financial reasons.[129] Goltz Pasha began his *layiha* with a complaint about the unpaid salaries of the Ottoman officers, and after suggesting a reduction in the number of active army personnel, he recommended an increase in the *Redif* army. In his *layiha* he wrote:

> I certainly believe that it is also possible to increase the strength of the Army through a reduction in military expenditures. The best and simplest way to achieve to this aim is, however, to reduce the number of the regular troops, whereas in the case of a war it is necessary to increase of the number of the reserve army [*redîf*].[130]

The following figure (Figure 2.3), based on a table produced by the Ministry of the Army, led by *Serasker* Rıza Pasha, illustrates how the total number of active troops changed between 1869 and 1904.[131]

After mentioning the shortages in some critical military materials, Goltz Pasha finished with a proposal for an increase in military materials purchases. He indicated that 'through the savings, which would be made through reducing the number of troops, the weapons and the other military materials required can be purchased'.[133] Apparently the reform plans suggested by Goltz Pasha and by the other German advisers served very effectively to promote and advance German political and economic interests in the Ottoman Empire. The strong correlation between the reform of military regulations and the arms procurement was clear to Goltz Pasha. In the end, however, the number of troops was increased, and consequently the needs of the army (military materials and other supplies) rose. After two years of the new regulations, an Ottoman officer (Hüseyin Tevfik Pasha) submitted a report to Yıldız Palace pointing to the link between the increased troop numbers and needed rifles.[134] During the 1886 negotiations over the army regulations and the new rifle procurement,

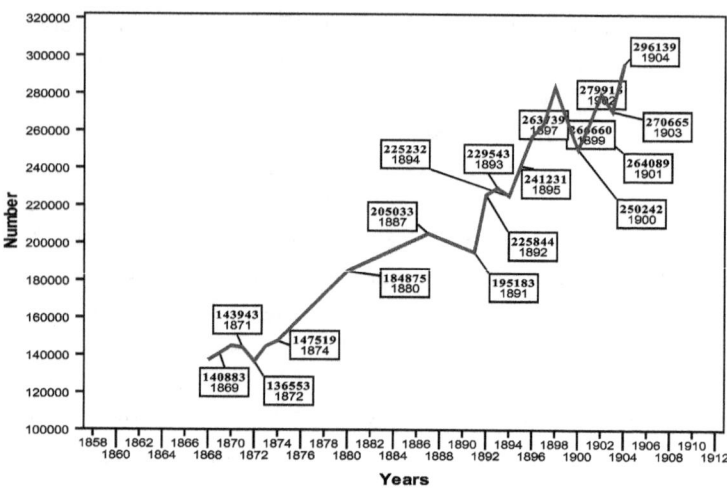

Figure 2.3 Change in Total Active *Nizâmiye*-Troops[132]
Source: Rıza Paşa, *Hülâsa-ı Hâtırâtım* (İstanbul 1325/1909), Mukâyese-Ekler.

Goltz Pasha, the architect of the regulations, sent a letter to Berlin. In it, he explained to the German Ministry of War the new recruitment law and its potential to benefit German industry. In his correspondence, Goltz Pasha requested official confirmation of the similarity between the Mauser rifles used in the German Army and those that would be used in the Ottoman Army. However Goltz's argumentation to pursue the Ministry was well formulated:

> This *sui-generis* circumstance could on the one hand impede the interests of the German industry, and on the other hand, jeopardize the much-desired procurement of Mauser rifles (M82) by the Ottoman army, the number of troops of which were significantly increased after the new recruitment law.[135]

He believed that the prospect of an increased number of troops needing supplies would whet the German arms makers' appetites. Along with his military abilities, Goltz Pasha possessed a clear and strategically astute commercial instinct. The Ottoman government was not unaware of the consequences of the increased number of troops or the fortification of the Straits, both steps suggested by the German military advisers. A report dated 7 March 1887 implied that the reform suggestions of Goltz Pasha and the other advisers had paved the way for the arming of the Ottoman soldiers and fortresses with German weapons.[136]

There were four particular occasions on which Goltz's influence was decisive and direct: first, the fortification of the Straits with Krupp guns in 1885–6; second, the new recruitment system, which increased the number of active troops; third, the contracts signed in 1886–7 with the Mauser Company for 500,000 rifles and 50,000 carbines, for which subsequent negotiations continued until 1896; and fourth, the operation of 1891, in which Goltz demonstrated his multilateral skills in diplomacy and in the marketing of German-made war materials.[137] These operations perfectly exemplify the German Style of War Business, in which the non-commercial players' personal influence proved to be more crucial and effective than the commercial factors. The German military advisers' connections with Ottoman bureaucrats and officers and their simultaneous co-operation with the GAFs paved the way for many lucrative contracts.

In brief, from his very first days onwards, Goltz Pasha used his considerable abilities to execute the duties Bismarck had clearly described in 1880, long before the first mission was despatched to İstanbul.[138] During his 12 years' services in the Ottoman Army, Goltz Pasha introduced the Mauser Company to the competitive Ottoman rifle market at every opportunity, which stimulated German financial institutions' operational interest in the Ottoman market. He lobbied within Ottoman military circles on behalf of Krupp and intensely supported the *Bagdadbahn* project; at the same time, he tried to manipulate the Sultan's response to some political matters, like the Egyptian question in 1891.[139] As a matter of fact, he acted to pursue Germany's peaceful penetration strategy in the Ottoman Empire. In addition, he helped to create a new elite perspective among the young Ottoman officers who were educated in the military academy according to Goltz Pasha's military and political doctrines. Over the course of time, he came to be known as 'the father of the Turkish Army'.[140] Finally the chief editor of the *Ottoman Lloyd*, Grunwald, who according to Lowther's 'unverified account' received a subsidy from the German government of 30,000 marks for the undertaking,[141] gave a very interesting account of the reasons for Goltz's influence and success: 'His biggest success here [in İstanbul] has certainly been acquired through his psychological sensitivity [*psychologisches Feingefühl*].'[142] Goltz Pasha became seen as a hero to everyone.

CHAPTER 3

ARMS ORDERS AND CONTRACTS: THE FIRST FRUITS OF PERSONAL DIPLOMACY

'It would be best for us to win over Colonel Mahmud [Şevket] Bey. It seems that the agreement cannot be reached without him.'

August Huber to Paul Mauser, 8 December 1892

Coastal Fortification with Krupp Guns in 1885–6

When the German military mission arrived in İstanbul in 1882, the Ottoman military industry consisted of five principal state-owned establishments, all of which were located in İstanbul and administered by the Ministry of Imperial Ordnance (*Tophâne-i 'Âmire Nezâreti*): *Tophâne-i 'Amire* (Imperial Gun Factory); *Tüfenkhâne-i 'Âmire* (Imperial Small Arms Factory); *Baruthâne-i 'Amire* (Imperial Powder Factory); *Kırkağaç Fişenkhânesi* (Cartridge Factory); and the *Zeytinburnu Fabrikâyi Humâyun* (ImperialFoundry).[1] During the period under consideration, the manufacturing capabilities of these factories gradually declined. For example, in 1881, the Tüfenkhâne-i 'Âmire was capable of producing (*ihzâr*) the following number shown in Table 3.1 of rifles within the given weekly period.

Table 3.1 Rifle Production in Tüfenkhâne-i 'Âmire in 1881

Number of Rifles	31 May–7 June
306	Springfield rifles with fixed-bayonets (System-Snider)
181	Enfield rifles with fixed-bayonets (System-Snider)
200	Martini-Henry rifles with bayonet
50	Winchester rifles

Number of Rifles	3 July–17 July
349	Springfield rifles with fixed-bayonets (System-Snider)
10	Enfield rifles with fixed-bayonets (System-Snider)
624	Martini-Henry rifles with fixed-bayonets
216	Martini-Henry rifles with bayonet

Source: BOA, *YPRK.ASK.* 7/31 (10.07.1298/08.06.1881) and BOA, *Y.PRK. ASK.* 7/74 (20.08.1898/18.07.1881).

The reports of Captain Domville, the British naval attaché in İstanbul, shed light on the dramatic change in Ottoman domestic production after the arrival of the Germans in 1882. According to him, in 1888 Martini-Henry rifles were being made [t]here at the rate of a hundred a week,[2] whereas [in 1890] less work appeared to be going on than at the time of his last visit and only ten Martini-Henry a week were being made.[3] In 1894, the situation of Ottoman domestic production became even worse. According to Captain Egerton, the new British naval attaché, 'there was no work in hand in the small arms factory except making gauges and dies for the manufacture of Mauser rifles'.[4] It seems that other types of military production were in a similar state. Egerton reported that in all of the above-mentioned imperial factories there was either very little work or 'no work had been done for years'.[5] Between 1881 and 1894, the Tophâne–made military materials gradually disappeared, while the German armaments firms (the GAFs) penetrated and reshaped the Ottoman arms market. As a matter of fact, we can posit a significant relationship between the increase in the German supply for the Ottoman Army and the decrease in Ottoman domestic military production.

Table 3.2 Ottoman Artillery Orders from the Krupp Company (1861–75)

Calibre	Year of Order										Total
	1861	1863	1864	1867	1868	1870	1871	1873	1874	1875	
7.85 cm, L/25					127	78	8	214	178	100	753
8.70 cm, L/24			48							100	100
9.15 cm, L/22	1	48	12	48		10	170	120	52		461
12 cm, L/24								120			120
15 cm, L/14								50			50
15 cm, L/26								230			230
21 cm, L/22								28			28
24 cm, L/22								50			50
26 cm, L/22								10			10
28 cm, L/22								12			12
35.5 cm, L/22										1	1
Total	1	48	60	48	127	88	178	834	231	201	1,816

Source: Verzeichnis der von der Gußstahlfabrik und vom Grusonwerk von 1847 bis 1912 gefertigten Kanonen, in: HA, Krupp: 5a VII f. 862: 44–44a.

In 1885, when Goltz Pasha was assigned to head up the German military mission, the German armaments firms were barely active in the Ottoman market. The Krupp Company had previously established a monopoly position in Ottoman field artillery, but it had won no new orders from the Ottoman government since 1875. At that time, Krupp's representative in İstanbul was Otto Dingler, whose service never satisfied Krupp.[6] Krupp's Ottoman business had begun as early as 1861, when it sent a sample gun to Sultan Abdulaziz.[7] Between 1861 and 1875, the Ottoman Empire purchased 1,816 guns in a variety of calibres from Krupp. However, after 1875 the firm had to wait 19 years to start supplying guns to the Sublime Porte once more. In the 1880s, when the German military mission entered Ottoman service, Krupp's good days resumed. Table 3.3 displays the list of Krupp guns purchased by the Ottoman Empire between 1861 and 1875.

The war of 1877–8 resulted in the destruction of a large portion of the Ottoman artillery, and prompted an investigation to provide a new calculation of artillery needs. For this purpose, the Sultan issued an order in August 1881 for an inventory of the existing war materials (including guns, rifles, ammunition, etc.) in the imperial arsenal and other locations. Accordingly, the Ministry of the Navy, the Ministry of the Army, and the Military Equipment Ministry (Techizât-ı 'Askeriye Nezâreti) submitted their reports listing the estimate of war materials to the commission headed by Gazi Ahmet Muhtar Pasha. According to a report dated 10 August 1881, the following superfluity of war materials was present in the Imperial Arsenal of Ordnance and Artillery, along with other equipment: 64 Krupp guns (5×12 cm; 42×15 cm; 12×24 cm; 2×26 cm; 3×28 cm); 24 Armstrong guns (4×300 lbs [pounds]; 4×250 lbs; 9×150 lbs; 3×115 lbs; 1×40 lbs; 3×12 lbs); 1,464 muzzle-loading guns (1,001 of them were in good condition (*sâlim*)); 101 six-chambered guns-rifles of various calibres (*şeşhâneli top*); 1,283,877 pieces of primer (*fünye*), and so forth.[8] From this report it became apparent that a large armament procurement was not an immediate priority.

Table 3.3 Ottoman Warships and the Krupp Naval Guns Orders (1883)

Name of the Ship	Number of order	Calibre (cm)
Nâm-ı celil Hazreti Pâdişâhiye mensub zırhlı Fırkateyn-i Humâyun [Hamîdiye]	10	24
	2	17
Mesûdiye	12	26
Âsâr-ı Tevfik	8	21
Feth-i Bülend	4	21
'Avnillah	4	21
Mu'in-i Zafer	4	21
Mukaddime-i Hayr	4	21
Sefâin-i Sâire (Others)	20	15
	20	12
	8	17
	4	21
	30	6 (pound)
	30	4 (pound)
	30	3 (pound)

Source: BOA, Y.PRK KOM.4/32 (27.01.1301/28.11.1883).

Subsequent to the German advisers' employment in the Ottoman service, however, new armaments orders entered the agenda of the Sublime Porte. Following the submission of the above-mentioned report, Otto Dingler, Krupp's İstanbul agent, submitted a proposal to the Sultan to acquire different calibre naval guns from Krupp on 2 June 1882. This proposal came just two days after Kähler's contract was signed, as if he had been waiting for the German military mission to enter Ottoman service.[9] However, the Sublime Porte did not take any immediate action to place an order. In November 1883, Krupp sent the Sultan another proposal, with some pictures of their new coastal and field guns. This time the Sultan demonstrated a keen interest in the guns and issued an order to investigate the most appropriate way to acquire modern and strong artillery.[10] Nevertheless, no concrete action was taken until 1885.

Some important steps had been taken to open the Ottoman market to the German armament firms. In November 1883, the Ministry of

Navy submitted a proposal concerning the demand for new armaments for some existing ironclads. The proposal offered to fit the existing armoured ships with 190 breech-loading Krupp-made naval guns to replace the existing mounted muzzle-loading Armstrong guns. Table 3.3 prepared by the Ministry of the Navy and submitted to the Military High Commission, lists some of the Ottoman armoured vessels and the number and calibre of the Krupp guns recommended for them.[11]

However, the request for such a large quantity of new guns was not accepted as reasonable by the commission headed by Gazi Ahmed Muhtar Pasha, who had actually been to Essen in 1883 as a guest of Krupp.[12] According to the commission, a further technical investigation was necessary to avoid any inconvenient financial consequences. Further investigations recommended the postponement of the negotiations and a delay of any potential orders. The commission also decided to investigate the possibility of transforming the existing muzzle-loaders into breech-loaders, as an alternative to purchasing new guns. This was not what the Krupp Company wanted to hear. For a large order, Krupp would have to wait for Germans to begin serving in the Ottoman Army. In 1887, four years after the commission rejected the first proposal submitted by the Ministry of the Navy, a new proposal was made suggesting that 66 guns should be ordered from the Krupp factory, while 130 guns were to be obtained from the Imperial arsenal.[13] It appeared that the Ottoman officers, free of any kind of pressure or external advice, were not ready to order military materials abroad, from Germany in particular. Given the financial state of the empire, the Sultan was also presumably in no hurry to place a large order for war materials.

However, the arrival of the German advisers and the perception of an increased threat from Bulgaria's increasing armament orders and a potential Russian threat paved the way for a change of heart. The method used by some German advisers was to create a 'tempting market'.[14] According to the German artillery advisers the Russian threat constituted a neither unimportant nor unlikely threat against the Ottoman coastal defences.[15] Germany and its allies (i.e. Austria-Hungary) desired a political conflict between the

Ottoman Empire and Russia. The Eastern Rumelia Crisis further strengthened the threat, which had the capacity to trigger a widespread conflict in the region. Almost all the arguments put forward by the Germans related to a probable Russian attack, against which the only precaution would be a strong fortification of the Straits – with guns provided by Krupp.

Even so, the German Foreign Office worried about the possibility of a rapprochement between the Ottoman Empire and Russia. They were well aware what the consequences of such a development would be. To this end, Şakir Pasha had suggested an alliance with Russia.[16] If this transpired, it would become pointless to fortify the Straits. Germany and her ally (Austria–Hungary) therefore were of the opinion that Goltz Pasha's presence in İstanbul was of great importance for ensuring that the Ottoman Empire would cement a friendship with Germany and her friends alone. As the Ottoman special commission had heard from Germany in 1881, the principle was *l'ami de nos Amis*,[17] and Russia was a friend of Germany and the Austria–Hungarian Empire. Goltz Pasha continued to elaborate on the concept of German–Austrian friendship and the Russian threat on many occasions. In 1887, for instance, when he returned from a Europe tour during which he had been received by Kaiser Wilhelm I and Bismarck in Berlin and by the Austrian Emperor in Vienna, he submitted to the Sultan a report on the topic.

In line with this concept, Goltz Pasha suggested establishing 'a supportive force' (*kuvve-i muzâhere*) that would be able to build 'a preventive rampart' (*sedd-i mümâna'ât*) against a possible Russian attack on either the Ottoman Empire or Bulgaria.[18] This was an obvious repolarization, and Goltz Pasha was seen as the person most likely to be able to manage it. Meanwhile, the creation of these alliances led to 'seething mistrust' between Russia and the Ottoman Empire.[19] As Albertini points out, through the control of the army and the railway construction, Germany had acquired a predominant position in the Ottoman Empire, which enabled 'her to prevent the realization of Russian traditional aspirations'.[20]

To this end, on 25 April 1885, 'the Sultan doubled the order to 60 mortars (20 each of 12, 15 and 21 cm calibre), added 2,400 shells and 3,000 percussion tubes for a total 922,600 marks, according to a report of Otto Dingler, Krupp's agent in İstanbul, cited by Cram.[21] The first proposal of the contract and the prices for the mortars were as follows: 10×12 cm mortars: OL 3,632.40; 10×15 cm mortars: OL 5,218.80; and 10×21 cm mortars: OL 10,404.80.[22] The negotiations continued from February to July 1885. Krupp's representative, Menshausen, came to İstanbul to sign the contract, and spent nearly three months in the capital.[23] According to an unsigned document dated 17 July 1885, Menshausen appealed to the German ambassador, Radowitz, to help by pressuring the Ottoman government to accelerate the process and threatened to leave İstanbul without finalising the contract.[24] After his threat, the Ottoman

Table 3.4   Krupp Guns and their Prices (Ordered in 1885)*

Calibre (cm)	Number of orders	Price for each (OL)	Total
35.5	7	30,972	216,804
24	22	7,461	164,142
7.5	39	450	17,550
8.7	389	480	186,720
Total	457		585,216

*Without 60 mortars.
Source: BOA, *I.MMS.80/3473* (12.10.1302/25.07.1885).

Table 3.5   Krupp Guns and their Prices (Ordered in 1886)*

Calibre (cm)	Number of orders	Price for each (OL)	Total
24	10	7,461	74,610
7.5	20	450	9,000
8.7	404	480	193,920
3.7*	4		
10.7*	2		
Total	440		277,530

*These guns were ordered by the Ottoman government in exchange of a price reduction by 20,000 OL, see in: BOA, *I.MMS. 82/3533* (13.04.1303/19.01.1886).
Source: BOA, *I.MMS.82/3533* (07.04.1303/13.01.1886).

government took concrete steps, and, as Table 3.4 shows, ordered 457 Krupp guns from Germany.

According to the document, the initial amount of payment was 605,283 OL,[25] which was reduced by 50,000 OL according to Abdülhamid's demand, with an agreement dated 27 July 1885.[26] However, the number of 24-cm guns ordered was increased from 12 to 22 in the final version of the contract.[27] As it turned out, 'the insistence of Goltz Pasha',[28] who declared the fortification of the Straits to be one of his most favoured preventive plans, proved to be an influential factor in the finalization of the contract, which was followed by another order in 1886.[29] The fortification of the Bosporus and Dardanelles defences with Krupp guns was, as the authors of *Denkwürdigkeiten* asserted, one of 'Goltz's special services to his fatherland'.[30]

Apart from the mortars – as Table 3.6 indicates – the total amount of the order was 891 guns (852 of them field guns). It was a magnificent comeback for the Krupp Company after 10 years of stagnation in the Ottoman business. 'The magnitude of this sale,' says Grant, 'can be appreciated when one considers that in the 1877–78 war, there were 590 field guns among the army in Europe.'[31] The British military attaché also shared some information concerning the guns ordered by the Ottomans with his government. However, the information he gave was not compatible with Krupp's published list or with a report submitted to the Sultan by Ali Saib Pasha, the *Serasker* (1886–1).[32]

According to the *Mübâya'ât-ı Mühimme Defteri*, the final agreement was signed on 1 August 1885 and modified on 30 January 1886, with an order for other materials.[33] As was noted in the *Mübâya'ât-ı Mühimme Defteri*, payment for the ordered artillery materials (guns and ammunition) was to have been completed within three years (by August 1888) and the total cost of the first contracts to the Ottoman Treasury amounted to 555,283 OL.[34] Together with the contracts signed on 30 January 1886 and 26 March 1887, the total amount owed to Krupp reached 1,108,213.94 OL (20,446,547 marks).[35]

Table 3.6 Ottoman Artillery (Guns and Mortars) Ordered from the Krupp Company

Calibre (cm)	Number given by the British Military Attaché*		Number given by the Krupp Company**	Number reported by Ali Saib Pasha***
35.5	7	50 steel projectiles to be supplied with each gun.	7	7
24	35		32	32
12	20	Mortars	20	
15	10		20	
25	20		20	
8.7	1,000	Field guns	793	793
7.5	100	Field guns (light)	59	59
Total	1,192		951	891

**For (1885 + 1886), in: *Verzeichnis der von der Gußstahlfabrik und vom Grusonwerk von 1847 bis 1912 gefertigten Kanonen*, in: HA, Krupp, 5a VII f. 862: 44a; and see also: *Bestellungen bei F.K. in den Jahren 1875–1887*, in: HA, Krupp, WA 4/749; ***without mortars, in: BOA, Y. MTV.29/102 (25.04.1305/10.01.1888).

Source: *Turkey: Coast Defences & c. in Europe, Asia, and Africa, 1889, in: NA, London: ADM 231/14: 30.

Payment was not easy to manage for the Ottoman government, especially when it was drawing on only the regular state sources. To meet the instalments, the *Meclîs-i Vükelâ* decided to apply for financial support from the Ottoman Bank on 6 August 1885.[36] Even so, the financial difficulties faced by the Ottoman Empire forced the Sublime Porte to seek other sources of funds in both 1886 and 1887.[37] Even in 1888, the Ottoman government was struggling to find a source to make the instalment payments. Finding the source to finance the war material procurement became a matter of the Empire's honour. According to a document signed by Süreyya Pasha, 'in order to protect the state's honour' the advance payment intended for the mining contract in Bulgar-dağı in 1888 was instead dedicated to the payment of the German firm's claims.[38]

As stated above, Krupp had sent a set of alluring pictures of the newly developed guns to the Sultan in 1883. By employing that strategy, he had anticipated that the Sultan would opt in favour of the German products. At the time, Abdülhamid was conscious of the inferior quality of Ottoman-made artillery materials. In a dictated document, the Sultan poked fun at the products of the *Tophâne-i 'Âmire*: 'As for our guns' shells, they are so far from reaching their targets among the enemy's army that it would seem they were meant for no other purpose than setting off a firework show for the purpose of welcoming the enemy.'[39]

Furthermore, Friedrich Alfred Krupp (1854–1902), who took over the leadership of the Krupp Company after his father Alfred Krupp (1812–87) died, was also confident in the expectation that the German military mission would support German commercial interests in the Ottoman market. On this occasion, however, the procured contracts were the result of a joint effort of the GAFs and GMAs, particularly Goltz Pasha, who was the most prominent figure in the operation.[40] Krupp's expectation was fulfilled. Goltz Pasha struggled to persuade the Sultan to fortify the Straits against a possible Russian threat. According to Griffiths, Goltz was of the opinion that an enemy who could seize the Straits would not only occupy the capital, but 'split the Ottoman forces which were divided between Europe and Asia'.[41] At first Abdülhamid II was not in favour of taking an action that could provoke the Russians. In fact, Abdülhamid II did not want to create greater uncertainty and instability in his empire's relationship with Russia. Some of Goltz's other suggestions, for manoeuvres and field exercises, were not followed because of the Sultan's perception of the need to keep stability within the region.[42]

Following Goltz Pasha's fortification strategy and related advice, the Ottoman government ordered in total 517 artillery weapons in 1885, and that was followed by an order for 440 guns in 1886. Krupp's total artillery sales to the Ottoman Empire from 1861 onwards reached 2,773 pieces by the end of 1886. Goltz's contribution to the procurement process was clearly mentioned by the *Denkwürdigkeiten's* authors. According to them, 'His [Goltz's] incessant pressure [*unausgesetzten Drängen*] succeeded in 1885 to prompt the order of a number of heavy guns, the heaviest for the Dardanelles, at the firm of Friedrich Krupp in Essen.'[43]

As the British military attaché rightly noticed, the above-mentioned orders led to a great advance 'in the remodelling of the defences of the Dardanelles and Bosporus'.[44] The first coastal guns ordered in 1885 were delivered to the Golden Horn in March 1886 and mounted on the several coasts and forts.[45] The largest guns, and some of the 24-cm guns, were mounted for the Bosporus and Dardanelles defence.[46]

Goltz Pasha's special service to the fatherland was not restricted to coastal defence. The German shipbuilding industry also took advantage of Goltz's ability to pressure the Ottoman government. Within the concept of the strategy of Straits defence, to which Goltz Pasha's contribution was clear, the Ottoman Empire ordered several torpedo boats from the Germania yards.[47] The justification provided by the Ministry of the Navy's Hasan Pasha to the Sultan for the torpedo boats order was compatible with Goltz Pasha's strategy. Hasan Pasha's formulation was based on the possible threat Russia and Greece posed against the Ottoman coasts through their growing naval forces. Accordingly, Hasan Pasha's *tezkire* informed the Sultan that, on 20 October 1886, an agreement was signed between the Ottoman Empire and the Germania yard for the torpedo boats.[48] In addition to Krupp's monopoly achievement in the Ottoman armaments market from 1885 onwards, Germany also gradually came to be a dominating force in Ottoman naval purchasing.[49]

In fact, during these years the four principal German companies (Germania, Schichau, Vulcan, and Howaldtswerke AG) competed with each other for the Ottoman torpedo-related orders (chasers and boats). On 13 September 1886, George Howaldt, the director of the Howaldtswerke AG, sent the Ottoman government a proposal in which he offered a lower price than his competitors. According to Howaldt's proposal, Schichau had offered OL 257,000, whereas Germania's first offer was OL 227,000. Following Howaldt's offer of OL 198,500, the Germania Company cut their price to OL 195,000, which was followed by Howaldt's last offer of OL 185,000.[50] In the end, the contract was obtained by Germania and the agreement for 12 vessels was signed between the parties on 20 October 1886.[51] The total amount scheduled for payment was 260,600 OL (4,808,070 marks) and the first instalment (20,000 OL) was to be paid on 20 November 1886.[52] The ordered vessels and their features were as follows:[53]

1 × Length 70 m torpedo chaser
1 × Length 57 m torpedo chaser
1 × Length 43 m torpedo boat
9 × Length 39 m torpedo boat

According to British Captain Cane, during the negotiation process, however, *baksheesh* was demanded 'by everyone... from the Minister of Marine downwards'.[54]

The Mauser Operations: Professional Team Work

'[Mahmud] Şevket [Pasha] is the most proper person [for your interest]; the others are working for your competitors.'
 Goltz Pasha's strategic advice to Paul Mauser in 1886[55]

'Since I knew from my childhood that the Turks always wage war... so I thought, that this can be a country to we deliver!'

Paul Mauser[56]

When the German military mission entered Ottoman service, they saw only British and American-made rifles in the Ottoman arsenal. In 1877 the Ottoman Army had 396,172 Snider, 339,160 Peabody-Martini, and 9,370 Winchester rifles.[57] In fact, in August 1873, the Ottoman government had decided to place an order with the American Providence Tool Company for 600,000 repeater rifles based on the British Martini-Henry rifle system, which were called Peabody-Martini rifles.[58] According to an 1881 enumeration of the war materials, however, the Ottoman arsenals already contained 67,974 Martini-Henry, 23,613 Snider, and 7,201 Winchester rifles as surplus stored as *Tophâne-i 'Âmire* and *Harbiye Nezâret-i Celîlesi Fazlası*.[59] In 1887, the inventory recorded 450,000 Henry-Martini rifles, which were described by Ottoman officials as obsolete and useless (*hiç bir işe yaramayan*).[60] Apparently, the good old days for the American and British rifle companies in the Ottoman market had ended; stocks of new rifles would come from the new favourite ally: Germany.

On 2 May 1886, three prominent German rifle producers, Paul Mauser, Ludwig Loewe and his brother Isidor met at the Frankfurter Hof in Frankfurt am Main.[61] The occasion for the meeting was the news that the Ottomans intended to place a large rifle order for 400,000 weapons of the Peabody-Martini system. The information about the Ottoman order probably came from the Huber Brothers, who were in İstanbul representing the British steel maker Continental Steel Works, based in Sheffield, whose owner, Joseph Jonas (1845–1921),was an industrialist born in Germany.[62] Before Paul Mauser was furnished with this information, however, Jonas sent a letter to the Loewe brothers regarding the Hubers' report about the Sultan's decision and asking whether they would be interested in the Ottoman business or not. Following this letter, Loewe invited Mauser to meet and negotiate in Frankfurt.[63] Thus, on 2 May 1886, they came together in the Frankfurter Hof.

During the meeting, the company leaders discussed the possibility of obtaining a contract from the Ottoman government, but instead of competing, as they had done previously, they agreed to a joint business arrangement. According to the proposal, if a contract was forthcoming, it would be signed under the name of Mauser. However, in 1889, after they had obtained a contract, the Loewe Company bought the shares belonging to Alfred Kaulla (1833–99), the director of the Württembergische Vereinsbank at Stuttgart, and consequently Paul Mauser lost the majority shareholding in his own company.[64] According to this initial agreement, the price for a rifle without bayonet would be 60 marks (325 Kuruş), including the freight cost and the 9 per cent commission for the representatives in İstanbul (the Huber Brothers). As planned at the conference, four weeks after the meeting Mauser sent a 9.5 mm rifle to the Ottoman Empire, after which they would wait for an invitation from İstanbul.

After the İrâde issued in November 1886 for the new recruitment regulation, Sultan Abdülhamid gave Goltz Pasha the directive to contact Paul Mauser in Oberndorf/Neckar and Isidor Loewe in Berlin. On 5 November 1886, however, Paul Mauser had already left for London on an unsuccessful mission to sell his newly developed 9.5 mm repeating rifle to the British government.[65] On 13 November 1886, Alfred Kaulla sent a letter to London, expecting that Mauser would still be there, and suggesting that before going to İstanbul he should come to Berlin and discuss some crucial points with regard to the joint business in the Ottoman market.[66] At that time Kaulla was the director of the Württembergischen Vereinsbank, the largest shareholder of the Mauser Company, and served as the Mauser Company's business manager.[67]

But Mauser was not in London on 13 November 1886. On hearing that the Ottoman government had finally issued instructions for a trial test of the rifles, he had immediately left London on 12 November and travelled via Oberndorf to İstanbul, where he would gain the greatest achievements in the history of his company. Before Mauser and Loewe arrived, an initial proposal and a telegram code had also been prepared and sent by Loewe to Kaulla.[68] After accomplishing the relevant correspondence between the two companies (Loewe and

Table 3.7 Names and their Encrypted Codes (in November 1886)

Name	Code	Name	Code
Abdülhamid II	*Ernst*	Mauser	*Robert*
The Ottoman Ministry of War	*Franz*	Kaulla	*Vicco*
The Ottoman Ministry of Finance	*Carl*	Loewe	*Max*
Goltz Pasha	*Friedrich*	Huber	*Anton*
The Ottoman Ambassador/Berlin	*Paul*	Werndl	*Georg*
The German Ambassador/İstanbul	*Wilhelm*	Azarian	*Bruder*
The German Foreign Office	*Otto*	Menshausen	*Eduard*
Deutsche Bank	*Koch*	Schulhof	*Peter*
Bleichröder/Berlin	*Julius*	Garbrecht	*Christoph*
The Imperial *İrâde*	*Rechnung*	Kühn	*August*
Schriever, Lüttich	*Gustav*	Derviş Pasha	*Alfred*
J.C.Jul. Möller	*Agent*	Hobe Pasha	*Heinrich*

Source: SA, Oberndorf: M-A8.

Mauser) and Alfred Kaulla, on 22 November 1886, Paul Mauser arrived in İstanbul and stayed there till 15 February 1887, returning to Oberndorf on 19 February 1886.[69]

One of the most interesting features of Mauser's first appearance in the Ottoman war business was the establishment of an encoded list of ciphered identifications and specifications. Within their first days in İstanbul, Paul Mauser and Isidor Loewe agreed with August Huber on a list of codes for key figures, institutions, and terms in the negotiation process.[70] As Table 3.7 illustrates, almost all the persons in the arms trade were given code names.

It is a matter of record that the names listed in the table included all the key determinants of the German Style of War Business in the Ottoman market: Abdülhamid II (*Ernst*) was the final decision maker and his *İrâde* (*Rechnung* – invoice) was the most crucial document that the German arms dealers were looking for; Deutsche Bank (*Koch*) and Bismarck's reliable banker Bleichröder (*Julius*) were the important financial factors to finalize the purchasing process; Goltz Pasha (*Friedrich*) was the man who had smoothly oriented the German arms dealers in the Ottoman market; Azarian (*Bruder*) the agent of the American rifle firms,[71] although he was encrypted as

ARMS ORDERS AND CONTRACTS

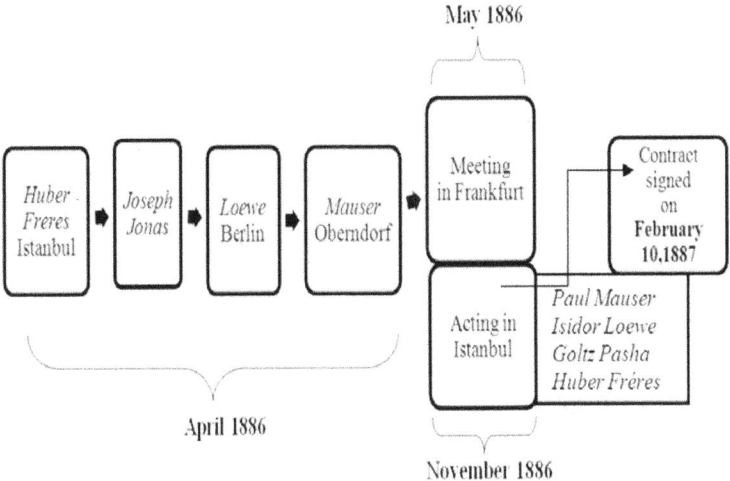

Figure 3.1 Mauser's Entrance into the Ottoman Market in 1886/87

Bruder (Brother), he was definitely one of the most powerful competitors of Mauser (*Robert*) and his agent Huber (*Anton*); Derviş Pasha (*Alfred*), the head of the test commission, was another important figure, described by the British ambassador as 'a very corrupt and dangerous man';[72] finally, the German Foreign Office (*Otto*), which proved to also be an influential and supportive instrument for the German firms' war business abroad, was codenamed Otto, most probably after Otto von Bismarck, who was also involved in his fellow citizens' war business in the Ottoman Empire at the very beginning of the negotiations. The codes used between the agent (Huber) and the firms (Mauser and Loewe) emerged as an effective and protective tool in their Ottoman business.

Figure 3.1 illuminates how the Mauser rifles entered the Ottoman arms market and also shows Goltz Pasha's timely presence in the Ottoman army for the sake of the Mauser Company. On his second day in İstanbul, Mauser met Goltz Pasha and Kamphövener Pasha. As the above given figure illustrates through Goltz Pasha's mediation, Mauser was able to participate in the test, in which the Belgian Mauser, Mannlicher, Martini-Henry and Hotchkiss also trialled.[73] Paul Mauser wrote about his first day in İstanbul and the first test as follows:

> I arrived on November 22 at 10 o'clock and was immediately led into the [Yıldız] palace where the negotiations soon began. Through the intervention [*Einwirken*] of the German officers, particularly Mr Goltz Pasha and Kamphövener, it was possible to immediately join in the tests.[74]

Goltz's presence in İstanbul and his authority in Ottoman military circles provided to the German armaments firms a series of conveniences and opportunities that the others did not share.[75] Goltz Pasha was well aware of the impact of his influential position on the finalization of the purchasing processes. In his memoir, he stated: 'I can claim that without my [intervention] the modernisation of the [Ottoman] Army with the German rifles would never have happened.'[76] Goltz was not mistaken. As the following figure illustrates, Goltz Pasha played a determinant role in the process as a non-commercial factor.

Test-shooting began on 8 December 1886. Goltz Pasha's influential assistance was revealed during the very first test. On that day, Goltz Pasha gave Paul Mauser critical advice relating to the particulars of doing business in the Ottoman Empire: establish close relations with the right person. According to Goltz Pasha, the best person for Mauser's business interest in the Ottoman Empire was Mahmud Şevket Bey (later Pasha) who was also present at the test as an observer. 'Şevket is the right person' uttered Goltz Pasha to Mauser, adding 'the others are working for your competitors.'[77] Goltz Pasha's instincts and experience were correct. During the negotiation Mahmud Şevket (later Pasha) and Goltz Pasha struggled together to promote Mauser's supremacy against the Serasker Ali Saib Pasha, who was inclined to purchase the Austrian-made Mannlicher rifles. The collaboration worked and the Mauser Company was consequently awarded the contract, which was one of the first triumphs that paved the way to the Germanization of the Ottoman Army.

While the tests were continuing, some German officers employed in the Ottoman service discussed whether it was permissible to sell to a foreign army a rifle initially developed only for the German army and labelled a state secret.[78] However, according to Goltz, these discussions aided Mauser's competitors, who claimed that the rifle tested in İstanbul was not identical to the rifle used in the German Army, and that the latter remained a secret.[79] These claims aroused suspicion in Yıldız Palace about Mauser's reliability. However, this unfortunate circumstance fully proved the sagacity of Goltz's advice to Mauser on the day of the test: 'Now everyone will want to be your friends, but be very careful, and beware of doing business with any of them, even if they are Germans. You need no one.'[80] Goltz Pasha's response showed he was more aware than the other Germans of the political and economic consequences of obtaining such a large order. He took immediate action to get written notification from the German Minister of War, declaring that the rifle submitted to the Sultan was identical to the rifles used in the German Army.

With this declaration Goltz Pasha hoped to basically eliminate the suspicions that had arisen from the rumours. In a letter dated 13 December 1886, five days after the first test took place, Goltz emphasised the significance of the expected notification from the Prussian Minister of War, Schellendorf. Goltz Pasha believed the rumour problem could easily thwart the procurement process of the Mauser magazine-rifle. German industry highly desired this contract, particularly after the significant increase in the size of the Ottoman Army brought about by the new recruitment law Goltz had helped to engineer.[81] Ultimately, the notification from Berlin arrived in İstanbul and thereby eliminated one of the most important obstacles to the contract. The Ottoman ambassador in Berlin, Tevfik Pasha, had communicated with both the Prussian Minister of War and also with Bismarck, who gave the same information and praised the Mauser rifles.[82]

The Mauser rifle may not have been the best rifle, but it was certainly the best-marketed rifle, with the following powerful figures lobbying on its behalf: German Chancellor Bismarck, Prussian Minister of War Schellendorf, Goltz Pasha, Kamphövener Pasha, Abdülhamid's first secretary Süreyya Pasha, Mahmud Şevket Bey and Ragıb Bey, who would be included in the team after the agreement was signed.⁸³ Goltz Pasha's relations with Mahmud Şevket Pasha and his influence on both the Mauser operation of 1887 and subsequent operations deserve further mention. As stated above, Goltz Pasha advised Paul Mauser to establish good relations with Mahmud Şevket, who Goltz Pasha had already chosen as a trustworthy pupil and friend. Goltz Pasha wrote a paper in 1913 about Mahmud Şevket Pasha, where he noted Mahmud Şevket Pasha's contribution to Goltz's endeavours in the military commission against the Austrian firm Mannlicher, which was Mauser's only serious rival and was supported by the Serasker.⁸⁴

Finally, on 6 February 1887, the Sultan issued an imperial *İrâde* approving the purchase of rifles from the Mauser Company.⁸⁵ After long negotiation, on 9 February 1887, the contract for 500,000 rifles (M/1887: 9.5 mm) and 50,000 carbines (M/1887: 9.5 × 60 mm) was signed between the Ottoman government and the Mauser/Loewe partnership.⁸⁶ On the day of the signing, the Ottoman government prepared a proposal relating to the conditions on price, delivery and payment.⁸⁷ Mauser and Loewe were to share the contractual obligations though, as Ball notes, Loewe's share eventually went to the Mauser Company.⁸⁸ At the outset of the negotiation, the unit price of the Mauser rifle (without bayonet) was 365 kuruş, but after the intervention of the Sultan, Mauser made a 2 kuruş reduction in the unit price.⁸⁹ The total value of this contract was 1,996,500 OL (36,835,425 marks).⁹⁰ Four days later, the Sultan awarded Paul Mauser an imperial order of *Mecîdiye (Nişânı)* for long-standing exceptional services, which were not actually defined or detailed in the document.⁹¹ On 15 February 1887, Paul Mauser departed from İstanbul with a contract valued at nearly 37 million marks.⁹² As Grant has noted, this order made the Ottoman Army the first to acquire the Mauser rifle in any significant quantity.⁹³

The contract included three important requirements, which Paul Mauser defined as 'big risks' for him.⁹⁴ These first of these three provisions obliged Mauser to inform the Ottoman government of any rifle improvement patented by him during the contract period.⁹⁵ The second important condition was that if the German Army was to adopt a new rifle during the course of the Ottoman delivery, the Ottoman Empire had the right to demand Mauser to complete the contract with the new model.[96] The third critical provision was a restriction for the Mauser manufactory. During the time the company was producing for the Ottoman Army, it would not be allowed to undertake orders from any other country.[97] These terms could be accepted as big risks for the Mauser Company and provided advantages for the Ottoman Empire.[98] In 1890, the Ottoman government took advantage of these conditions by demanding that Mauser halt the delivery of the initial model (cal. 9.5 mm) and complete the contract with a new developed one (cal. 7.65 mm).[99]

Nearly two weeks passed after the issue of the *İrâde*, and the Ottoman government was unable to make the deposit payment to Paul Mauser; the terms were set at 20 per cent on the date of signing the contract and the remainder on delivery. According to *The {London} Times,* Mauser became very angry and threatened to leave İstanbul. A new Finance Minister came into office and cut short the negotiations in progress for a loan; the contract could not be finalized because funds were lacking to pay the deposit. However, at that juncture Abdülhamid's personal intervention became significant. The Sultan invited Paul Mauser and the German ambassador, Radowitz, to dinner and a short delay in the payment process was probably arranged then.[100] The only way to overcome the existing financial difficulty was through foreign borrowing.[101] When Mauser left İstanbul he had the contract and a medal from the Sultan in hand – but not the money that he had expected.[102]

The contract to buy the rifles produced another headache for the Ottoman government. In March 1887, the government had to find a factory to which the cartridge and powder order could be conditionally awarded. The contract in question would involve 150,000 chests of cartridges. A commission established in the Ministry of War (Seraskerlik) discussed the issue in March 1887. The commission's first inclination was to give the contract to Wilhelm Lorenz of the Lorenz Company of Karlsruhe, which had technical superiority over their competitors and long-term experience in cartridge manufacturing.[103] However Mauser also wanted the contract to provide the required cartridges. On the day after the commission meeting, Kamphövener Pasha submitted a report to the Serasker in which he supported Mauser's interest.[104]

However, Serasker Ali Saib Pasha struggled to prevent the monopoly position of any single company. He intended to use his ministerial power to counter foreign attempts to monopolize the Ottoman market. He criticized the government's inclination to make contracts with a certain company without undertaking any comparative testing of the products. In his view, there had to be sufficient opportunity for all to compete. During the cartridge-purchasing negotiations in the Meclîs-i Mahsûsa, he opposed the purchase of the cartridges from the Mauser factory, and recommended purchasing from another German firm, the Lorenz Company (Deutsche Metallpatronenfabrik Lorenz).[105] His key argument against the Mauser factory was the lack of experience in cartridge production.[106] The Mauser had no strong background in cartridge production, which put them at a disadvantage against their major rival, the Deutsche Metallpatronenfabrik Lorenz.[107] The Lorenz offer was, according to Serasker Ali Saib Pasha, acceptable from a technical point of view, and at first the commission decided to place its order with the Lorenz factory.[108] As Mauser was not capable of producing cartridges, he had recommended Max Duttenhofer (later Max von Duttenhofer), the director of the Rottweiler Company, to the Ottoman Government. The Rottweiler factory had collaborated with Mauser for a long time and was located in Rottweil, only 18 km from Oberndorf – as Şakir Pasha reported in 1894, a mere 30-minute travel time from Mauser's location in Oberndorf.[109]

Paul Mauser and his business partner Loewe, as the government-supported arms makers, managed to overcome their disadvantage with an aggressive marketing strategy. Kaulla, Mauser's Company partner, submitted to the Sublime Porte a report defaming Lorenz as 'an inferior cartridge maker' (*Lorenz gibi 'âdi bir kovancı*).[110] While the Meclîs-i Vükelâ was discussing the issue, Isidor Loewe, Mauser's business partner, went into action. With the support of Kaulla and the Mauser representative in İstanbul, together with Max Duttenhofer, he tried to persuade Wilhelm Lorenz to give three-quarters of the contract to Duttenhofer and Loewe.[111] On 21 November 1887, based

ARMS ORDERS AND CONTRACTS

on Kraus' account Ludwig Loewe and Max Duttenhofer signed a partnership agreement for any future business starting with the here-mentioned Ottoman contract.[112] Consequently, Mauser, Loewe and Duttenhofer worked together against the Lorenz factory. However, to gain a share of the Ottoman cartridge market, they offered Lorenz a joint business venture. Aware of both their strong position in the market and their power in both the Berlin and İstanbul governments, Wilhelm Lorenz could not endure anymore the pressure coming from all side and subsequently accepted their offer.[113] Under this pressure, however, Lorenz was eventually forced to sell his factory to Isidor Loewe on 6 February 1889, for a payment of six million marks.[114] The delivery of the ammunition, which was started under Wilhelm Lorenz, continued after 1889 without him. Through this sale, Ali Saib Pasha's fears of monopolization of the Ottoman arms market became a reality.

On 7 July 1887, the final decision about the cartridges was announced in the Meclîs-i Vükelâ and, consequently, the process of signing a contract between parties began.[115] On 11 July 1887, the ministers signed a protocol designed to finalize this exhausting process. In the protocol a note was made of the unification of the Lorenz factory by means of the M&L partnership.[116] The contract was signed on 20 September 1887 (nine days after the official partnership between the Mauser and the Rottweiler companies had been signed) and ordered 100 million cartridges from Mauser and his business partners (*Mavzer ve şürekâsı*). The total amount paid for the cartridges was 473,875 OL (nearly nine million marks), which was more than what Isidor Loewe had paid to buy out the Lorenz factory.[117] Since Abdülhamid did not allow the army to train with live ammunition,[118] such large cartridge procurement was an extraordinary decision. As can be seen in Table 3.9c below, more that 60 per cent of all the cartridges purchased between 1892 and 1904 were stored in the Imperial Storehouse in Gülhâne for years.[119] According to Goltz Pasha's report to Paul Mauser the fact that the Ottoman Army rarely used live ammunition had to be taken into consideration while marketing powder to the Ottoman government.[120]

While the cartridge supply was being organized, powder supply became another important source of competition between firms. However, the German government made a clear choice to favour the Rottweiler Powder Company. Bismarck intervened in the process and sent the Ottoman Empire an official letter written in support of the Rottweiler Company, which affected the course of the decision.[121] Following Bismarck's letter, Radowitz also interfered in the marketing process. Radowitz's letter, sent on 21 April 1887, also amounted to a recommendation for that firm: 'According to the information from very reliable source located in Berlin, the best powder for the ammunition used for the Mauser rifles is the powder produced by Mr Duttenhofer from Rottweil.'[122]

Germany continued to assert pressure on the matter of the powder until the Ottoman government made a final decision. After the rifle order was awarded to the Mauser/Loewe companies, Goltz Pasha went to Germany following an audience at the Yıldız Palace with the Sultan on 12 March 1887.[123] During his stay in Berlin, he was received as a reliable informant, by several important personalities, including Kaiser Wilhelm I and Bismarck. The Prussian minister of War, Schellendorf, to whom Goltz Pasha sent an informative letter on 13 December 1886 regarding Mauser's struggle for the Ottoman rifle contract,[124] also received him and discussed the Ottoman military reform process. During the conversation the Minister asked for some information about the Sultan's decision for purchasing cartridges and powder. According to Goltz Pasha's report to the Sultan, Schellendorf was hoping that the decision would be made in favour of Mauser, Loewe and Duttenhofer. Goltz Pasha later recalled that the minister put special emphasis on the qualifications and competency of Mr Duttenhofer, the owner of the Rottweiler Powder Company.[125] Presumably Goltz instructed the minister with regard to the entire procurement process, in which only the powder issue remained unresolved. It appears that support for one of the GAFs' interests in the Ottoman market had become a matter of State. This was the nature of the German Style of War Business, as Menshausen, Krupp's influential representative (and later the director) illustrates in a letter addressed to the Unterstaatssekretär Richthofen, writing that 'the question of who obtained the contract is a political question of power or a result of a political trading-business'.[126]

However, contrary to the reports and letters praising the Rottweiler powders, Paul Mauser himself acknowledged that the tests were still continuing in November 1887 and that he did not have a clear result confirming the efficiency (*Leistungsfähigkeit*) of the new powder. In his response to Goltz Pasha, Paul Mauser reported the results: 'I will let the experiments taking place in Rottweil continue. Till this day I have heard of the report submitted to me that the performance of the new powder is not yet clear.'[127] The Ottoman Empire placed an order for the ammunition from the Lorenz Company, which the Loewe Company bought in 1889, with the powders from Rottweil and the rifles from the Mauser/Loewe co-operative. On 11 September 1887, the Loewe/Mauser partnership made an agreement with the Rottweiler Company to work in a close partnership.[128] In November 1887, when Goltz Pasha was informed of this partnership for the Ottoman market, he sent a letter to Paul Mauser and expressed his appreciation.[129]

While the powder issue was being vociferously discussed in Ottoman military circles, a French firm also showed interest and sent powder samples to the Ottoman Empire for testing. Goltz Pasha, as an open supporter of the German industrial interests, gathered confidential information about this French powder. As he wrote in a letter to Paul Mauser, he obtained the technical details of this powder from a reliable source (*aus sehr guter Quelle*). As stated above, Goltz Pasha played an essential role as mediator of the information flow from the Ottoman officers/officials to the German arms makers. His relations with the Ottoman officers and bureaucrats gave him access to this critical information, which was obviously assumed to be secret. To all intents and purposes, Goltz's behaviour amounted to industrial espionage carried out for the sake of his country and its industry.[130] In the last notification regarding the technical specification of the French powder, Goltz Pasha wrote that 'perhaps this message leaves you [Paul Mauser] in a position to determine to what extent a similar powder for our rifle has to be considered'.[131] Mauser replied, 'your description for the

French powder exactly matches with that I have now in my hand. I hope to write you on this matter even more'.[132]

Goltz Pasha wrote to Paul Mauser that 'as far as the chemical analysis has yet determined that the storage capacity of [this] powder is to be regarded as favourable',[133] but one year later, he submitted to the Sultan a *layiha* in which he argued against the French powder's durability. Referring to documented (*mevsûk*) information from an (anonymous) competent person (*Erbâb-ı vukufdan bir zât*), Goltz Pasha asserted that 'the French powder, the quality of which was exaggerated, was not as durable [*dayanıklı*] as desired'.[134]

In addition to this kind of technical material, Goltz Pasha sent Mauser up-to-date information on other subjects, including the payment status of the Ottoman government for the rifles ordered, and rumours circulated in Ottoman government and military circles about the Mauser Company and its products. In November 1887, for instance, when a rumour circulated in İstanbul saying that Paul Mauser would sell his company and give up his office, the Sultan instructed Goltz Pasha to ask Mauser if these rumours were true. For the purposes of verification, Goltz Pasha sent Mauser a telegram on 23 November 1887.[135] The following day, Mauser responded to Goltz's question: 'The Mauser factory still exists and will definitely continue to exist. I am the head [of the company] and I will be remaining on the top.'[136] However, one month later, on 28 December 1887, Isidor Loewe took over a major share of the Mauser Company, and Paul Mauser lost his position as the major shareholder. Despite this takeover, the rifle contract remained in the name of Paul Mauser as the firm's executive director.[137] The change did not negatively affect Mauser's Ottoman business.

The real challenge facing Paul Mauser was the Ottomans' inability to make payment on the contracted date. Mauser's agent, August Huber, visited the Ottoman Ministry of Finance several times to seek payment.[138] For this purpose, Abdülhamid's private secretary, Ragıb Bey, sent a private letter to Paul Mauser and explained the reason for this default as the 'lack of money in the State Treasury' (*der Geldmangel, an welchem die kaiserliche Schatzkammer leidet*). In his letter, Ragıb Bey also tried to reassure Mauser: 'Currently the work is done with the best will to pay you as soon as possible in order to obtain your wonderful rifles earlier. Do not let yourself be discouraged, but continue to work with your usual energy.'[139]

As it turned out, six months after the contract had been signed the Ottoman government managed to pay the first instalment. The 'bearer of joyful tidings' for the Mauser Company was Goltz Pasha. In a letter dated 22 November 1887, Goltz Pasha wrote that a sum of at least 100,000 OL (1,845,000 marks) was ready for payment.[140] However, three days later Goltz Pasha sent Paul Mauser another letter in which he expressed his regret that because of financial difficulties the Ottoman rifle orders could not be handled quickly; as a consequence, Goltz Pasha warned him that might experience problems with the payment.[141] In July 1888, Goltz received a letter from Mauser referring to the payment problems.[142] It is a matter of record that similar problems occurred over and over during the course of the order-delivery process.

After many debates, discussions and revisions, the first manufactured rifles were ready for test-firing in December 1887; consequently, on 30 May 1888, 'the first railroad car loaded with 1,305 rifles began its journey' towards the harbour.[143] The first group (*kâfile*) of rifles arrived in İstanbul on 17 June 1888, transported by a ship called the *Jupiter*.[144] As of January 1889, even though the rifles were still being manufactured, and despite the 36,400 Mauser M/87 cal. 9.5 mm rifles already stored in the Imperial Arsenal (*Silah-hâne*), the debates in Ottoman military circles about the features of the Mauser rifle had not ceased.[145] In November 1887, as Goltz Pasha reported to Paul Mauser, the Ottoman Military Commission had been inclined to alter the contract to switch from the M/87:9.5mm model to the newly-developed, smaller-calibre rifle (M/87:8mm), which had actually failed during its test firing.[146] The most common complaints about the Mauser rifle related to its calibre and the powder used for it. To counter these complaints, Goltz Pasha submitted to the Sultan several reports rejecting the criticisms and praising the M/87:9.5mm rifle.[147] In January 1889, in one of his reports, Goltz Pasha admitted that the decision in favour of the Mauser rifle had not been made unanimously; however, he specifically reminded the Sultan that the contract decision was final and irreversible. After this reminder, he asserted that 'I certainly guarantee that even until today there are no rifles superior to these [Mauser] rifles [M/87:9.5mm].'[148] While Goltz Pasha was struggling to focus the Sultan on the M/87:9.5mm, he was simultaneously asking Paul Mauser to provide him with the test results of the new Belgian Model/89:7.65mm.[149]

Serasker Ali Saib Pasha was the foremost person to keep criticizing the Mauser rifle and comparing it with the Austrian-Mannlicher rifle.[150] As a consequence of these debates, which were based on several points of dissatisfaction with the Mauser rifles, and the news that Mauser had developed a new rifle (in a smaller-calibre of 7.65 mm) for the Belgian government, in 1890 the Ottoman government took advantage of the conditions mentioned above by demanding Mauser halt production of this model (cal. 9.5 mm) and complete the contract with a newly developed model (cal. 7.65 mm).[151]

Interestingly, Paul Mauser and his agent, August Huber, opted to keep the technical development of the M/87:9.5mm a secret as long as possible. However, they were forced to change their strategy because of a letter sent by the Ottoman diplomat Caratheodory Pasha to the Ministry of War. The letter revealed that the Belgian government had adopted a new model of Mauser M/89:7.65mm that was manufactured in the Fabrique Nationale plant in Belgium under Mauser's patent, and intended to offer this new model to the Ottomans. After being informed of this letter, August Huber suggested to Mauser that he take immediate action to send one of the new model rifles produced in Oberndorf so that the Ottomans could see it before the Belgian model arrived.[152] Consequently, the Mauser Company reluctantly informed the Ottoman government about the new model, which they would later adopt.

This development served to prove Ali Saib's earlier assumption that the government had decided precipitously in favour of the Mauser Company, even though the decision was taken by the Sultan's own initiative. August Huber sent a letter to Oberndorf on 8 December 1892 in which he claimed that 'reliable sources' in the Yıldız Palace had said that the Sultan had regretted making such a quick decision regarding the first Mauser order and doing so on his own initiative.[153] At the earlier stage of the contract, the Sultan looked on the contract given to Mauser 'as his own act and deed'.[154] Apparently, the Sultan's own inclinations, which were the basic factors shaping both the Empire's foreign and defence procurement policies, proved to be a greater determinant than the Empire's military and economic priorities. As Mahmud Şevket said, the Sultan's benevolence (*Wohlwollen seiner Mejestät des Sultans*) was actually the principal factor behind the contracts being given to the Germans.[155]

On 21 July 1890, the Ottoman Military Commission decided to stop the production of the Model 1887:9.5mm at the number of 220,000 rifles and 4,000 cavalry carbines.[156] According to the Mübâya'ât-ı Mühimme Defteri, by 12 March 1891 the number of M/87:9.5 mm rifles delivered totalled 218,765 (through 177 delivery lots).[157] Together with one more group, the total number of rifles delivered reached 220,000.[158] The last group of carbines (M/87:9.5mm) arrived in İstanbul on 12 February 1891.[159] After that, the company began supplying the new Model/90:7.65mm.[160] Olson asserts that the new Model/90 was generally similar to the Belgian Model/89, which was officially adopted in Belgium on 23 October 1889.[161] Although the Meclîs-i Vükelâ tended to accept the conditions provided by the Mauser Company with regards to modifications, the Sultan had waited till the last minute to issue the *İrâde*.[162] The Loewe Company had made the 31 July 1890 the last day for notification.[163] Following the Sultan's approval, the amended contract was signed on 6 August 1890.[164]

When the last group of long rifles (M/87:9.5mm) was sent to İstanbul on 2 March 1891, the Mauser factory had already begun manufacturing the new Model/90:7.65mm.[165] In January 1892, the daily production rate of the new model amounted to 300 units and daily production was contractually planned to increase to 500 pieces by July 1892.[166] Modification in the rifle model led to a subsequent revision of both the cartridge and powder systems. Because of this change, the entire factory had to be re-equipped for manufacturing the Model/90. The Ottoman Empire had to contribute to cover some of the expenses involved in the updating of the factory, and was also obliged to pay 17,500 OL (322,875 marks) towards the cost of modifying the machines.[167]

The changeover of the models and the increase in daily production caused Paul Mauser both administrative and manufacturing difficulties. Based on these technical hitches, Mauser wrote a letter defining the problems he faced to his İstanbul agent, August Huber, in November 1892. He asked for Huber's opinion about the possibility of finding an alternative way to meet the conditions determined by the Ottoman government.[168] Huber, in his response, stressed the importance of ensuring that the Ottomans would not realise that Mauser was in breach of the modification request. He then wrote:

> In response to your secret request about whether successful results of the 9.50 mm calibre-rifle tests could have disruptive effects on possible subsequent orders of the rifles cal.7.65mm, we reply to you politely that this could easily be possible. This is because the Sultan places great value on having the 9.50 mm calibre rifle enhanced with as many of the same good features as the 7.65mm. Should this be achieved, they could easily suspend any subsequent order. They will then say, we now have 550,000 new good rifles, which will for the time being be enough, especially since we cannot make any more financial sacrifices.[169]

An important postscript to his letter pointed out the challenging situation: 'From Şakir Pasha we heard that a barrel of the Model/87:9.5 mm broke up during the test-firing, which means relating to this issue [persuasion of the Sultan] there is a lot more to it than that.'[170] Along with these notes, Huber suggested a course of action that drew on the key instruments of the German Style of War Business: drawing on close personal relations with influential officers/officials and exploiting their needs. In this instance, the officer targeted by Huber was Mahmud Şevket, one of Goltz Pasha's best cadets, who was present in Oberndorf at that time.[171] As the British military attaché Chermside noted, Huber understood very well 'how to manage the Turks by the judicious distribution of gratuities'.[172] Huber, as a competent dealer and persuader, suggested Paul Mauser adopt the following method:

It would be best for us to win over Colonel Mahmud Bey. Since we have not had the opportunity to associate with him for years, we do not know if this is possible and should therefore think hard, together with Mr Groneky [Director of the factory], who is located there, as to how best you can get close to him. Mr Mahmud Bey has been with you for so long now and has sacrificed so much, that we are inclined to assume that he would be prepared and expecting to earn something decent. Should you after your investigation [*Sondierung*] come to the conclusion that your findings are positive and useful, we consider it vital to reach an understanding with the named [Mahmud Şevket Bey], as it seems that the agreement cannot be reached without him.[173]

At the end of his letter, Huber strongly emphasized the importance of acting carefully and with deliberation.[174] Huber proved to be one of the few people in the business who understood the influential power of *baksheesh* as a facilitating factor in critical operations.[175] As indicated by an anonymous letter from an informant who might have been employed in the Ottoman service (he appeared to be an official servant in the Ottoman financial department and able to write in fluent German), Huber was inclined to offer money for the purpose of solving critical issues and persuading people.[176]

Baksheesh had become the most common tool used for winning a contract. The following statement, in a letter sent from Berlin to Paul Mauser, highlights how *baksheesh* became an accepted part of the war business in the Ottoman market: 'Of course, we are happy to cooperate to the necessary *Baksheesh* and the appropriate fee [*Honarar*].'[177] Huber's statement in the first letter might presumably also contain an implied suggestion for the judicious distribution of gratuities. He pointed out that the best way for Mauser to achieve its goal – to manipulate the Ottoman contract in favour of the factory – was to win Mahmud Şevket Pasha over to their support. However, Huber forewarned Mauser to carefully determine the most appropriate way of dealing with Mahmud Şevket. Huber emphasized Mahmud Şevket's sacrifices which, according to him, had to be rewarded: 'Mahmud Bey has been there [Oberndorf] for a long time

Table 3.8 Mauser Rifles in the Ottoman Army (1886–1908)

Model	Manufacturing Period	Number	Price for Each* (in *Kuruş*)
M/87;9.5mm (1887)	11.03.1887/16.03.1891	220,000	373
M/87;9.5mm (carbine)	19.01.1890/29.12.1890	4,000	363
M/90;7.65mm (1890)	01.01.1891/05.12.1893	280,000	383.35
M/93;7.65mm (1893)	05.12.1893/16.03.1896	200,100	365
M/93;7.65mm (1893)	27.08.1896/21.09.1896	1,800	325
M/03:7.65mm (1903)	1903–1908	207,700	315
Total	1887–1908	913,600	

*Rifles with Bayonet: BOA, *Y.MTV.240/128* (23.11.1320/21.02.1903).
Source: Seel, Wolfgang, 'Mauser-Gewehre unter dem Halbmond, Türkenmauser', *Deutsche Waffenjournal* 5 (1981a), pp. 1423, 1582.

and he also made some sacrifices so we are inclined to believe that he would probably deserve to earn something decent.'[178]

Huber considered it was essential to reach an agreement with Mahmud Şevket [Bey]. We can offer no further documentary proof as to whether or not Mauser was able to do so, but we do know that the Sultan was determined to obtain the rifles as quickly as possible. At the end of July 1890, when he finally issued the imperial *İrâde*, he emphasized his desire to obtain the rifles in the fastest way, and earlier than the Bulgarians, who had ordered 67,000 rifles from the Austrian–Mannlicher firm.[179] It appears that despite Huber's strategy and Mauser's endeavours, the Sultan had not been convinced to wait. As Table 3.8 indicates, between 2 July 1891 and 5 December 1893 the Mauser factory finished manufacturing the 280,000 (M/90:7.65) rifles contracted.[180] According to Serasker Rıza Pasha's report, the delivery of the 280,000 M/90 rifles was accomplished on 2 April 1894.[181]

The Ottoman Empire's desire to purchase the most recent military materials stimulated the arms makers' interest and gave them a focus for their marketing attempts. Paul Mauser was inclined to exploit this opportunity, and he was one of the prominent arms makers who benefited from the Ottomans' 'vested interest in new improvements' in arms technology.[182] On 30 April 1893, before delivery of the

Table 3.9a Places to Which the Purchased Mauser Rifles Were Sent (M/90:7.65)

Date of Dispatch	Place	Numbers of Rifles
12.03.1896	The Sultan's Household	1
04.04.1892	Arsenal in the Sultan's Household	10
03.1895–02.1896	Military School	20
02.1899–08.1899	The Third Army	116,000
	Others	25
[19.01.1904]	Imperial Storehouse in *Maçka*	163,944
	Total	280,000

Source: BOA, Y.PRK.ASK.211/40 (01.11.1321/19.01.1904).

M/90:7.65 mm rifles was completed, Paul Mauser travelled to İstanbul to present his 'best customer', the Sultan, with the newly developed model that had been ordered by the Spanish government.[183] Following Mauser's visit, the Ottoman government decided to place another order, this time for 200,000 rifles of the new model. Mahmud Şevket Pasha, the head of the Ottoman Purchasing and Inspection Commission, arrived in Oberndorf on 22 December 1893, and defined the contract as 'benevolent of the Sultan'.[184] The cost of the Sultan's *Wohlwollen* (benevolence) to the Ottoman Treasury was (along with the cartridge orders) nearly 1 million OL. As Table 3.8 shows, from 1887 to 1908 the Mauser Company manufactured more than 900,000 rifles for the Ottoman Army.

These Mauser rifles were purchased at the cost of increasing the Ottomans' foreign debt and budget deficit. However, from the military point of view, the impact of the procurement appeared limited. As Uyar and Erickson assert, – 'only one out of 10 divisions that took part in [the Greco–Turkish War of 1897] hurriedly armed themselves with these new rifles; all the others used the veteran Sniders and Martinis'.[185] Also Nevinson, who had been in the field during the war, asserted that the Ottoman soldiers 'were armed with Martini rifles of a cheap quality'.[186] The same unfortunate reality was revealed again during the Balkan Wars. 'On the last day's fighting', wrote M. H. Donohoe, the *Daily Chronicle's* correspondent with the Ottoman Army, 'I came across

Table 3.9b Places to Which the Purchased Mauser Rifles Were Sent (M/93:7.65)

Date of Dispatch	Place	Numbers of Rifles
12.03.1896	The Sultan's Household	1
05.06.1896	Arsenal in the Sultan's Household	1,350
06.02.1895–19.03.1895	Military School	20
27.02.1897–22.03.1897	The Second Army	89,000
28.04.1897	The Second Division	10,000
28.04.1897	The First Division	4,919
06.05.1897	Divisions in the Black Sea Fortification	896
20.02.1899	*Hassa* Army: Redif Battalion	51,200
29.07.1903	*Hamidiye* Cavalry (1. & 2. Regiments)	1,200
	Others	7,569
[19.01.1904]	Imperial Storehouse in *Maçka*	33,345
	Total	199,500

Table 3.9c Places to Which the Purchased Cartridges Were Sent (M/90–93:7.65)

Date of Dispatch	Place	Numbers
07.02.1897	The Second Army	11,232,000
02–03.1897	The Third Army (in Total)	42,902,400
20.02.1897	*Hassa* Army	15,360,000
	Others	10,866,922
[19.01.1904]	Imperial storehouse in *Gülhâne*	141,606,061
	Total	224,967,383

Source: BOA, *Y.PRK.ASK.211/40* (01.11.1321/19.01.1904).

instances of reserves ignorant of the manipulation of the mechanism of the Mauser rifle.' Donohoe added, 'Anatolians mostly use muzzle loaders, and had never seen a magazine rifle. Their weapons had to be loaded by their officers or better instructed comrades.'[187] It seems that the Mauser rifles, which were not inexpensive, were complex for the ordinary Ottoman soldiers, by whom the Mauser rifles were not capable of being operated under such unexpected conditions. Moreover, the other point that should also be highlighted, as Tables 3.9a–c show, the imported rifles were mostly stored in the imperial arsenals, rather than being distributed to the troops for training purposes: 58 per cent of the M/90:7.65mm Mauser rifles, for instance, and 16 per cent of the Model M/93:7.65 mm were just stored in the depots, and more than 60 per cent of the cartridges remained in the Imperial Storehouse in Gülhâne. The above tables allow us to analyse the efficiency of the Ottoman procurement policy.

Mauser's lucrative business, conducted at the expense of Ottoman financial stability, had begun at the end of 1886 under Goltz Pasha's guidance and continued until Goltz Pasha's last days in the service of the Ottoman Army in 1895.[188] Whenever Goltz Pasha declared his intention to terminate his service in the Ottoman Army, the Germans argued against it. The main factor that made him so indispensable to the state was his contribution to the German war business and to Germany's influence on the Ottoman Army. This fact was clearly stated by Radolin in 1893, when Goltz Pasha's last contract ended. In a letter to Chancellor Caprivi, Radolin expressed his opinion about the importance of Goltz's service in the Ottoman Army: '... for our influence in the Ottoman Army and for our further war materials delivery to Turkey [Goltz Pasha] is invaluable'.[189] A document dated 13 August 1895 confirms Radolin's view, revealing that between 1886 and 1895 the number of Mauser rifles supplied to the Ottoman Army totalled 625,650 and the number of cartridges reached 182,790,000 pieces.[190]

During those years, the Mauser Company became, like the Krupp Company in artillery, a second German monopolistic (industrial) power, in the market for Ottoman infantry rifles. Krupp and Mauser became almost the sole suppliers of military materials for the Ottoman Army. The exceptional power they established in the Ottoman market and the massive profits gained through the war business were directly attributable to the teamwork mostly led by Goltz Pasha. As a letter Paul Mauser sent to Goltz Pasha proves, Mauser recognized and acknowledged Goltz Pasha's multidimensional and influential position with regards to the Sultan. In his letter, Mauser openly requested Goltz Pasha to make use of his access to the decision maker:

> It is well known to me that your Excellency has regularly been the adviser to His Majesty the Sultan. I now think that I am doing nothing more than my duty if I ask you very humbly to make His Majesty the Sultan aware of the aforementioned communication [with regards to some modification of the Mauser rifles], at the next opportunity.[191]

A copy of the letter was sent to Mr Huber, who was told by Goltz Pasha that 'he would do what needed to be done'.[192] Accordingly, Goltz Pasha submitted a report to the Sultan regarding Mauser's request.[193] As many other examples show, Goltz Pasha guided his fellow countrymen during and also after his service in the Ottoman Army, and contributed effectively to their 'energetic compulsion/attack on the [Yıldız] Palace'.[194] He proved to be more influential than the German ambassadors as a supporter of German interests in the Ottoman Empire.[195] Even after he terminated his service in the Ottoman Army he was keenly propagating the superiority of the Mauser rifles. On 18 February 1900, during the second Boer War, Goltz Pasha wrote to one of his best-known cadets, Pertev Pasha, that the very first lesson of this war was 'the Mauser rifle proves itself excellently'.[196] In his report (*layiha*) Kamphövener Pasha, the German infantry officer, who was still in the Ottoman Army during the Boer War, stated the German-made Mauser rifles and Krupp guns used by the Boers proved better than those the British had.[197]

In summary, the Mauser Company's entry into the Ottoman market in late 1886 was a *sui generis* operation supported by the German government and the German military mission in the Ottoman service. In particular, the close relations between the German industrialists and the military personnel contributed to the success of the GAFs. As Goltz Pasha wrote in his condolence letter for Paul Mauser, who died on 29 May 1913, he and Paul Mauser had worked together for the purpose of the 'strengthening of the German name and German efficiency in the Orient'.[198]

CHAPTER 4

KAISER WILHELM II AND THE POLITICAL ECONOMY OF PERSONAL DIPLOMACY (1898–1914)

'As a professor, I tended to think of history as run by impersonal forces. But when you see it in practice, you see the difference personalities make.'[1]

Henry A. Kissinger, January 1974

Kaiser Wilhelm II's Second *Orientreise* in 1898 as Multidimensional Personal Diplomacy

Eight years after Bismarck was forced to resign, the Kaiser paid another visit to Abdülhamid II in İstanbul in October 1898, a tour that was organized by the well-known British firm Thomas Cook and Son.[2] The visit was more influential than the first one, which Bismarck had opposed.[3] In contrast to the first visit, nine years previously, there was no sign of disagreement from the German governmental apparatus.[4] This can probably be attributed to the fact that after Bismarck's dismissal, Kaiser Wilhelm II effectively became his own chancellor and Foreign Minister.[5] Chancellor Prince Hohenlohe, who was favourably inclined toward the Kaiser's Ottoman policy, publicly supported the Kaiser's second *Orientreise*. As the Kaiser stated in his memoir, 'Hohenlohe hailed with much joy the [Kaiser's] trip to Constantinople and Jerusalem. He was pleased at the strengthening of [German] relations with Turkey and considered the plan for the Baghdad Railway arising from them as a great cultural work worthy of Germany.'[6]

Kaiser Wilhelm II began his second *Orientreise* on 18 October 1898, when he arrived in İstanbul.[7] The planned arrival date was delayed because of adverse weather.[8] As during the first visit, the Ottoman press showed keen interest in the Kaiser's visit and asserted that it would further strengthen the friendly relations that existed between the Ottoman Empire and Germany. For instance, the newspaper *Sabah* published a special 176-page book dedicated to the visit. This edition gave detailed information about the Kaiser's programme and shared observations and anecdotes about the close friendship between the Sultan and Wilhelm II.[9] In addition, the 'unusual preparations' made before the Kaiser's arrival were widely reported by the European newspapers.[10] Diplomats in Istanbul also reported on the preparations to their Foreign Offices. The US ambassador, James B. Angell, was one of those who mentioned the flurry of activity in the capital city, stating that 'unusual preparations are already going on to give great splendour and significance to the occasion'.[11] In addition, he expressed his thoughts about the possible consequences of the Kaiser's visit – he believed the second *Orientreise* would strengthen the intimacy between Wilhelm II and the Sultan.[12]

On their first day in İstanbul, the Kaiser and the Kaiserin visited a German school, where they engaged in a long conversation with the teachers and children.[13] According to *The New York Times*, Kaiser Wilhelm remarked that there were a large number of foreign children in attendance at the school and said this demonstrated the 'victorious force of *Germanism*'.[14] During their İstanbul visit, they made several excursions,[15] which led the Kaiser to conclude that during the nine years since his last visit, the decay of the Ottoman Empire had advanced rapidly.[16] On all occasions, the Kaiser expressed his gratitude and pleasure with the Sultan. For his part, the Sultan tried hard to prove his sincerity by showing calculated hospitality to the Kaiser and the Kaiserin and giving them some special presents. Wilhelm II, whom Naumann called 'the Sultan of the Germans',[17] and the Kaiserin were impressed by the preparations and courteous welcomes during the *Orientreise*. The *New York Times* provided some interesting detail about the presents given to the German delegation:

> Apart from the regular presents, the Sultan of Turkey gave a number of others. For instance, the coverlet on the Empress's bed had the imperial crown and her monogram in the centre, embroidered with diamonds and pearls. On Her Majesty expressing admiration, the coverlet was immediately presented to her. Two magnificent Saxe vases adorned the salon of the Yıldız Kiosk, and the Sultan asked Baron von Bülow, the German Minister of Foreign Affairs, if he admired them as products of his own country. Von Bülow shrewdly replied that he would like to have a similar pair, whereupon the Sultan ordered them to be placed with the German Minister's baggage.[18]

According to a document dated 3 November 1898, the transportation of the gifts presented to the Kaiser and the Kaiserin became a challenge, for which they requested help from the Ottoman government.[19] The presents aside, the total cost of the Kaiser's visit to the Ottoman Empire was quite high. From the new rooms specially built in the Yıldız Palace and the modernization of the roads over which the Kaiser would travel, to the purchase of new clothes for the cadets in the Military School (which the Kaiser visited) and the salaries for those who accompanied the Kaiser during his Jerusalem visit, the total outlay amounted to 20,095.57 OL (370,763 marks).[20]

The most noteworthy 'gift' presented to the Kaiser was Abdülhamid's permission to acquire a plot of land on Mount Zion in Jerusalem, known as *La Dormition de la Sainte Vierge*, 'as an expression of intimate friendship'.[21] Because of this meaningful gift and the Kaiser's subsequent strategic presentation of the acquired ground to German Catholics, France lost her prestige as the protector for the Catholic subjects in the Ottoman Empire. According to White, the British ambassador at İstanbul, since Bismarck's time the German government had been paying increasing attention to the German Roman Catholic establishments in the Ottoman Empire, without in any way neglecting its Protestant ones. White asserted that even 'Prince Bismarck was by no means disposed to allow France to claim [...] her protectorate of Roman Catholic interest but wished her to confine herself to the care of purely French interests'.[22] As a consequence of this increased attention, Germany gained crucial influence with regards to the Catholics – especially the German Catholics – living in the Ottoman Empire. Over the years, French diplomats had tried to acquire that piece of land in Jerusalem from the Sultan, but they were unable to secure possession.[23] As a result, the Kaiser's strategic push to make a profound impression on the Catholics would deal a blow to French interests in the Ottoman Empire.[24] Prince Bülow submitted a report to Kaiser Wilhelm II on 4 June 1898, clearly spelling out the probable consequences of acquiring the *Dormition*. According to him, it might be generally useful to support anything that could demolish French prestige in the Levant; on the other hand, this might cause German antagonism against the French Catholics in the Orient to be kept alive (*wachhalten kann*).[25]

In fact, that antagonism was behind an unspoken cold war between French and German interests in the Ottoman territorial area. Abdülhamid II was observing this struggle very cautiously; in 1898 he described French complaints and comments regarding the Germans' increasing influence over the Catholic subjects of the Ottoman Empire as 'indescribable arrogance'.[26] Kaiser Wilhelm's Ottoman policy did have the goal of undermining French influence in the Empire. Apparently the foreign policy elaborated by Bismarck, which was formulated on the proposition of France's isolation, was reshaped and reformulated by the Kaiser. Consequently, Wilhelm's present of the land (the Virgin's Abode) to the Catholics was regarded 'as a clever move' among contemporary observers.[27] By way of example, Field-Marshal Waldersee, who according to Menne was one of the Emperor's friends,[28] noted in his diary on 11 November 1898 that 'it has a special significance because, through [the acquiring the *Dormition*] the patriotic feelings of the [German] Catholics will be stimulated and encouraged'.[29]

Although the Kaiser aimed to create a favourable impression among Catholics and Protestants, he was later criticized by some religious commentators outside of Germany, especially following World War I and its consequences, which sparked criticism of the friendship between the Kaiser and the Sultan. For instance, Newell Dwight Hillis, a Congregationalist minister and the author of *The Influence of Christ in Modern Life* (1900), strongly criticized Kaiser Wilhelm's friendship with Sultan Abdülhamid. He wrote 'so the Kaiser took his train, lived in the Sultan's palace, signed this treaty, and hired the Sultan's knife and club, just as the Chief Priest Annas chose Judas to be his representative upon whom he could load the responsibility for the murder of Jesus.'[30]

Hillis' criticism represents one strain of international perception of the Kaiser's personal friendship with the Sultan. In particular, the critics focused on the Kaiser's position on 'The Armenian Question'. According to the British annual report for the Ottoman Empire for 1907, the Kaiser visited Sultan Abdülhamid when he 'was under the odium and cloud of the Armenian massacres'.[31] In fact, the Kaiser's visit was an obvious sign of opposition to the European Concert line on this issue. The report asserted that Kaiser did not gainsay the decision of the European powers. Nonetheless, the Kaiser did not hesitate to show himself as the personal friend of the Sultan.[32]

While the Kaiser was in İstanbul, other European governments were strongly criticising the Sultan's position on the Armenian question. They had already begun to support anti-Ottoman organizations and movements within their borders, and strongly protested the Sultan's policy towards the Armenians. Wilhelm II's supportive visit to the Ottoman Empire and his open declaration of neutrality on the Armenian question and the Crete issue were promptly recompensed by the Ottoman Empire. According to a document dated 30 October 1898, the Kaiser had noted that during a conversation with Nazım Pasha, the Governor of Damascus, he did not take seriously the complaints of the Armenians who visited him while he was in Damascus.[33]

Additionally, on the occasion of an official dinner, the Kaiser provocatively voiced his opinion that there was a British hand behind the Armenian and Crete issues.[34] Interestingly, the Kaiser, who provoked the Ottoman government against the British position in Crete, had also held a critical conversation with the British ambassador to Berlin, Sir Frank Lascelles, on 1 February 1898. According to Bülow's 'top secret' report, at the conclusion of a lengthy conversation, Kaiser Wilhelm openly declared his position on the Crete question, remarking that it was all the same to him (*allerhöchst ihm geleichgültig sei*) what happened in Crete. This statement may have astonished the British ambassador, who replied, 'So is it, Your Majesty, really the same?' The Kaiser's response was clear: '*Ja, ich mache mir nichts daraus*, if your fellows take Souda Bay [A bay on the northwest coast of Crete Island].'[35] Furthermore, Bülow pointed out in his final remarks that the Kaiser authorized him to telegraph to Hatzfeldt the secret message that he would not be opposed to an English occupation of Crete in any form.[36] When the Kaiser talked to the Ottoman officials about 'the British hand in the Crete question', he had already been well informed. Apparently, the Kaiser positioned himself as an honest mediator between the two sides, while encouraging one to another in private.

However, the remarks addressed by the Kaiser during his visit were welcomed by Abdülhamid II, who believed he had won the 'allegiance' of Germany in discouraging further concerted action by the other European powers on the Armenian issue.[37] The British annual report for the Ottoman Empire revealed the real anxiety of the European powers. The report opined that 'if the policy of Germany was neither humane nor creditable, [Kaiser Wilhelm's visit] was at all events positive and material. It secured [Germany and Germans] the concession of the Baghdad Railway, a monopoly on all orders for military munitions for the Turkish Army, and a privileged position for all industrial and commercial concessions which it was in the power of the Sultan to bestow upon his friend and patron.'[38] At the same time, Hillis's account shows his irritation over the outcomes of the Kaiser's visit, and summarizes the European and American perceptions of the motives behind the Kaiser's second *Orientreise*:

> Everyone knew that the Kaiser wanted to build a German railroad through to Baghdad and the Persian Gulf; this would give him an outlet for surplus goods to be sold in India. Serbia lay straight across the path, and he had to work out some scheme to attack Serbia. Then he needed the Sultan's friendship, and the end justified the means – and the end was the Baghdad Railroad. But the Turk tired of being the Kaiser's tool; he [the Kaiser] wanted more land.[39]

Hillis was not alone in contrasting the *Orientreise*'s spiritual image with its concrete outcomes. Harrison wrote, 'but if in its spiritual aspect it left nothing abiding, from the secular standpoint it was entirely successful. Apart from the purely political value of such a coup de theatre economically much was achieved.'[40] In 1902, Ray S. Baker asserted that 'the Kaiser's visit was one of the epochs of recent Turkish history, the full effects of which are not yet appreciated by Westerners'.[41] 'The youthful Kaiser' according to *The {London} Times*, 'the modern representative of the temporal power of the Holy Roman Empire, is following the footsteps of Barbarossa, of Henry VI, and of Frederick II to the Holy Land, and the end of the nineteenth century is witnessing a pacific crusade.'[42]

After a week's stay at Yıldız Palace in İstanbul, the Kaiser's party sailed into Haifa. Müşir Mehmed Şakir Pasha was their host throughout the second stage of their journey, from Haifa via Jaffa to Jerusalem, and from thereon to Damascus via Beirut.[43] Interestingly, and maybe intentionally, the second stage of the *Orientreise*, beginning with the Kaiser's arrival at the port of Haifa on 25 October 1898,[44] marked the 30th anniversary of the arrival of the first German Templar, George David Hardegg, in Haifa in October 1868.[45] It was also the anniversary of the Lutheran Reformation of 31 October. The month of October was in all respects a memorial date for the Templars of Haifa. Based on an official account of the Kaiser's trip, Röhl says that the Kaiser's landing in Haifa was 'the first time since the visit of Friedrich II of Hohehnstaufen in 1228 that a German emperor had set foot on the soil of the Holy Land'.[46] After spending two days in Haifa, the Kaiser left via Jaffa, where he delivered a speech to the German colony about their important role in the improvement of Ottoman–German relations.[47] He arrived in Jerusalem on 29 October 1898.[48]

The Kaiser and his party's Jerusalem programme was organized for the comfort and safety of the German delegation by the Kudüs Mutasarrıfı (Governor of Jerusalem), Tevfik Pasha (later Biren), who obtained a first-class Prussian cross medal,[49] and Muhammed Servet Bey, the Chief of Police.[50] Reporting on the Jerusalem visit, *The New York Times* noted that 'no private persons were allowed to stand in the streets along the line of march – as the streets of Jerusalem are narrow – so as to guard against any possible attack, and the crossings were strongly guarded by police and soldiers, who also lined the streets on the route'.[51]

Prince Bülow's memoirs also provided more information on the Kaiser's *Orientreise*, especially about the Kaiser's enthusiasm for what he observed and experienced throughout his trip and about the international reactions to 'his enthusiasm for the Sublime Porte, the Koran, and the Sultan'.[52] Bülow wrote, 'the homage of the populace, the courteous welcomes of the municipalities, the conviction that he enjoyed the real friendship and respect of all Turks, nay; of all adherents of Islam all this produced such an effect on William II that almost every day he felt constrained to express his delight and gratitude to the Sultan by telegraph.'[53] During the Kaiser's visit to Jerusalem, Bülow had the task of drafting these telegrams, 'owing to the need for a certain variety of phraseology'. Nevertheless he 'gradually exhausted the whole available stock of expressions and idioms in the French language for the ideas of appreciation, pleasure, and gratification'. More detail of this remarkable side of the *Orientreise* can be gleaned from Bülow's following account:

> Whenever the exclamation fell from His Majesty's lips, and it was a constant occurrence that 'that really was the finest experience we have yet had, Bülow, send the Sultan a telegram

of thanks', I took up my pencil and flogged out a new variant. My friend Knesebeck said to me one day: You know those pamphlets for lovers, The Model Letter-writer; you ought to bring out a model letter-writer for polite correspondence with Sultans, for use during a Near East tour.[54]

From Jerusalem, the Kaiser and the Kaiserin went to Damascus, where Wilhelm II delivered a highly influential speech. At that time, Damascus was the centre of French influence in the Ottoman territories, and the speech was also important in this light. On 8 November 1898, Kaiser Wilhelm II addressed his Damascus audience by saying: 'Let me assure His Majesty the Sultan [Abdülhamid II] and the 300 millions of Muslims who, in whatever corner of the globe they may live, revere in him their *Khalif*, that the German Emperor will ever be their friend.'[55] While visiting the tomb of Saladin, Wilhelm II laid a crowned wreath on the tomb

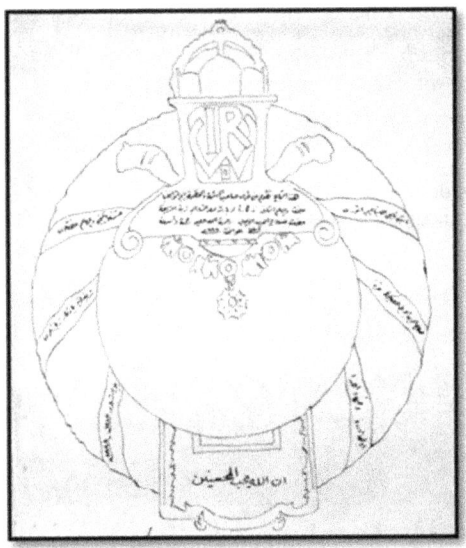

Image 4.1 The Wreath Laid by Kaiser Wilhelm II on the Tomb of Sultan Saladin (in 1898)
Source: BOA, Y.EE.91/51 (1315/1898).

while expressing admiration for Saladin; a sketch of the item he laid (see below) was submitted to the Sultan.[56]

Kaiser Wilhelm's Damascus speech and his deeds resounded throughout the Muslim world. Even nine years later, Abdülhamid II recalled the speech with gratitude and mentioned to the German ambassador, Marschall, the deep impression that the speech had left among Muslims. According to Marschall, Abdülhamid II said that he could not thank Kaiser Wilhelm II enough for the speech he delivered in Damascus and for another he gave in Tangier[57] in which he expressed Germany's concern over the independence of Morocco and the need to protect a Muslim empire against foreign invasion.[58] The Sultan stated that these two speeches would always remain in his memory and that of all Muslims.[59]

Among the other important political and emotional consequences of the *Orientreise*, the Kaiser's speech in Damascus declaring his admiration for the Sultan and his Empire ranked among Abdülhamid's most remarkable political coups, the price of which had been paid in advance by the arms contracts and the railway construction agreements signed with German firms. Arminius Vambéry, one of Abdülhamid's unofficial advisers, described the Kaiser's attitudes in a striking way:

> The Emperor William II admires the talent of the ruler in his friend, which is its autocratic bearing he would like to imitate if it were possible; but [Kaiser Wilhelm II] is clever enough to discount the reward for this admiration in various concessional privileges, & c. Well-paid appointments for German officers, consignments of arms, concessions for railway lines, manufactures.[60]

In effect, the Kaiser's two *Reise nach Osten* (Travels to the East) served as 'a new and memorable starting-point' in the *Drang nach Osten* (Drive to the East) policy, which was framed within the peaceful penetration strategy.[61] As Bülow declared, it was a successful start to the cultivation of good relations between Germany and the Ottoman Empire.[62] The Kaiser's Damascus speech was just one step of a determined programme.[63] It was said that there was *muhabbet* – affection – between the Kaiser and the Sultan; the *Orientreise* and the speeches delivered during the trip provided an excellent opportunity for both sides to demostrate and deepen this *muhabbet*.[64]

During and after the second *Orientreise*, German entrepreneurs successfully concluded some important agreements and extracted promises from the Ottoman government for new orders. As Prince Bülow pointed out, 'the Baghdad Railway scheme was a result of the Emperor's journey to Palestine... which was in every respect so successful'.[65] During the Kaiser's *Orientreise*, German diplomats pursued what Archibald J. Dunn called 'untiring German diplomacy'.[66]

It was after the Kaiser's trip that the railway project became more of a political instrument than an economic investment. As Barth revealed, the board of Deutsche Bank had intended to sell off the bank's shares in the Ottoman railways to Russia on 22 November 1896, without first informing the German government.[67] The board's plan suggests that the railway construction was not an indispensable investment for German financiers. But the issue was not solely economic; the political image the project created was as important as the economic benefits. The Deutsche Bank's plans did not become reality, and it continued to play a role in the Ottoman railway business due to the politicization of an economic venture. As Barth asserts, the Deutsche Bank's relative freedom in Ottoman affairs came to an end through Kaiser Wilhelm's second *Orientreise*.[68]

The *Orientreise*, as a 'romantic incident' of an export-oriented expansionist strategy, provided a guaranteed and facilitated *Absatzmarkt* for German products, especially those whose trade required governmental approval and support.[69] For that reason the Kaiser's trips, especially the second one, can properly be categorized as business trips.[70] According to the *Neue Freie Presse*, the Kaiser went to the Ottoman Empire – Germany's best customer for war materials – as a business traveller promoting Germany's economic advantage, and his journey was like a customer visit (*Kundenbesuch*).[71] Indeed, as Bode rightly asserted, on the Kaiser's second *Orientreise*, Kaiser Wilhelm – the 'Managing Director of the German Empire' (*Geschäftsführer*) in Carl Peters' formulation – was personally interested in all aspects of German economic expansion in the Ottoman Empire.⁷²

Alldeutsche Blätter, an important pro-colonialist paper, summarized the feasible goals of the Kaiser's *Orientreise* in two points: political influence and economic benefit. The newspaper argued that the first success of the trip was to eliminate any possible doubts on the part of the Sultan and his advisers about Germany's posture on general Ottoman political affairs, about which the German government had already declared their disinterest (*für politische Bestrebungen, welche den Bestand des türkischen Reiches gefährden*). As the newspaper pointed out, even the mere elimination of distrust was a success for the trip. The second successful outcome of the *Orientreise* was the mutual economic benefits from the contributions of German industry, trade and capital (*Großkapital*) to both states' prosperity. The newspaper suggested that Germany desired the continued existence of the Ottoman Empire as an ally and market.⁷³ Meanwhile, Friedrich Naumann also suggested a framework within which German capital should be invested (*Kapitalanlage*) in a broader context – that of a labour/working force [*arbeitende Kraft*] in the Ottoman Empire:

> If the Germans want to support the Ottoman state, they must provide a working potential for her. This force is a capital investment in the broadest sense of the word: it includes people, money, peasants, craftsmen, military personnel, civil servants, rails, banks, and machines. All these investments must, as the Kaiser [Wilhelm II] said in Bethlehem, be given freely with no expectation of immediate return, that is, with the full knowledge that they cannot pay off immediately...
> The endpoints of our work seem to be: military reform, financial reform, and agricultural reform. The first point has already been achieved, and much done towards the second, but progress in the third as good as nothing.⁷⁴

In the meantime, the diplomats of other nations watched the expanded influence of Germany and the deepening friendship between the two Empires with suspicion. For instance, James

B. Angell, the U.S. Minister to the Ottoman Empire, emphasized three main points in his observation report in regard to Germany's thriving influence in the Ottoman Empire, all of which are relevant to the discussion of the consequences of the Kaiser's visit. First, he noted that Germany was the nation that enjoyed the highest favour in İstanbul. Second, he mentioned his predictions about the probable outcomes of the Kaiser's visit in these terms: 'whether the German Sovereign is actuated by a desire to enlarge the commercial advantages of his people, or whether he has political aims in doing so much to secure the friendship of the Sultan, or whether, as is probable, he has both ends in view, time will disclose'. Finally, he pointed to Germany's emergence as an influence on the Ottoman Empire: 'certainly it is that Germans are now in the ascendant here. German officers are employed to instruct the army, German professors are called to teach in the Imperial Medical College, German contractors have the best chance to furnish munitions to the Government.'[75] Everything Angell had listed fell within the concept that Naumann had formulated for German efforts in the Orient.[76]

Aside from everything that Kaiser Wilhelm said and did on the trip, his presence in the East, especially in Jerusalem, was a political stunt and part of a well-constructed diplomatic plan.[77] In fact, the plan was part of the German Foreign Office's methodology for the progress of relations with the Ottoman Empire. The German method (*die Deutsche Methode*), as it was called by Marschall, was later imitated by the other Great Powers.[78] Thanks to the *die Deutsche Methode,* the mutual friendship, and the expressions of goodwill, the door was opened wide for the exchange of German finished industrial products for Ottoman raw materials. The first of the outcomes Angell considered appeared immediately (by 1898) with the economic motivation that went hand in hand with political and military influence. The Kaiser's second *Orientreise* started the gradual process of developing bilateral trade-based foreign relations. This was the second wave of the German expansionist strategy, in which Germany immensely strengthened and broadened its sphere of influence in the Ottoman Empire. In addition to that, the concrete outcomes of the second *Orientreise* provided tangible proof that the personal diplomacy launched by both the Sultan and the Kaiser, who might have strongly believed in the effectiveness of personal factors, could be an essential part of the economic foreign policy.[79]

The Concrete Outcomes of the Kaiser's Second *Orientreise*: Some Critical Concessions

The second wave of Germany's expansionist policy towards the Ottoman Empire furthered the processes set in motion by the German industrialists, traders, diplomats and politicians during the first wave. However, since the mutual trust and friendship between the two heads of state was the dominant determinant of this progress, the economic gains made through the Kaiser's visits were almost all in fields for which governmental approval was needed, such as the purchase of military equipment (artillery, rifles and warships), the construction of railways, and the laying of telegraph wires. Although Germany broadened her position in all of these sectors, the most significant progress was made by the German armament industry. The only market where the Germans held a monopoly position was the arms market. That achievement was the result of the German method of building good personal relations, and its application in the German Style of War Business. Having said that, however, following this trip, German total trade with and the direct investment in the Ottoman Empire incrementally improved. Before discussing the arms trade exclusively it is also crucial to understand how German economic influence in the Ottoman Empire rapidly increased under the shadow of this declared reciprocal friendship.

It is important to recognize, as Osman Nuri noted, that the Germans began their trade journey in the Ottoman Empire from scratch;[80] the starting point was the mutual governmental support determined by the personal diplomacy of the Kaiser and the Sultan.[81] When Wilhelm II was visiting the Ottoman Empire and taking strong steps to reinforce his nation's position in the Ottoman market, *The* [*London*] *Times* reported to its readers: 'Political considerations incline the Turkish Government to grant facilities for the expansion of German commerce and financial enterprise; the Sultan regards the

KAISER WILHELM II AND THE POLITICAL ECONOMY   147

Kaiser as his only friend, and German applicants for valuable concessions are, as a rule, preferred to their competitors.'[82] The comment was accurate. The direct influence of high-ranking personalities on bilateral relations is what makes the extraordinary jump in the foreign trade indicators shown below comprehensible. Table 4.1 and Figure 4.1 clearly demonstrate how the foreign trade indicators between the two countries changed dramatically, especially after Wilhelm II's visits.

As seen in Figure 4.1, the Kaiser's initial visit to İstanbul in 1889 marked the arrival of German commercial actors in the Ottoman market, and the next significant increase came after the Kaiser's second *Orientreise*. The second visit was obviously more productive with respect to commercial aspects. A deeper investigation of the data behind this graph gives us a clearer picture. This sharp increase in the total trade volume mostly involved materials whose importation required governmental approval and support. The iron and steel industry benefited the most from these developments. The railway built across Asia Minor, the war materials purchased from the

Table 4.1   Ottoman Trade with Germany, 1895–1912 (in Marks)

Years	Export	Import	Years	Export	Import
1895	22,000,000	39,000,000	1904	43,500,000	75,300,000
1896	25,900,000	28,000,000	1905	51,600,000	71,000,000
1897	30,500,000	30,900,000	1906	55,100,000	68,500,000
1898*	29,500,000	37,100,000	1907	55,100,000	81,700,000
1899	28,900,000	32,600,000	1908	47,600,000	64,000,000
1900	30,200,000	34,300,000	1909	57,300,000	78,900,000
1901	30,100,000	37,500,000	1910	67,400,000	104,900,000
1902	36,600,000	43,300,000	1911	70,100,000	112,800,000
1903	37,600,000	50,200,000	1912	77,600,000	112,800,000

*New orders placed during the Kaiser's visit (1898) are reflected in the trade statistics two or three years later. See Figure 4.1 below.
Source: Birken, Andreas, *Die Wirtschaftsbeziehungen zwischen Europa und dem Vorderen Orient im ausgehenden 19. Jahrhundert* (Wiesbaden, 1980), p. 176.

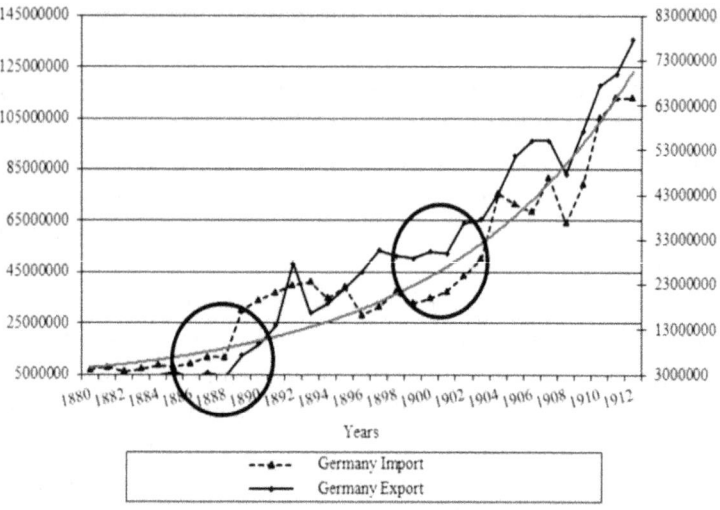

Figure 4.1 Ottoman Trade with Germany, 1878–1913 (in Marks)
Source: Birken, *Die Wirtschaftsbeziehungen zwischen Europa und dem Vorderen Orient*, p. 176.

German factories, and the telegraph cable construction dramatically increased Germany's market share in the Ottoman Empire. Krupp, which enjoyed a monopoly on the provision of artillery for the Ottoman Army, was also the chief rail supplier for the construction of the Baghdad Railway.

The dramatic increase shown in the figure above resulted mainly from the concessions obtained by the German syndicate headed by the Deutsche Bank.

Among the most important results of the Kaiser's second visit was the Baghdad Railway, one of the most-discussed operations of the German expansionist strategy towards the Ottoman Empire. A detailed discussion of the Baghdad Railways project is beyond the scope of this book, so I will discuss it only briefly within the framework of the concrete consequences of the Kaiser's second *Orientreise*.[83] Prince Bülow clearly illustrated the link between the *Orientreise* and the Baghdad Railway scheme in his memoirs. As he stated, the Baghdad Railway was a result of the Emperor's journey to

Palestine. The railway project was described by Paul Rohrbach, the semi-official spokesman of German imperialism, as a political life insurance policy for Germany.[84] Scherer argues that the line between Eskişehir and Konya, which opened in 1896, was the first step of the Baghdad Railway.[85] However, the Baghdad Railway scheme had existed as an idea and a favourite plan (*Lieblingsplan*) of Sultan Abdülhamid long before the first section ever reached Eskişehir. Numerous documents demonstrate that a rail line that would extend to Baghdad was one of Abdülhamid's long-cherished dreams.

Germany was never mentioned in the negotiations that occurred before 1887, although Russia, France and Britain were. The Germans entered the race for the Ottoman railway construction contracts in 1888 and obtained their first concessions in 1889 (for the Anatolian Railway).[86] The Germans' entry into the competition as an unexpected rival devastated the balance of calculations made by the French and

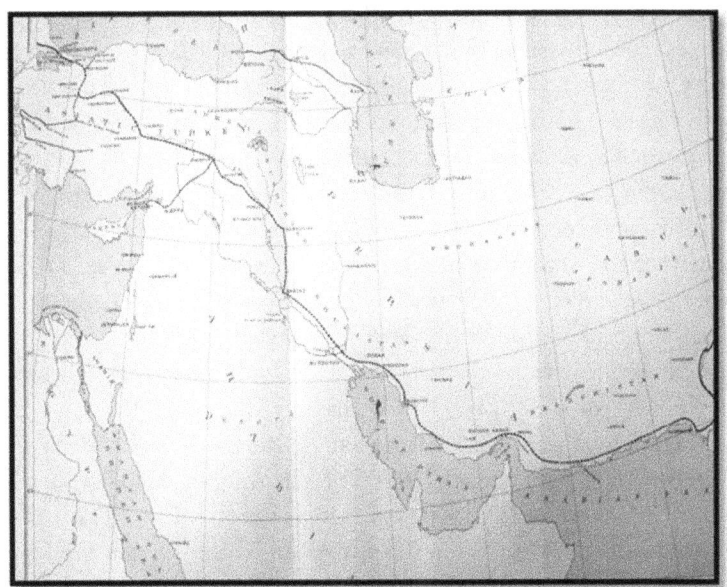

Map 4.1 Haydarpaşa–İzmit Railway with its Projected Extensions through Asia Minor up to the Persian Gulf, dated 4 February 1885. Source: NA, London: FO 78/4264:10.

British companies that had already invested in Ottoman lands. In 1887, before the German entrance, British Ambassador White sent a report to Lord Salisbury, the British Prime Minister, in which he wrote, 'Your Lordship will no doubt be glad to learn that W. Seefelder, the Representative of the İzmit–Haydarpaşa Railway Company at Constantinople, has succeeded in concluding a preliminary arrangement with the Ottoman Government for the construction of a railroad to Ankara and Diyarbakır and ultimately to Baghdad.'[87]

Two years later, on 24 December 1889, Pendleton King, the first secretary in the American Legation, sent a report entitled 'German commerce and influence in Turkey', stating that the rail line built by the German group from İzmit to Ankara 'will be continued to Baghdad'.[88] This information suggests that Abdülhamid's idea of giving German capital and industry the concession to extend the existing railway to the Persian Gulf evidently emerged during the Kaiser's first visit to İstanbul in 1889, even though it was during the Kaiser's second visit to the Sultan in 1898 that the Germanization of the Ottoman–Baghdad railway project became a concrete political objective. The initial step towards the Baghdad railway was taken as early as 1888, when the Deutsche Bank was awarded the first railway concession by Abdülhamid II, who clearly harboured distrust of the British and French firms that were already active in Ottoman railway construction. According to a telegram sent from the Kaiser to the *Reichskanzler* (German Chancellor) on 9 December 1891, Abdülhamid requested Wilhelm's support (*Schutz*) for countering the American, French and British interest in obtaining railway contracts to implement his *Lieblingsplan,* namely the Baghdad Railway project.[89] A report Goltz Pasha sent to Kaiser Wilhelm II on 28 October 1891 supports this assertion. During an audience at the Yıldız Palace on 25 October 1891, the Sultan told Goltz Pasha that the extension of the railway from Ankara to the Persian Gulf via Baghdad was his old favourite plan (*alter Lieblingsplan*), the implementation of which would be of high military and political significance, providing a way to transport the army to the defence of İstanbul and draw traffic from India to the Ottoman Empire.[90] In

Goltz Pasha's report, he quoted Abdülhamid's expectations for the construction of a railway from İstanbul to the Persian Gulf:

> Through the opening up of these lines, especially in the case of a war, I [Sultan Abdülhamid] will be able to utilize the whole of my armed forces from the Asian provinces, from whichever direction the enemies may come. At the same time [by opening up these lines], the commerce of India, which must then take the direction of Basra to Constantinople, will increase the welfare of my countries.[91]

After seven years of requests, when Kaiser Wilhelm II was still in İstanbul in October 1898, Sultan Abdülhamid mentioned his intention to award the concession to build the new railway to a German group.[92] The idea of a rail line that would connect Berlin to the Persian Gulf and that would be built with German capital and industry filled the Kaiser with enthusiasm. According to Friedrich Rosen, who accompanied the Kaiser during the trip and was later appointed as consul in Jerusalem, the concession was a guest-gift of the Sultan (*Gastgeschenk des Sultans*) to Kaiser Wilhelm.[93] In fact, this *Gastgeschenk* was almost like a hidden gift, which Abdülhamid left waiting for more than ten years until the second *Orientreise* provided the right time to present this gift to the right person: Kaiser Wilhelm II.

News of the conversation and the award quickly spread through Europe via the newspaper correspondents, but in a mostly agitated way. For instance, the Austrian newspaper *Neue Freie Presse* compared the achievement of the concession by the German firms with the military occupation of the Bay of Kiaochow by the German Admiral Diederichs in 1898, by which, according to *The New York Times*, three of Europe's great powers – England, France and Russia – were directly threatened.[94] 'It is a tremendous perspective', said the Austrian newspaper, 'with more enormous background than those which had been acquired through the occupation of Kiaochow.'[95] So the *Orientreise* came to represent a new form of penetration and occupation that was greater in scale and intensity than those pursued for many years by the other imperialist European powers: that is, the form created by means of the German Method [*die Deutsche Methode*].

As early as May 1899, an agreement to fund the Baghdad Railway was reached between the Deutsche Bank and the Imperial Ottoman Bank.[96] The preliminary concession (*Vorkonzession*) was signed by Georg von Siemens, the director of Deutsche Bank and president of the Anatolian Railway Company, on 27 November 1899.[97] For the concession, the Deutsche Bank deposited an advance of 200,000 OL in the Ottoman Treasury.[98] The Sultan approved the concession by the *İrâde* issued on 16 January 1902, and the final agreement was signed on 5 March 1903 by the Ottoman government and the director of the Deutsche Bank, Arthur von Gwinner, Siemens' successor.[99] On the day the *İrâde* was issued, Kaiser Wilhelm II sent a letter to the Sultan in which he expressed his appreciation regarding the news. The words he used in the letter were clearly meant to highlight his satisfaction:

> I would most sincerely congratulate your Majesty the Sultan on your success in establishing such a beautiful and exalted order for public works. The day of 6 January 1902, on which his Majesty's *İrâde*, with regards to the concession, was issued, will be forever remembered as the day of happiness [*yevm-i mes'ûd*] for the history of his Empire's progress.[100]

Table 4.2 Financial Participation of Foreign Financiers in the Baghdad Railway (1903)

Shareholders	Percentage (%)
Deutsche Bank	40
Banque Impériale Ottomane	30
Anatolische Eisenbahn-Gesellschaft	10
Wiener Bankverein und Schweizerische Kreditanstalt	7
Banca Commerciale Italiana	5

Source: Lothar Gall, *Die Deutsche Bank, 1870–1995* (München, 1995), p. 78.

Kaiser Wilhelm had every right to be pleased because, as the following table indicates, the Sultan's *İrâde* put the Baghdad Railway, which had initially been pursued by the British companies, into the hands of a German syndicate. The Kaiser knew that it was a German victory gained, quite literally, at the expense of British industrial and financial groups.

The position the Deutsche Bank obtained through the Anatolian and Baghdad Railway concessions was both politically and economically significant.[101] Germany's involvement in the Baghdad Railway was a combination of private and public initiatives.[102] However, according to *The Standard* newspaper of 23 August 1899, over time the Baghdad Railway Project became of more political than commercial significance.[103] Abdülhamid II was well aware of the principal rationale of the Baghdad Railway construction for the interested European parties. In 1900, the Sultan wrote in his diary: 'In spite of all the denials it is only too obvious that these large construction projects such as the rail line are undertaken not only for economic purposes, but they also have a political significance.'[104] It was no surprise, then, that the ambassadors of the European states had shown keen interest in the Ottoman railway construction. Their lobbying was even more intense than those of the financial or industrial investors. Abdülhamid II described their aggressive involvement as follows: 'the competition for the Baghdad Rail line has become absolutely *grotesque*... It is a great pleasure to be present to witness the spectacle. I can wish nothing more favourable than to witness all four of them devour one another. Whatever the outcome, it is to our advantage!'[105]

As a commercial/financial operation, the Baghdad Railway was inextricably and closely intertwined with the expansionist strategy of the German Foreign Office. But from that point of view, the Baghdad Railway was not an exceptional case given the German government's tendency to intervene in commercial matters abroad. The complex intertwining of foreign trade and investment with foreign policy and also military strategy became the main characteristics of the German Style of War Business – particularly in the Ottoman Empire – during the reign of Kaiser Wilhelm II. Pointing to this interrelation between the political and economic questions, Marschall said in 1907 that 'the economic interests are so much in the forefront of international life, that any attempt to separate them from the political questions would be necessarily in vain'.[106]

Another noteworthy concrete outcome of the second *Orientreise* was the right granted to the German Anatolian Railway Company to build a harbour, quay and bonded warehouses at Haydarpaşa, site of the Anatolian Railway Company's terminus on the Bosporus. The convention for the concession was signed on 23 March 1899, by Zihni Pasha, Minister of Commerce and Public Works, and Dr Zander, Chairman of the Anatolian Railway Company,[107] under the name of Société du Port de Haidar Pacha.[108] However, both the Anatolian Railway Company and the Société du Port de Haidar Pacha meant in practice the Deutsche Bank, which acted as the chief financier of these two projects.[109] This concession to the Germans irritated both the French and British, and was opposed especially strongly by the French government in the interest of the French Quay Company.[110]

According to a report by the British ambassador at İstanbul, Sir Nicholas O'Conor, submitted to Lord Salisbury on 8 February 1899, the French company claimed a monopoly right to build 'quais, docks, et entrepôts' in the port of Constantinople. O'Conor also wrote that the French ambassador, Constans, had energetically protested against the Haydarpaşa Harbour concession as a contravention of the privileges and rights already accorded to the French government.[111] In fact, the Germans had already been guaranteed the concession as a result of Kaiser Wilhelm's direct request during his second visit. Therefore, the objections of French ambassador Constans and other ambassadors were not effective, since the Kaiser's efforts had already tipped the decision-making process in favour of Germans.[112] The Kaiser's good relations with Abdülhamid prompted the Sultan to grant him precious concessions. In the words of a young Ottoman officer, who was interviewed by *The New York Herald*'s correspondent in 1908, 'German amity was onerous'.[113]

From the commercial and technical points of view, this concession provided many significant advantages to Germany.[114] It also had important effects on British commercial interests in the Ottoman

Empire. In his report, O'Conor summarized the possible contributions the Port of Haydarpaşa concession would make to the economic advantage Germany had gained already through the Anatolian Railway.[115] O'Conor argued that the principal importance of the concession lay in the increased control it gave the Germans over Asia Minor's export and import traffic. The export trade in Asia was, according to O'Conor, already largely controlled by the German-operated Anatolian Railway Company. The British ambassador emphasized that 'the German hold on the trade passing along the Sea of Marmara will thus be fortified, and if, in addition to this, Germany obtains an outlet at Smyrna [İzmir], she will be in a position to exercise an overwhelming influence over the entire carrying trade of Asia Minor'.[116]

Philipp Holzmann, a German construction company based in Frankfurt/Main that enjoyed close connections to the Deutsche Bank,[117] obtained the Haydarpaşa Harbour contract as one of its first international ventures.[118] Construction began in September 1900 and finished in April 1903. By then, the Haydarpaşa Harbour had a 600-metre breakwater with a lighthouse at its end, as well as large quays, warehouses, granaries and cranes. The new port handled 6 per cent of the Ottomans' trade and received about two-thirds of rail-shipped wheat.[119] The harbour, and later the railway station at Haydarpaşa – the start point of the Baghdad Railway, designed by Hellmuth Cuno and built by the German firm Philipp Holzmann in 1905 – made a remarkable contribution to the growth of German economic influence in the Ottoman Empire.[120] The construction of the Haydarpaşa harbour and station and their connection to the Persian Gulf through the German-made Baghdad Railway occupied an important place in Marschall's vision of the future (*Zukunftsbild*). Lindow cited the following statement written by Marschall in a report dated 1899:

> The port of Haydarpaşa, which was mostly supplied by German goods carried on German ships; the railway line from there to Baghdad, [for whose construction] a German company uses only German materials is at the same time – for both goods and

people – the shortest way from the heart of Germany to her East Asian possessions [*Besitzungen*]. So that the previous view, which [identified with] the famous dictum that the whole East was not worth a single Pomeranian grenadier, is in contradiction with the present events and is just an interesting historical memory, but no longer a current reality.[121]

Like railway construction, the installation of telegraph lines became another investment area for German entrepreneurs. German cable companies had demonstrated their interest in the Ottoman telegraph network during and after Kaiser Wilhelm's *Orientreise*.[122] England was the dominant supplier of the Ottomans' telegraph requirements until 1899. As a result of energetic intervention by the Kaiser, who made a direct request to the Sultan to provide the concession rights to German firms, the concession for a telegraph cable line from Berlin to İstanbul via Bucharest and Constanta was given to German companies.[123]

Among the activities of German capitalists following the Kaiser's second visit to Ottoman territory, the establishment of the German–Palestine Bank (GPB) deserves particular mention. The bank was founded in 1899 by Bankhaus von der Heydt & Co to promote trade between Germany and Palestine and the bank's branches.[124] The GPB took over the assets and premises of Deutsche Palästina und Orient-Gesellschaft (Limited) in Jerusalem with a capital of five million marks.[125] The GPB initially opened branches in Jaffa and Jerusalem and an agency in Gaza and, according to Tschoegl, in the following years it added more branches in Haifa, Beirut, Damascus, Tripoli and Alexandretta, as well as agencies in Nazareth and Nablus. However, Riesser asserted that in 1911 the GPB had just four branches – in Jaffa, Jerusalem, Beirut and Hamburg.[126] The GPB continued to operate till 1914, when it was absorbed by the Deutsche Orient Bank.[127] German banks spread all around the Ottoman Empire. The German traders, who had previously worked with the Austrian Bank in their Ottoman businesses, began to use the German banks established in the Ottoman Empire instead. Unsurprisingly, this shift was of great importance for German capital investment in the Ottoman Empire.[128] The German capitalists' interest in the Ottoman market gradually increased over time. In 1913, after the French, the Germans became the second largest holders of Ottoman bonds (with a market share of 20.1 per cent), while the share of the previous largest holder, Britain, declined to the level of 6.9 per cent.

The concentration of German capital investment is also important. According to Pamuk, German capital investment – outside the public debt – was concentrated in Ottoman railway construction. He asserts that by 1914 more than 80 per cent of German direct investment in the Ottoman Empire had gone to railway construction. According to the author, at that time only 40 per cent of British direct investment and 60 per cent of French direct investment had gone into railways.[129] Moreover, the concessions for the most valuable minerals in the Ottoman territorial area had been secured by the German banks (Deutsche Bank, Disconto Gesellschaft, Darmstaedter Bank, Dresdner, and National Bank) for their metallurgical subsidiaries in Germany.[130]

The close political relationship between the two heads of state promoted German investment in the Ottoman Empire – and the

Table 4.3 The Bondholders of the Ottoman Converted Debt, 1898–1913 (in %)

	1898	1913	Change in %
France	44.9	49.5	+4.6
Britain	10.9	6.9	−4.0
Germany	12.2	20.1	+7.9
Belgium	17.9	11.0	−6.9
Netherlands	4.5	3.0	−1.5
Italy	1.3	1.0	−0.3
Austria–Hungary	1.9	1.3	−0.6
Ottoman Empire	6.4	7.2	+0.8
Total	100	100	

Source: Alexander Schölch, 'Wirtschaftliche Durchdringung und politische Kontrolle durch die europäischen Mächte im Osmanischen Reich (Konstantinopel, Kairo, Tunis)', *Geschichte und Gesellschaft*, 1/4 (1975), p. 440.

closer the Kaiser and the Sultan became the more contracts Germany obtained. As a result of the Kaiser's visits, the Germans considerably increased their sphere of influence compared to other states. Being encouraged by this visit, Ambassador Marschall and the other German civil servants in İstanbul acted in a more obvious way to support their countrymen's business entrepreneurship in the Ottoman Empire. In 1906, for instance, when the Ottoman government was planning to place an order for French Hotchkiss machine guns, Marschall got involved in a very aggressive way in the matter and successfuly tried to cancel the French order, arguing the inferiority of the French machine guns, whereas praising the Germans. As he noted, in Marschall's presence right after his conversation, the Grand Vizier wrote a letter to the Minister of War, in which he exactly portrayed Marschall's arguments and reiterated that he considered the French plan definitely failed.[131]

Another noticeable example of this kind of support emerged at the expense of the British investor Sir Ellis Ashmead-Bartlett and his attempt to win a concession for electric lighting at İzmir. According to a report in *The Standard* on 7 June 1899, his application for the concession was rejected because of opposition from a German company, which had been trying to obtain it for nine years.[132] However, six days later, Ashmead-Bartlett sent the editor of *The Standard* a letter that corrected some points given in the report; his letter also drew attention to the strangeness of the concession award process:

> First, I did not ask for the electric concessions of Smyrna [İzmir] and Salonika. I was offered and promised these concessions by the Turkish Government in November last. Three of these have now been completed. Second, the Smyrna Electric Lighting was not refused me by the Council of Ministers: but, in consequence of the severe pressure of the German Ambassador, [the] Minister asked me to give a guarantee against a possible claim for damages on the part of a German competitor. This I naturally declined to give and the *Mazbata* [final report] was, therefore, postponed... The German Ambassador made three personal visits to the Porte

in opposition to my concession, and sent his first Dragoman every day both to the [Yıldız] Palace and the [Sublime] Porte. Ministers themselves assured me that my competitor's claim had no force in law, and that they wished to complete my lighting concession, but were afraid of the German Ambassador. I replied that the Sultan and not the German Ambassador was Sovereign of Turkey, and that there were other Ambassadors besides the German in Constantinople. The British and French Ambassador are supporting my rights; it remains to be seen with what results.[133]

After recounting the process, Ashmead-Bartlett sharply criticized his government's Ottoman policy from the perspective of an investor: 'The whole business is an excellent illustration of what we have lost and what Germany has gained by our foolish anti-Turkish policy of the last six years.' He concluded his letter with a striking statement: 'The Germans are eating up everything in Turkey – a country which is by nature richer, safer, and far better worthy of the attention of British investors than China.'[134] Ashmead-Bartlett's letter was also published in the *Pall Mall Gazette,* and it created a tremendous impression in the German colonisation-oriented newspaper *Alldeutsche Blätter*, which described Ashmead-Bartlett's statements as a *Jammer* (Moan). After quoting Ashmead-Bartlett's statement 'The Germans are eating up everything in Turkey' the *Alldeutsche Blätter* replied: 'Hold up a minute, Mr Bartlett, we Germans are not English!'[135]

Ashmead-Bartlett's case demonstrates that the businessmen and investors were perhaps more aware of the shifting balance in Ottoman foreign policy and its concrete consequences in many aspects of the bilateral relations than were the policy makers. In the years that followed, Germany's relations with France and Britain did not improve; on the contrary, from 1890 onwards political friction among the European states increased steadily.[136] As was apparent in the case of Ashmead-Bartlett, who noted that the British and French ambassadors supported his rights against Germany,[137] the British and French ambassadors had begun to act together against Germany after the latter's aggressive penetration of the Ottoman market.

Kaiser Wilhelm II and his Contribution to the German Style of War Business

Through the *Orientreise*, Kaiser Wilhelm had realised one of his major aims: to 'open a new market for German energy and initiative [*der deutschen Energie und der deutschen Tatkraft*]'.[138] One of the most prominent representatives of German energy and initiative abroad was unquestionably the armament industry, which played an important role in the expansion of German influence in foreign countries. Essentially, Germany's aggressive expansionist foreign economic policy towards the Ottoman Empire was correlated with an increase in armaments exports and a strengthening of the arms makers' position with respect to the German state.[139] Before moving on to the Kaiser's role in the German arms makers' business strategy in the Ottoman market, it is illuminating to focus on his relations with the arms makers, especially to the Krupp family. The concept of the 'German Style of War Business' gains its meaning from the arms makers' personal connections with the German state apparatus and the government's contribution to their successful business abroad. Among these connections, Kaiser Wilhelm's friendship with Krupp, the leading industrialist of his time, was of the utmost significance.

The strong relationship between the Krupp family (The House of Krupp) and the Kaiser's family (The House of Hohenzollern) had a long and interesting history that went back to the time when Wilhelm I was the King of Prussia. Manchester describes the bond between Alfred Krupp (1812–87) and Wilhelm I (1797–1888) as an 'unbreakable link' and adds 'Alfred wanted to make guns, Wilhelm wanted to buy them. It was a marriage of convenience, perhaps of necessity, and not even death could end it; each of Wilhelm's successors was bound to be allied with the senior Krupp of his generation.'[140] In July 1853, Prince Wilhelm demonstrated his satisfaction by awarding Alfred Krupp the Order of the Red Eagle Fourth Class, which was described by Showalter as 'the first link in a chain which would bind the two dynasties for over a half century'.[141] Wilhelm II continued the friendship between the two dynasties. He was, as *The New York Times* argued, personally very fond of

F. A. Krupp.[142] Isabel V. Hull comments that Wilhelm II found F. A. Krupp 'personally very attractive because his personality echoed parts of Wilhelm's own'. Hull adds that 'Krupp and Wilhelm shared an avid interest in technological progress and inventions of every sort'.[143] Wilhelm II frequently visited Krupp, spending nights with the Kaiserin at the Villa Hügel on the Krupp family estate in Essen. *The New York Times* asserted that the Kaiser never visited that part of Germany without seeing Krupp.[144]

Wilhelm II believed that the Krupp firm was of tremendous importance for Germany. He was of the opinion that the international reputation enjoyed by German workers and German industry was exclusively the result of the work produced by the Krupp factory. On F. A. Krupp's death in 1902, the Kaiser wrote to his daughter Bertha Krupp, saying that the work of the Krupp family was 'God given'.[145] Thus, thanks to his strategic contacts, the owner of the 'God-given' factory, Mr Krupp, achieved the position of a sacrosanct personality in the German Empire. The unfortunate fate of J. Ludwig von Verdy, the Prussian War Minister (1889–90), may throw light on the influence of the Krupp family on the German government. On 20 July 1890, Verdy had notified the Kaiser that:

> The prices paid by the military authorities to the Krupp works up to now have been very high, precisely because the monopoly granted by the military authorities to the firm... The Krupp works have in this respect, in their relations with the Ministry of War, acted in their own business interests in the most extensive way, and the Army authorities are in a total state of dependence on them in the matter of price.[146]

Afterwards Verdy refused to purchase the artillery in question from the Krupp factory. As a possible consequence of this act, Verdy was removed from office.[147] However, the relationship between the two personalities (F. A. Krupp and the Kaiser) was not based solely on friendship. Their shared interest was to expand their influence as widely as possible. Krupp was a prominent supporter of Germany's economic expansionism strategy, which was one of the major parts of the Kaiser's political vision. In one respect, the deeds of the Kaiser and Krupp might be described as different reflections of the same intention. In the Kaiser's opinion, Krupp's success in business abroad brought international prestige for Germany to a degree that had never been gained by other German firms. In a speech made in Essen, where the seat of the Krupp Company was located, the Kaiser praised the company as follows: 'The Krupp factory has provided German workers, German industry with a world-wide fame, as no other company has done.'[148]

With respect to Bismarck's concept of economic war, the Krupp Company and its founder and directors were the most influential and successful fighters for the name of German industry and German enterprise (*Unternehmungsgeist*) in the 'economic war' in the *Weltmarkt*.[149] Moreover, it appears that Kaiser Wilhelm II saw Herr Krupp as the commander of the German business army fighting in the battle of commerce and he was called by some authors the 'second head to the State'.[150] Based on this approach, the common belief in German governmental circles was that Krupp's authority must not be weakened by any possible commercial attack, even if the attack came from another German firm. In 1899, Kaiser Wilhelm clearly demonstrated his bias in favour of Krupp against another German company: Heinrich Ehrhardt's Rheinische Metallwaren und Maschienenfabrik. Ehrhardt wanted to enter the Ottoman market through a fair competition for recoil guns previously supplied by Krupp. The Prussian Minister of War Heinrich von Gossler and Marschall advised the government that it should be neutral in this German–German competition on the Bosporus. However, Wilhelm II disagreed and made his position clear in a note made in the margins of a report by Marschall, who proposed an equal balance between the German competitors, especially between Krupp and Ehrhardt.[151]

Kaiser Wilhelm II was unequivocal in his open support for the Krupp Company, and wrote: 'No, the other company [Ehrhardt] must be sharply warned [*gehörig auf den Deckel kriegen*], and Krupp, under all circumstances, must be awarded this order.'[152] It was well known that Krupp, who did not hesitate to join with his other most prominent rivals, the French Schneider-Le Creusot and the British firm of Vickers, Sons & Maxim Limited[153] in order to eliminate the *Düsseldorfer* firm from competition, was a close friend of the Kaiser.[154] In 1908, the Krupp Company, the directors of which were well aware that the Company's 'power' was fed by the Kaiser's support, protested to the German ambassador to İstanbul about his support for the Ehrhardt Company during the process of a new artillery order. In fact, the Krupp Company had been 'almost a national institution', but not only in the later years of Wilhelm II, as Burchardt argues, but it is crucial to keep in mind that the Krupp family's close relationship with and patronage of the German Emperor dates from the personal friendship between Kaiser Wilhelm I and Alfred Krupp.[155] Taking courage from that traditional patronage, in a remonstrative letter, that was sent from the Krupp Company to Schoen, Staatssekretär des Auswärtigen Amts, the Krupp directorate strongly demonstrated the firm's discontent about the efforts of the German ambassador in İstanbul in favour of Ehrhardt's Company:

> We cannot assume that such steps had been really taken by the Imperial Ambassador [at İstanbul], because they would be inconsistent with the repeatedly and verbally advised statements about the attitude of the imperial representatives abroad in the case of the several German competitors' applications for orders in foreign markets. Still, the concern of our representatives, as declared by them, has become so great that we believe it justified to take the liberty of making this communication to your Excellency, and to ask to be informed after hearing from the Imperial Ambassador, so that we may hope to eliminate that anxiety.[156]

Krupp's exclusive position at the top level of German politics and its concrete consequences in the Ottoman market were also reported by the British military attaché, Colonel Surtees. In a despatch that G. Lowther forwarded to Edward Grey, Colonel Surtees reported that the Ottoman government had placed an order for more than 250,000 OL worth of field artillery ammunition with the German firm of Ehrhardt. The report, entitled 'Messrs Krupp – a Menace to

England', also included the statements of Ehrhardt's representative in İstanbul. Colonel Surtees transmitted the agent's expressions along with his own conclusion as follows:

> The endeavours of the German Emperor during the past ten years, have [the Agent] says, been mainly devoted to helping Krupp. In Turkey the Emperor has repeatedly used his personal influence with the Sultan to help Krupp... Through such assistance Krupp has made enormous profits, compared to those of any other German trading firms. Their profits must have been over 1,000,000 OL per annum more than shown on their balance-sheets. The Emperor has always opposed Ehrhardt in Germany in order to give Krupp a monopoly. Today Krupp has a complete monopoly of the trade in naval guns and mountings in Germany.[157]

In the world's arms market, where German firms were struggling to sell their products, Krupp had the support of the Kaiser himself and the government. As Forbes quotes from a memorandum by the Councillor of the German Legation to Brazil, Kries, it had become the practice for German officials abroad, in all cases when Krupp competed with other German firms for foreign orders, to use official influence exclusively on Krupp's behalf.[158] The explanation made by Kries throws light on the Kaiser's comments stated above. Kries wrote in his memorandum that the government provided exclusive support to the Krupp Company 'because of the strong competition offered by France and England in the armaments business; the government's support was concentrated on the one German firm best fitted to meet this competition'.[159]

Krupp was well aware of the influence of the Kaiser's name on the successful outcome of securing business abroad: therefore, he did not hesitate to market his closeness with the Kaiser, and also the Kaiser's influential friendship with Abdülhamid II, in his Ottoman business. However, other prominent armament firms also exploited the Kaiser's influence in the Ottoman market. The Kaiser's significant *Orientreise* created a profitable opportunity for the efforts of several

German arms firms, activities that were attentively observed by their competitors. For example, the *Neue Wiener Journal*, located in Austria, where one of Germany's foremost rivals in the Ottoman small-arms market, namely the Steyr-Mannlicher Company, published some 'instructive stories' [*lehrreiche Geschichtchen*] under the title 'How does Kaiser Wilhelm support German Industry?' The published information, about the Ottoman government's order for 100 million cartridges from German arms and munitions factories (*Deutsche Waffen-und Munitionsfabriken* – DWM)[160] in Karlsruhe, was provided by a careful observer: Max Mauthner, the president of the Austrian Chamber of Commerce. Mauthner reported:[161]

> For quite some time, the supply of 100 million cartridges in readiness for the Turkish army has been proposed. Several German and Austrian cartridge factories applied for the supply and – at the last moment – the Karlsruhe cartridge factory received the order despite having asked for a higher price. This happened in the following way: Emperor Wilhelm turned to the Sultan with his own handwritten letter making reference to the friendship of many years between Germany and Turkey. The prompt consequence of this intervention was the assignment of the cartridge supply to the Karlsruhe factory.[162]

Mauthner was right, and the case he described was not exceptional. As emphasized above, personal relations and Abdülhamid's change of position based on the Kaiser's direct intervention were key influences on the finalizing of the contract in favour of German industry. In fact, the Kaiser's closeness to the Krupp family and the firm had led to speculation that he was one of 'the large stockholders in Krupps'.[163] In 1915, Murray, for instance, pointed out the Kaiser's relation to the firm as a shareholder:

> Friedrich A. Krupp died in 1902, and left the works to his eldest daughter, Bertha. On 1 July 1903, the whole concern was floated as a company with a capital of £9 million, the shares being held mainly by members of the Krupp family, though it

is well known that Kaiser Wilhelm II, the friend of Friedrich Alfred, is one of the largest shareholders. But perhaps his Imperial Majesty regards himself and is regarded by the Krupps as one of the family.[164]

Another example of the Kaiser's influence, or rather his name's impact on German success in the Ottoman arms market, appears in Huber's correspondence with Abdülhamid's second secretary, İzzet Bey. In his letter, Huber gave some information about the recommended prices and quantities of the Krupp artilleries and Mauser rifles.[165] According to the documentation, dated 1900, Huber was suggesting a price of 3.00 OL (54.90 marks) for each rifle, but on the condition of ordering a quantity of 200,000 rifles. After writing this offer, he sharply criticized those people who claimed the price was too high, and informed the Sultan accordingly. Huber accused these people of being inexperienced and of being motivated by their own interests. He further claimed that the price he offered was an exceptional price that had never been offered to any other government. Huber knew how to affect İzzet and manipulate the purchasing process. He tried to influence İzzet Bey through emphasizing the connections between the Sultan and the Kaiser. Finally, he asserted, 'in order to know for certain, the Sultan could ask this issue directly to the Kaiser'.[166] Thus, in the hands of arms dealers, the names of the Kaiser and the Sultan became an integral part of the course of arms trade negotiations.

Apparently, the Kaiser saw Krupp's trade activities in the Ottoman Empire as not solely a trade activity, but rather a multifaceted endeavour with political consequences that had to be supported for political reasons. Krupp's success or failure in obtaining a contract would affect the Kaiser's political attitudes towards the Sultan and the Ottoman Empire. The operation from 1891 provide evidence that the success of the GAFs, especially Krupp, in the Ottoman market was one of the principal achievements of the Kaiser's expansionist strategy as applied in the Ottoman Empire with the able assistance of Goltz Pasha. Goltz was in the middle of the information flow from the Sultan to the GAFs, and was also corresponding with Kaiser Wilhelm II. On 28 October 1891, three days after he was received by the Sultan, he sent the Kaiser a lengthy letter about various critical issues discussed during his audience with the Sultan. One of the crucial subjects addressed in the communication, and that had been found worthy to be mentioned by Goltz Pasha in his report to the Kaiser, was that the Sultan intended to order a warship and guns from French firms. Goltz was concerned that such a deal could pave the way for a closer relationship between the Sultan and the French.[167] But the most essential subject, he wrote, was the naval guns order from the French firm of Canet. Goltz warned the Kaiser that the introduction of the Canet system of naval guns into the Ottoman Navy would 'perforate the Krupp's monopoly position' in the Ottoman market.[168]

In one of his letters to Kiderlen, Goltz Pasha mentioned that Krupp's agent, Menshausen, had also been informed of the Ottomans' purpose in placing an order for guns from the Canet Company, one of Krupp's strong competitors, both by Goltz Pasha and by other 'confidential' sources.[169] After being informed, Krupp took steps to prevent the Sultan from finalizing the contract with France. Krupp immediately held a long conversation concerning the issue with the Kaiser, 'the friend of the Sultan'. After the conversation with Krupp, in which they discussed Sultan Abdülhamid's decision to give French firms a concession to arm Ottoman cruisers and an order for new artillery, the Kaiser sent a telegram to the Chancellor on 19 November 1891. In it, he detailed the conversation with Krupp and shared with the Chancellor the following information, which F. A. Krupp gave him:

> After a lengthy conversation with Mr. Krupp, the latter pointed out how momentous was the Sultan's decision to grant France an order for some cruiser-ships and cannons. His secret information was originally based on the verbal consent of the Sultan – given to Admiral Duperré at an audience held this past summer, which I in my own way have regarded as binding. However, [the Sultan's verbal consent] is most energetically pursued and exploited by the French Ambassador.[170]

The Kaiser's obvious intention was to stimulate the Foreign Office to warn the German ambassador at İstanbul. His telegram was immediately forwarded to the Foreign Office, which admonished the ambassador (Von Radowitz) to work harder on Krupp's behalf. According to Menne, Alfred Krupp looked on the German ambassador in Constantinople as an unofficial representative of his firm.[171] In a letter sent to his board in Essen, Krupp confirmed this view: 'Undoubtedly the Ambassador, who can easily discover our relations with the Emperor even if he does not already know of them, will give any necessary advice, indicate ways and means or act as intermediary himself.'[172] The Kaiser's telegram was a directive issued to support Krupp's interest in the Ottoman Empire. His targets were Radowitz, who had not been as active as Krupp wished, and Abdülhamid II, who placed an order from the French firm instead of from Krupp or other German firms. The Kaiser made the following explicit directions, and the somewhat threatening tone of his statement testifies to the unique patronage the Krupp Company enjoyed:

> Mr Krupp sends once again a representative [Menshausen] to Constantinople, in order to make again an attempt [to persuade] the Sultan. It would be very useful for this purpose if Mr Radowitz acts the opposite way from how Mr Cambon [Pierre Paul Cambon, the French Ambassador at İstanbul] has acted, and gives his support to Mr Krupp's last attempt. The ambassador [Radowitz] could point out among others to the Sultan that such a concession [given to] France, which would *ipso facto* damage the German industry, could not be entirely without political consequences and would alienate [the German capitalists and industrialists] here.[173]

As the Kaiser wrote in his notification in the last week of November 1891, Krupp's representative travelled to İstanbul and met the Serasker nine days after this conversation, on 28 November 1891.[174] While Menshausen was conducting a series of meetings during his stay in İstanbul, the Sultan instructed the Ottoman ambassador to Berlin, Ahmed Tevfik Pasha, to communicate with the

Kaiser. Acting on the Sultan's order, Ahmed Tevfik Pasha notified the German State Secretary, Marschall, of his request for an audience with the Kaiser. According to a statement by Marschall, who at that time was the State Secretary of Germany (de facto Foreign Minister), the agenda of the audience was to be the construction of the Baghdad Railway.[175] But this petition for an audience provided the Kaiser with an opportunity to state Krupp's request. Six days after submitting the petition, on 9 December 1891, the Kaiser received the Ottoman ambassador. During the audience, the Kaiser clearly demonstrated that the arms trade was considered an inseparable part of German foreign policy shaped by his expansionist desire.

The Kaiser's audience summarized the principal combination of the determinants of his Ottoman policy in a most effective manner. Wilhelm II, who was richly furnished with confidential information regarding the warships and naval guns ordered from France by the Sublime Porte, apparently formulated his arguments on the basis of the Ottomans' obvious dependency on financial and political collaboration with Germany. As the following quotation from the Kaiser's telegram highlights, Kaiser Wilhelm used unambiguously menacing language to extort an order for the Krupp Company. After communicating his thoughts on two main issues – the Baghdad Railway and Germany's financial and political support for it, and the assignment of two German civil and military doctors in the Ottoman service – Kaiser Wilhelm II came to the critical point:

> I called the Ambassador's attention confidentially to the point that it is currently not easy to persuade the German capitalists to open their wallets if he himself is worried. After that, I cannot conceal from the Ambassador that certain rumours are running around in the circles of the German industrialists and capitalists that Abdülhamid soon intends to turn away almost absent-mindedly from the proven German industry and contemplates entrusting the French with orders for ship construction and cannons.[176]

Through these words, the Kaiser demonstrated that he was well aware of the Sultan's decision, which had preferred French firms at the expense of German interests in the Ottoman military market. The Kaiser illustrated the possible consequences of such an order as follows:

> Well, the ambassador could probably judge for himself the horrible and upsetting impression this rumour made on the German capitalists. If the Sultan, despite his satisfaction over many years with proven deliveries, and the progress of railroad construction undertaken by German industry, puts the German interest behind the French interest, German capital would have no reason to take risks to accommodate the Sultan's private wishes or to continue their efforts supporting his country's progress.[177]

These statements amounted to a deliberate threat to the Sultan, implying that the result would be severance of political and economic relations. On hearing this obvious threat, Ottoman Ambassador Ahmed Tevfik Pasha felt compelled to remind the Kaiser that the Sultan had already made a decision to award an order for cannons to Krupp and an order for ships to the German firms Vulcan and Schichau. Ahmed Tevfik Pasha's reply was accepted by the Kaiser as a definite promise that would have to be fulfilled in time. After having extorted promises in favour of German military industry, Kaiser Wilhelm was proud of the result, as his own words demonstrate: 'It would be a great pleasure to me, if I could help again to secure some sales for our national industry.'[178] Through the Kaiser's effective intervention, three major military companies (Krupp, Schichau and Vulcan) had been guaranteed new orders from the Ottoman government, at least verbally. In this case, the concrete steps towards a successful war business deal were made by Kaiser Wilhelm II himself, the dominant representative of the German Style of War Business.

After Kaiser Wilhelm II's threatening interferences and provocative statements, Sultan Abdülhamid found himself in a difficult situation. Meanwhile Krupp's representative, Menshausen, sent by Krupp to İstanbul in order to solve this issue, continued to act effectively to manipulate the process. As an element of the German Style of War Business, this tactic proved to be unique and pioneering in its characteristics. Menshausen advised the Foreign Office that Bleichröder, one of the prominent bankers in Ottoman financial circles, who enjoyed a close relationship with the German Foreign Office, as was well known by the German arms firms, especially the house of Krupp – which was identified 'by the closest kind of connection with the centres of finance'[179] – must refuse the new financial combination of the Ottoman Bank, which was ready to solve the financial problem of the contract for the warship ordered from France. If possible, Bleichröder should prevent the contract being finalized, so that the Sultan would be able to mention the financial difficulties as a pretext to the French ambassador, if he again tried to pressure the Sultan with regard to the ships.[180]

On the day following Ahmed Tevfik Pasha's above-mentioned audience, Kiderlen-Wächter (later the Secretary of Foreign Affairs) sent a letter from Berlin to Goltz Pasha informing him of what had taken place regarding the French order. After warning him to treat the letter as highly confidential and to destroy it after reading, Kiderlen wrote that 'the audience took place in a way that we wished; it is now only to be anticipated that [Ahmed] Tevfik Pasha (whose mentality was well known by you) would exactly report [to the Sultan] what he has been told [by the Kaiser]. Presumably, you are in a position through which you are able to control and correct his report, if you would be notified by the higher position [Yıldız Palace]. It would be very interesting to know the impression of Tevfik's report over there.'[181]

On 16 December 1891, Goltz Pasha was received by the Sultan at Yıldız Palace.[182] During the audience they discussed a number of critical issues, including the Baghdad Railway, the military materials issue, and Ahmed Tevfik Pasha's report. According to Menshausen, who met with Goltz Pasha immediately after the audience, the Sultan went to great pains to clarify that nothing had happened yet (no order was placed).[183] Goltz Pasha also told Menshausen that the

Sultan had declared to him that he would never change his pro-German policy to one that favoured France.[184] His reassurances meant that the Kaiser's latest push in the arms trade had worked, because, once again, the GAFs had strengthened their position, and Germany did not lose her best customer to French military industry.[185] As the Kaiser noted, he secured his industrialists' interest in the Ottoman market through direct and aggressive intervention. Following the Sultan's promise for a placement of new orders from the GAFs, this temporary crisis was resolved. This case also illustrates that Germany's friendship might be described as arms-trade-dependent. It highlights Hirst's assertion that 'to push the armament trade in [the Ottoman Empire] [was] one of the functions of modern diplomacy.'[186] Germany was probably the first country to realise the importance of this 'function' and used it most effectively. Accordingly, the Sultan promised to place an order with Germany, though he did not cancel the order he gave to the French firms.[187]

Kaiser Wilhelm II's personal intervention in the war business helped the German armament firms to maintain their monopoly position in the Ottoman arms market for years. In 1899, when the Sultan sent some officers to Berlin to inspect the quick-fire 96 cm Krupp guns, Kaiser Wilhelm II facilitated the procedures required to order them. The Ottoman ambassador to Berlin, Ahmed Tevfik Pasha, and the inspection commissars, Rıza Pasha and Miralay Hurşid Bey [later Pasha], were affected by the interest shown by the Kaiser and the German officers, to whom several Ottoman medals were granted in recognition of their assistance.[188] Ahmed Tevfik reported to the Sultan on the Kaiser's facilitation of the technical investigation of the Krupp cannons. As he wrote, after being received in an audience by His Majesty, Rıza Pasha and Colonel Hurşid Pasha were invited to banquet at the troops' casino and dining hall in Potsdam. The following day, the two Ottoman officers completed the technical investigation and their examination of the quick-fire Krupp guns; they also obtained the information about the guns' technical features they needed in order to be able to make a recommendation. In his report, Ambassador Ahmed Tevfik Pasha noted that 'everything related to the artillery was thoroughly explained to the Ottoman officers in a way that nothing remained secret'.[189] Ahmed Tevfik Pasha particularly emphasized the Kaiser's role as a facilitator, which had enabled the Ottoman representatives to obtain all the information they needed about the Krupp guns under consideration.

Based on the 'consumer point of view' discussed above, the Kaiser's likely intention was to achieve customer satisfaction by providing a high standard of hospitality. His intervention in the business with the Ottoman Empire served to promote the interests of the GAFs. At the same time, the Ottoman government tried to take advantage of the Kaiser's friendship with the Sultan in the course of their negotiation with Krupp and other German manufacturers. Naturally, both parties were acting to secure their perceived advantage. Ottoman documents indicate that the Ottoman government attempted to use this close relationship to obtain several advantages, such as price reductions, guarantees of faster delivery for ordered war materials, and favourable terms on the issue of delayed payments.[190] As one of the GAFs' best customers, the Ottoman government tried also to play one supplier off against the others in an attempt to take advantage of such benefits.[191]

During his second *Orientreise*, without giving Krupp any advance notice, Kaiser Wilhelm II had promised a gift to the Sultan: a modern, quick-firing Krupp gun, one of the types being tested for Russia. His promise was transmitted to Essen as a command to begin to manufacture. In the following days, however, Krupp sent the Kaiser a letter in which he indicated that accomplishment of the task was not feasible (*nicht angängig*) for the following reasons:

> On account of a number of issues, such as the calibre of bullet, the weight of the barrel, ammunition cases – limber cases – and cartridge, and the internal layout of the barrel and placement of the cartridges, the powder type, the gauge, etc. are exactly as prescribed by the Russian artillery and produced by my factory, and therefore are considered the exclusive right of the Russian artillery forces.[192]

However, Krupp made the Kaiser an alternative offer, which he found acceptable. Consequently, on 25 January 1899, Krupp reported that the *Modellkanönchen* was sent to İstanbul.[193] Wilhelm's endeavour to bring the name of Krupp onto the Ottoman artillery agenda resulted in crucial promises made by Abdülhamid II. As *The New York Times* reported on 17 January 1899, an imperial *İrâde* was issued ordering 162 Krupp field guns and 30,000 shrapnel shells and, according to the newspaper, this order was undoubtedly the outcome of the Kaiser's action.[194] Immediately following an additional meeting with Abdülhamid II on 21 October, Wilhelm II had telegraphed to Essen that the Ottoman army's gun purchases would be made solely from Krupp.[195] The Kaiser, who was successful in gaining the order for the German arms maker, was also successful in following up on the arrangements that he had made during his *Orientreise*. For example, the Ottoman ironclad *Âsâr-ı Tevfîk* was sent first to Italy for modernizing and overhauling, but through the intermediation of Wilhelm II it was redirected to the Krupp-Germania yard in Kiel. The switch was the fruit of long and hard negotiations between the Ottoman government and the Krupp Company, and it is clear that, at the final stage, the Kaiser's direct involvement played an important role. In addition to making these kinds of marketing contributions to Krupp's success, the Kaiser provided support for Krupp against an attack made by one of its disappointed customers, the Russian Tsar Nicholas II, Kaiser Wilhelm II's cousin. A letter the Kaiser sent to the Tsar indicates his almost infinite trust in the House of Krupp. In it, he praised the German arms makers while accusing British and French companies of feeling anger towards Germany due to 'the fact that German companies provided the Russian government well and better than the French and British could do it'.[196]

During the Kaiser's involvement in the war business, he also tried to unify the three German yards to make them better able to compete in the Ottoman naval market against British interests.[197] When Sultan Abdülhamid II and his naval ministry wanted to modernize the Empire's Navy, the Sultan invited Krupp's engineers in 1897 to investigate the state of the old battleships. The investigation was completed on 29 November 1897, and it recommended spending a small fortune – 3,400,000 OL (62,730,000 marks) – a number by which the armament firms were seduced.[198] For this massive order, Kaiser Wilhelm II recommended a unification of the three leading shipyards: Krupp-Germania, Schichau, and Vulcan (*Vereinigung der drei großen deutschen Kriegsschiffsbauwerften*). According to Grant, the reason behind the Kaiser's attempt was 'not to want German prestige to suffer by letting the Turkish business fall into British hands'.[199] However, the unification was not successful in the end.[200]

The contract for the modernization of the two warships neither went to Germany nor to England, but to the Italian firm Ansaldo. Although this result was at first perceived as a defeat for German industry (*Mißerfolg der deutschen Industrie*), according to Krupp the net result was a triumph [*ein Triumpf*] against the British, for which '... German diplomacy and industry had fought hand in hand'.[201] Two battleships went to Italy to be overhauled and modernized, but Krupp did not give up its struggle for one of the ships (*Âsâr-ı Tevfîk*). For the purpose of obtaining the contract, he took advantage of his friendship with the Kaiser to push the German embassy in İstanbul to lobby for his firm. This was not a simple price offer, which could be made during a regular supply–demand process, but rather a blatant attack intended to disrupt a finished contract between Ansaldo and the Ottoman Naval Ministry.[202]

The Kaiser's second *Orientreise* was a godsend for Krupp. Following this visit, one of the ships sent to Italy, *Âsâr-ı Tevfîk* was redirected to the Krupp–Germania yard. The reason was not as simple as Grant's claim, that '... this was only because Ansaldo had been unable to complete the work in 1899'.[203] To the contrary, an extremely complicated interrelationship affected the whole decision-making process, which resulted in a decision in favour of the Krupp–Germania yard. The Kaiser's support and Abdülhamid's personal trust in Krupp's work might have been among the most crucial determinants of *Âsâr-ı Tevfîk*'s journey from Genoa to Kiel. Additionally, the race to supply armaments for eight ironclads became another competition in which the close personal relationship had an impact on the negotiation process, and the economic cost became less important than the possible political advantages of the contracts. A comment published in *The Daily News* on 21 June 1900 summarizes the process, which ended in Krupp's favour: 'Krupps are supported by the influence of the German Government and Embassy, the belief prevails that they will practically force the Turkish Government to reject the lower offer for the more valuable article.'[204] In addition to the modernization of *Âsâr-ı Tevfik* and the armaments for eight ironclads, the Krupp–Germania also obtained a contract for two new torpedo boats, which cost more than 220,000 OL.[205]

The solicitation of foreign trade for Krupp was, as Boelcke noted, one of Kaiser Wilhelm's main contributions to Krupp's profits.[206] However, as mentioned earlier, support for the arms makers' business in the foreign markets was almost a tradition of the Kaiser's family, who were well aware of the fact that the increase in production capacity of the German armament firms was closely related to their foreign sales. As the German arms firms' Ottoman business clearly indicated, there was a strong correlation between the German armament firms' successful war business and the obvious and generous patronage of both the Kaiser himself, and the apparatus of the German state in general.[207]

CHAPTER 5

SULTAN ABDÜLHAMID II AND HIS BUREAUCRATS (1876–1909)

'[Osman Nizami Pasha] has used his whole influence in order to make Germany the unique supplier for all Turkish arms orders.
[He] is a Turkish patriot, but in his mind throughout [in seiner ganzen Geistesrichtung] he is more German than Turkish.'
Marschallvon Bieberstein to Chancellor Bülow,
25 October 1908

Sultan Abdülhamid II and the Arms Trade in the Shadow of Personal Trust

'Your Majesty [Sultan Abdülhamid II] is not only Sultan of Turkey but Caliph of the Mussulmans.
Your office is now the highest and the most important in the world,
for every Mussulman State is oppressed,
and the Powers of Europe are joined in a league with the Oppresser.
It is not competent to the Caliph to become the vassal of the European Powers for the oppression of Mussulmans.'
Foreign Affairs Committees of England, 1879[1]

'Sultan Abdülhamid never forgave us for our intervention in Egypt.'

John Holland Rose (an influential British historian)[2]

Abdülhamid II (1842–1918) became the 34th Sultan of the Ottoman Empire in 1876 and ruled for 33 years, until he was deposed in 1909.[3] During these three decades, the Empire was faced with territorial occupation by successive European states including Britain (Cyprus 1878, Egypt 1882), France (Tunis 1881), and Austria–Hungary (Bosnia 1878). These attacks changed the Empire's domestic and foreign policy priorities. Defending the Empire against foreign invasion and protecting Ottoman territory became the chief aims of Sultan Abdülhamid's agenda. During his reign, therefore, the following defence policy instruments served as the cornerstones of a comprehensive military reform programme and decisively shaped Abdülhamid's military-based foreign policy:

- Outside assistance to modernize the army.
- Importation of war materials.
- Dispatch of military officers to Europe for training.
- Reform of the military school with the assistance of foreigners.
- Railway construction for military purposes, financed largely by foreign capital.[4]

At the beginning of his reign, Abdülhamid II faced serious external difficulties. The first vital challenge was the Russian–Turkish War in 1877–8, which caused the Empire to lose two-fifths of its extensive territories and one-fifth of its population.[5] 'In common with earlier losses in Europe', indicates Quataert, 'these provinces possessed the most advanced agriculture, commerce and industry in the Empire.'[6] Because of the defeat, the Ottoman Empire also lost the substantial state revenues that were allocated for the amortization and interest on the debt for the war indemnity.[7]

However, as Griffiths argued, the Empire's defeat in the 1877–8 war did not reflect the real potential of the Ottoman Army.[8] Its military equipment was not significantly inferior to the Russians.[9] On the contrary, the Ottoman Army had a technological advantage over them.[10] Ottoman artillery was equipped with breech-loading steel Krupp cannons, which were superior to the Russians' bronze pieces.[11] According to a British report Gazi Osman Pasha, the hero of the Siege of Pleven, said that the Krupp's 'guns not only carried further than the Russian ones, but the precision of their fire was quite remarkable while the destructive power of the shells was double that of the ordinary shells'.[12] The Ottoman infantry had obtained American Remington breech-loading arms, and just before the war the Empire ordered 600,000 American-made Martini-Peabody arms. By July 1877, 442,240 the ordered rifles had arrived in İstanbul.[13] The general appearance of the Ottoman infantry and artillery was, according to Captain Herbert, who was present in the Ottoman Army during the war, as follows:

> The clothing [of the Ottoman infantry] was of a good make and material, except the boots; these were execrable... The equipment consisted of a Martini-Peabody rifle and sword-bayonet... The armament is a heavy sword, Winchester repeating carbine, and revolver. Lances are carried only by regiments belonging to the Guards. Some regiments had still (in 1877) the Circassian sword... The horses were bad, and their supply was insufficient... The equipment [of the Artillery] consists of cavalry sword and revolver. The guns were of modern Krupp manufacture. The horses left much to be desired, as regards both quality and numbers; often the live-stock of a battery was incomplete. There are six guns to the battery. The ammunition carts, of which there should be six to the battery, were often deficient.[14]

However, the organization and training of the Ottoman soldiers were not as efficient as their weapons. As Shaw indicated, the Ottoman officer corps had still not completely developed at the time of the war, and some political rivalries appeared among the officer corps.[15] In 1878, Great Britain occupied Cyprus and Austria–Hungary occupied Bosnia-Herzegovina; in 1882 France occupied Tunis and Great Britain occupied Egypt, a development Marriott described as 'the final blow to a traditional friendship [between the Ottoman Empire and Britain]'.[16] Afterwards, an independent Bulgaria was established under Russian protectorate, and in 1886, Bulgaria annexed East Rumelia. Yasamee is especially revealing concerning the general picture of the empire's vulnerability to foreign attack: 'It could not ensure the actual defence of an Empire which stretched across three continents, and which faced the possibility of attack by five of the six Great Powers, four of the five Balkan states, and various minor powers in Asia and North Africa.'[17]

At the beginning of the nineteenth century, as Grant also indicates, the Ottoman Empire was self-sufficient in arms production, but by the middle years of the century the Empire could not keep up with the technological innovations abroad in armaments and remained dependent on foreign arms suppliers.[18] This dependence on outside assistance was to continue until the Empire's last days. When the Sultan realised these major inferiorities in military organization, the training of soldiers,[19] and the development of new weapons technology, he decided, as his predecessor had,[20] to invite military advisers from Europe to assist in military reform and modernization, including rearmament with modern weapons and technology. As has been discussed, Sultan Abdülhamid preferred to seek help from the Germans for his military reform and modernization project. This was in large part because of the reputation the German arms makers had gained during the Franco–Prussian War in 1870–1 (especially for the Krupp guns). The Sultan's preference for German arms was not an extraordinary or a unique phenomenon in this period. In fact, the Sultan was, in Schiff's words, sharing in 'the worldwide respect for German military success'.[21] The Prussian military system became, to quote Sater and Herwig, 'the envy of, and the model for, much of the world', especially after the Franco–Prussian War.[22]

In addition, Germany had not indicated any official colonial interest in the Ottoman territories, unlike Britain, France, Italy, Austria–Hungary and Russia.[23] Unquestionably this was of paramount importance for the Ottoman rulers. Mehmed Ferid Pasha, known as the Pro-German Grand Vezier, emphasized that approach in a very clear way in responding the questions addressed by several members of the CUP after the Young Turk revolution in 1908, why his policy had been so pro-German, as follows: 'Weil Deutschland niemals "un pouce de territoire" von uns verlangt hat.'[24]

For the pursuit of her own economic and political interests in the East, moreover, Germany favoured a militarily and economically strong Ottoman Empire.[25] That said, some sectors of the German public had expressed a colonial interest towards the Empire – some nationalist pressure groups and some segments of German society promoted the idea of colonization of the Orient to make Germany an influential world power – *Weltmacht*. The Ottoman lands were one of the most attractive targets for them.[26] Newspapers and periodicals, such as the *Alldeutsche Blätter*, were driving the idea of colonization of the Orient.[27] In fact, as Pears summarized in a particularly revealing way, the German interest in the Ottoman territory had a relatively deep-rooted tradition. 'German writers and thinkers', he wrote,

> had long hoped to find a place in the sun for their country in the Turkish Empire... In 1846, List proposed the construction of a railway to Baghdad. In 1848, Roscher claimed that the heritage of the Turkish 'sick man' ought to fall to Germany. In 1886, a German Oriental scholar, Sprenger, described Babylonia as 'the most ruminative field for colonisation' and as 'the only country not yet occupied by great Powers'. Many German writers advocated the establishment of a Protectorate in Asia Minor. Dr Seton Watson has traced the growth of the idea in Germany of domination over all the territories between Berlin and Baghdad, and has shown how Germany's thinkers gave the nation a conception of a world policy that would aim at such a result.[28]

After unification in 1871, Germany's impressive industrial expansion and solid military strength had an ineluctable effect on the European balance of power. Because of its growing production supply and rising capital, the new industrialized German economy raised the first signal of the coming clash of interests. As an 'active foreign policy maker', Abdülhamid was also observing the European power-struggle and trying to take advantage of it.[29] According to Marriott, Abdülhamid 'was one of the shrewdest diplomatists that ever ruled the Ottoman Empire'.[30] Abdülhamid realised that with Germany's emergence on the scene as another European great power, any possible clash of interests in the Ottoman territory would make him less vulnerable to foreign interference. Germany's growing industrial production fascinated many countries, including the Ottoman Empire. This fascination focused particularly on the output of the iron and steel industry, in which arms materials were one of the most noteworthy products. It was during this period that Germany became one of the world's leading producers and exporters of war materials, especially in the field of guns and rifles. Initially, the Sultan's decision to select Germany over the other European powers seems to have been merely an attempt to keep up with the changing times. As Sater and Herwig argue, several governments turned to Germany for military help and weapons at that time.[31]

In addition to Germany's solid reputation for military success and its support for Ottoman territorial integrity, it is also important to emphasize the Sultan's personal actions as an authoritarian ruler as a factor that tipped the balance in favour of the Germans. This study examines Sultan Abdülhamid's personal preferences in order to help clarify the emergence of Germany as a player in the Ottoman military modernization process. The following paragraphs demonstrate the Sultan's personal conviction about the Germans and his description of the German state, firstly by quoting from his political memoirs, edited by Ali Vahbi Bey during the Sultan's alive.[32] Archival documentation also highlights the important decisions made by the Sultan in favour of German companies, rather than other European or American firms. These sources help establish the motivations behind the Sultan's favour for the German arms firms, and its role in allowing the energetic and successful German penetration of the Ottoman arms market.

As has been pointed out earlier, Germany's emergence onto the international stage as a new industrial power was one of the most striking developments in world events on the eve of Abdülhamid II's succession to the throne. As a matter of fact, even before he came to power Abdülhamid may have harboured an inclination towards a German-friendly foreign policy. When he was still a prince in 1867, he travelled to Europe with his uncle, Sultan Abdülaziz, giving him an opportunity to observe European countries first-hand.[33] Goltz Pasha informed the Kaiser that Abdülhamid had said he had been positively impressed by the Germans and their states during his tour across Europe.[34] Along the same lines, Graf von Hatzfeld, the German Ambassador at İstanbul from 1881 to 1885, noted that 'since he [Sultan Abdülhamid] ascended the throne, he is determined in the idea of more and more rapprochement with Germany and her friends'.[35] This approach was also mentioned by the British military attaché, Colonel Chermside. In a memorandum dated 25 May 1893, he wrote that 'the Sultan... ever since 1878 has looked to Germany as a military model as well as a dominant but disinterested military power to be conciliated in every way'.[36]

There might have been personal considerations behind the Sultan's inclination towards Germany, along with the political aspirations. Abdülhamid's opinion about the Germans and Germany was initially very positive. From his point of view, the German people were a strong nation, one that would never accept being protected by another state.[37] According to Goltz Pasha, the Sultan stated that 'the German people [*Volk*] were, among all of the European peoples, the one whose features most inspired him'.[38] In Abdülhamid's view, the Germans and Ottoman Turks had similar characteristics: he considered them brave, honest, and hospitable.[39] Abdülhamid also believed that tranquillity, cautiousness, and patience were common characteristics of the two nations and that both acted with deliberation and only when the time was right. Additionally, the Germans were, according to him, loyal and honest, hardworking and unwavering people.[40] According to the Sultan, the Turks were called 'the Germans of the Orient [*les Allemandes de l'Orient*]', much like the Greeks were named 'the French of the Levant [*Français du Levant*]',[41] and he further claimed that both countries, the Ottoman Empire and Germany, had similar histories and had both squandered their potential in the past.[42] Sultan Abdülhamid's good opinion of Germany and the Germans was also noticed by one of the members of the German Military Mission in İstanbul, Strempel. According to him, the Sultan's first circle advisers and secretaries were conscious of Abdülhamid's strong consideration (*felsenfest überzeugt*) of German discipline.[43]

However, the Sultan also knew that his closeness to Germany annoyed France. He wrote that he had good reasons for adopting that position. According to the Sultan, the Kaiser's personality alone was enough to attract his sympathy for the Germans.[44] The Sultan also expressed his belief that compared to the French, the Germans were more sympathetic, more obstinate, and did not waste their time by playing politics as the French did.[45] However, while making all these positive statements, the Sultan also criticized Germany's foreign policy as 'an incompetent policy that allows England to establish its supremacy over France'.[46] He was also critical of Germany's earlier colonial policy of giving priority to the colonies that, according to the Sultan, 'never gave a result'. Instead, Abdülhamid suggested, 'Germany must deliberately spread its influence to the Persian Gulf', which was more favourable for both Germany and for the Ottoman Empire.[47] Although Abdülhamid defined Germany as 'an honest ally in restraining the other European countries' imperialist ambitions',[48] he was well aware that Germany was a country that had achieved success with a peaceful expansionist policy toward the East.[49] On the other hand, the Sultan believed that Germany had to be restrained from her possible colonial interest in the Ottoman territory.[50]

According to the Sultan's memoirs, Germany constituted the right choice for an ally that could contribute to the empire's survival in the European power struggle. For that reason, he availed himself of every opportunity to influence Germany and to obtain and maintain her support and friendship. For this purpose, probably, he transferred his personal capital investments from French banks to German banks. As he stated in his memoirs, he did not trust the banks in İstanbul, which were 'still far from being at the desired level'. He found it more reasonable to invest in a safe place abroad rather than keep it in İstanbul.[51] The 'safe places' where the Sultan invested his money were the German Reichsbank and Deutsche Bank.[52] According to a report written by Radowitz, German ambassador at İstanbul, the Sultan wanted to transfer the deposits he had made privately for his children's benefit from a French bank to the German Reichsbank. The amount transferred was more than 400,000 OL (7,376,000 marks).[53] In a document dated 16 July 1887, Sultan Abdülhamid summarized the conditions for transferring and/or depositing his private savings to the German banks; the savings consisted of German, English, and French Treasury bonds, as well as his newly-purchased German state bonds, which were obtained in exchange for the accrued interest payments from previous treasury transactions.[54] The decision to transfer his money from France to Germany may have been a sign of a change in Ottoman foreign policy that was shaped mostly by Abdülhamid's personal inclination. In this context, Tahsin Pasha's words provide an insight into the intention of the Sultan's decisions concerning capital investments abroad. According to Tahsin Pasha, the Sultan believed that money could buy every conscience, or at least could moderate some hearts and win them over.[55] In the end, a great deal of the Sultan's savings would remain in German hands, as a sign of his trust, until his days of exile in Salonika.[56]

A fuller understanding of Sultan Abdülhamid's system of rule may provide further insight into the complete picture of the successful German war business in the Ottoman market.[57] In fact, the ruling system played a decisive role, particularly in the arms trade. Grant outlines its impact on the arms trade process:

> With the importer states, the arms procurement process resided at the intersection of business, politics and foreign policy. Here the regime type played a determining role in how the arms trade interacted with the buyer country... Variations existed among autocratic states, depending on whether the autocrat personally intervened in the procurement process.[58]

Abdülhamid II was an autocratic sultan who directly intervened in the arms trade. Abdülhamid II, as a successor of Mahmud II (reg.1808–39), followed his predecessor's project of centralizing state authority. Griffiths argues that Mahmud II's centralization efforts were a pre-condition for success in his drive to modernize the army. According to Griffiths, without first 'achieving' a centralized authority in the empire, a modern military organization would have been impossible.[59] Centralization of authority was therefore the first thing that Abdülhamid II tried to achieve. During the course of his reign, his personality became central to his system of policy making and administration. According to Sultan Abdülhamid's first secretary, Tahsin Pasha, the Sultan gathered control over all administrative, military, political, religious and social affairs at the Yıldız Palace, where he established a centralized autocratic administration.[60] The Sultan's administration of government and offices was, as Baker wrote in 1902, 'reorganised like great business enterprises, with numerous departments and bureaus, each supreme in its own sphere, consulting the sovereign only in the greater affairs of State policy'.[61]

As part of this process, Abdülhamid set up a military commission system that gave him the opportunity to wield power over the military administration.[62] As his future activities would prove, he wished to be informed of even the smallest detail in military-related subjects. As an authority figure, he involved himself in almost every military affair, especially the purchase of war materials. This involvement derived from the fact that he viewed and managed the arms trade as an instrument of his foreign policy. As Erickson also pointed out, the Sultan took a personal interest in military reform and was responsible for many of the developments in that field.[63]

Because the final decision for the purchase of war materials depended on the Sultan's İrâde, the war business was unquestionably interconnected with the political environment and the strategies pursued as part of the Empire's foreign affairs, which was practically in the hands of the Sultan. He understood that the international perception of the Empire could be balanced with large armaments orders from abroad. Based on this strategy, the arms trade and various political issues co-existed on the same agenda, a fact that was well known to those people who had reliable contacts within Yıldız Palace. Krupp's agent, August Huber, was among those who could gather vital information from the Palace. Thanks to his length of service and his business activities related to the Palace, he was well informed about the Ottoman war business and its nature. According to Huber, based on his former experiences (*alter Erfahrungen*), Abdülhamid's principal motivation in the arms trade was shaped by some 'political ulterior motive [*ein politischer Hintergedanke*]'.[64]

The Sultan's response to an American claim for indemnity for American properties damaged during the Armenian uprisings in 1895–6 was one of the remarkable cases supporting Huber's assertion of existing *politischer Hintergedanke*. After the Armenian uprisings in some towns in eastern and central Anatolia in the 1890s, the Ottoman military used force to put down these uprisings. In doing so, however, they severely damaged some American colleges and the houses of some American missionaries, mostly in the towns of Harput, Maraş and Merzifon. The American government claimed the Ottoman government was responsible and demanded a total of \$90,000 in indemnity.[65] Despite the fact that the Americans officially demanded this amount several times, starting in 1895 and continuing until 1901, the Ottoman government refused to accept responsibility and rejected the claims for indemnity.[66] Their refusal made the Americans unhappy. According to Reed, US Ambassador Angell, in a telegram to Washington D.C. on 18 December 1897, suggested that the American fleet be sent to İstanbul to 'rattle the Sultan's windows' and also that 'the fleet seize the port of İzmir and collect Turkish customs until the indemnity claim was paid'.[67] Angell was convinced that the Sultan would pay no attention to the claim unless it was backed by a show of force.[68]

On 23 September 1899, the US minister to İstanbul, Oscar Straus, submitted a report regarding the indemnity negotiations to Secretary of State John Hay.[69] The report began with a statement about negotiations with the Ottoman bureaucrats for guns purchases from the Pneumatic Torpedo and Construction Company of New York, rather than mentioning the indemnity issue first. According to Straus, negotiations 'were promptly resumed under the cover of which, it had been frequently stated by the Sultan's secretary and by the Minister for Foreign Affairs, the indemnity claims would be paid'. Straus noted that the contracts had suddenly been dropped, just before the point of gaining approval from the Sultan. Straus provided the following details of his 'unofficial conferences' with the Minister of Foreign Affairs, to whom Straus expressed his demand of an audience with the Sultan. 'I told the Minister,' wrote Straus,

> the matter of the guns did not concern me, nor my Government, our demand was for indemnity for losses sustained by our citizens, that payment had been promised last December and my Government had patiently waited for the Sultan to make his promise good. If His Majesty wished to screen the payment under other transactions that was not our concern and could not be regarded as a valid reason to defer payment.[70]

In September 1899, the Minister of Foreign Affairs informed Straus that the Sultan would receive him on Friday after the ceremony of *Selamlık*.[71] That day Straus had an audience of more than an hour's duration, of which he gave the following summary in his report:

> [Abdülhamid II] opened the conversation by saying... the *İrâde* for the purchase of a war ship in America had been sent to the Minister of Marine and with the making of the contract the American claims would be paid, or literally translated, 'Wiped out', and that he would request me not to discuss with him this matter further, as it is arranged for. Knowing the Sultan's temperament and his horror of this question, I did not directly go further into the subject, but brought the conversation around to it several times, by asking what answer I should give my Government as to when these claims would be 'wiped out' and when the *İrâde* for the rebuilding of the Harpoot School

buildings would be given. He replied as soon as the contract for the ship was concluded, which would be done shortly.[72]

On one hand, the Sultan was determined not to concede the indemnity claim, but on the other, he declared that he intended to buy a new cruiser from an American firm. From the financial point of view, the indemnity was more reliable than the cruiser. But the Sultan's priority was his Empire's image in the international political arena, and he was again ready to sacrifice his Empire's weak economic resources for the sake of its external image.

The Empire's financial state was unquestionably shaky, and the Sultan knew it. According to Straus, the Ottomans were actually unable to pay the salaries of civil and military officials at that point; they were nine to twelve months in arrears. Additionally, he wrote, nearly all of the tangible sources of revenue had been conceded or pledged for advance loans. After adding some more reasons why any expectation of an earlier payment for the indemnity claim was not realistic, Straus wrote:

> We have the Sultan's promise made and repeatedly confirmed. But when? I am unable to answer. It will require time, patience and tactful pressure, or the other extreme. The other extreme, the show of force, which too often, by untoward circumstances, leads to the most serious consequences, I certainly would not recommend.[73]

Straus argued that 'by pushing the [indemnity] matter further, nothing would be gained, except to aggravate [Abdülhamid] and perhaps bring about a rupture'.[74] It seems that Sultan Abdülhamid achieved his aim; he was successful in postponing the indemnity payment to a later date, at which time its political consequences would not be as destructive. The negotiations for the contract to purchase a cruiser from Cramp of Philadelphia proceeded till the end of 1900, but the contract was not signed.

The cruiser order allowed Abdülhamid to transform the Americans' demand for indemnity into a part of a package, which provided him with time to postpone and maybe to liquidate the indemnity payment. The Sultan's tactic did not go unnoticed by Oscar Straus. On 7 October 1899, Straus sent a telegraph in which he noted that 'The Sultan requests me to telegraph the President of Cramp's shipbuilding, Philadelphia, to come here with drawings, and if possible a model, to negotiate purchasing a cruiser... [The] Sultan seems in earnest to make contract and thereby liquidate at the same time the indemnity claims.'[75] Through this operation, Sultan Abdülhamid showed his strategy of sacrificing his Empire's economic interests in order to avert possible political pressure, which could further damage his Empire's international prestige. Since paying the indemnity could be perceived as acknowledgement of blame, he intended to reduce the negative effects of such an appearance through a late payment.

By these methods, the Sultan managed to postpone paying the indemnity until 1901, without actually giving any contract to the Cramp Company. The negotiations, the mutual visits of technical delegations, the production of drawings and models, and so forth took a long time, and during their course it became clear that the Sultan had played well for time.[76] A provisional contract was finally signed in December 1900, and included the indemnity payment.[77] The American Legation was tired of waiting for a final agreement, though, and to this end, Lloyd C. Griscom, the American chargé d'affaires, sent a letter to Tahsin Pasha, the Sultan's first secretary, in January 1901:

> The signing of the Contract for the purchase by the Imperial Ottoman Government of a cruiser from Messrs. Cramp of Philadelphia, the price of which includes the sum of £19,000 which Messrs Cramp are to deliver to the United States Government to cover the damages suffered by American citizens during the troubles of 1895, has been for the fourth or fifth time postponed... I would ask that Your Excellency obtain the necessary Imperial İrâde inviting the Minister of Marine to immediately sign the said contract.[78]

In June 1901, the problem of indemnity was resolved in favour of the Americans through 'the show of force'. According to Erhan, an American cruiser was sent to the harbour in İzmir with orders to sustain pressure on the Ottoman government until the payment was made.[79] However, from the war business point of view, this pressure on the Sultan actually hurt the interests of the USA and her armament firms. As a result, the American arms makers' existence in the Ottoman market became barely perceptible. These political interventions damaged the reputation they had gained over many years, and caused a gradual divergence away from American products, which served to promote the interest of Germany. The latter appeared absolutely disinterested in Ottoman internal affairs and, in some cases, willing to lend support to the measures taken by the Ottoman government.

This matter was not the only case in which the Sultan played the military contracts card for a political purpose. By signing a contract with an Italian firm to rebuild the ironclad *Mesûdiye*, Abdülhamid II hoped to satisfy Italian claims for damages arising from property destroyed during the same Armenian uprisings in 1895–6.[80] In addition, the Ottomans' order for eight large armoured vessels from Krupp's Germania yard in Kiel was regarded as a reward for Germany's threat to blockade Greece during the Greco–Turkish war of 1897.[81] Another example of Abdülhamid's use of military contracts to gain political support was reported by Goltz Pasha. Goltz reported that by placing an order with a French firm for a warship and some naval guns in 1891, the Sultan intended to win France's support in the issue of the British evacuation of Egypt.[82] The Sultan achieved his goal. Without referring to the armament negotiations, Colin L. Smith wrote that 'France... appeared to be the Power most likely to support the Sultan in the stand he was taking about Egypt.'[83]

On the other side of the ledger, though, the expensive war materials orders caused an increase in the Empire's budget deficit. As the following document – a statement dictated by the Sultan – demonstrates, even the simple implication about the Empire's financial and military weaknesses was enough to anger him, and he treated it as an excuse for not placing a war materials order. He was decisively aware of the Empire's deficiency in the field of domestic war materials production.

> The enemies have surrounded us on all four sides. As for our guns' shells, they are so far from reaching their targets among the enemy's army that it would seem they were meant for no other purpose than setting off a firework show to welcome the enemy. While it was necessary to find a remedy either by purchasing [from abroad] or – if it is possible – by producing in the factories here, despite the urgency of this matter there is [as yet] no [project] that has been proposed to the Council of Ministers [*Meclis-i Vükelâ*]. This must be considered by the Council. So, what do your acts mean? Who gave you this right? Who appointed you to this [task]? Alongside my astonishment about the return of the drawings [of the Krupp guns] with the hint [i.e., excuse] that such plans are beyond our means and that the State is poor and the treasury is empty, the thought that you [the sender] would have the effrontery to send such a [negative] report never even occurred to me in the wildest of my dreams.[84]

The great cost of the military stemmed from the maintenance of the regular forces, the purchase of weapons from abroad, the building of fortifications, and the stocking of war reserves.[85] Accordingly, Sultan Abdülhamid turned increasingly to foreign borrowing to finance the ordered war materials and the growing number of troops. Germany was the most prominent source of the borrowed money. According to Griffiths and based on a British report, between 1890 and 1896 the Ottoman government borrowed 27,014,906 lira. After repayment of earlier loans totalling 18,339,700 lira, successive payments of more than OL 3 million to the German arms firms left a debt of about OL 6 million.[86]

In spite of that grim reality, the Sultan did not refrain from making one order after another from the German armaments firms. One of the most conspicuous reasons might have been his belief in the existence of a positive correlation between the arms trade and the external image of his

Empire. In his view, Ottoman military expenditure abroad probably served as a demonstration of the financial strength of the Empire.[87] He did not restrict arms imports despite the financial shortages that persisted from the first years of his reign until his dethronement in 1909. He refused to accept the Empire's financial state as an excuse for not moderzising his army. Through purchases from abroad, he struggled to give the impression that the Empire was still strong. A report by Alexander W. Terrell, who served as American minister to the Ottoman Empire (1893–7) on the eve of the Greek–Ottoman War, suggests that Sultan Abdülhamid was successful in giving the above-mentioned strong impression. Terrell reported the following information to the Secretary of State, John Sherman:

> I have obtained more accurate data from two of my colleagues regarding the small arms purchased and already delivered from Germany. Turkey now has one million stand Mauser rifles, with ammunition and accoutrements complete. This may be of interest to the Department. This 'Sick man' if confronted with only one power, would certainly prove the most vigorous invalid of modern times.[88]

Goltz Pasha, who probably knew the strengths and weaknesses of the Ottoman Army better than other foreign observers, made a similar statement.[89] The 'Sick man,' wrote Goltz Pasha, 'still possesses a rich quota of vital force; he must not be diagnosed according to external symptoms such as those we are familiar with.' As a well-known military strategist, Goltz Pasha added that 'often in the past the weak have been oppressed by the strong; but there can be no doubt that the means for salvation are forthcoming. It is only a question of making good use of them.'[90] Placing orders for military materials was an expensive image management tool, but it proved to be cheaper than costly wars. The Sultan's intention was to provide the Ottoman Empire with a reputation of being determined and able to modernize its Army, thus ensuring that it would be regarded either as a strong ally or an enemy who should be avoided. Furthermore, Abdülhamid had rejected the idea that a reduction in military expenditure might benefit the economy.[91] The

Sultan even used the indemnity of the War of 1897 to buy new weapons and ammunition for the army from Germany.[92] All the while, European and American arms producers competed to win orders from the economically emaciated Ottoman Empire. As a careful observer, Abdülhamid II was well aware of the arms makers' and their governments' fierce competition. A simple cruiser order, for instance, could become an important topic in the correspondences of the various Foreign Offices.[93] Accordingly, the Sultan attempted to turn his Empire's weakness in military technology into a political strength, using it as a potential bargaining tool in the marketing race.

One of the fiercest contests for Ottoman military contracts occurred between French and German companies.[94] Following defeat in the Franco–Prussian War, France also lost her reputation of having a model army, and consequently, steadily lost her status as the Ottomans' chief arms supplier, military adviser and modernization model.[95] In this way, France lost one of her major arms markets to her traditional rival, Germany. The reorganization and rearmament of the army had become an excellent tool for Sultan Abdülhamid, allowing him to keep the European powers divided. Abdülhamid was aware of this competition, and in his memoirs he persistently and particularly compared Germany with France. In 1901, Sultan Abdülhamid noted:

> Unfortunately, our relationship with France does not go well. France appears to be very angry and they do not forget the Kaiser's visit with us. During the last centuries, we turned our attention completely to France. Turkish–French friendship started after the speech of Louis XIV to the brave Ottomans saying that they cannot collaborate with any other European state. We are doubtlessly thankful to the French Officers that they reformed the army, and especially the artillery. During later years, there were always some French Officers in our army, and the Crimean War in particular generated a kind of brotherhood between the soldiers of the two nations. The last century of our history could even be called the 'French century'. During the reforms carried out by my grand predecessor

Abdülaziz and sainted father Abdülmecid, the French people inspired it all. Until recent years, France had a clear influence on our army, schools, and language. France built the first railways. To observe Germans now being settled in the Ministries as advisers or military trainers is obviously painful for these sensitive people. They do not accept the rising influence of Germany.[96]

Although French capital investments in the Ottoman Empire told a different story, he was generally right. France had increased her share of foreign capital investment in the Ottoman Empire from year to year. As a consequence, by 1898 French investors held at least 50 per cent of the total Ottoman debt.[97] But during the course of German emergence in the Ottoman market, France began to lose her influence in the government-supported fields of trade and investment, particularly in the military-based trade. As the German embassy reported to Berlin, 'in Paris everyone is very nervous about our position here [in İstanbul].'[98] However, the whole of the Ottoman foreign trade picture had not changed dramatically during this period. German investors' capital interest in the Ottoman market was still not as high as the French investors'.[99] Still in the 1890s Germany's trade with the Empire was well behind that of Britain, Austria, and France.[100]

However, the Sultan's personal trust in Germany and its remarkable and concrete outcomes were demonstrated through the armaments purchasing process. According to Marschall,[101] the Sultan told him during an audience that 'it was a settled principle of his [*feststehendes Prinzip bei ihm*] to order war materials from Germany and he would never forsake that [principle]'.[102] Moreover, on several occasions Abdülhamid expressed his admiration for the German products. According to Alexander W. Terrell, the US minister plenipotentiary to the Ottoman Empire, when he was received by the Sultan at the Yıldız Palace on 19 October 1894, the Sultan had described the Mauser rifles as 'the best rifle', even though the minister plenipotentiary had brought an old American Ferguson rifle as a gift to be presented to the Sultan.[103] Throughout his entire reign, Sultan Abdülhamid was the best customer of the German arms makers, especially Krupp and Mauser. In one of his letters to Von Einem, the Prussian War Minister, Paul Mauser admitted that: 'I can only thank his Majesty the Sultan [Abdülhamid] for his gracious attitude and personal trust to me and my company for the delivery of more than 900,000 rifles over the past 20 years.'[104] Mauser was right to express his gratitude to the Sultan personally, whose 'benevolence' was actually the main factor behind the contracts given to the Germans.[105] Furthermore, as has been stated above, the Sultan looked on the arms trade and the signing of crucial contracts as 'his own act and deed', and had 'a settled principle' in favour of the German firms. The Sultan personally intervened in the arms trade and was instrumental in the decisions to place crucial military orders with German firms, even though some of his ministers disagreed.[106] Through his acts and deeds he became to be known as the best customer of the German armaments firms.

Through the Sultan's support, German firms gradually came to dominate the Ottoman arms market. A document dated 11 September 1895 further illustrates Abdülhamid's personal consideration about the German arms companies, especially Krupp and Mauser: 'While it is evident that His Imperial Sovereign [Sultan Abdülhamid] could buy the firearms [*esliha*] from anywhere he wants and even if required [he could also purchase] from American factories, however, because of his trust in [*i'timâd*] and favour for [*teveccühât*] the Krupp and Mauser factories [these factories] will be preferred.'[107] Moreover, Marschall, in one of his reports submitted to the German Foreign Office, referred to the Sultan's intention to place an order for coastal guns (24 cm) as follows: '... The Sultan talked about the subjects related to the military, troop training, etc., and he expressed that he intended to place an order for 24 cm coastal guns "of course with Krupp".'[108] The parenthetical expression, given in quotation marks in the original document, demonstrates Marschall's confidence in the Sultan's inclination towards the Krupp factory specifically and towards the GAFs generally. A letter sent to Krupp by Paul Horn,[109] a German civil adviser in the Ottoman service, whose status Pendleton King defined as 'a very important position',[110] gives another indication of the Sultan's personal trust in Germany and its positive impact on the GAFs' position in the Ottoman market. According to Horn, 'if perchance there was still no danger for the German position acquired in the Ottoman Empire, it was exclusively indebted to the Sultan's *engouement*/infatuation with Germany'.[111] The Sultan, who intervened directly in price negotiations,[112] payment procedures[113] and delivery processes[114] for guns, rifles and gunboats ordered from abroad, lent his personal support almost exclusively to German firms. A report Marschall sent to Hohenlohe, demonstrates the Sultan had acted in favour of German arms manufacturers. 'On his own initiative', wrote Marschall, 'the Sultan increased the amount of the cartridges order – from 100 million to 200 million units with a purchase price of approximately twenty million Marks – he will order 250,000 new rifles from us [...]'[115] Expressions such as 'his own act', 'his own deed' or 'his own initiative' highlight Sultan Abdülhamid's authority in the Ottoman arms trade.

France, which lost its former dominant position to Germany, was quite late in realising the strong position its rival had achieved in the Ottoman market and understanding the methods used to achieve it. In 1904, the Ottoman government had to turn to Paris to obtain French support to sign a new debt arrangement and put the Ottoman state bond on the French market. Ernest Constans, the French ambassador to İstanbul, imposed some preconditions for the requested approval: guns and destroyers must be ordered from a French firm, Schneider's Le Creusot, a prominent rival of the Krupp Company.[116] Because of this condition, the Ottoman government was constrained to purchase four destroyers from Schneider's Le Creusot.[117] Subsequently, in 1905, a loan agreement for 60 million francs was signed between the two parties. According to the agreement, 20 million francs would be used to pay for French industrial goods. 'Ultimately,' says Fulton, 'Schneider delivered ships worth about 13,500,000 Francs.'[118] Langensiepen and Güleryüz assert that the reason for this order was to create a diplomatic and financial balance between the great powers.[119] However, the true motivation was not a balanced policy, as Langensiepen and Güleryüz suggest; on the contrary, the aim behind the French order proved to be French financial extortion.[120] The German arms makers and their agents in İstanbul were anxious about the fallout of these possible orders.[121] But the German influence in the Ottoman market was not as superficial as the French might have expected.

Constans' belated personal attempt to regain influence in the Ottoman Empire on behalf of French interests was shaped mostly by economic considerations.[122] But Germany and her businessmen had realised much earlier than the French that the road to success in the Ottoman Empire was found in the intertwined features of politics, economics and personal diplomacy. Paul Graf Wolff Metternich, the German Ambassador in London (1903–12 and later in İstanbul 1915–16), alluded to doing business in the Middle East, specifically in the Ottoman Empire, in a revealing manner: 'The foreign influence in the [Middle] East is of an economic or political nature. In general, both are intertwined. Who even has the strongest political influence, will most likely receive concessions and its merchants will be favoured.'[123] Thanks to the personal trust of the Sultan, most of the lucrative concessions and contracts, for which several countries were competing, went easily to the Germans.

However, towards the end of Sultan Abdülhamid's reign, the German government came to realise that 'the German influence is not as strong as it was before'. The truth of this statement could be attributed to another crucial development: the rising power of the Young Turks. In fact, thanks to the German factors in Ottoman civil and military circles the German government was better informed than the other arms-supplier countries about any political development in the Sublime Port.[124] Based on the information flow coming from Ottoman military and civil circle, the Germans were not utterly unprepared for the coming power shift. In fact, German policy makers saw no reason not to be 'on equally good terms with the Young Turks as with Sultan Abdülhamid'.[125] The following passage from an article published in *Deutsche Zeitung* on 9 July 1907, confirms that the Germans were making preparations for a possible replacement of Abdülhamid II. According to the article, 'based on human calculations, the fate [was] not far off, when Abdülhamid's line to life will be cut'. The newspaper argued that 'one may not expect much from him because of his illness, his administrative acumen and reluctance to any reforms'.[126] The newspaper's calculation was based on the expectation of a power shift in imperial sovereignty, after which the Young Turks would become the most powerful party in the Ottoman Empire.[127] The newspaper's prediction was right, although its calculation was wrong. On 17 April 1909, Sultan Abdülhamid was deposed by the Young Turks, but he did not die until 10 February 1918 – 11 years after this article was published.

The Ottoman Bureaucrats: Personal Ties with the Arms Makers

In his book *The Political Economy of War*, Francis W. Hirst defined the nature of the arms trade. Hirst argued that governments are 'the only customers of the [armament] firms' and defined ministers and subordinate officials of the governments as authorities who 'have no interest in [the] economy, and have even been [known to] yield to bribery'. Based on this assessment, Hirst asserted that 'the ordinary theory of supply and demand cannot be applied rigorously to the

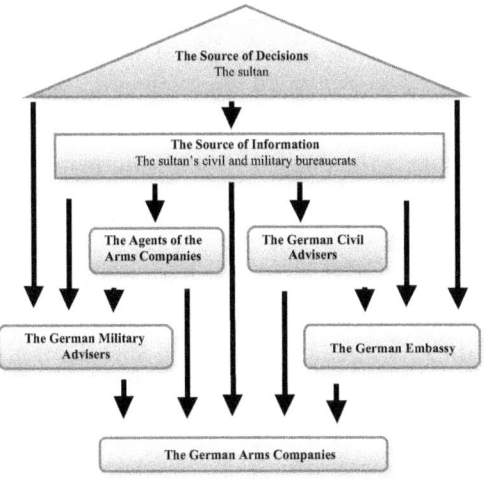

Figure 5.1 The Information Flow towards the German Arms Companies

armament trade'.[128] Presumably, if Hirst had examined the late nineteenth century Ottoman case as an example of the inapplicability of ordinary market theory to the arms trade, he would have confirmed his assertion. More or less in line with Hirst's formulation, the Germans' success also relied on a multiple-stage information flow, as Figure 5.1 below indicates, between the source of decisions, namely Abdülhamid II and the German arms companies, with Ottoman civil and military bureaucrats, as the sources of information, were situated under the decision maker: the Sultan.[129] During Sultan Abdülhamid's reign, some ministers and subordinate officials of the Ottoman government were directly involved in the arms trade and tried to influence the purchasing process in favour of the Germans by using two basic methods: submitting reports to the Sultan for the purpose of influencing armament policy, followed by recommendations for the GAFs, and directly sharing crucial information with the GAFs and the German civil and military advisers.

The *lâyiha*s submitted to the Sultan suggesting an increase in the import of war materials helped to stimulate the growth of German influence in the Ottoman arms market. However, the need to increase armaments was basically shaped by the new perception of a war threat, on which the German military mission's impact was obvious.[130] 'Since the demand for armaments is greatest during the war,' wrote Hirst, 'war is the ultimate aim of private armament firms; or, if not the actual aim, it is their *raison d'être*, the end and purpose for which they exist.'[131] Similarly, if war was not anticipated to be imminent, then either the threat of war or information about other states' procurements could be instrumental in creating a new market for manufactured war materials. That was, in fact, what had happened in the case of the Ottoman arms purchasing process during Abdülhamid's reign. The threat of war forced the Ottoman authorities to maintain a close watch on the armament policies adopted by other nations, especially those countries from which a possible attack seemed most likely: Russia and the Balkan states (Greece, Bulgaria, Serbia and Rumania). As an example, Ottoman military officials, in a report dated 19 October 1886, argued that the Ottoman government should take into consideration the fact that the

Russians and Greeks were strengthening their naval forces. The report's consequent suggestion was to take immediate action to finalize the purchasing process for the torpedo boats ordered from the Germania yards.[132]

All the while, political instability in the Balkans and rumours of a European war loomed large in Ottoman debates.[133] The Ottomans' arms-import priorities were shaped by the technological innovations of the European arms industry and the perceptions of a new threat to peace.[134] The result was a conviction in Ottoman military circles that 'whoever wins the armament race may very well win the war'.[135] On that basis, they felt compelled to follow very closely the armaments strategies of their potential enemies.[136] One of the most debated sources of threat was the increased armament of Bulgaria, whose friendship was also of enormous importance for the Krupp Company and Germany.[137] Subsequent events justified the officials' concern about the Bulgarian war preparations. At the end of 1894, it was reported that two tugboats of the Danube Steam Shipping Company (*Donau-Dampfschiffahrts-Gesellschaft*) were transporting war materials produced by the Krupp factory to Bulgaria.[138] Furthermore, a document dated 20 January 1898 demonstrates that Bulgarian officials visited the Krupp factory for the purpose of placing new gun orders.[139] A decade later, on 10 August 1903, the Ottoman government signed an agreement with the Krupp company for 186 guns (31 batteries),[140] which was reported by *The New York Times* as 'Turkish war preparations' against Bulgaria.[141] Furthermore, on 1 December 1903, Hurşid Pasha, who was officially sent to Germany to inspect the cannons ordered from the Krupp Company, submitted a report to the Ottoman Minister of War informing him that the Krupp factory had provided the Bulgarian Army with 26,304 pieces of shrapnel, and a French company had sold them 15,430 pieces.[142] Presumably, Hurşid Pasha obtained this information directly from the Krupp Company, as part of its strategy to encourage the Ottomans to place orders for more guns and related materials.

This was a sound marketing strategy, designed to ensure that the more war materials the Bulgarians bought from Krupp, the more the Ottoman Empire would order. That was a natural instinct of an arms maker: if he could persuade one government to increase its armaments, then more orders could be secured from others.[143] In February 1905, a year after Hurşid Pasha submitted his report, important information reached the Ottoman Government: the Bulgarian government had placed an order valued at 4.5 million francs (ca. 197,541 OL) with the Krupp Company and 2,200,000 francs of the total amount had been paid in advance.[144] According to the 'Report on Changes in Foreign Armies during 1905' published by the British War Office, the Bulgarian artillery was composed of 7,874 men (the peace strength) and supplied with 602 field guns (486 Krupp field guns and mountain guns; 54 Krupp 7.5 cm quick-firing field guns; 54 howitzers; and eight Le Creusot 7.5 cm. quick-firing field guns),[145] whereas the Ottoman artillery consisted of 40,000 men (the approximate peace strength) and 1,650 field guns, almost all of which were made by Krupp.[146]

The Ottomans' immediate reaction to the Bulgarian artillery orders was followed by the European press. *The {London} Times*, for instance, reported the Ottoman reaction: 'The recent purchase of quick-firing guns by Bulgaria has created a deep impression at Yıldız Kiosk, and it has been decided considerably to augment the Ottoman artillery. To this end negotiations have been opened with a financial group represented by the Ottoman Bank, for a loan of OL 3 million, for the purchase of new armaments... The project causes much concern in German circles, and attempts are being made to obtain an order for arms for German firms.'[147] The Sublime Porte then accelerated the negotiations for a new guns order from the Krupp Company; consequently, on 6 April 1905, the Ottoman government signed a new agreement with Krupp for 546 guns (91 batteries). The total cost of these guns amounted to 1,967,634.37 OL (more than 36 million marks).[148]

According to a protocol prepared by a member of the Military Commission and considered when it assembled on 5 December 1905, the artillery emplaced in Rumelia amounted to 848 guns, and the Bulgarian Army already had 972 guns, which meant that in the case of a war against Bulgaria the Ottoman Army would face a difficult situation. Based on this comparison, the commission suggested –

after praising the Krupp guns – more gun orders from an appropriate firm.[149] Another comprehensive comparison of the number of guns recently ordered by both the Ottoman and Bulgarian governments was made by the sub-Ministry of Techizât-ı Askeriye in 1907.[150] According to this report, up to August 1907 the total number of the guns recently ordered by the Ottoman government amounted to 732, whereas Bulgaria's contracts amounted to 324 guns. In short, this report reflected the conviction widely held in Ottoman military circles that 'whoever wins the armament race may very well win the war'.[151] But numerical superiority in armaments did not necessarily translate into superiority on the battlefield. The Balkan Wars demonstrated that this conviction misled Ottoman decision makers. The Ottoman Army was defeated by the Bulgarian Army during the First Balkan War in 1912.[152]

During the reign of Abdülhamid II, the power of every European state was determined by its military and naval strength. As a consequence of this determination, Ottoman military officers followed the military–technological developments and armament strategies of the European states through translated books, newspaper articles and reports written by Ottoman officers who had been sent to Austria, Germany, France, England and Spain. The articles and books translated by the Translation Office in the Sublime Porte (*Bab-ı Ali Tercüme Odası*) were investigated in detail by Ottoman bureaucrats and discussed afterwards in the Meclis-i Vükelâ.[153] Additionally, the purchasing commissioners abroad and the inspection commissioners in İstanbul submitted reports (*lâyiha*) and comparative statements about the new military technology developed by European arms producers. In most of these reports, when war materials were compared the verdict was in favour of the German-made war materials. The reason was mostly the great success of the Prussian–German Army in the Franco–Prussian War (1870–1). This kind of argumentation played a decisive role in Ottoman bureaucrats and officers' support for the German style of military reform in Abdülhamid's military modernization plan. As an outcome of this war, France was replaced as the foremost military power in Europe and the position as leader in military technology and strategy passed to Germany.[154] Ottoman officers and bureaucrats, who propagandized the superiority of German war materials, used this war and its political consequences as a significant example. The German victory over France was portrayed as clear evidence of Germany's military strength and the quality of the German weapons used in this war.[155]

The reports, which related to the reorganization and rearmament of the army, merely represented a simple bureaucratic confirmation of the Sultan's well-known inclination towards Germany. The archival documents relating the rearmament of the Ottoman ironclad *Âsâr-ı Tevfîk* with Krupp guns give illuminating examples. According to a document dated 7 December 1899, Sultan Abdülhamid had particularly preferred the Krupp guns to the Armstrong guns in armouring the *Âsâr-ı Tevfîk*.[156] Halil Ibrahim Pasha (1862–1917), who was the naval officer responsible for the inspection of the restoration process of the ironclad in Geneva,[157] argued that the Sultan's personal preference for the Krupp Company was, from a technical point of view, very appropriate. Accordingly he defined the Sultan's decision to arm the Ottoman ironclads with Krupp guns as 'a decision which is a result of an inspiration of God (*ilhâm-ı rabbânî*)'.[158] Halil Pasha's remarks in his report, which might deserve to be called an obsequious statement, were a natural outcome of the Sultan's well-known inclination towards and complimentary view regarding both German-made war materials and the German military system.[159] Halil Pasha or the other officials should be well aware of the fact that the Sultan did not give much credence to reports which were unfavourable to German-made war production,[160] and sometimes he became very angry with officials who did not pay enough attention to offers made by German arms companies, particularly the Krupp or Mauser Companies.[161] As a result, the reports were typically and unsurprisingly biased in favour of Germans, because the officials understood the Sultan's inclination towards Germany. The Sultan's control over the purchasing process and his orientation towards Germany during the ordering process was, as mentioned earlier, very conspicuous. He seemed to have gladly accepted reports or statements that were prepared in favour of German suppliers.

The following view, elaborated by Grant, makes Halil Pasha's report all the more interesting. Grant asserts that in the 1910s, Halil Pasha 'had pro-British sympathies' and had 'entered into secret and unauthorised negotiations with Armstrong for the purchase of two dreadnoughts'. In fact, Halil Pasha's action was unexpected at that time, when he submitted to the Sultan the report in which he described as 'a wonder work' (*Kerâmet*) the Sultan's decision about the arming of *Âsâr-ı Tevfîk* with Krupp guns, rather than British-Armstrong. However, the Young Turk revolution brought about a change in political affairs and also in the attitude and approach of the officers. Halil Pasha, despite being trained in the British Navy for years, in 1899 an obvious opponent of arming the ironclad with Armstrong guns, by 1910 was fighting with 'the ardent pro-German war minister', Mahmud Şevket Pasha, to buy warships from Armstrong. Grant asserts that when Halil came forward with his plans, Mahmud Şevket Pasha feared that the failure of the Germans to supply warships would be regarded as his personal defeat. Consequently the Grand Vizier, who was said to be 'very anti-English',[162] forced Halil to resign on 29 May 1910.[163]

The official reports by the Ottoman commissions, on topics such as German-made rifles and cannons, military organisation and equipment, and new techniques developed by the German manufacturers, were influenced by the civil or military bureaucrats' personal opinions, which could be easily altered and/or manipulated with gift-giving. But *baksheesh*, as a tactic, was prevalent before and after the reign of Abdülhamid II as well. Abdülhamid himself complained about corrupt officers, and especially about the penchant of high ranking-officials to accept bribes.[164] The Ottoman Empire was not an exceptional case in this regard. As Grant pointed out, in many markets the armament companies 'offered the native officers, off the record, a share in the armaments contracts through the payment of commissions or other financial blandishments'.[165]

In the case of the Ottoman Empire, the Sultan himself mentioned corruption in his memoirs as a matter that reduced the Empire's credibility among foreign investors.[166] As Arthur von Gwinner expressed in a self-explanatory letter, *baksheesh* was almost a common feature of doing business in the Ottoman Empire in those days. Gwinner was a member of the board of managing directors of the Deutsche Bank (1894–1919) and 'an active promoter of the Baghdad Railway'.[167] According to Gwinner, £120,000 had to be paid as *baksheesh* for the concession of the Baghdad Railway Company. As he stated in a letter dated 7 November 1930, just a year before he died, 'indeed it is known to all who ever had to do with Turkey that it was even impossible to pass a donkey charged with gold for the Treasury into Stambul [İstanbul] without paying *Bagsheesh* [sic] a way of the Sultan's of paying his ministers and officials'.[168] The German firms' profitable war business in the Ottoman market was always conducted with *baksheesh* as a tool. In September 1906, the *Leipziger Neuesten Nachrichten* published an article about *baksheesh* in the Ottoman war business. As the title of the article (*Politische Übersicht: Eine Bakschischgeschiechte*) exposed as well, in the end *baksheesh* came to be regarded as a political instrument which the Germans used effectively – with varying political consequences. The article argued that 'It is a well-known fact that in İstanbul business could be run effectively through *Baksheesh*.'[169]

In the same vein, bribery of the officials involved in the awards process of the arms contracts seems to have been a typical feature of the war business during this period. As some similar cases indicate, corruption was an inevitable by-product of the strong emergence of German manufacturers into the world arms market. There was a direct correlation between the strong position of the GAFs and the methods they employed to persuade officials who could manipulate the decision-making process on armament purchases. The American ambassador to İstanbul, John Leishman, reported: 'I am creditably informed that Krupp's sales here during the past 30 or 40 years amount to over 20 millions of pounds, and it is quite safe to assume that at least five to 10 per cent of this amount has been distributed among certain officials in the shape of *baksheesh*.'[170] As Scott generalized, 'bribery was not accidental or occasional, but essential and systematic in every field of commerce'.[171] Because of its importance, Sampson's illuminating explanation is worth quoting:

The great majority of orders were from governments, where the decision could well depend on one or two individuals, whose support was therefore essential. The advantage of buying one warship or gun, as opposed to another, was often uncertain, and arguments could thus easily be swayed. The orders were often very large, so that a single decision was more critical for an arms company. And the sales were usually conducted in secrecy for reasons of national security. Moreover, as the commission increased, officials might well favour bigger orders, beyond the capacity or needs of their country, to ensure that their share would be greater.[172]

Based on this scenario, it can be said that the process of modernizing and rearming the Ottoman Army with German-made war materials was not necessarily a solely military-oriented or economically sound one. On the contrary, the personal influence and attitudes of the officials and officers played a decisive role. Although Marschall expressed the view that the Ottoman statesmen had no impact on the Sultan's decisions,[173] the following statements from his report confirm that at least some decisions relating to the arms trade were not solely the province of the Sultan. This documentation also provides some more evidence about how the system worked and how the Germans became the Ottomans' chief arms suppliers. Responding to an information request relating to Osman Nizami Pasha, the newly-appointed Ottoman Ambassador to Berlin in 1908,[174] Marschall wrote the following about his contribution to the German arms supply to the Ottoman Army:

> [Osman Nizami] has always proven his pro-German sentiments by his actions. During my residency here [in İstanbul] for eleven years he has been a loyal friend and adviser of our military reformers and he has been a reliable informant for the German military mission. He has used his whole influence in order to make Germany the unique supplier for all Turkish arms orders... Osman Nizami is a Turkish patriot, but in his mind

throughout [*in seiner ganzen Geistesrichtung*] he is more German than Turkish.[175] He deserves therefore my full trust.[176]

Deutsche Zeitung, reporting in 1907, endorsed Marschall's conclusion about the contribution of Ottoman statesmen to Germany's political and economic progress in the Ottoman Empire. The article indicated that thanks to the active support of the pro-German Grand Vizier, Halil Rıfat Pasha – who had been rewarded with the Black Eagle medal by Kaiser Wilhelm II for '[his] services and friendship' – German influence in the Ottoman Empire had gradually risen.[177] The following report by Ahmed Rıfat Bey, the son of Halil Rıfat Pasha, gives us another revealing glimpse of the importance of the bureaucratic contribution to German success in the Ottoman Empire. Ahmed Rıfat Bey, who was also educated in Germany, sent the German ambassador an article published in the *Süddeutsche Zeitung* on 9 July 1907, entitled *Deutschlands Einfluss auf die Türkei muß wieder steigen* [Germany's influence on Turkey must rise again] and declared that:

> I request from your Highness to be allowed to submit the enclosed newspaper clippings. They were sent to me from a friend, who – as can be derived from the content – seeks for the improvement and strengthening of the German–Turkish relations. The latter was the chief aim of my deceased father, who regarded it the highest luck to have contributed to its realization as the Grand Vizier. May both our nations be destined for a blessed future![178]

Ahmed Rıfat Bey was one of the many students who trained in Germany and in later years became 'Germany's apostle' in the Ottoman Empire. The appeal of Germany and her military model was strongest among the younger officers. But the admiration was obvious in the upper ranks as well, especially among those who had trained in the War Academy or who been to Germany for some reason. Over time, these students became loyal representatives of German culture in the Ottoman Empire. In addition to their role in promoting cultural transfer, these cadets made a significant contribution to the political and economic links between the two Empires. In reports prepared for the government, they enthusiastically complimented German military organization and strategy. Their overt contribution to the German name, prestige, and influence in the Ottoman Empire was well observed by the German foreign office and its staffs located both in Berlin and İstanbul. Referring to the other governments' 'intriguers against the Sultan's decision to ask for sending the Ottoman military officers to Germany in 1907' Kiderlen warned the foreign office for an immediate 'approval' and conveyed that 'in terms of German influence and prestige in Turkey such a transfer [Kommandierung] is of great importance'.[179]

Among these officers were three future war ministers (later Pashas): Ali Rıza, Mahmud Şevket and Ahmed İzzet.[180] These students proved to be loyal representatives and an inseparable part of the German penetration strategy towards the Ottoman Empire. However, their impact on the decision-making process seems to have been restricted during Abdülhamid's reign, but in the long term they acted as life insurance for the German penetration strategy towards the Ottoman Empire.[181] Although Abdülhamid was a personal supporter of Germany, when he lost power after the Young Turk revolution, Germany and the German arms makers did not lose their marketing power as a result, as had been predicted. On the contrary, the Young Turk revolution brought German-trained officers into key command positions.[182] 'As long as the Army remained in power in Turkish policy,' wrote Wangenheim proudly, 'Germany will remain in a preferred position against the countries with which it's competing.'[183] Wangenheim's evaluation was correct, and historical events supported his statement.[184] The German advisers, especially Goltz Pasha, were successful in creating a pro-German cadre of young officers in the Ottoman Army.

Based on this fact, Wangenheim noted as late as 1912 that 'The majority of the Turkish officers still believe in the absolute superiority of our military capabilities.'[185] In fact, even before the revolution the pro-German officers had already begun playing their important role in the Empire's military reorganization and rearmament policies.

Further examples demonstrate the impact of the German-trained officers in creating a pan-German climate in the Ottoman Empire's ruling circles. Ahmet İzzet Pasha, for instance, one of the foremost of Goltz Pasha's cadets, graduated from the Ottoman War Academy in 1887 and received advanced military training in Germany in 1891–4.[186] After his return to İstanbul, he became one of the leading friends of the German military advisers in the capital. In 1898 he visited Germany again, and on his return to İstanbul he prepared a report setting out his observations about Germany's military system and its organizational skills. He mentioned in the report that he had been invited to observe infantry and cavalry manoeuvres in Berlin. According to him, the main characteristics of German soldiers were their discipline and obedience to their commanders. He recounted a conversation with Count Alfred von Waldersee, who had a lengthy background in the artillery and cavalry. Waldersee was a well-known cavalry commander[187] and, in Menne's words, a 'doubtless well-informed friend of the Emperor'.[188] İzzet also gave detailed information about manoeuvres in which he took part.[189]

Although Ahmed İzzet did not comment explicitly in favour of the Mauser rifles or the Krupp guns, his report might be regarded as a statement of manifest admiration for the German military system. Unquestionably, these kinds of conclusions facilitated the strengthening of German influence in the Ottoman Army. Ahmed İzzet, in coordination with Goltz Pasha and Mahmud Şevket Pasha, altered the education system for general staff officers, introduced model troop regiments, erected training areas for officers, worked on transportation and mobilization schemes, and arranged manoeuvres.[190] These developments were based on his experiences during his stay in Germany. The German arms makers took advantage of Germany's increasing influence in the Ottoman Army to gradually win more contracts from the Ottoman government.

Mahmud Şevket Pasha was one of the pro-German officers, and he was well known for having a particular influence on the

Sultan Abdülhamid II and his Bureaucrats

arms-purchasing process.[191] The entrance of the Mauser rifle into the Ottoman Army was an illustrative example. In the last days of 1886, when the Mauser Company was struggling to enter the Ottoman market, Mahmud Şevket Pasha proved his pro-German sentiments with his vigorous advocacy on behalf of the German-made rifles. Serasker Ali Saib Pasha opposed the German offer and was inclined to recommend the Austrian-made Mannlicher rifles instead.[192] In the commission, where the German advisers, including Goltz Pasha, were observing the discussion as 'spectators and technical advisers', Mahmud Şevket Pasha – the commission's youngest member[193] – came onstage to represent German interests and criticize the approach put forward by the Serasker.[194] Goltz Pasha used the following words to explain Mahmud Şevket's important contribution to the Germanization of the Ottoman arms market:

> At first, nobody dared to speak against him [Ali Saib Pasha] and a deep silence followed. After a short pause, the youngest of all the members, Mahmoud Schewket [Mahmud Şevket Pasha], started talking and objected to the Minister in a quiet but very impressive way. His remarkable memory helped him immensely at this. He repeated sentence by sentence the news articles as quoted and proved the superficiality of these press attacks, and briefly yet effectively went over the comparison of the competing rifles. It was a brilliant speech of irresistible logic, at the end of which the speaker accepted with great warmth the attacked weapon factory and its directors [and] *Kommerzienrath* Mauser. He finished with a very particular [expression]: '*Vallâhi doğru söylüyorum!*' – 'By God, I speak the truth!' The general impression was enormous. All eyes turned to the young, otherwise taciturn officer, from whom no such vigorous and energetic speech was expected [but at the same time] no one did expect [from him] such a venture.[195]

Despite the apparent opposition of the Serasker, the commission decided in favour of the Mauser rifles. Consequently, in 1887, the Goltz–Mahmud collaboration provided one of the first triumphs that paved the way for the Germanization of the Ottoman arms market. In the years that followed, Mauser obtained a virtual monopoly in the Ottoman small-arms market, as Krupp had done in artillery and naval guns. The monopolization of the Ottoman arms market by the GAFs was a first step towards the Germanization of the army, which led eventually to the 'Brothers in Arms' concept of World War I. A statement Mahmud Şevket Pasha made on the eve of World War I becomes very illuminating in this respect. In a conversation with Cemal Pasha, Mahmud Şevket, who often corresponded with Goltz Pasha after the latter's departure for Germany[196] said: 'Now we cannot salvage ourselves from the German style of war [application]. For more than thirty years the German instructors have been found in our army, our officer corps had been completely trained according to the German method, in short, our army generated a familiarity with the spirit of German instruction and discipline. Now it is impossible to change all that now.'[197]

This statement was also valid for the Ottoman arms purchases, especially the artillery. On 6 April 1905, the Ottoman government had signed a new contract with the Krupp company for 558 guns, for which it owed 1,967,634.37 OL (36,302,854 marks).[198] According to Grant, through this contract the Germans 'achieved their greatest sale'.[199] By 1906 the Germans became almost the only artillery supplier to the Ottoman Army. The military commission investigated the competing systems (French/Canet and German/Ehrhardt), visited the factories where they were being made, and came to a solid conclusion that the Krupp guns were perfect.[200] After writing favourably of the Krupp products, the commission – led by Hurşid Pasha – echoed Mahmud Şevket's statement, demonstrating the Germans' monopoly position in the Ottoman arms market. The commission pointed out that for a half-century the Ottoman artillery unit had been armed with the Krupp guns and in that time it had developed a familiarity with the Krupp weaponry; any change in the system, from the commission's point of view, might cause a disaster in a possible war.[201] As Mahmud Şevket said, 'now it is not possible to change.'[202]

Apart from the above-mentioned high-ranking military officers, the Sultan's secretaries, advisers and other officials at the Yıldız Palace also had a clear influence on the arms trade.[203] The Yıldız officials, particularly the Sultan's secretaries, who were selected by the Sultan himself, were the most influential among these others.[204] As Goltz wrote, 'the *Başkâtib*s [Chief Scribes] of the Sultan have in reality more influence on state affairs than the Grand Vizier' [and they] were 'best able to discover the snares and pitfalls which lurk under the surface, and this makes [them] indispensable.'[205] According to British Ambassador White, 'every Ministerial report [was] criticised and openly attacked by these persons before the Sultan, and as they [were] much nearer his presence than his Ministers they [had] greater facilities in working on his imagination or prejudices.'[206] Their influence on Ottoman administrative affairs was also noted by *The Times of India*, which wrote on 10 August 1908 that 'all real power was vested in the Sultan and his secretaries and under-secretaries.'[207]

The political importance of the secretaries is highlighted by the example of the most remarkable figures among them, the second secretary İzzet Bey, who was also called 'Arab İzzet', 'İzzet Holo', and 'İzzet Al 'Âbid'.[208] Some foreign observers identified him, after Sultan Abdülhamid himself, as the most interesting personality in the Ottoman Empire. He was also described as 'the avatar of the Hamidian system',[209] the 'Machiavelli of Turkey'[210] and 'the mouthpiece of the Sultan'.[211] As Farah points out, İzzet Bey was the Sultan's most trusted confidant during his 15 years of service in Yıldız Palace.[212] In fact, he acted as the Sultan's chief of advisers.[213] Sultan Abdülhamid made him a member of all commissions concerned with controlling and accounting for financial outlays; in particular, he was a critical member of the financial reform commission. Through these positions he was able to exert a visible influence on the empire's financial affairs, including the armament orders and their financing through foreign loans.[214] So having a close and good connection with İzzet Bey meant having an excellent conduit to the Sultan and the opportunity to affect him. The Germans, better than most nations, recognized the necessity of this close relationship; to quote from an official report written by the German ambassador to İstanbul: 'Because of his influence on the Baghdad railroad project, İzzet [Bey] is for us an indispensable man.'²¹⁵ Furthermore, Marschall described the information given by İzzet Bey as 'the most confidential [*höchst vertraulich*]'.²¹⁶ Mr Huber, the representative of Krupp and Mauser in İstanbul, corresponded directly with İzzet Bey. In one of his informative letters to İzzet Bey, he mentioned some information about the recommended prices and quantities of the cannons and rifles ordered from Krupp and Mauser.²¹⁷ Documentation proving İzzet Bey's direct intervention in the war business in favour of the Germans has not been found. However, Kössler asserts that the French armaments firms gave İzzet Bey more *baksheesh* than the Germans.²¹⁸

The manipulative power corrupt officials had and used to change the balance of the arms trade in favour of the GAFs was undeniable. However, some writers have overstated the role played by *baksheesh* traffic in the development and maintenance of relations between the German military mission and Ottoman officials.²¹⁹ In fact, the offering of bribes to Ottoman officers in order to open up the Ottoman market to the German arms industry and to guarantee business success might not have been a major concern of the German military missions. On the contrary, the arms makers had their own ways of establishing access, and there was more than one way to manipulate Ottoman officers. Other tactics might include a warm and friendly reception and generous hospitality during a visit, or small token gifts. Such simple instruments served to create considerable influence.²²⁰ The companies were aware that the first key to success in business in the Ottoman market might lie in the hands of Ottoman officers. Therefore, the arms makers concentrated assiduously on hospitality during visits by Ottoman military purchasing commissions to their factories and their cities, especially in Oberndorf/Neckar and in Essen.

As the Krupp Company had already settled into the Ottoman market and held the monopoly position in the Ottoman artillery supply since 1870s, most efforts by the German military advisers and their Ottoman connections were dedicated to a successful penetration of the Mauser rifles into the Ottoman small-arms market. Therefore, the case of the Mauser Company in the Ottoman market provides a comprehensive example of the impact of personal influence.²²¹ After obtaining his first major order in 1887, Mauser started to establish more personal relations with some Ottoman officials, as the Krupp Company had been doing since its first days in the Ottoman business.[222]

As already pointed out, the Sultan's secretaries were fully aware of the Sultan's inclination towards German-made weapons. For this reason, the reports and activities of Abdülhamid's private secretaries, and other secretaries are revealing. For instance, Süreyya Pasha's justifications and arguments cited below indicate the characteristics of this kind of report. The arguments in the report are based on roughly three points, which defended the German style of military organization and armament strategy. The report was an example of insider marketing of German-made military materials. It underlined the possibility of war in Europe and the political changes which would follow. Based on this approach, the *layiha* asserted that the reorganisation of the Ottoman Army and a new rearmament policy were essential:

> Across Europe the procurement of armaments is being carried out in an excessive way. According to the speeches given in the European parliaments and the contents of the newspapers, with respect to the current political development it is obvious that the dreadful wars that will take place are not far away. In order not to be unprepared, *Devlet-i 'Ali* [the Ottoman Empire] needs to begin an immediate procurement of the war materials.[223]

The second point of this report addressed the actual state of the Ottoman Army and the weapons in the army's possession. The writer's expressions were very negative about the existing weapons, which were provided by non-German companies, e.g. Henry-Martini, Snider and Winchester. According to the *tezkire*, the Ottoman Army's first and foremost need was to ensure that every soldier sent into battle had a rifle; this would involve arms purchases, to comply with the reforms introduced by Goltz Pasha, who had recommended changes in the recruitment system and an increase in the number of troops.[224] 'Since there are [in the hands of the Army] only 450,000 Martini rifles,' wrote

Süreyya Pasha, 'in the case of war breaking out, more rifle supply will be inevitable.' According to him, 'there would be no other alternative way than providing the soldiers with the useless Snider and Winchester rifles.'[225] To avoid this unsuitable situation, he suggested buying 550,000 new rifles and giving financial preference to spending on these rifles over any other expenses. After a sharp critique of the rifles made by non-German firms, the third argument concerned Germany's reputation as a military power and the quality of the rifles produced in Germany. According to the *lâyiha*, German military superiority was undisputed:

> Germany is regarded by authorities from everywhere as being superior to all other states in terms of military affairs and military supplies. After five–ten years of experience, Germany has adopted the Mauser repeating-rifles in preparation for an unprecedented war with France and distributes these rifles with the numbers of 500,000 to her soldiers with the intention of equipping its whole army with these rifles. According to the newspapers, however, the French Government, which is in the process of getting machines from America for the purpose of manufacturing the repeating-rifles, is fearful and in a rush due to Germany's possession of the Mauser rifles.[226]

Interestingly, Süreyya Pasha, in the following pages, advocated for the Mauser rifles while sharply abusing the other companies' representatives. Through these statements, the Sultan's bureaucrats reduced the burden borne by Mauser and his agent in marketing their rifles. The following statements, which were written and submitted to the Sultan one month before the contract was given to the Mauser company, were determined signs of the final decision in favour of the Mauser rifle. Süreyya Pasha, firstly, accused Azarian (alias *Bruder*),[227] the representative of an American factory in İstanbul, of engaging in several intrigues that were, according to Süreyya, well-known to everyone in İstanbul, and then he claimed further:

The same person [Azarian] who is the partner of an American commissioner, Mr. Hartley, submitted an offer made by Hartley to the Ministry of War saying that he [Hartley] could provide rifles the same as Mauser's or maybe better than Mauser's rifle for only 345 *Kuruş*. As a matter of fact, this [man] Hartley... was not a [armaments] producer but a simple commissioner, who has damaged the [Ottoman] state [treasury] at one time.[228]

According to Süreyya Pasha, the patent right owned by Mauser proved that Azarian's statement – that Hartley was able to produce the same rifle as Mauser – was definitely wrong. Thanks in part to Süreyya Pasha's strong arguments and lobbying on behalf of *Mösyö* Mauser, who met with Abdülhamid on 17 November 1886, just a month before this *lâyiha* was submitted to the Sultan,[229] the government placed an order for 500,000 rifles and 50,000 carbines with the Mauser Company on 9 February 1887.[230]

Another prominent figure at the Yıldız Palace was Ragıb Bey, who definitely deserves special mention here. Ragıb Bey, or 'Robert' as Menshausen called him, was one of the key personalities who made possible the information flow from the Sultan to the GAFs and vice versa.[231] Although Ragıb wrote in one of his *tezkire*s submitted to the Sultan that 'until today I have never worked for/served anyone other than *Efendimiz* [Abdülhamid II] and God willing [*inşâ'Allah*] henceforth I will never act dishonestly by serving for someone else [*namussuzluğuna irtikâb etmem*]',[232] his service to the Germans was remarkable and – as is indicated below – was praised by them several times. Ragıb Bey was, as British Ambassador White described, 'an active and enterprising Turk whom the Sultan liked'. He became very rich, especially from his enterprises in the mining industry, which provided him a good deal of revenue apart from the commissions he earned through his participation in several contracts.[233] Abdülhamid noted in his memoirs that Ragıb Bey also made some extraordinary speculative profits in the South African gold market on behalf of the Sultan.[234] At this time, the Sultan had set Ragıb Bey the task of dissuading Goltz Pasha from his decision to leave Ottoman service. According to the Austrian military attaché in İstanbul, Joseph von

Manéga, Ragıb Bey met with Goltz Pasha almost every day trying to change his mind.[235] In foreign diplomatic circles Ragıb Bey was infamously known as a person who took every opportunity to fill his own pockets[236] and who was extremely corrupt.[237]

During the course of time, as the German firms came to realise his enterprising character and his power and influence in the Yıldız Palace, they tried to establish friendly relationships with him. Ragıb reciprocated and began corresponding directly with Paul Mauser, who introduced his newly-developed rifles to the Ottoman government in November 1886. To provide an accurate insight into the dimension of personal ties in the war business, the following words of Ragıb Bey, written in a letter to Paul Mauser, are very telling: 'Please accept my apology that I have not written to you until now. But be assured that I always remember you. It is unnecessary to say that I have the greatest respect for you. Your heart [kindness] has bound me and I hope you believe the words of a man with whom you have interacted for months.'[238] What Ragıb meant by 'having interacted for months' is not clear from this letter, but it can be assumed that during the negotiations they built up a close relationship, through which Paul Mauser could obtain crucial information about the Sultan's concerns related to the rifles that were being tested. Based on their closeness, as Sir William White wrote, it was generally believed that Ragıb received gratuities from the Mauser Company.[239]

Krupp's agent, Menshausen, described Ragıb Bey as 'the only friend of the Triple Alliance'[240] and the Krupp firm at the Yıldız Palace.[241] As the Operation 1891 shows, Ragıb Bey intervened in the negotiations in favour of German interests. In fact, as both Goltz Pasha and Menshausen also admitted, Ragıb's contribution to the German war business in the Ottoman market was much more essential and obvious than the contribution of the German ambassador, Radowitz.[242] Therefore, the expression used by Marschall for Osman Nizami could also apply to Ragıb Bey, who demonstrated by his pro-German sentiments and actions that he deserved to be called 'more German than Turkish'. Like the other pro-German officials, he also used 'his whole influence in order to make Germany the unique supplier for all Turkish arms orders'.[243] According to Menshausen's letter to Krupp, if they wanted to accomplish a desired result through Ragıb Bey's intervention, the support of the German ambassador was indispensable. An Ottoman bureaucrat was fighting to ensure things went Germany's way, whereas their ambassador was disregarding the importance of obtaining armaments contracts.[244] As Menshausen noted, Radowitz's disinterest in Krupp's interests could endanger the full support of Ragıb Bey, who was 'the only influential contact of the Krupp Company at the Yıldız Palace'.[245]

The Germans understood that information about the Sultan's approach, intentions, and decisions could best be obtained with Ragıb Bey's help. On the day following Goltz's audience with the Sultan on 16 December 1891, when Goltz Pasha relayed the Kaiser's trenchant statement regarding the Sultan's intention to place an order with French gun and ship makers at the expense of the Krupp Company, Menshausen paid a visit to Ragıb Bey in his private residence at 3 am. Menshausen's aim was simple: to get reliable information about the Sultan's reactions to the Kaiser's severe statement and to discover the nature of any possible guns or ship orders. As expected, Ragıb gave detailed information concerning these questions.[246] Based on the information Ragıb Bey provided, Menshausen noted the Sultan's first reaction as follows: 'The information provided by Goltz Pasha put the Sultan in most embarrassment [...] [Sultan Abdülhamid] tried to apologize to all directions, [the Sultan] said that so far nothing had happened... Under no circumstances he would move politically to the French [geçmeyeceğim].[247] Ragıb Bey was also Goltz Pasha's source of information.[248] The expression Goltz Pasha used was similar to Menshausen's. In his report, dated 23 December 1891, based on both his own observation and the information provided by Ragıb Bey Goltz Pasha described Sultan Abdülhamid's feelings and reactions after hearing the Kaiser's response: '... the Sultan was embarrassed during the audience itself, and helpless in the next two days.'[249]

The Sultan had established a strong spy system,[250] so it was not difficult to keep track of his secretaries' doings. It was even speculated that he might have used his secretaries' personal relations with certain countries and companies as manipulative instruments for his own purposes. According to Menshausen's letter, Sultan Abdülhamid was well aware of Ragıb's doings in favour of Germany. 'It is also important to mention,' wrote Menshausen: that '... the Sultan told Robert [Ragıb Bey] that everyone around him was for the French and worked for their interest, while he alone was operating for German interest. Robert [Ragıb Bey] responded with great dexterity that he was not working for Germany but for Turkey and that he was, in fact, standing alone with this.'[251] In short, Ragıb Bey and the other palace officials played an effective role in the arms trade negotiation and purchasing process. According to Mahmud Muhtar Pasha, who was the Commander of the First Army Corps in 1908, all money used for the purpose of bribery had gone to palace officials who had assisted the entry of German-made war materials into the Ottoman arms market.[252] The Germans expertly exploited their penchant for accepting bribes, as well as their critical positions as facilitators of the information flow from the Sultan to the GAFs.

The Ottoman Inspection and Control Commission in Germany: Inspectors or Friends?

Following the agreement signed between the Ottoman government and the Mauser Company on 9 February 1887 for 500,000 rifles and 50,000 carbines, the first group of the Ottoman inspection and control commission – consisting of six officers – arrived at Oberndorf, where Mauser had its headquarters, on 11 March 1887.[253] Paul Mauser met the Ottoman delegation at Stuttgart train station and they travelled together on another train to Oberndorf, where he hosted a lavish dinner for them. The local newspaper, *Schwarzwälder Bote*, which published several accounts of the commission members' stay in Oberndorf, welcomed them: 'May the gentlemen from the far off Golden Horn be well in our little town of Schwarzwald and may their task benefit our region.'[254] Following this first group, another 13 officers plus a child aged 13, a relative of one of the commission members, came to Oberndorf on 9 September

1887.²⁵⁵ The first group was headed by Tevfik Pasha, who was later replaced by Mahmud Şevket Pasha.²⁵⁶

As has been stated, the Ottoman Army became the first army to be equipped with the Mauser rifle in large numbers.²⁵⁷ The contract had a value of about 37 million marks, which represented a very good start for the factory. However, Mauser had reason to expect further lucrative orders from the Ottoman Empire. The existence of the German Military Mission and its patronage was likely to guarantee the sustainability of the orders. Paul Mauser realised that the Ottoman Empire could be a steady and loyal customer, whose satisfaction was of vital importance to him. With that in mind, in March 1887 Mauser commissioned the construction of a special residence and headquarters for the Ottoman officers; called the *Türkenbau* (Turkish Building), it was located near the factory site.

The *Türkenbau* was another clear demonstration of the German approach to the war business in the Ottoman Empire. It enabled Mauser to strengthen his customers' loyalty. Although another country's flags sometime waved on the roof of the *Türkenbau*, the

Image 5.1 *Türkenbau* in Oberndorf am Neckar built in 1887
Source: SA, Oberndorf: 793.32/13.1 Mauser Werke/Türkenzeit.

Ottomans — whose number fluctuated between 20 and 30 — knew that there was a Turkish-named residence in Oberndorf where they could stay as long as they needed to.[258] That was naturally a strategic advantage for Mauser's likelihood of winning future contracts. The *Türkenbau* enabled the Ottomans to stay much longer during the manufacturing process, during which careful investigation was necessary. Later on, 30 young volunteer cadets who went to Oberndorf in March 1895 to be trained in the Mauser factory also resided in the *Türkenbau*.[259]

Schmid wrote that 'The Turkish officers and volunteers have quickly acclimated in Oberndorf and took an active part in the daily life of the town, and so the festivities in Oberndorf took on a colourful character.'[260] In fact, over time, some of the Ottoman officers started families in Oberndorf and had children born there, while others died and were buried there.[261] For instance, İbrahim Bey, who arrived in Oberndorf on 9 September 1887 with the second group of the first committee, died on 3 September 1888, and was buried in Oberndorf.[262]

Image 5.2 Turkish Young Volunteers in *Türkenbau* in Oberndorf am Neckar
Source: SA, Oberndorf: 793.32/13.1 Mauser Werke/Türkenzeit.

Image 5.3 Playing Cards in the Pavillion Rosenberg/Oberndorf am Neckar (c.1893)
Shown from left to right: Ottoman Major Azmi; standing: Ottoman Colonel Zeki; Magistrate (*Amtsrichter*) Jahn; Magistrate Abek; Secretary Schmidheini.
Source: SA, Oberndorf:793.32/13.1 Mauser Werke/Türkenzeit.

The first commission inspected the manufacturing and delivery process of the following models: M/1887: cal. 9.50 mm; M/1890: cal.7.65 mm; M/1893: cal.7.65 mm. They stayed in Oberndorf for nearly ten years and supervised the delivery of 550 rail wagon-loads of rifles to İstanbul.[263] According to Seel, the last three members of the first commission left Oberndorf on 15 May 1897. Two of them had been among the first group that arrived on 11 March 1887. On 2 June 1897, Hüseyin Hüsni Bey, the last Ottoman officer of the first commission to Oberndorf, departed.[264] After five years, on 23 April 1903, another commission led by Hüseyin Tevfik came to Oberndorf to inspect and supervise the manufacturing process of 200,000 newly ordered rifles (M/1903: cal. 7.65mm).[265] Paul Mauser and the town's notable figures, who were already aware of the importance of the Ottoman orders to Oberndorf's economic life, developed close relations with the members of the Ottoman commissions. As Image 5.3 demonstrates, the duration of the officers' stay in Oberndorf enabled them to develop personal ties with Mauser and the local elites. Abdülhamid's accession to the throne and his birthday were formally recognized and celebrated in Oberndorf, and the Ottoman officers joined in the celebrations to mark those events. In 1894 for instance, according to Şakir Pasha's report, in honour of the anniversary of Sultan Abdülhamid's accession to the throne, the Mauser Company organized a firing competition.[266]

The Germans realised that the Ottoman arms market was not just lucrative, but also highly competitive. To ensure success, they employed every known marketing strategy and instrument. They transformed every relevant event or occasion into an opportunity to win potential or existing customers' hearts. Donations to worthy causes was another marketing tool the Germans used to gain Ottoman public support. In 1893, for instance, through the mediation of the Ottoman delegation in Oberndorf, the Mauser factory workers donated 250 OL (4,612 marks) to the Ottoman *Dar-ül 'aceze* (Poorhouse)[267] and later on, as the *Sabah* newspaper reported, the workers gave 472 OL (8,708 marks) to help the victims of the 1894 İstanbul earthquake.[268]

The methods employed by the Mauser Company had already been in use by Krupp for many years. Krupp developed, as Sater and Herwig wrote, 'a complex protocol [to] cultivate potential customers'.[269] These kinds of marketing instruments acquired vogue among the German arms makers during that time. The German arms marketing strategy applied to the Ottoman Empire was essentially the same as those used for some Latin American countries such as Argentina, Brazil, Mexico and Chile, and even other Middle Eastern and North African countries.[270] As a result, the GAFs gained a monopoly position in both markets through the application of the same tools and methods. Furthermore, the arms trade's encouragement of closer mutual economic–political relations transpired in both locations. The similarities are such that scholars who focus on German interests in Latin America use almost the same language, concepts and arguments as those who deal with German–Ottoman relations in the same period.[271] Both groups of scholars agree that there was a complex and multidimensional interrelationship between the military advisers, arms makers and political actors, a dynamic that can be described with the concept of the German Style of War Business. However, my research shows that the Ottoman arms market was one of the first markets where this type of German strategy was applied. According to Sater and Herwig, Krupp developed a complex protocol to attract potential – customers from South America. In the case of selling to the Chilean Army, Sater and Herwig give the following detailed information about the protocol, which was used beneficially by Krupp as a simple marketing strategy to gain customers:

> The company [Krupp] wined and dined foreign officers and local military attachés... Krupp literally rolled out the red carpet for those foreigners... who came to Germany to pick up orders. These buyers received the best of treatment: tours of the Rhine, the Harz Mountains, and Berlin. Chilean officers visited Krupp's mansion, the Villa Hügel at Essen-Bredeney, where they dined on Chilean national dishes and consumed its wine. On such occasions, Chilean flags were flown on the grounds of the mansion and were placed at each setting in the dining hall.[272]

The Ottoman purchasing commissions and visiting delegations were always welcomed as guests of honour. In the same way that the officers in Oberndorf became close with their hosts, the Ottoman officers who stayed in the Villa Hügel in Essen became good friends with Herr Krupp and his family. For instance, Sabit Pasha, who visited Germany in 1879, 1885, 1888 and 1891,[273] was one of the prominent figures who became a 'personal friend' of F. A. Krupp and his family. The exchange of photographs between F. A. Krupp and Sabit Pasha also deserves mention. After receiving the photos, Sabit Pasha wrote a letter of thanks to Herr Krupp for the dispatch.[274] The dates on which the photo exchange took place were critical for the finalization of contracts with the Krupp Company. In one letter sent to F. A. Krupp in December 1885, months after the Ottomans had placed a large order with the Krupp factory, Sabit Pasha expressed his pleasure at being Herr Krupp's 'personal friend', and he continued:

The warm welcomes with which you have received me both in 1879 as well as today have filled me with sincere appreciation... I feel and remember your kindness, especially at the thought that I will have to reside at my current location for a long time to receive the delivery of the currently manufactured large number of guns... As a faint sign of my gratitude and admiration please kindly accept the enclosed two photographs of me. The bigger one with frames I ask you to kindly hang in your office, as I send it not as a luxury but rather as a sign of sincere friendship.[275]

This was the same Sabit Pasha who had been sent to France as the head of a purchasing commission to inspect the French gun factories and get reliable information about the French firms' prices and the quality of their products. While Sabit Pasha was in France carrying out his assigned tasks, he telegraphed Ali Saib Pasha with a report on his negotiations and inspections in the French artillery factories in Paris and Le Havre. Ali Saib Pasha informed the Sultan about Sabit Pasha's message, which included a claim that Canet's factory did not have a polygon for firing tests.[276] However, it appears that Sabit Pasha and his delegation did not consider it worthwhile to wait for the results of Mr Canet's experiments. This lack of esteem for Canet's production was not based on technical failure. Evidently, the purchasing commission was conscious of the Sultan's preference for Krupp productions before any French-made artillery. It is probable, then, that based on this awareness, Sabit Pasha and his companions were keen to go to Essen to see Sabit Pasha's 'very close friend [*liebster freund*]' F. A. Krupp and his products.[277] This short French visit and its consequences were reported to Carl Menshausen by Goltz Pasha. According to him, the major reason why Sabit Pasha cut his French visit short was his consciousness of the superiority of the German-made guns. As the following passage indicates, Goltz Pasha also wrote:

> Although the same alleged that Sabit Pasha himself reported to the War Minister saying that he left France during the first visit only because Canet did not have a polygon, not because they

Table 5.1 The Technical Comparison of the World's Major Contenders/Gun Producers (1889)

	France*	British	German	Russian	United States
Weight of gun/pounds	9,532	11,200	9,048	9,114	10,192
Lengthy of gun/inches	212	192	176	140	196
Weight of projectile/pounds	88	100	112	86	100
Weight of charge/pounds	42	42	33	18	50
Muzzle velocity/feet per second	2,165	1,920	1,624	1,463	2,105
Muzzle energy/foot per tons	2,841	2,556	2,055	1,276	3,072
Muzzle penetration of iron/inches	12.3	12.1	11.0	8.4	13.4

*The Canet factory in France.
Source: *The New York Times*: 27.10.1889.

did not have any heavy (for the program-suitable) guns, it appeared to me however that even [Sabit Pasha] reached the conclusion that France could for the time being not compete with Germany in the field of gun production.[278]

While the Ottoman purchasing commission did not consider it worthwhile to wait for the firing results for another customer (Japan) at Canet's factory, Canet was, according *The New York Times*, 'a formidable continental rival of the Krupp factory'.[279] According to the newspaper:

> The factory occupied a large plot of land... which affords space for the future extension of the works, on the west by the company's old machinery and shipbuilding workshops... Connected with the factory, but nearly four miles from the town, is the proving ground, which is known as the Hoc. Here are four firing platforms situated on the seashore and used for high-angle firing. Above the platforms runs an overhead travelling crane, which can raise and carry a weight of eight tons, and the whole ground is covered with a network of railways, for which a specially massive plant of engines and trucks has been built... there is no better found or more convenient proving ground in the world than the Hoc.[280]

The article also gave table (see Table 5.1) comparing the technical details of the productions of the main artillery suppliers in different countries.

From the perspective of Sabit Pasha and other Ottoman officers, the technical features were not the first priority when it came to making decisions about the arms trade. Sabit Pasha's report, which apparently contradicted *The New York Times*' information, was a reflection of the personal opinion of an officer who had close connections with the German gun maker Krupp. Sabit Pasha paid another visit to Essen in 1902, during which he fell ill and was treated in Germany.[281] During this treatment, F. A. Krupp covered the entire cost of his treatment, which was paid back by the Ottoman government in the years following his death in Germany.[282]

Briefly, the German Style of War Businesses was mostly shaped by decision makers' personal influences, which were deliberately developed through direct relationships that could be manipulated by personal satisfaction or dissatisfaction. Goltz Pasha, who was well aware of this fact, suggested that the allocation of supplies for the Ottoman Army was not decided through objective means, but instead through personal influence. Inevitably the question arises, what happened when the above-mentioned personalities lost their position and the power shift occurred and how did the Germans reacted to this change correspondingly? The next chapter deals with these vital questions.

CHAPTER 6

THE POWER SHIFT AND ITS CONSEQUENCES (1908–14)

'We have no eternal allies, and we have no perpetual enemies. Our interests are eternal and perpetual...'
Lord Palmerston, 1 March 1848

The First Episode: The Old Regime and the Old Friend (1908–9)

'The old regime had not only deprived us of our liberty but also of what is equally important – British friendship [...] Long live the great British nation!'
Talat Pasha, London, 22 July 1909[1]

On 24 July 1908, Abdülhamid II proclaimed the re-establishment of the Constitution of 1876, which was suspended by the Sultan himself in 1878. In fact, the proclamation of the Constitution was a forced consequence of several rebellious uprisings in the Third Army and in some Ottoman Balkan cities, which joined in protest against Sultan Abdülhamid's system of governance. This so-called revolution led by an exiled group of political liberals and mostly educated in France and England prompted the Sultan to concede the re-establishment of the Constitution.[2] However, when the Constitution was declared in 1908, the Germans became anxious about maintaining the position they had held since the 1880s, when Bismarck had praised the Sultan's decision to abolish the parliament due to the ethnic diversity of Ottoman society.[3]

It was widely expected that this swift and almost radical change in the Ottoman ruling and decision-making system, from which the Germans had enormously benefited for almost 30 years, would place the Ottoman–German relationship in jeopardy.[4] Because Germany enjoyed the support of the Sultan and his bureaucrats at Yıldız Palace, the attack on Yıldız's authority seemed to threaten the many personal ties with Germany and the GAFs in the Ottoman Empire. For instance, Fairfax L. Cartwright, who later became British ambassador to the Austria–Hungarian Empire before World War I, pointed out the impact of the close relationship between the Kaiser and the Sultan on Germany's strong position in the Ottoman Empire, as follows:

> If in any sense of the world one can talk of a political influence exercised by Germany in Turkey, this influence is merely due to the confidence which the Sultan has in the personality of the Kaiser, and the prestige which the German army generally enjoys among the governing classes in Turkey, a prestige which is so great that it overcomes even the intrigues which are rampant at *Yıldız* Kiosk.[5]

As a consequence of such an approach, a blow for the Sultan came to be regarded as a simultaneous blow to Germany's influence in the Ottoman Empire. The Germans' successful entrepreneurship was reliant on governmental support and guarantees. The strong foundation of the German penetration of the Ottoman market notwithstanding, the position seemed vulnerable to any shift in the balance of power within the Empire. In 1907, for instance, an article based on an interview with an 'anti-Abdülhamid official in İstanbul', published in an Indian newspaper that was characterized by the German Ambassador to Simla as pro-British, indicates the fragility of the Germans' influence in the Ottoman Empire: 'As to the fate of the present Yıldız gang there will be a clean sweep of them. Many will be killed like dogs, others expelled from the Empire, and within twenty-four hours there will not be a German official in the country... England has but to lift her little finger and we would expel every German from Constantinople tomorrow and install her in her old position.'[6] The Belgian ambassador at Berlin, Baron Beyes, reached a similar conclusion too: 'The fall of absolutism at Constantinople was in itself a serious blow to German influence there, which was based upon Abdülhamid II's friendship.'[7]

Subsequently, this power shift became a test for the durability of the German method. In accumulation of future events, however, it is not accurate to say that German influence ended with this power shift. The Germans had invested wisely to cultivate the Ottoman market; they reaped the benefits even after the power shift until World War I. Since the leading military staff of the new ruling class had been educated and trained under the German military system and doctrines, the Committee of Union and Progress (CUP) (İttihat ve Terakki Cemiyeti) continued to maintain a close relationship with Germany and purchased large quantities of German-made rifles and guns. The German military advisers remained in the Ottoman service. Kiderlen sent a telegraph to Bülow informing him of current circumstances in İstanbul after the Sultan's dethronement: 'It is stated in the press and, as I understand from a report sent to me from the Imperial ambassador in Vienna, also commonly believed that the Young Turk movement is pro-English and anti-German. This is a grave mistake [irrtum].'[8] Kiderlen was correct in his conclusion. The actual situation was better summazised by the later German ambassador to İstanbul, Wangenheim, who said that: 'The power which controls the army in Turkey will be supreme. As long as we control the army, no anti-German government can long remain in power.'[9] Kaiser Wilhelm was also convinced that both Abdülhamid's presence as the Sultan and the German-trained military officers as the leading figures in the army would secure Germany's position in the Ottoman Empire. Claiming to take credit for the 'military revolution' led by the so-called 'Action Army [Hareket Ordusu]' composed of military units from the Third Army and some volunteers coming from different ethnic groups in the Empire's Balkan provinces,[10] Kaiser Wilhelm was of the opinion that 'the revolution was not led by the "Young Turks" out of Paris and London, but rather by the army alone, and naturally by the so-called "German Officers" trained in Germany: a pure military revolution. These officers are at the helm and are absolutely on Germany's side.'[11] The new government's subsequent decisions concerning some political and military issues suggested the Kaiser was right.

As a matter of truth, there was no reason for the German government to get so frustrated at not having 'influential friends' among the leaders of the newly established regime; on the contrary, the vast majority of the military wing of the CUP were looking at Germany with a proven loyalty that would later provide the asset, strength and also perseverance essential to establish German–Ottoman war alliance. Wangenheim was right, when he wrote in 1912 that the majority of the Ottoman officers still believe 'in the absolute superiority of [Germany's] military capabilities'.[12]

So it was quite premature for Pears and *The Times of India* newspaper in August 1908 to declare that: 'It is, of course, no longer true that Turkey looks on Germany with a friendly eye. Young Turkey is enthusiastic for the Western Powers and especially for England. Germany's influence for the present has suffered a quite remarkable eclipse.'[13] The commentator was clearly misled by Sultan Abdülhamid's loss of power, which had – as the writer contended – a strong link with the German success. 'The collapse of the Camarilla,' noted the writer 'brings down the whole edifice of German designs in the Near and Middle East like a pack of cards... The foundations of German influence have been swept away. It is not Marschall von Bieberstein, who so long dominated the Ambassador at İstanbul, who is hailed as the patron of the new regime, but Sir Gerald Lowther, the British representative.'[14] However, two years later, in July 1910, Sir Gerald admitted that such predictions had been premature:

> The early days of the Constitution were marked by considerable enthusiasm for Great Britain and France, the former owing to

the fact that we stood before the world as the representatives par excellence of constitutional government and because we had been the stoutest opponents of the hated Hamidian regime, the French because it was in their country that prominent Young Turks, like Ahmed Rıza [...] had found a refuge and a congenial atmosphere for developing their plans [...] In the initial stages of the constitutional government Germany, thanks to her very intimate connection with Abdülhamid, was looked upon with some suspicion by the civilian elements of population, but the administration of the army, which has necessarily been the backbone of the movement, and on which it must continue to rely, is as deep as ever. A very large number of Turkish officers have been educated in Germany, and the military organisation of that country appeals warmly to them [...] The Turks think, rightly or wrongly, that Germany has at any rate in the near future no political designs in this country and that her aspirations are purely commercial [...][15]

The German arms industry, especially the Krupp Company, had obviously been apprehensive about their future business. After the Young Turks came to power in 1908, there was initial discord between the new regime and the previously favoured German arms companies, Mauser and Krupp, which had prospered thanks to the support of Abdülhamid and his palace officials. Mahmud Muhtar Pasha told the British Ambassador, Lowther, on 8 December 1908, that the new Ottoman Government had called on Huber to supply it with 'a list of names of all those who under the old regime had taken bribes in return for orders, and implied that unless this list was forthcoming no further orders would be given to Krupp'.[16] If what Mahmud Muhtar Pasha told the ambassador was true, such an exchange might have taken place successfully, because Krupp had regained its old position sooner than expected.

The new regime found itself caught in a predetermined format of relationships between Germany and the Ottoman Empire. These relationships had been mostly shaped by military officers educated in Germany or according to a German military doctrine inculcated in the Ottoman Army, particularly by Goltz Pasha. One of the most telling statements concerning the continuity of German influence in the Ottoman military administration and in the war business was made in 1908 by Marschall, who said: 'Today, the War Minister, the Undersecretary of the Ministry of War, Chief of General Staff, the commanders of the Guards Corps and other important commands are in the hands of the officers who have served in Germany.'[17] These optimistic statements made by the Germans were conditioned by Abdülhamid's existence as the Sultan. Ironically, however, on 27 April 1909, 'the German officers' as the Kaiser called them, pulled off the overthrow of the Kaiser's personal friend: Sultan Abdülhamid II.

The Second Episode: The New Regime and the Old Friend (1909–14)

'Now we cannot salvage ourselves from the German style of war [application].
Now it is impossible to change all that.'
Mahmud Şevket Pasha (1911–12)[18]

On the very same day of his dethronement by the Young Turks' army, which was called by Goltz's best cadet Mahmud Şevket 'the guardians of freedom',[19] Sultan Abdülhamid was exiled to Salonika 'in a mad hurry'.[20] 'Soon after' noted Marschall von Bieberstein, 'the Sultan's palace [Yıldız Palace] was ransacked by an amount of the Young Turks for money, jewellery, and also for some classified papers'.[21] While this was happening, the Germans in their anxiety were just waiting for what would happen next. Huber, the Krupp's agent who might have supplied the new governing authorities with 'a list of names of all those who under the old regime had taken bribes in return for orders'[22] had already reasons to be worried for his future armaments contracts; Marschall was paying careful attention to any information coming from Yıldız Palace and also was watching closely the activities of the representatives of other Great Powers. As McGarity wrote, Marschall accepted the new situation 'with masterly grace and set about repairing Germany's position with uncommon political acumen'.[23]

In August, three months after Abdülhamid's exile to Salonika, Marschall described the old regime as a regime 'in which the entire state power concentrated on one man, who in his nervous and anxious character could not resist against even tiny pressure coming from abroad [*der in seiner nervösen und ängstlichen Eigenart jedem Fingerdruck von Aussen nachgab*]'.[24] Marschall's written sentiment about the new regime was also noteworthy. According to him, the new regime was constituted of young and inexperienced people who were, as a result of the continuing banishments of foreign countries, arrogant and pathologically nationalist. Therefore, he suggested that these young people must be treated pathologically.[25] Through this dethronement, according to Marschall's consideration, the power had shifted from a 'paranoid' and 'coward' Sultan to the inexperienced young people with some pathologic problems.[26] Fortunately for Germany, however, immediately after this power shift, in May 1909, German-trained members of the older generation of the revolutionary group lead by Mahmud Şevket requested a new military mission from Germany.[27] Following the official invitation made by the new Sultan, Mehmed Reşad V (1844–1918), on 16 May 1909, Kaiser Wilhelm II asked Goltz Pasha to embark on that project accordingly.[28] Goltz Pasha was regarded a hero for everyone 'under the old regime' and had almost a quasi-spiritual and charismatic influence on the military wing of the leaders of these 'pathologically nationalist young people' who deposed the 'paranoid' Sultan. It was so overt that after all this turmoil the only losers were Sultan Abdülhamid II and his first circle men, most of whom were infamously known as corrupt and 'German tools'. The others gained their previous status sooner or later. On 12 July 1909 Goltz arrived in İstanbul almost like a spiritual leader of the revolution for serving four months a year in the Ottoman army, so that within months Goltz Pasha became the vice-president of the Supreme Military Court (Mühim Askeri İşler Meclisi) that was established at the War Ministry on 14 August 1909.[29] It was so clear that from the standpoint of Germany, things began gradually slotting into place.

As highlighted in the previous chapters, Germany's successful war business, especially Krupp and Mauser's monopoly in the Ottoman market, was firmly indebted to Sultan Abdülhamid for his support. It was very clear that the Ottoman arms market, without this sole and potent decision maker, would become more competitive for German companies. At least price, quality, or technical features of competing war materials, which were seemingly not as decisive as they deserved to be during the old regime, would be among the major topics of the negotiation process. Henceforth the process would be a bit longer and more challenging. With this regard, a premonitory remark came from Mauser and Krupp's highly experienced agent August Huber. On 10 November 1909, in his letter to Paul Mauser, he acknowledged the new era as follows: 'The monopoly, which we conquered [*eroberten*] together with you [Paul Mauser] after severe fighting in 1886 and which we were able to hold it for 23 years, had [now] been broken.'[30] In the following circumstances, Huber's anxiety was quite justifiable. In July 1910, when the Ottoman government decided to purchase more than 100,000 rifles, Major Mahmoud Fethi, who was also a member of the second and third Ottoman purchasing commission sent to Oberndorf in 1903 and 1908[31], was appointed to pay several visits to the European rifle companies, including Paul Mauser's factories in Oberndorf. In the meantime, however, Major Mahmud Fethi, informing the Mauser Company about his proposed visit to the factory, particularly emphasized that he would not make any deal with the Company's Istanbul agents, Huber Brothers.[32]

When Mahmoud Fethi was still in Europe the Ottoman War Ministry did shooting trials in which the Mauser pistol was competing with the Browning. On 9 August 1910, Huber informed Paul Mauser that the Browning pistol won this competition and got priority.[33] Four days after that disappointing news, on 13 August, Huber sent another letter giving the technical detail of the trial and based on his perceptions (*Wahrnehmungen*) he remarked that it would be pointless to attempt further efforts to try to change the decision made at the expense of the Mauser pistols. He suggested they abandon their hopes on this contract and that he considered the process as 'done'.[34] Huber perceived that any kind of pressure, which used to work very well in the old days, would be unavailing. However as the future events mentioned in the following pages show, this attitude towards Huber Brothers directly and towards the Mauser Company indirectly seemed to be provisional and cannot be regarded as a generally accepted approach towards German military industry.

Keeping their options open with the French, as Grant notes, the Young Turks preferred German arms makers for their armaments order.[35] On 22 September 1909, Mahmud Sevket Pasha was in Düsseldorf to visit Rheinische Metallwaaren-und Maschinenfabrik of Heinrich Ehrhardt, Krupp's most prominent rival from his own country.[36] According to Ehrhardt's agent in İstanbul, as reported by the British military attaché Surtees in December 1908, because his firm (Ehrhardt) was in sympathy with the 'Constitutional Party' in Germany, 'he received the good-will of the members of the Young Turkish party, who have been delighted to place orders independently and without having their hands tied by the receipt of orders from the Palace to give the business to [the] Krupp [company]'.[37] In fact, the process of finalization of negotiations for this contract for a large supply of field and mountain artillery ammunition was more complex than that the firm's agent indicated. The key factor behind that success was not their political position but the price they offered. As this instance illustrates, after a long time of ineffectiveness, ultimately the price as a functioning factor began to play its essential role in the process of an arms contract.[38] In order to distinguish how the above-argued change in the process of armament contracts took place, the following quotation from the Ottoman Grand Master of Artillery, which was translated by the British foreign office for the use of Sir Edward Grey who was in contact with J. M. Falkner of Armstrong Company, is illuminating especially for how the process was carried out:

> During the last week the first minimum price having been offered by the firm of Krupp, the other manufacturers were asked in their turn to make offers. Armstrong's representative then made a sealed tender offering a reduction of [OL] 6,000;

THE POWER SHIFT AND ITS CONSEQUENCES (1908–1914) 239

and, in conformity with established customs, the 'Grand Master of Artillery' asked the other manufacturers to make reductions. Some Austrian manufacturers gave up the contest. The German firm of Ehrhardt made a reduction of [OL] 9,000, while the firms of Armstrong and Krupp sent in a declaration signed by their representatives that they could not make any further reduction on their last offers. Therefore the orders in question were left with the firm of Ehrhardt at the price of [OL] 316,000. Subsequently, Krupp's representative having offered a reduction of 5 per cent on the forementioned sum, and this offer being in conformity with established custom, this new reduction by Krupp was accepted, and tenders were again called for [...] as proposed by Armstrong's representative, the tenders were to be made under seal and no new reduction beyond them was to be accepted. This decision was communicated to the representatives of the arms manufacturers and published in the newspapers. On November 28th, in the presence of the 'Grand Master of Artillery' and of all the representatives, the conditions laid down with regard to the tenders were read again, and the lowest price called for. The sealed tenders were opened one at a time, and each representative signed the table on which he had himself written down his price. The result was that Armstrong offered [OL] 319,000; Krupp [OL] 300,200; Schneider [OL] 299,000; Coventry Ordnance [OL] 290,000; Ehrhardt [OL] 277,700. Consequently, the orders in question were awarded to the firm of Ehrhardt.[39]

So although the Krupp Company lost its position for a while, its fellow countryman, the Ehrhardt Company, carrying the German name, remained successfully in the race. Moreover, as Mahmud Fethi Bey's above-mentioned letter reveals, where one of the German companies explicitly lost their previous monopoly of power to penetrate the decision makers' circle and manipulate the purchasing process, the Ottoman government was still ready and willing to make the arms deal with German companies. Although it seems that the good old days were over for the Krupp Company, the Krupp name was still on the Ottoman government's suppliers list. At least for artillery, the Krupp Company protected its market share against its rivals for several more years. In August 1909, Lewis D. Einstein, the chargé d'affaires at the American embassy in Istanbul, described the fact in a clear manner. 'In view of the fact' wrote Lewis 'that all the material for the Turkish artillery has come from Krupp, it is unlikely that any change will now be made in future orders for similar supplies'.[40] He had been proved correct; in 1910, after a two-year break, a contract for the 106 guns (90 field guns and 16 naval guns) was awarded to the Krupp Company.[41] In 1911, again, Krupp signed a new agreement to provide the Ottoman army with 88 field guns and two mountain howitzers.[42] In addition to these orders, in 1911 the Ottoman government placed another order for the 680,000 rifle sight-covers from another German Company.[43]

While the Young Turks government continued to increase the Empire's military strength through new armament contracts, on 29 September 1911, Italy declared war on the Ottoman Empire.[44] From the very first days of the war, from 30 September 1911 to late February 1912, Italian warships sank three Ottoman torpedo boats bought during the reign of Abdülhamid from the Ansaldo shipyard, in Italy (*Hamidiye, Alpagot* and *Ankara*), six gunboats, an armoured corvette *Avnillah*, and six lighters.[45] In addition to its military, political and territorial costs, the financial outcomes of this war were also put the Empire in a detrimental situation. According to Beehler, during the middle of June 1912, to finance the battle against Italy, the Ottoman government was forced to decree some extra war taxes that increased income tax, ground tax and industrial tax (25 per cent), and the military exemption tax.[46] The Italia–Ottoman War revealed the delicacy of the Ottoman defence capacity that might encourage the Balkan states to unify and wage war on the weakened Ottoman Empire even before the Italia–Ottoman war ended in October 1912. On 8 October 1912 the Balkan states, including Bulgaria, Greece, Serbia and Montenegro, declared war on the financially collapsed, militarily demoralized and tired Ottoman Empire.[47] At the end of the First Balkan War the Ottoman Army was, as Erickson points out, decisively defeated in detail. According to him, 'unable to achieve the necessary mass, portions of their armies were isolated and beaten in widely separated campaigns'.[48] During the First Balkan War, the Ottoman Empire lost almost its entire territory on the European continent. Following the lost counter-attack of the Ottoman forces, the Bulgarian Army succeeded to occupy the old capital city of the Empire: Edirne. In addition to these territorial losses, much of the recently bought military equipment were also captured or destroyed by the Balkan States. The Second Balkan War, nonetheless, gave the Ottomans the opportunity to regain some lost territories, including Edirne.

The defeat in the First Balkan War was regarded as a disaster for both the Ottoman military forces and also for the German system and equipment applied by the Ottomans.[49] According to the Germans, however, the reason of this defeat was the Turkish officers' ineffectiveness and unprofessional attitudes during the battles.[50] In November 1912, the *New York Times* published an interview with an unnamed 'officer of Kaiser's Army' under the title of 'French guns proved better than German'. The conclusion of this interview was simple: The war proved the superiority of the French Creusots guns over the German Krupp's employed by the Ottoman army.[51] However, the fact was that the Balkan states were also among Germany's best costumers and most materials, especially the Bulgarian artillery or the Serbian small-arms, employed in the battle against the Ottoman forces, were labelled as 'German made'.[52]

A well-known German propagandist for an economic and cultural expansionist foreign policy, Ernst Jäckh, who was of 'certain' opinion that 'under the skilful, superior diplomacy of Sultan Abdülhamid it would never happen such a Balkan War',[53] articulated that the technical quality of military materials employed by both parties were equally good. His argument clearly voiced the widely expressed opinion in Germany. In his book where he described the Bulgarian as 'Prussians of the Balkans', Jäckh arrogated the Bulgarian victory to the German influence on the Bulgarian army. His conclusion was clear and accurate: both sides were Germany's clients. Krupp guns, Mauser rifles, Köln-Rottweiler powder were used by both sides in the battle.[54] Eventually, from the German point of view the outcome of the Balkan War might be summarized as follows: one of Germany's best costumers was defeated by the others but the ultimate victory belongs to the German arms manufacturers. As stated above, the Balkan states captured a number of Ottoman rifles and artilleries. According to British War Office's notes on the Balkan states, during the war Bulgarian forces captured from the Ottoman army in addition to several rifles and machine guns, 274 Krupp field guns in various calibres; 11 Krupp mountain guns; 6 Krupp field howitzers; and 14 Krupp siege howitzers[55]. In terms of Ernst Jäckh's above-mentioned formulation, these captures might be called just an involuntary transfer from the defeated to the victorious client. After the war ended some of these materials were repurchased by the Ottoman government.[56] In the meantime, moreover, the Ottoman Navy also lost two gunboats, two armoured corvettes, two torpedo boats and one armed steamer.[57]

These successive wars and defeats overtly revealed the weak state of the Ottoman army and paved the way for the ruling government to apply new preventive measures containing new orders for armament and warships, and inviting new military advisers from Germany: the very same preventive measures applied by the dethroned Sultan. As a consequence of the Ottoman request, in June 1913 Kaiser Wilhelm II approved Liman von Sanders as the head of the military mission to work in the last Army of the Ottoman Empire. He arrived in Istanbul on 14 December 1913 as the President of the Reform Commission.[58]

Running contrary to this fresh desire to reinforce Ottoman military forces through using the old methods, the Empire was in an extremely unfavourable financial condition. As usual, the way the government applied to finance this effort was through foreign loans. On 28 October 1913, the German ambassador in İstanbul, Wangenheim, submitted a report to the German Foreign Office referring to his communication with August Huber, the Krupp's representative, to inform 'that France is making her financial assistance conditioned on seventy-five per cent of all army contracts being placed with French firms'. According to Wangenheim, Huber's suggestion in this regard was that 'Turkey be told frankly that we are unable to tolerate any agreements under which the monopoly of such contracts is reserved for other States.'[59] It seems that after a short 'drawback' the old days' struggle for selling arms to the Ottoman Empire had re-emerged just on the very eve of World War I.

In February 1914, according to the German chargé d'affaires at the German embassy, Gerhard Mutius, the Krupp Company, for the sake of German military industry's victory over the French, got involved in this race through offering credit of 2.5 million lira for the Ottoman's payment for already purchased materials from the Krupp, Deutsche Waffen- und Munitionsfabrik, Mauser and Köln-Rottweiler Powder factories; and another 2.5 million lira for new orders, and also 2 million lira cash credit.[60] The French government, nonetheless, was not pleased with this financial package and according to the Minister of Finance, Cavid Bey, French threats (*Drohungen*) blocked the Krupp's offered package.[61] Meanwhile, Talat Bey gave the guarantee to the Germans that once the ongoing favourable Paris negotiations were terminated, the Ottoman government was determined to accept the Krupp's offer. According to Talat Bey, moreover, the Ottoman government was of the view that it might be beneficial for the Ottomans to be bound by long-term orders from Krupp in order to prevent any new fights and upsets for each small order.[62] Talat's verbal confirmation seemed to be, if it was not just a conciliation tactic, an obvious offer for a monopoly position for the Krupp Company.

Following the negotiation with France, however, which was described by Talat Bey as 'favourable', the Ottoman Finance Minister approved the contract for 376 mountain guns, 50 million bullets, two submarines, and six torpedo boats.[63] This sale was materialized through a new French loan, the use of which was restricted only to payment of orders placed to the French firms.[64] 'Having lost some ground to the French,' writes Grant, 'the Germans recovered between February and May of 1914. First, Krupp moved to open Ottoman long-term credit and as a result acquired a large order. The Ottomans then placed massive orders in Germany for guns, rifles and bullets.'[65] In addition to these foreign sources the Young Turks government was also utilizing several other domestic means to cover the cost of purchased military materials. Among others, these following were almost exclusively used for the German orders: ex-Sultan

Abdülhamid's personal investments saved in German banks for years;[66] hypothecation of some museum pieces;[67] and collecting donations from the public in July 1909 through the established charitable trust organization for the Navy, Donanma-yı Osmanî Muavenet-i Millîye Cemiyeti.[68]

The reinforcement of the Ottoman naval force was elevated to one of the most imperative priorities of the Young Turks government. At least any development in the Navy came to be regarded as a proof that a very fundamental shift would happen from Abdülhamid's modernization policy that was accused of neglecting the Navy. From the beginning of this shift both German policy makers and German military industry realized that in order to protect the influence and strong position they had in the Ottoman political, military and economic spheres, a fundamental modification of and an enrichment strategy for both foreign policy instruments and the product range offered to the Ottoman army had become an indispensable precaution. Although Germany had never gained a monopoly in the Ottoman naval market, as illustrated above, Germany still had several influential 'friends' within the Ottoman decision-making circle, which could facilitate German penetration of the Ottoman naval market that was extensively occupied by non-German ships. In May 1910 the office of the Grand Vizier was still occupied by a person (İbrahim Hakkı Pasha) who was known as 'very anti-English'[69] and forced the pro-British Minister of Marine Halil Pasha to resign on 29 May 1910.[70] Sir Lowther's note about Halil Pasha's successor Salih Pasha was short, clear, noteworthy: '[Salih Pasha] spent some time in Germany.'[71] Later on, on the grounds of the ill-health of Salih Pasha, Mahmud Muhtar Pasha, who remarked in September 1908 that the German Army was the best in the world and the reorganization of the Ottoman army must follow the German way,[72] was appointed Minister of Marine.[73] In his letter to Edward Grey, Marling added, that 'it is to be hoped that the German sympathies of the new Minister of Marine will not produce friction in his relations with Admiral Williams, [the head of the British naval mission].'[74] In addition to this list, the Minister of War of this cabinet was a well-known pro-German officer within the military circle, Mahmud

Şevket Pasha, who hoped that 'the revolution might eventually open the way to a new Triple Alliance, to be formed by Germany, Austria–Hungary and the Ottoman Empire.'[75] It was so obvious that there was no need for Germany to be so alarmed about losing their market share in the Ottoman market for a long period of time; on the contrary, as indicated below, thanks to these influential military personalities who had immense power over the political decision-making process, Germany soon began to challenge Britain's longstanding monopoly in the Ottoman Navy.[76]

At the beginning of 1910, the Ottoman government decided to purchase two old Brandenburg-class battleships from Germany.[77] The former *Kurfürst Friedrich Wilhelm* and *Weißenburg* were renamed *Barbaros Hayreddin* and *Turgut Reis*.[78] This procurement was, essentially, a part of a proposed ten-year improvement programme of the Ottoman fleet, which was to be equipped with six dreadnoughts, six small-cruisers, 12 submarines, 24 torpedo boats, 24 gunboats, and two floating docks.[79] For that purpose the Ottoman government dispatched some officers to Europe. According to the *New York Times*, after the British Admiralty refused to negotiate, the Ottoman officers found the authorities in Berlin willing to sell these battleships 'which were about to be removed from the effective list of the German Navy'.[80] Indeed, this comment was based on some verified official statement. The similar remark was also mentioned in Gerard Lowther's telegram dated 10 January 1910.[81] Another argument concerning Germany's real purpose behind this sale was that the emerging necessity of replacing the two warships, which were launched in 1891, would have the result of 'speeding up' the German Dreadnought programme.[82] Citing from the Russian newspaper *Novoe Vremya*, *The {London} Times* also shared similar comments on that matter.[83] In this manner, the semi-contribution of the Ottoman government to the so-called German Dreadnought programme amounted to more than 18 million marks that was paid for these warships on 30 August 1910.[84] The price paid for these two old warships was called exorbitant by almost all observers. According to one observer 'although it was a bad bargain for Turkey, it must have been a very good bargain for the negotiators'.[85] Concerning the purchase, there were also domestic critiques published in Ottoman magazines and newspapers. The German embassy monitored closely and collected some of these publications. The humourous magazine, named after one of the leading characters of the Turkish shadow play, *Karagöz* (*The black eye*), was one of those putting emphasis on the age and shabbiness of the warships and underlined Germany's desire to re-enter the Ottoman market through this sales operation.[86]

Image 6.1   The Sale of German Warships, Karagöz and Kaiser Wilhelm II.
Kaiser Wilhelm II: Please, Mr. Karagöz, accept this pair. They are used items, but still waterproof. As you know, we have not been in business for a while.
Karagöz: Actually, I do not want to buy such used items anymore, but I am barefoot! In order not to get nail in my feet, I have to buy it. God willing, I will be soon able to order [some new] from a good master.
Source: *Karagöz*, 17 August 1910, in: PA.AA.13312.

THE POWER SHIFT AND ITS CONSEQUENCES (1908–1914) 247

The sale of these warships to the Ottoman government was regarded by the European Great Powers as a successful attempt by Germany to regain their power and influence in the Ottoman Empire after the short 'drawback' period. According to the chargé d'affaires of the German embassy, Miquel, Germany's comeback with this sales operation in the navy strongly annoyed the other Great Powers. Miquel reported that these countries began, with 'a strong jealous feeling', to try agitating the Ottomans through insulting remarks against these warships' technical features and against Germany.[87] Russia was particularly interested in this sale and was overtly opposed to that transaction happening. Whereas the Russian formulation was based on the possible threat the Ottoman Empire posed against Russia through her growing naval forces, the British government's major consideration was its market share and monopoly in the Ottoman Navy.[88]

For the Ottoman government, however, Germany's willingness to sell these warships was a clear and strong sign of the permanence of mutual trust and friendship between the two Empires. Furthermore, the Ottoman rulers considered this procurement as an enormous step for the Ottoman Navy.[89] The sultan was also proud of that dealing with Germany. Dressing in a navy uniform Sultan Mehmed Reşad received the German delegation both before and after the official delivery of the warships took place.[90] After his grateful thanks to the Kaiser, who visited Sultan Mehmed Reşad on 15 October 1917 as his third visit to the Ottoman Empire, for his authorization to send these warships to the Ottoman Empire, he said that '[the Ottoman Empire] would never forget such a service provided by Germany, particularly during such critical times'.[91] As Miquel reported Ottoman ministers, who were also at the dinner, were all well aware of the hard attacks (*Angriff*) coming from both domestic and international circles regarding the procurement of these 'expensive and old warships'. Although the entire cabinet were subjected to such attacks, as Miquel quoted from the Minister for Foreign Affairs, Rıfat Pasha, it was 'not the complaints that already began to be silenced but the complaisance of Germany and the success of the Ottoman government' that would be remembered within a couple of days.[92] Mahmud Şevket Pasha, the War Minister, also put emphasis on the other governments' unwillingness to 'support [*Unterstützung*]' the Ottoman Empire, whereas the German government declared its enthusiasm for the Ottomans' request and subsequently provided help, which would, according to Şevket Pasha, never be forgotten (*Das werde man nie vergessen*).[93] Similar sentiments were published in some of the Ottoman newspapers, like *Sabah*, *Tanin* and *Tasvir-i Efkar*.[94]

It is also noteworthy to state that after this successful sales operation, the Ottoman Empire started to be considered a profitable market for second-hand ships. Consequently several other firms in Germany became interested in selling their second-hand ships to the Ottoman government. One of these firms was Norddeutscher Lyod that expressed, via Deutsche Bank, its eagerness to sell some of their mail-ships, which were said to be still quite powerful and in good condition, but could not offer the required luxury and comfort at a reduced price.[95]

The reign of Sultan Abdülhamid II has been widely criticized, with a superficial interpretation, as the 'dark age of the Ottoman navy'.[96] According to the Young Turks' ruling elites, for most of the years of Sultan Abdülhamid's reign the warships were not utilized and due to not performing any significant naval mission the bulk of the Ottoman fleet remained anchored in the Golden Horn.[97] A radical shift from that negligent naval policy to an impetuous aggressive procurement-based naval policy profoundly shaped the Empire's very last years' foreign policy at the hand of the Young Turks. In the meantime, just as Sultan Abdülhamid had elevated the arms trade to one of the very key determinants of his foreign policy, the Young Turks tried to do the same, but for naval procurement. Unfortunately, however, the new strategy did not produce the expected effect that the Young Turks naively calculated. On the contrary, both the Ottoman financial state and the supplier countries' political and strategic priorities hindered the new regime to achieve their calculated success.

In the meantime within a couple of months following delivery, the Ottoman government realized the renovation and moderniz-

THE POWER SHIFT AND ITS CONSEQUENCES (1908-1914) 249

ation effort that would be needed to bring *Barbaros Hayreddin* up to the standard of the proposed naval development programme. Since the Germans did not accept any responsibility after official delivery took place, they rejected the Ottoman's claim for 'free renovations'.[98] So consequently, even until September 1911, the Ottoman government was struggling to find a way to manage the repair cost of *Barbaros Hayreddin*.[99] More interestingly, however, according to Childs' argument, the Ottoman Navy had difficulty in even manning these two ships.[100] Briefly to say, the power shift increasingly facilitated the German penetration of the Ottoman Navy which was, due to Abdülhamid's well-set balance strategy, quite impossible during the old regime. In Abdülhamid's set of policies, the German name was strong and almost exclusively associated with Ottoman land forces, whereas the Navy was mostly dominated by Britain. It seems that the power shift somehow enlarged the German naval share in the Ottoman market. Although, regarding the Ottoman naval contract, Germany was still far behind Britain and France, the rise of German naval competition might not be what the British government expected from the Young Turks government.

As an 'irony of fate', furthermore, the very last symbol of both the German–Ottoman friendship and Germany's third and last expansionist wave towards the Ottoman Empire was the Ottoman procurement of two other German warships on 16 August 1914: the battle-cruiser *SMS Goeben* and light-cruiser *SMS Breslau*, which were renamed as *Yavuz* and *Midilli* respectively. Soon after *SMS Goeben* 'successfully shelled the Black Sea port Sevastopol' on 29 October 1914, as German Admiral Wilhelm Souchon reported, the Ottoman Empire entered the war on the side of Germany.[101] Bombardment of the Russian facilities became the pretext for Ottoman participation in the war on the side of Germany against Russia. However, as this book has tried to indicate, the very first domino had fallen when military advisers were dispatched to the Ottoman Empire during Bismarck's chancellorship. As has been pointed out in the first chapter of this book, Bismarck's support for the Ottoman Empire through sending military advisers and providing weapons proved to be a forewarning for Russia that Germany was able to counter any Russian threat by building closer relations with the Sultan.[102] Bismarck's foresight would be realized just five years after the dethronement of Sultan Abdülhamid, who had somehow been able to impede this conflict for years mostly based on his carefully balanced diplomacy, by the recently bought German battle-cruiser's attack on Russian naval facilities.

It is also interesting to remember Bismarck's advice in 1887 about waging war on Bulgaria to prevent the Russian attack towards the Balkans,[103] or Goltz Pasha's provocative suggestions regarding the armament and fortification of the Straits as a preventive measure against a possible Russian attack[104] had not been enough to induce Abdülhamid, in whose mind the memory of Ottoman army's severe defeat by Russia in 1877–8 had still been very fresh, to have any aggressive adventure. This had not been the case for the Young Turks, who had just experienced two successive severe defeats by Italy and the Balkan States, nevertheless.

SMS Goeben's bombardment was the triggering moment, the consequences of which would verify the accuracy of Goltz Pasha's fortification strategy he worked on during his service in the Ottoman army for the defence of the Straits.[105] Shortly after that event, according to Aksakal's account, Enver Pasha received an encouraging and reassuring letter from Goltz Pasha, 'Bravo! Old Turkey now has the opportunity' wrote the 'father of the Turkish Army'[106] 'in one fell swoop, to lift itself up to the heights of its former glory. May she not miss this opportunity?'[107] In fact, as Corrigan also indicates, German ambitions in the Ottoman Empire 'had come to be more easily realizable in the context of a successful European war'.[108] Gradually, the War became to be regarded by German decision makers as an indispensable instrument to achieve the ultimate goal of being a *Weltmacht*, whereas for the Young Turks, the War could pave the way for regaining the 'former glory'.[109]

As a final remark for this chapter, these very last encouraging words coming from Germany, namely from Goltz Pasha, were remarkably similar to those Bismarck made during his communication with Reşid Bey 33 years previously, in 1881. Whereas Goltz

Pasha regarded the coming war as an 'opportunity' to lift the Empire up to 'the heights of its former glory', according to Bismarck, as the quotation cited in the first chapter reveals, 'diminishing of the influence and significance of and assimilation of [the Empire's] Christian subjects' were the necessary acts in order to regain the 'former glory'.[110] The new regime, the Young Turks, tried to follow both these ways, guided by the old friend with an aim to regain the former glory and greatness that had existed several centuries previously. The result was not what they dreamt of, but the collapse of the Empire.

CONCLUSION

'Show me who makes a profit from war, and I'll show you how to stop the war.'

Henry Ford (1863–1947)

Germany's unparalleled success in the Ottoman Empire before World War I has been widely discussed among historians, but mostly in the particular context of the Baghdad Railway and its financing by the Deutsche Bank. Given this limited agenda, scholars who have examined the relationships forged between the Ottoman Empire and Germany before the World War I have not paid sufficient attention to the Ottoman Empire's arms purchases from Germany; moreover, they have almost entirely neglected the impact of personal relations and personal influence on the arms trade. Both the link between personal influence and the German armament firms' success in the Ottoman Empire and the arms trade's importance in the formation of bilateral relations have been largely disregarded in the literature. Furthermore, as this study has demonstrated, the arms trade itself was one of the most powerful determinants that shaped German–Ottoman rapprochement in the late nineteenth century, creating the *Waffenbrüderschaft* that emerged in World War I.

As Pamuk indicates, by the start of the nineteenth century, as an agrarian economy, the Ottoman Empire had been integrated into the world economy, as a result of which Ottoman foreign trade increased

CONCLUSION 253

more than tenfold between 1820 and 1914.[1] European countries, especially Britain and France, were the most important partners in Ottoman foreign trade during that time. During the 1870s, there was almost no German interest in the Ottoman market. However, Germany's arms manufacturers, especially the Krupp Company, were an exception. Krupp's discovery of the Ottoman market in the late 1860s opened a financial and commercial gateway for other German investors. In 1869, when Krupp opened a representative agency in İstanbul, the Ottoman army had already acquired 284 large-calibre Krupp guns.[2] By the end of the 1870s, Krupp's cumulative sales to the Ottoman Empire amounted to 1,816 guns. Through large-scale gun sales to the Ottoman government, Krupp introduced a new and profitable market to other German industrialists and capitalists, who would later finance the arms trade by lending money to the Ottoman government. Both the Empire's financial state and its continual armaments purchases from Germany offered great opportunities for German banks, especially the Deutsche Bank, which had a close relationship with the Krupp Company. After a while, the Deutsche Bank held the top spot as the primary financier for Ottoman arms imports from Germany.[3]

Based on archival research in four countries, this study examined the successful war business of German armament firms (especially Krupp and Mauser) in the Ottoman market for the period of 1876 to 1914, and tried to answer the question of how German firms obtained this monopoly position and held it for decades. The answer was initially sought in a comparison of the technical features of war materials purchased by the Ottoman government and the prices demanded by the armament firms. However archival documents clearly demonstrate that these two vital factors did not play as crucial a role as has been assumed. Despite the fact that the German rifles (Mauser) or guns (Krupp) were not necessarily superior to the French, American, British or Austrian products, and moreover that in some cases German war materials were more expensive than the others, the Ottoman government clearly preferred German firms for decades during and after the reign of Sultan Abdülhamid. The archival documents, especially the handwritten letters and reports of several influential personalities, including Kaiser

Wilhelm II, Chancellor Bismarck, Goltz Pasha, Paul Mauser, F. Alfred Krupp, Ottoman bureaucrats, and German military and civil advisers employed in the Ottoman service, highlight the motivations that lay behind Germany's exceptional success in the Ottoman arms market. These documents clearly demonstrate that, personal influence, which stemmed from close personal relationships, and the political considerations of both governments were much more decisive factors for the awarding of lucrative contracts than the technical features and the cost of the war materials offered by German firms. In fact, the Ottoman Empire serves as an instructive example of the intertwined relationship of political, military and business factors, as well as 'a good measure of personal interest'.

One of the main contentions of this book is that arms exports had a decisive impact in stimulating and strengthening Germany's political, economic and military expansionist mechanisms. The relationships between political, financial and military players all came to bear on the finalization of an armaments contract. In the hands of Germany, as the exporting country, arms sales proved to be a multipurpose tool for both domestic socio-economic policy and military-based foreign policy. Based on this strategy, the German government supported the arms makers' export-oriented production, while the other countries' government did not provide such intense and open support. As has been indicated, especially British manufacturers were angry with the British government and embassy's disinterest in their business in the Ottoman market. *The Daily News* blamed the British embassy for this failure and argued that 'The English Embassy does not consider it with its province to support demands made the British subjects for large contracts with the Turkish Government. But the German Embassy and Government do.'[4] The present study, therefore, argues that the German armament firms' success in international arms trade was a natural outcome of three principal planks of German expansionist policy: economic/industrial, military and political interests.[5]

In this respect, German foreign diplomacy openly facilitated and supported the arms makers' business activities in foreign markets. The German government provided significant political and financial support to companies exporting military materials. As Boelcke has asserted, war business activities triggered foreign policy actions, and vice versa. Indeed, the 'foreign policy objectives pursued by the German government frequently reflected such a strong commitment to economic concerns that their priorities were virtually indistinguishable from those pursued by the German arms makers.'[6]

The multidimensional impact of a foreign contract was well understood by German policy makers. As a result, the German government did not hesitate to support the domestic and international activities of the armament firms. Over the course of time, German policy makers realised that Germany's aggressive expansionist strategy could utilize the German arms makers' successful business activities abroad as an influential tool to gain access to the circles of foreign military decision makers and, by extension, create a controlling position within foreign military markets. According to archival records, the German arms makers' marketing strategy in the Ottoman market, though dependent on governmental support, was unquestionably well planned. For that reason, in contrast to many other German entrepreneurs, investors and traders in the Ottoman Empire, the arms makers and their representatives in İstanbul never failed to realise the profits of the war business.[7] In fact, the Germans held this absolute advantage only in the war business, and not in other business activities.

The political considerations and manoeuvres of German statesmen served as crucial components of a comprehensive expansionist strategy towards the Ottoman Empire, one that proved more productive and profitable than the arms makers' own unsupported marketing endeavours. From Chancellor Bismarck to Kaiser Wilhelm II, and also from Goltz Pasha, the leading figure in the German military mission employed in the Ottoman service, to the representatives of the German Foreign Office, the German government actively supported the business activities of the German armament firms in the Ottoman market within the concept of the peaceful penetration strategy.

The most effective tool of this strategy was the German military mission. Military advisers serving in the Ottoman Army were instrumental in achieving the concrete outcome of the 'virtual monopoly' of German armament firms in the Ottoman arms market. This study has portrayed the German experience in the Ottoman Empire as the beginning of the age of peaceful penetration and, in this regard, considered Bismarck, Kaiser Wilhelm II and Goltz Pasha among the leading figures of this age.

Based on comprehensive archival research, this study has demonstrated that the successful German war business was born and then quickly flourished in the Bismarckian era. It was during these years that Germany took major steps to monopolize the Ottoman arms market. As a matter of fact, Bismarck gave open patronage to the German arms makers and their business in the Ottoman arms market. Bismarck's recommendations in favour of German war materials and his open patronage of the German arms industry gave the German firms an insurmountable advantage against their competitors. However, despite Bismarck's massive contribution to Germany's increasingly influential position in the Ottoman Empire, scholars have viewed his policy towards the Ottoman Empire under the shadow of his famous speech of 1876, in which he gave his opinion that Ottoman affairs, within the context of the Eastern Question, were 'not worth the bones of a single Pomeranian grenadier'. This approach tends to underestimate the importance of Bismarck's crucial strategic steps towards the German expansionist strategy during his late Chancellorship. It was at this time that Germany began to send military advisers to the Ottoman Empire, starting in 1882 and continuing after Bismarck was dismissed by Kaiser Wilhelm II in 1890.

Contrary to the common argument that Bismarck was not interested in a friendship with the Ottoman Empire, the evidence shows that Bismarck tried to make the Sultan believe that Germany was a friend and supporter of the Sultan and his policy, which had attracted sharp criticism from other European powers. The two Ottoman reports dated 24 December 1881, which record Bismarck's conversations with the Ottoman delegation sent by Sultan Abdülhamid II to obtain a commitment on military advisers and to investigate the possibility of an alliance between Germany and the Ottoman Empire, demonstrate that Bismarck was not indifferent towards Ottoman affairs, nor was he disinterested in the Sultan's friendship. This conversation in 1881 might therefore be regarded as the definitive beginning of the change in Germany's foreign policy towards the Ottoman Empire. In fact, during the conversation with the Ottoman delegation (led by Ali Nizami Pasha and Reşid Bey), Bismarck took the significant step of offering them some very forceful advice. Particularly significant was the comment in which he categorized the Sultan's Muslim/Turkish Ottoman subjects as reliable and the non-Muslim/non-Turkish (*mezahib-i sa'ire efradı*) subjects as unreliable, and suggested governing these non-Muslim subjects 'with lion's claw hidden in a silken glove'. In addition, his congratulations to the Sultan upon the latter's decision to dissolve the parliament was the sort of approving statement the Sultan had been hoping to hear from a European politician at that time. Through such remarks, Bismarck gave support to the strategic efforts that aimed to win the Sultan's trust and friendship. As has been shown in this study, the Sultan's friendship was the most crucial factor for opening the doors of the Empire's markets to German financiers and industrialists, especially to German armament firms.

The policy of dispatching German military advisers to the Ottoman Army also supported the German arms manufacturers' marketing efforts or, to put it another way, reduced their marketing costs. From the military point of view, the advisers had a limited impact during the first years of their service in the Ottoman Army, but they lobbied intensively for their fellow countrymen's business interests. The members of the German Military Mission in İstanbul established an operative link between Ottoman military decision makers and the German arms makers. During the course of their presence in Ottoman service, the military advisers became an indispensable part of, and an effective instrument of, Germany's expansionist strategy towards the Ottoman Empire. During the period under consideration, the advisers' effectiveness – in terms of creating political, economic and military control over a foreign country – was so great that it created a model for other governments. Moreover, the multidimensional effectiveness and global potential of this strategy of sending military missions abroad to reorganize foreign armies made the Ottoman case a sort of pilot project for an approach that was later applied in other countries. The military advisers in general Goltz Pasha in particular performed a significant service for their fatherland. Their service was not restricted to the training of a potential military ally for future wars, but also aimed to produce an ally that was increasingly dependent on German financial support and military equipment.

This study specifically emphasized the crucial role played by Goltz Pasha, the pre-eminent figure among German military advisers, who devoted most of his efforts to establishing a German sphere of influence on behalf of arms makers. He was the key figure in the creation of the close links between the military advisers and the arms makers. His information net provided him with excellent opportunities to manipulate the process by which the armaments contracts were awarded. The lucrative contracts signed with Krupp in 1885 and Mauser's entrance into and rapid monopolization of the Ottoman market for infantry rifles in 1887 were both the results of Goltz Pasha's direct personal intervention into the negotiation process. He was, in the strictest sense, a 'businessman in uniform'.

The case of Mauser's entrance into the Ottoman market offers an enlightening example for revealing the importance of personal influence and its impact on military contracts. At the very outset in 1886, when Paul Mauser was first informed about the Ottoman proposal to order new rifles from abroad and during the peak period of Ottoman orders in the late 1890s, the individuals and their spheres of influence were more important than the technical features of the products. The correspondence between the Mauser Company and Goltz Pasha and also between the company's official agent in Istanbul, August Huber, and Paul Mauser provide ample evidence of how the Germans used both the German military advisers' position and the friendship between the Sultan and the Kaiser for the sake of their war business. The success of the German Style of War Business in foreign countries was reliant on governmental support. This current study tries to indicate that Germany's success in the Ottoman arms market cannot be fully explained without taking into

CONCLUSION 259

consideration the personal friendship between the Kaiser and the Krupp family.

Drawing on unpublished archival documents, this study has shown how Kaiser Wilhelm II's direct intervention in the German war business strengthened the position the German armament firms had gained in the Ottoman market during Bismarck's chancellorship. During and after his first two visits to the Ottoman Empire (in 1889 and 1898), Kaiser Wilhelm II also established a close political and personal relationship with Sultan Abdülhamid II. Wilhelm II's personal diplomacy with the Sultan also provided German entrepreneurs, especially arms makers, with advantages inaccessible to their competitors.

To emphasize the impact of the German state apparatus and German military advisers in the war business, this study has also clarified the role of domestic factors in the German armament firms' successful business in the Ottoman arms market. Comparative archival research in Turkey and Germany shows that the personal involvement of both Sultan Abdülhamid and some of his corrupt bureaucrats and officers had a conspicuous impact on the arms business, strengthening the German position in the Ottoman arms market. The letters and reports of these bureaucrats clarify their crucial role during the finalizing of arms contracts. These highly significant documents also demonstrate the methods the Germans used to manipulate Ottoman officers and bureaucrats during and after the negotiation process. According to these documents, some of the Ottoman officers who were sent to Germany to observe the production and delivery of the war materials established close personal relationships with Paul Mauser and F. A. Krupp, and also with the people of the cities where the factories were located, Oberndorf and Essen. Some of the Ottoman officers got married in Germany and started families with their spouses, while others died there after a long stay. This study has argued that such close and personal relationships may explain why the final decisions with regard to armament contracts – in particular for rifles and guns – were generally made in favour of the German companies, even though the German offers were not the most economically and/or militarily advantageous for the Empire. The German arms makers' experiences in the Ottoman market paved the way for the fruitful financial and commercial involvement of other German investors. As Howerth pointed out in 1906, 'armies and navies were the effective instruments for opening doors to business enterprise'.[8]

Sultan Abdülhamid's intention to modernize the Ottoman Army at the start of his reign opened doors for German armaments companies and consequently for German capitalists who would provide the necessary financial support. The German armament firms, especially the Krupp and Mauser Companies, deserve to be called the pioneers of the German expansionist strategy towards the Ottoman Empire. They were the commercial agents that pursued German political and economic interests in the Ottoman market. As this book has argued, the arms trade that emerged in the context of personal connections was the triggering factor for Germany's increasing influence in the Ottoman Empire during the late nineteenth and early twenty century. Collaboration of the military advisers with the arms makers, and also establishing influential friendships facilitated and strengthened the foundation of the German Style of War Business. In Germany or under the German system trained and educated officers became the 'natural' supporter of the German interest in the Ottoman Empire. As a consequence of that strong and steady establishment, even after Sultan Abdülhamid II and his first circle men, the most supportive factors behind the German success, lost their power, the Germans could manage to re-establish their old position much earlier than expected. This was mainly because Germany took the necessary step long before this power shift took place, namely since the end of Bismarck's pretended disinterest policy in 1880s. So as Chirol pointed out, the growth of German influence in the Ottoman Empire was 'one of the most remarkable political phenomena of the closing years of the nineteenth century. Never [had] a great European Power acquired so rapidly and with so little apparent effort a position of authority and privilege in a decadent Oriental state with which its previous connections and actual community of interests seemed so slender.'[9]

Finally, it is true that Germany had never colonized the territory of the Ottoman Empire nor became the Ottomans' leading trade and financial partner but Germany gained the monopoly in the Ottoman arms market throughout the period under review and became the doctrinal model for the young Ottoman officers, the military leaders and elites of the next generation. Briefly to say, the short drawback in 1908–9 did not massively affect Germany's position and her strong establishment; on the contrary, the 'drawback' triggered the Germany's third and final expansionist wave, the force of which systematically threw the Ottoman Empire into the her last battle: World War I.

NOTES

Introduction

1. Naumann, Friedrich, *Asia: Eine Orientreise über Athen, Konstantinopel, Baalbek, Nazareth, Jerusalem, Kairo, Neapel* (Berlin, 1913), p. 164: 'Wir müssen das Land wirtschaftlich von uns abhängig machen, um es später politisch *"kontrollieren" zu können*.' Friedrich Naumann (1860–1919) was – as Smith pointed out – one of the prominent 'academic imperialists' and the leader of the German National–Social Association (1896–1903). Smith, D. Woodruff, *The Ideological Origins of Nazi Imperialism* (New York, 1986), p. 156; Zimmermann, Moshe, 'A Road not taken-Friedrich Naumann's Attempt at a Modern German Nationalism', *Journal of Contemporary History*, 17/4 (1982), pp. 689–708.
2. McGarity, James Madison, *Foreign Influence on the Ottoman Army*, Ph.D. Thesis: American University (Washington, D.C., 1968), p. 35.
3. Marschall to Hohenlohe, 23.09.1899, in Lepsius, Johannes, Mendelssohn-Bartholdy, Albrecht, and Thimme, Friedrich W. K. (eds), *Die große Politik der Europäischen Kabinette 1871–1914: Sammlung der Diplomatischen Akten des Auswärtigen Amtes*, 40 vols (Berlin, 1922–6), Vol.12-2, p. 583: 'Der Sultan wird sich, wenn er heute freundliche Worte von einer Seite vernimmt, die ihm früher keine Demütigung erspart hat, erinnern, daß Deutschland ihm gegenüber stets die Grenzen internationaler Höflichkeit eingehalten hat, und daß es die deutsche Methode ist, welche andere Großmächte nachahmen, wenn sie sich in ihren Beziehungen zu der Türkei urbaner Formen befleißigen.'
4. Translation of portions of an article from *'El Alem el Islami'*, 9 June 1905, in: NA, London: FO. 78–5396.

5. Wallace, William K., *The Trend of History: Origins of Twentieth Century Problems* (New York, 1922), p. 289; for the definition of the 'Eastern Question' see also Seymour's book published in 1916, in which he defined the Question as 'the Near Eastern Question'. He argued that 'the Near Eastern Question is as old as history or legend.' Seymour, Charles, *The Diplomatic Background of the War 1870–1914* (New Haven, 1916), p. 194.
6. McMurray, S. Jonathan, *Distant Ties: Germany, the Ottoman Empire, and the Construction of the Baghdad Railway* (Westport, 2001), p. 7.
7. Luxemburg, Rosa, *The Crisis in the German Social-Democracy, The "Junius" Pamphlet* (New York, 1919), p. 41.
8. Türk, Fahri, *Die deutsche Rüstungsindustrie in ihren Türkeigeschäften zwischen 1871 und 1914: Die Firma Krupp, die Waffenfabrik Mauser und die Deutschen Waffen- und Munitionsfabriken* (Berlin, 2006).
9. According to Türk's calculations, in 1873 the Ottoman Empire had paid 123,354,312 marks for 834 guns while in 1905 the Empire paid 9,506,876 marks for 668 guns. Türk, *Die deutsche Rüstungsindustrie*, p. 168.
10. Türk quotes from the following document: Alfred Krupp's Notes 13.04.1876, in: HA, Krupp: WA IXa 170. Türk, *Die deutsche Rüstungsindustrie*, pp. 177–8. However during my research in the Krupp Archive in Essen I saw a document in which there was the exact same statement written by Krupp and quoted by Türk in his dissertation: *Prokura*, 20.04.1876, in: HA, Krupp: FAH 2M/78/15 (previously as WA IV.341).
11. Grant, Jonathan A., *Rulers, Guns, and Money: the Global Arms Trade in the Age of Imperialism* (Cambridge, MA, 2007), pp. 81–91.
12. Griffiths, Merwin Albert, *The Reorganization of the Ottoman Army under Abdulhamid II. 1880–1897*, Ph.D. Thesis: University of California (Los Angeles, 1966); McGarity, *Foreign Influence*.
13. Wallach, Jahuda Luther, *Anatomie einer Militärhilfe. Die preußisch-deutschen Militärmissionen in der Türkei 1835–1919* (Düsseldorf, 1976); Wallach, Jahuda Luther, *Bir Askeri Yardımın Anatomisi*, translated by Fahri Çeliker (Ankara, 1985). In this study the Turkish edition of Wallach's book has been used.
14. Yasamee, F. A. K., 'Colmar Freiherr von der Goltz and the Rebirth of the Ottoman Empire', *Diplomacy and Statecraft* 9/2 (1998); Akmeşe, Handan Nezir, *The Birth of Modern Turkey: The Ottoman Military and the March to World War I* (London and New York, 2005).
15. Jastrow, Morris, *The War and the Bagdad Railway the Story of Asia Minor and its Relation to the Present Conflict* (Philadelphia and London, 1917); Earle, Edward Mead, *Turkey, The Great Powers, and The Baghdad Railway A Study in Imperialism* (New York, 1924); Blaisdell, Donald C., *European Financial Control in the Ottoman Empire* (New York 1929); Bode, Friedrich Heinz, *Der Kampf um die Bagdadbahn 1903–1914: Ein Beitrag zur Geschichte der deutsch-englischen Beziehungen* (Breslau, 1941); Schölch, Alexander, 'Wirtschaftliche Durchdringung und politische Kontrolle durch die europäischen Mächte im Osmanischen Reich (Konstantinopel, Kairo, Tunis), *Geschichte und Gesellschaft*, 1/4 (1975),

pp. 404–6; Ortaylı, İlber, *İkinci Abdülhamit Döneminde Osmanlı İmparatorluğunda Alman Nüfuzu* (Ankara, 1981); Kössler, Armin, *Aktionsfeld Osmanisches Reich: Die Wirtschaftsinteressen des Deutschen Kaiserreiches in der Türkei 1871–1908* (New York, 1981); Önsoy, Rifat, *Türk-Alman İktisadi Münasebetleri 1871–1914* (İstanbul, 1982); Rathmann, Lothar, *Berlin–Bagdad, Die imperialistische Nahostpolitik des kaiserlichen Deutschland* (Berlin, 1962); Trumpener, Ulrich, 'Germany and the End of the Ottoman Empire', in M. Kent (ed.), *The Great Powers and the End of the Ottoman Empire* (Oxford and New York, 1996); Schöllgen, Gregor, *Imperialismus und Gleichgewicht, Deutschland, England und die orientalische Frage 1871–1914* (München, 2000); McMurray, *Distant Ties*; Franzke, Jurgen (ed.), *Bagdadbahn und Hedjazbahn. Deutsche Eisenbahngeschichte im Vorderen Orient* (Nürnberg, 2003); Jerusalimski, A. S., *Die Außenpolitik und die Diplomatie des deutschen Imperialismus Ende des 19. Jahrhunderts* (Berlin, 1954); Kampen, v. Wilhelm, *Studien zur deutschen Türkeipolitik in der Zeit Wilhelm II* (Kiel, 1968); Soy, H. Bayram, *Almanya'nın Osmanlı Devleti Üzerinde İngiltere ile Nüfuz Mücadelesi 1890–1914* (Ankara, 2004); Gencer, Mustafa, *Imperialismus und die Orientalische Frage. Deutsch-Türkische Beziehungen 1871–1908* (Ankara, 2006); McMeekin, Sean, *The Berlin-Baghdad Express: The Ottoman Empire and Germany's Bid for World Power, 1898–1918* (London, 2010).
16. Yorulmaz, Naci, 'Krupps weitreichende Kanonen. Bewertung der Quellen im Osmanischen Archiv zu den Aktivitäten der Fa. Krupp im Osmanischen Reich', in C. Schönig, R. Çalik and H. Bayraktar (eds), *Türkisch-Deutsche Beziehungen: Perspektiven aus Vergangenheit und Gegenwart* (Berlin, 2012). pp. 192–216.
17. Seel, Wolfgang, 'Mauser-Puzzle', *Deutsches Waffen-Journal* 1 (1993), pp. 43–7.

Chapter 1 The German Expansionist Wave and the Political Economy of German Style of War Business in the Ottoman Empire (1880–98)

1. Cited in McMurray, *Distant Ties*, p. 39.
2. Barker, J. Ellis, *Modern Germany: Her Political and Economic Problems, Her Foreign and Domestic Policy, Her Ambitions, and the Causes of her Success* (London, 1909). p. 30.
3. Wallace, *The Trend of History*, p. 289. See also: Kössler, *Aktionsfeld Osmanisches Reich*, p. 102. Kössler quotes Bismarck's statement from the *Verhandlungen des Deutschen Reichtages*, 5 December 1876, 2. Leg. Per., IV. Session 1876, Bd.1:585: 'Ich werde zu irgendwelcher aktiven Betheiligung Deutschland kein interesse sehe, welches auch nur – entschuldigen Sie die Derbheit des Ausdrucks – die gesunden Knochen eines einzigen pommerschen Musketiers werth wäre'.
4. *The New York Times*, 25 September 1922.

NOTES TO PAGES 16-20   265

5. Wilhelm II, *The Kaiser's Memoirs, Emperor of Germany 1888-1918*, trans. by Thomas R. Ybarra (New York and London, 1922), p. 28.
6. Ismail Kemal Bey, *The Memoirs of Ismail Kemal Bey*, Sommerville Story (ed.) (London, 1920), p. 85; see also Wallach, Jahuda Luther, 'Bismarck and the "Eastern Question"—A Re-Assessment', in *Germany and the Middle East 1835-1939* (Tel Aviv, 1975), pp. 23-30.
7. Blowitz, Henri G.S. de, *Memoirs of M. de Blowitz* (London, 1903), p. 148.
8. Marschall to Bülow, 26 December 1907, Consular Correspondence, British National Archives, London: German Foreign Ministry Microfilm, 10/11.
9. Ismail Kemal Bey, *Memoirs*, p. 84.
10. Ibid, p. 102.
11. Yasamee, F. A. K., *Ottoman Diplomacy: Abdulhamid II and the European Great Powers 1878-1888* (Istanbul, 1996), p. 74.
12. Griffiths, *The Reorganization of the Ottoman Army* pp. 47-9; Wallach, *Anatomie einer Militärhilfe*, pp. 29-30.
13. Yasamee, for instance, asserts that Bismarck warned the Ottoman envoys that there could be no question of the appointment of military advisers. Yasamee, *Ottoman Diplomacy*, p. 80; Hajo Holborn, *Deutschland und die Türkei 1878-1890* (Berlin, 1926), p. 22; see also Ortaylı, *İkinci Abdülhamit Döneminde*, p. 59; McMurray, *Distant Ties*, p. 27.
14. Başbakanlık Osmanlı Arşivi (referred to subsequently as: BOA), Yıldız Esas Evrakı (referred to subsequently as: Y.EE) 7/6, 02.01.1299 in hegira calendar/ 24.12.1881 in the Gregorian calendar. Hereafter the dates will be given as follows: 02.01.1299/24.12.1881.
15. Ismail Kemal Bey, *Memoirs*, p. 84, 102.
16. *Projet des conditions d'engagement du personnel composant la mission militaire et civile allemande en Turquie*, 14.07.1880, in: Politisches Archiv des Auswärtigen Amtes Berlin (referred to subsequently as: PA.AA.) R13233.
17. Hohenlohe-Schillingsfürst, Chlodwig K.V. *Memoirs of Prince Chlodwig of Hohenlohe Schillingsfürst*, edited by Curtius, Fridrich, translated by George. W. Chrystal (London, 1907). Vol. 2, p. 268.
18. Ibid.
19. Ibid.
20. Cited in Wallach, *Bismarck and the Eastern Question*, p. 27.
21. In 1908, 18 years after Bismarck's statement, Marschall described the new Ottoman ambassador to Berlin, Osman Nizami Pasha, as a reliable informant for the German military mission and an officer who had used his whole influence in order to make Germany a unique supplier for the Ottoman's arms order. This kind of justification confirms Bismarck's prediction. Marschall to Bülow, 25.10.1908, in: PA.AA. R 13746.
22. Hohenlohe-Schillingsfürst, *Memoirs of Prince Chlodwig*, vol. 2, pp. 267-8.
23. Lepsius et al., *Die große Politik der Europäischen Kabinette*, vol. 3, p. 403.
24. BOA, Sadaret Hususi Maruzat Evrakı (referred to subsequently as: Y.A.HUS.) 169/24 (15.01.1299/07.12.1881).

25. BOA, Yıldız Perakende Evrakı (referred to subsequently as: Y. PRK) Mabeyn Başkitabeti (referred to subsequently as: BŞK).5/40 (18.01.1299/10.12.1881); See also Yasamee, *Ottoman Diplomacy*, p. 80; Hürmen, Fatma, R. (ed.), *Bürokrat Tevfik Biren'in II. Abdulhamid, Meşrutiyet ve Mütareke Hatıraları* (İstanbul, 2006), vol.1, p. 55, 88; Griffiths, *The Reorganization of the Ottoman Army*, p. 50.
26. Bolayır, Ali Ekrem, *Hatıralar*, Metin K. Özgül, (ed.) (Ankara 2007), p. 203.
27. BOA, Y.PRK. *Tahrirat-ı Ecnebiye ve Mabeyn Mütercimliği* (referred to subsequently as: TKM) 4/60 (22.01.1299/14.12.1881). Kirakossian argues the purpose of sending of Reşid Bey to Berlin was to know the German position on the Armenian Question. He asserts, 'to that purpose, the Sultan had sent one of his confidantes, the young Reşid Bey, as an emissary to Berlin'. Kirakossian, Arman D., *British diplomacy and the Armenian question: from the 1830s to 1914* (Princeton, 2003), p. 134. Although the main purpose was not that what Kirakossian claims, Bismarck's remarks about the non-Muslims within the Empire, including the Armenian population, were very straightforward and illuminating.
28. BOA, Y.PRK.BŞK.5/40 (18.01.1299/10.12.1881); BOA, Y.EE.7/6 (02.02.1299/24.12.1881); see also *The History of the Year, A narrative of the chief events and topics of interest from Oct. 1, 1881, to Sept. 30, 1883* (London, 1882), p. 242.
29. BOA, Y.EE.7/6 (02.02.1299/24.12.1881).
30. Ali Nizami's report: BOA,Y.EE.7/5(02.02.1299/24.12.1881); Reşid Bey's report: BOA.Y.EE.7/6 (02.02.1299/24.12.1881); Bismarck's memorandum: *Aufzeichnung des Reichskanzlers Fürsten von Bismarck: Hiesige Stimmung über die in Berlin anwesende Türkische Spezial-Mission*, PA.AA.R.13427, 22.12.1881: *Ich habe die beiden türkischen Würdenträger, jeden besonders empfangen, ihnen gegenüber aber dieselbe Sprache geführt, wie dies auch von Seiten des Grafen Hatzfeldt geschehen ist'.*
31. Hohenlohe-Schillingsfürst, *Memoirs of Prince Chlodwig*, vol. 2, pp. 267–8; see also Evans Lewin, *The German Road to the East; An Account of the 'Drang nach Osten' and of Teutonic Aims in the Near and Middle East* (New York, Doran, 1917).
32. BOA. Y.EE. 7/6 (02.02.1299/24 Dec. 1881). Parenthesized comment of Reşid Bey was in his original submission to the Sultan.
33. BOA.Y.EE. 7/6 (02.02.1299/24.12.1881).
34. Rose gave this conversation based on the statement of Oppert, the correspondent of *The {London} Times* at Berlin. Rose, John Holland, *The Origins of War 1871–1914* (New York 1915), p. 98; according to Blowitz, Prince Bismarck said to Beaconsfield: 'Why are you opposed to Russia? You might come to an understanding with her. It would be to the interest of both countries. Why do you not take Egypt? France would not bear you any ill-will on that account for very long. Besides, you could give her a compensation Tunis or Syria, for instance and then Europe would at last be free from this question of Turkey, which is constantly bringing her within an ace of a fresh war. Beaconsfield did not reply, but I saw that my words had not fallen on a

NOTES TO PAGES 22–28

deaf ear'. Blowitz, *Memoirs of M. De Blowitz*, p. 148; see also Baykal, Bekir Sıtkı, 'Bismarck'ın Osmanlı İmparatorluğu'nu Taksim Fikri' *Ankara Üniversitesi Dil ve Tarih-Coğrafya Fakültesi Dergisi* 5 (1943), pp.3–12.

35. BOA.Y.EE. 7/6 (02.02.1299/24.12.1881).
36. BOA, Y.EE. 7/5 (02.02.1299/24.12.1881).
37. Wehler, Hans Ulrich, '*Bismarck's Imperialism*, 1862–1890', *Past and Present*, 48 (1970), 128.
38. BOA. Y.EE. 7/6 (02.02.1299/24.12.1881).
39. Gooch, P. George, and Harold W. V. Temperley (eds), *British Documents on the Origins of the War 1898–1914*, 11 vols (London, 1927–1936), vol. 5, p. 43.
40. Lord Ampthill to Lord Granville, 17.12.1881, in Paul Knaplund (ed.), *Annual Report of the American Historical Association*, vol. 2, p. 239.
41. Hohenlohe-Schillingsfürst, *Memoirs of Prince Chlodwig*, vol. 2, pp. 267–8.
42. Peters, Carl, *Lebenserinnerungen* (Hamburg, 1918): pp. 73–4. See the full 'Charter of Protection' in German on pp. 74–5; see also Graudenz, Karlheinz and Hanns-Michael Schindler (eds), *Die Deutschen Kolonien: 100 Jahre Geschichte in Wort, Bild und Karte* (Augsburg, 1988), p. 98; and for the English translation see Pollard, Sidney and Holmes, Colin, *Industrial Power and National Rivalry 1870–1914* (London, 1972), pp. 157–8.
43. Peters, *Lebenserinnerungen*, p. 253.
44. Bismarck addressed the following speech to the Reichstag on 10 January 1885: 'Our colonies are at present important in my view first of all as markets for the products of our industry.' Pollard and Holmes, *Industrial Power and National Rivalry*, p. 172.
45. Wehler, 'Bismarck's Imperialism', p. 125.
46. According to Hill, Bismarck's statement was quoted by Bülow. Hill, David Jayne, 'Economic Imperialism: Germany's Self-revelation of Guilt', *The Century: Illustrated Monthly Magazine* 44 (1917), p. 359.
47. Wilhelm II, *The Kaiser's Memoirs*, p. 8.
48. Wehler, 'Bismarck's Imperialism', p. 127.
49. In one respect, Bismarck's prescience was attested by the outbreak of World War I. The former US ambassador to Germany, Hill put forth the following argument that overlaps with Bismarck's foresight: 'Beyond dispute it was economic imperialism that caused the present war World War I and plunged all Europe into it.' Hill, 'Economic Imperialism', p. 357.
50. Barker, *Modern Germany*, p. 30.
51. Wehler, 'Bismarck's Imperialism', p. 127.
52. Sampson, Anthony, *The Arms Bazaar in the Nineties: From Krupp to Saddam* (London, 1991), p. 58.
53. Hirst, Francis Wrigley, *The Political Economy of War* (London, 1916), p. 92.
54. For more discussion about the influence of technology on the European expansionism Trebilcock, Clive, 'Spin-Off' in British Economic History: Armaments and Industry, 1760–1914', *The Economic History Review* 22/3 (1969), pp. 474–90; Trebilcock, Clive, 'Legends of the British Armament

Industry 1890–1914: A Revision', *Journal of Contemporary History* 5/4 (1970), pp. 3–19; Gillis, J. R. (ed), *The Militarization of the Western World* (New Brunswick, 1989); Hacker, Barton C., 'Military Institutions, Weapons, and Social Change: Toward a New History of Military Technology', *Technology and Culture* 35/4 (1994), pp. 768–834 and Hacker, Barton C., 'Military Technology and World History: A Reconnaissance', *The History Teacher* 30/47 (1997), pp. 461–87; Headrick, R. Daniel, 'The Tools of Imperialism: Technology and the Expansion of European Colonial Empires in the Nineteenth Century', *The Journal of Modern History* 51 (1979), pp. 231–63.
55. Warner, C. D. (ed.), *Library of the World's Best Literature, Ancient and Modern* Vol. 5 (New York, 2008; first published 1896), p. 1957; see also Manchester, William, *The Arms of Krupp 1587–1968* (London, 1969), p. 175.
56. Warner, *Library of the World's Best Literature*, p. 1956.
57. Ibid., p. 1955.
58. Wehler, 'Bismarck's Imperialism', p. 122.
59. Ibid., p. 129.
60. Wilhelm II, *The Kaiser's Memoirs*, p. 7.
61. Menne, Bernhard, *Blood and Steel: The Rise of the House of Krupp* (New York, 1938), p. 88.
62. Menne, *Blood and Steel*, p. 78.
63. Cited in Menne, *Blood and Steel*, p. 79.
64. Ibid., p. 80: 1,250,000 thalers (1 mark = 0.33 thalers).
65. Ibid., p. 80: 2 million thalers.
66. Bontrup, Heinz-Josef and Zdrowomslaw, Norbert, *Die deutsche Rüstungsindustrie, vom Kaiserreich bis zur Bundesrepublik* (Heilbron, 1988), p. 53.
67. Türk, *Die deutsche Rüstungsindustrie*, pp. 160–3.
68. Epkenhans, Michael, 'Krupp and the Imperial German Navy 1898–1914: A Reassessment', *The Journal of Military History* 64 (2000), p. 335.
69. Klass, v. Gert, *Die Drei Ringe* (Tübingen and Stuttgart, 1953), pp. 112–23; Lehmann, Karin, 'Der Funktionswandel der öffentlichen Haushalte im Deutschen Reich vor dem Ersten Weltkrieg', in L. Zumpe (ed.), *Wirtschaft und Staat im Imperialismus* (Berlin, 1976), p. 96.
70. Manchester, *The Arms of Krupp*, p. 121.
71. Riesser, Jacob, *The German Great Banks and Their Concentration in Connection with the Economic Development of Germany* (Washington, D.C., 1911), p. 484; see also Gall, Lothar, *Die Deutsche Bank, 1870–1995* (München. 1995), p. 32, 50.
72. Riesser, *The German Great Banks*, p. 484; in fact, this transaction was one of the major earlier indicators of the existence of an alliance for the support of the armaments industry. According to Lehmann, the loan was underwritten by financially strong parties of the bourgeoisie, senior officials and the military leaders, and the bond was guaranteed by a consortium of great banks. See Lehmann, 'Der Funktionswandel', p. 96.
73. *The New York Times*, 1 November 1887.

74. Kraus, Jörg, *Für Geld, Kaiser und Vaterland: Max Duttenhofer, Gründer der Rottweiler Pulverfabrik und erster Vorsitzender der Daimler-Motoren-Gesellschaft* (Bielefeld, 2001), p. 64; see also Radolin to Caprivi, 06.02.1893, in: PA.AA. R13286. The contract awarded by the Ottoman government to the Germans was a joint contract in which the Waffenfabrik Mauser and Loewe & Co. were the co-producers for the Ottoman Empire. Having said that, in referring to this and other contracts awarded to this joint venture, most of the Ottoman archival documents refer to Mauser's name for the chief supplier company. Although on 4 November 1896 the Mauser Company became a part of The German Arms and Munitions Factories (Deutsche Waffen-und Munitionsfabriken A.G.: known as DMW) in the present study, regarding the contracts and other commercial issues happened even after this date 'the Mauser Company' or 'Mauser' will generally refer to the mentioned partnership.
75. BOA, *Y.MTV.29/19* (13.01.1305/31.10.1887).
76. The *Pulverfabrik Rottweil-Hamburg* was renamed in 1890 as *Vereinigte Köln-Rottweiler Pulverfabriken AG* and finally merged into the in 1896 established *Deutsche Waffen- und Munitionsfabriken*.
77. Kraus, *Für Geld, Kaiser und Vaterland*, p. 36.
78. Kraus, *Für Geld, Kaiser und Vaterland*, p. 36.
79. BOA, *Y.PRK.EŞA.6/61* (19.04.1887).
80. Vagts, Alfred, 'Bismarck's Fortune', *Central European History* 1 (1968), p. 216; cf. Stern, Fritz, *Gold and Iron: Bismarck, Bleichröder and the Building of the German Empire* (London, 1980), p. 298; Kraus, *Für Geld, Kaiser und Vaterland*, pp. 30–52.
81. Stern, *Gold and Iron*, p. 298; Cf. Vagts, 'Bismarck's Fortune', pp. 216–7.
82. Pflanze, Otto, *Bismarck: Der Reichsgründer* (München, 1998), p. 587.
83. Vagts, 'Bismarck's Fortune', p. 217.
84. Busch, Moritz, *Bismarck: Some Secret Pages of His History* (Vol. 2) (London, 1898), p. 158. The interview with Bismarck might have taken place on 18 October 1877.
85. Busch, *Bismarck: Some Secret Pages of His History*, p. 158.
86. Seel, Wolfgang, 'Mauser-Gewehre unter dem Halbmond, Türkenmauser', *Deutsche Waffenjournal* 1 (1981a), p. 802.
87. Unsigned to Salisbury, 27.01.1887, in: NA, London: FO 78/4002.
88. Salisbury's note on the same paper 28.01.1887, in: NA, London: FO 78/4002.
89. White to Foreign Office, 30.01.1887, in: NA, London: FO 78/4002.
90. See Mauser to the Waffenfabrik Oberndorf, 26.05.1893, in: SA, Oberndorf: M-A7.
91. BOA, *Y.A.RES.37/2* (01.05.1304/26.01.1887); BOA, *Y.A.RES.37/2* (05.05.1304/30.01.1887).
92. White to Sir Julian [Pauncefote], 12.03.1887, in: NA, London: FO 78/4022.
93. Sanderson to Fergusson, 12.05.1888, in: NA, London: FO 78/4095. In addition, according to an Ottoman document Mr. Kinok [Kynoch] made an offer to the Ottoman government for supply the cartridges which were

actually cheaper than the Mauser Company's demand. BOA, *Y.MTV.* 27/59 (26.11.1304/16.08.1887).
94. Bayard to King, 26.01.1887, in: NARA-Microfilm, College Park: M77/165.
95. Bayard to King, 26.01.1887, in: NARA-Microfilm, College Park: M77/165: On the following day, on 27 January 1887, a second telegram, at the same line was sent to İstanbul: 'You may unofficially use proper good offices to secure for Winchester and Union Metallic Company's agents full opportunity to submit bids and obtain contracts on equal footing with any other competitors.' Bayard to King, 27.01.1887, in: NARA-Microfilm, College Park: M77/165.
96. Bayard to King, 29.01.1887, in: NARA-Microfilm, College Park: M77/165.
97. BOA, *Y.PRK.EŞA.6/61* (19.04.1887).
98. King sent a long letter to Yıldız Palace regarding to the rifle and cartridges order. BOA, *Y.A:RES. 36/17* (07.06.1304/01.02.1887).
99. Hirsch to Blaine, 10.04.1890, in: NARA-Microfilm, College Park: M46/50.
100. Seel, 'Mauser-Gewehre' (1981a), p. 802.
101. Mitchell, Nancy, *The Danger of Dreams: Germany and American Imperialism in Latin America* (Chapel Hill, NC, 1999), p. 149.
102. Bode, *Der Kampf um die Bagdadbahn*, p. 2: See also McMurray, *Distant Ties*, p. 22.
103. BOA, *Y.PRK.HR.10/23* (13.04.1304/09.01.1887).
104. BOA, *Y.A.RES.40/36* (07.03.1306/11.11.1888).
105. Bode, *Der Kampf um die Bagdadbahn*, p. 3.
106. Barth, B., 'The Financial History of the Anatolian and Baghdad Railways, 1889–1914', translated by J. C. Whitehouse, *Financial History Review* 5 (1998), p. 117.
107. Pamuk, Şevket, *The Ottoman Empire and European Capitalism 1820–1913* (Cambridge, 1987), pp. 75–81.
108. Yasamee, *Ottoman Diplomacy*, pp. 173–8.
109. Kössler, *Aktionsfeld Osmanisches Reich*, p. 122. BOA, *Y.PRK.BŞK.13/41* (06.04.1305/22.12.1887).
110. Smith, L. Colin, *The Embassy of Sir William White at Constantinople 1886–1891* (Oxford, 1957), p. 93.
111. BOA, Y.EE.115/6 (24.08.1887); See also Yasamee, *Ottoman Diplomacy*, 245–50.
112. Menne, *Blood and Steel*, pp. 134–5.
113. Cited in Yasamee, *Ottoman Diplomacy*, p. 246.
114. Menshausen to Richthofen 18.01.1898, in: PA. AA. R13291: 'Wer den Auftrag erhält, ist eine politische Machtfrage oder das Ergebnis eines politischen Handelsgeschäftes'.
115. Kössler, *Aktionsfeld Osmanisches Reich*, pp. 122–3.
116. Cram, Robert Gordon, *German interests in the Ottoman Empire, 1878–1885* (Ph.D. Thesis: University of London (London, 1989), pp. 205–23.
117. For more detailed information about the relations between Bismarck and Bleichröder, see: Busch, *Bismarck: Some Secret Pages of His History*, pp. 70–147; Stern, *Gold and Iron*; Illich, Niles Stefan, *German Imperialism in the Ottoman*

Empire: A Comparative Study, Ph.D. Thesis: Texas A & M University (College Station, TX, 2007), pp. 141–3.
118. Stern, *Gold and Iron*, p. 419.
119. Vagts indicates that Bismarck had chosen Bleichröder as his banker in 1862 on the advice of Frankfurt Rothschild. Vagts, 'Bismarck's Fortune', p. 219; see also Stern, *Gold and Iron*, p. 304.
120. Illich, *German Imperialism*, p. 142.
121. Stern, *Gold and Iron*, p. 307.
122. Stern, *Gold and Iron*, p. 309.
123. Stern, *Gold and Iron*, p. 405.
124. Epkenhans, Michael, 'Military-Industrial Relations in Imperial Germany, 1870–1914', *War in History* 10/1 (2003), p. 14.
125. *The {London} Times*, 15 December 1881.
126. Windelband, Wolfgang, *Bismarck und die Europäischen Großmächte 1879–1885* (Essen, 1942), p. 320.
127. *The New York Times*, 8 November 1885.
128. Smith, Munroe, 'Military Strategy versus Diplomacy', *Political Science Quarterly* 30 (1915), p. 69; *Neue Freie Presse*, 20 October 1898; for Kaiser Wilhelm and his way of doing foreing policy also see Röhl, C.G. John, *Wilhelm II: the Kaiser's Personal Monarchy 1888–1900* (London, 2004), pp. 732–65.
129. Smith, 'Military Strategy versus Diplomacy', p. 69.
130. *Berliner Tagesblatt*, 2 January 1882, in: PA.AA. R13427: 'Es ist wohlbekannt, dass der Sultan seit langer Zeit in Wirklichkeit sein eigener Minister der auswärtigen Angelegenheiten geworden ist'.
131. Röhl, *Wilhelm II: the Kaiser's Personal Monarchy*, pp. 732–65.
132. Kohut, Thomas A., *Wilhelm II and the Germans: A Study of Leadership* (New York, 1991), p. 122.
133. Passant, Ernest James, *A Short History of Germany 1815–1945* (Cambridge, 1959), p. 101.
134. McMeekin, *The Berlin-Baghdad Express*, p. 9.
135. Bülow, Prince, von, *Memoirs of Prince von Bülow*, 2 vols, translated by F. A. Voigt (London and New York, 1931), Vol. 1, p. 266.
136. Barker, *Modern Germany*, p. 282.
137. *The Outlook*, 5 August 1905, in: NA, London GFM 10/11.
138. Trumpener, 'Germany and the End of the Ottoman Empire', p. 111; for more detailed discussion about the question of Kaiser Wilhelm II's personality and its impact on his ruling system, see Lerman, Katharina A., 'Wilhelmine Germany', in Mary Fulbrook (ed.), *German History since 1800* (London, 1997), pp. 199–227; Hull, Isabel V., *The Entourage of Kaiser Wilhelm II 1888–1918* (Cambridge, 1982).
139. Cited in Fuller, Joseph V., *Bismarck's Diplomacy at its Zenith* (Cambridge, MA, 1922), p. 3.
140. However, Wehler asserts that Wilhelm II's world policy was based on the deliberate and calculated use of foreign policy as an instrument for achieving

domestic political ends. Wehler, Hans Ulrich, *The German Empire 1871–1918*, translated by K. Traynor (Oxford, 1991), pp. 176–177.
141. Angell to Sherman, 07.12.1897, in: NARA-Microfilm, College Park: M46/63.
142. Peters expressed the Kaiser's award of title Commissar *(Reichskommissar)* with pension rights *(Pensionsberechtigung)*. Peters, *Lebenserinnerungen*, p. 102.
143. Peters, Carl, *Zur Weltpolitik* (Berlin, 1912).
144. Ripley, Z. William, 'The Commercial Policy of Europe', *Political Science Quarterly* 7 (1982), p. 634.
145. On 10 December 1891, Caprivi addressed the following speech: 'Wir müssen exportieren, entweder wir exportieren Waren oder wir exportieren Menschen. Mit dieser steigenden Bevölkerung ohne gleichmäßig zunehmende Industrie sind wir nicht in der Lage, weiterzuleben'. Schmidt-Richberg, Wiegand, 'Die Regierungszeit Wilhelms II', in Militärgeschichtliches Forschungsamt (ed.), *Handbuch zur deutschen Militärgeschichte 1648–1939 5, Von der Entlassung Bismarcks bis zum Ende des Ersten Weltkrieges 1890–1918* (Frankfurt am Main, 1968), p. 33.
146. For a detailed study on the terms of *Lebensraum* see Smith, D. Woodruff, 'Friedrich Ratzel and the Origins of Lebensraum', *German Studies Review* 3 (1980), pp. 51–68 and Smith, D. Woodruff, *The Ideological Origins of Nazi Imperialism* (New York, 1986).
147. Kaiser Wilhelm's speeches were edited and published by Johannes Penzler. Penzler, Johannes, *Reden Kaiser Wilhelms II. in den Jahren 1896–1900*, vol. 2 (Leipzig, 1904), pp. 9–10.
148. Ibid., pp. 9–10.
149. Naumann, *Asia: Eine Orientreise*, pp. 144–5.
150. Earle, Edward Mead, 'The Importance of the Near East in Problems of Raw Materials and Foodstuffs', *Annals of the American Academy of Political and Social Science* 112 (1924a), p. 183.
151. 'Germany and her Future', in: NA, London: GFM 10/11: The document (the newspaper article) was undated and also the name of the newspaper was not given on the document.
152. Ibid.
153. Feis, Herbert, *Europe the World's Banker, 1870–1914: An Account of European Foreign Investment and the Connection of World Finance with Diplomacy before the War* (New Haven, 1930), p. 60.
154. Helfferich, Karl, *Germany's Economic Progress and National Wealth 1888–1913* (Berlin, 1913), p. 14.
155. Maddison, Angus, 'Historical Statistics of the World Economy: 1–2008 AD', http://www.ggdc.net/maddison/; Helfferich: *Germany's Economic Progress*, p. 14.
156. Naumann, *Asia: Eine Orientreise*, p. 144.
157. Ibid., p. 144.
158. Howe, Frederic Clemson, *The Only Possible Peace* (New York, 1919), p. 6.

NOTES TO PAGES 50–55   273

159. Seymour, *The Diplomatic Background*, p. 202.
160. Helfferich, *Germany's Economic Progress*, p. 64. According to Passant, in 1910 Germany's steel output was 14,794,000 tons. Passant, *A Short History of Germany*, p. 107.
161. Passant, *A Short History of Germany*, p. 107.
162. Pollard and Holmes, *Industrial Power and National Rivalry*, p. 77.
163. Naumann, *Asia: Eine Orientreise*, p. 144.
164. Ripley, 'The Commercial Policy of Europe', p. 640.
165. Zucker, D. Richard, 'Germany's Industrial Position', *Ind. Eng. Chem.* 11 (1919), p. 777; Moulton, H. G., 'Economic and Trade Position of Germany', in *Annals of the American Academy of Political and Social Science* 114 (1924), p. 2.
166. Earle,'The Importance of the Near East in Problems of Raw Materials and Foodstuffs', p. 183.
167. Marschall to Bülow, 26.12.1907, in: NA, London: GFM 10/11.
168. Penzler, Johannes (ed.), *Fürst Bülows Reden nebst Urkundlichen Beiträgen zu seiner Politik: 1897–1903*, vol. 1 (Berlin, 1907), p. 100.
169. The Kaiser paid three visits to İstanbul; two of them were during the reign of Abdülhamid II, in 1889 and 1898. During the reign of Sultan Mehmed Reşad, on 15 October 1917, upon the Sultan's invitation, the Kaiser paid his last visit when the Ottoman Empire was still in the war on the side of Germany.
170. BOA *Y.PRK.ASK.58/49*/07.03.1307/01.11.1889); White to Salisbury, 07.11.1889, in: NA, London: FO 78/4207; BOA, *Y.A.HUS.229/45* (07.01.1307/ 03.10.1889); Wilhelm II, the Kaiser 1922: 28.
171. White to Salisbury, 07.11.1889, in: NA, London: FO 78/4207.
172. BOA, *Y.PRK.NMH.4/42* (08.01.1307/04.09.1889).
173. BOA, *Y.PRK.NMH.4/43* (9.01.1307/05.09.1889).
174. McMurray, *Distant Ties*, p. 28.
175. Kössler, *Aktionsfeld Osmanisches Reich*, pp. 124–5.
176. The publications of the Newspaper *Sabah* about Kaiser's visits were studied in detail by Gözeller. Gözeller, Ali, *Osmanlı-Alman Yakınlaşmasının Basına Yansıması: Sabah Gazetesi Örneği (1889–1895)*, M. A. Thesis: Marmara University (İstanbul, 2005).
177. Ibid., p. 99.
178. Ibid., p. 27; BOA, *Y.PRK.SRN.2/68* (08.03.1307/02.11.1889). According to this document the Ottoman brass band played some German march during the Kaiser's parade.
179. *The Levant Herald and Eastern Express*, 3 November 1889, in: NARA-Microfilm, College Park: M46/50.
180. Röhl, *Wilhelm II: the Kaiser's Personal Monarchy*, p. 125.
181. Cited in Röhl, *Wilhelm II: the Kaiser's Personal Monarchy*, p. 125.
182. Röhl cites that on the Kaiser' departure the Sultan 'presented the Kaiser with an "extraordinarily costly sabre" and the Kaiserin with gifts including a piece

of jewellery which alone was valued at £10,000.' Röhl, *Wilhelm II: the Kaiser's Personal Monarchy*, p. 125.
183. Wilhelm II, *The Kaiser's Memoirs*, p. 28.
184. McMeekin, *The Berlin-Baghdad Express*, p. 8.
185. See Cram, *German interests;* McMeekin, *The Berlin-Baghdad Express*, pp. 7–9; McMeekin Sean, 'Benevolent Contempt: Bismarck's Ottoman Policy', in M. Hakan Yavuz and Peter Sluglett (eds), *War and Diplomacy, The Russo-Turkisch War of 1877–1878 and the Treaty of Berlin* (Salt Lake City, 2011), pp. 79–97.
186. Bismarck to Solms-Sonnenwalde, 15.10.1889, in Lepsius et al., *Die große Politik der Europäischen Kabinette*, vol. 6, p. 360; According to Robolsky, Bismarck looked at the Kaiser's trip as a junket (*Vergnügungsreise*). Robolsky, Hermann, *Drei Jahre auf dem Throne 1888–1891* (Leipzig, 1891), p. 29.
187. BOA, Y.PRK.PT.5/96 (10.03.1307/04.11.1889).
188. White to Salisbury, 08.11.1889, in: NA, London: FO 78/4207.
189. White to Salisbury, 07.11.1889, in: NA, London: FO 78/4207.
190. BOA, Y.PRK.EŞA.10/24 (14.03.1307/08.11.1889).
191. Bismarck to Solms-Sonnenwalde, 15.10.1889, in Lepsius et al., *Die große Politik der Europäischen Kabinette*, vol. 6, pp. 360–1.
192. Smith, 'Military Strategy versus Diplomacy', p. 48.
193. *The Levant Herald and Eastern Express*, 03.11.1889, in: NARA-Microfilm, College Park: M46/50.
194. The Kaiser stayed in İstanbul between the November 2th and 6th of 1889. White to Salisbury, 07.11.1889, in: NA, London: FO 78/4207; BOA, Y.PRK. ASK.58/49 (07.03.1307/01.11.1889); BOA, Y.PRK.ASK.58/65 (13.03.1307/07.11.1889).
195. Marriott, John Arthur Ransome, *The Eastern Question: An Historical Study in European Diplomacy* (Oxford, 1917), p. 342.
196. Gözeller, *Osmanlı-Alman Yakınlaşmasının Basına Yansıması*, p. 14.
197. McMurray, *Distant Ties*, p. 28.
198. King to Blaine, 24.12.1881, in: NARA-Microfilm, College Park: M46/50.
199. Gözeller, *Osmanlı-Alman Yakınlaşmasının Basına Yansıması*, p. 31.
200. *The New York Times*, 31 January 1898.
201. BOA, Y.PRK.NMH.4/42 (08.01.1307/04.09.1889).
202. BOA, Y.PRK.PT.5/95 (10.03.1307/04.11.1889).
203. BOA, Y.PRK.PT.5/106 (13.03.130/07.11.1889).
204. *The {London} Times*, 8 November 1889.
205. Copy of the Kaiser's telegram in Turkish: BOA, Y.PRK.PT.5/82 (8.03.1307/02.11.1889): 'İşbu dakîkada Dersa'âdet'e muvâsalat eyledim. Havâ' pek latîfdir. Manzara ta'rîf edilemeyecek derecede güzeldir'.
206. Earle, *Turkey, The Great Powers*, pp. 29, 31. See also Helfferich, Karl, *Die deutsche Türkenpolitik* (Berlin, 1921), p. 154; Shaw, J. Stanford and Ezel K. Shaw, *History of the Ottoman Empire and Modern Turkey: Reform, Revolution and Republic, vol. 2: The Rise of Modern Turkey 1808–1975* (Cambridge, 1977),

p. 227; McMurray, *Distant Ties*, p. 22; Gencer, *Imperialismus und die Orientalische Frage*, p. 104. Earle stated that the first arrival of the Oriental Railways in İstanbul was on 12 August 1888. According to him, the Oriental Railways placed the Ottoman capitol in direct communication with Vienna, Paris, Berlin and London (via Calais).
207. Shaw and Shaw, *History of the Ottoman Empire*, p. 227.
208. Woods, H. Charles, 'The Baghdad Railway and Its Tributaries', *The Geographical Journal* 50/1 (1917), p. 35; Earle, *Turkey, The Great Powers*, p. 30.
209. Smith, *The Embassy of Sir William White*, p. 123.
210. Cf. 'Remarks applying to different British schemes for the construction of Turkish Railways in Asia' 02.07.1887, in: NA, London: FO 78/3999.
211. Jastrow, *The War and the Bagdad Railway*, pp. 82–3.
212. O'Conor to Salisbury, 02.02.1899, in: NA London, FO 78/5000; Earle, *Turkey, The Great Powers*, p. 31.
213. Gencer, *Imperialismus und die Orientalische Frage*, p. 103.
214. *Statistiques du Service des Recettes (Du 1er Janvier au 31 Décembre), Société du Chemin de fer Ottoman d' Anatolie* 1892: 57, in: PA. AA. 13451.
215. Earle, *Turkey, The Great Powers*, p. 33; Quataert, Donald, 'Limited Revolution: The Impact of the Anatolian Railway on Turkish Transportation and the Provisioning of Istanbul, 1890–1908', *The Business History Review* 51/2 (1977), p. 141; Pohl, Manfred, *Philipp Holzmann: Geschichte eines Bauunternehmens 1849–1999* (München, 1999), p. 100.
216. Woods, 'The Baghdad Railway', p. 35.
217. Quataert, 'Limited Revolution', p. 143.
218. O'Conor to Salisbury, 02.02.1899, in: NA, London: FO 78/5000.
219. *Sociéte du Chemin de fer Ottoman d'Anatolie, Bureau du Contrôle Haidar Pacha, Statistiques du Service des Recettes* 1893: 57 (25.02.1893), in: PA.AA. 13451.
220. Barth, 'The Financial History of the Anatolian and Baghdad Railways', p. 121.
221. Quataert, 'Limited Revolution', p. 159.
222. HA, Krupp WA 4/757.
223. Gall, *Die Deutsche Bank*, p. 74.
224. Önsoy, *Türk-Alman İktisadi Münasebetleri*, p. 26.
225. Ibid., pp. 27–8.
226. Ali Vahbi Bey collected the memoranda dictated by the Sultan and translated them into French and published in France under the title of *Avant la débâcle de la Turquie: Pensées et Souvenirs de l'Ex-Sultan Abdul-Hamid* when the Sultan was still alive in 1913. Ali Vahbi Bey (ed.), *Avant la debacle de la Turquie: Pensées et Souvenirs de l'ex-Sultan Abdul-Hamid* (Paris, 1913). Karpat argues that Ali Vahbi's collection is the most reliable collection that can be regarderd as a memoir of the Sultan. Karpat, Kemal, *The Politicization of Islam: Reconstructing Identity, State, Faith, and Community in the late Ottoman State* (New York, 2001), p. 445. See also Birinci, Ali, 'Sultan Abdülhamid'in Hâtıra Defteri Meselesi' *Divan İlmî Araştırmalar* 19 /2 (2005), pp. 177–94.

227. As it appears in his memoirs, Abdülhamid was content with the progress of the railway construction and its concrete economic outcomes. He detailed the positive contributions of the finished railroads to the regional macroeconomic indicators in a very optimistic way. Ali Vahbi Bey: *Avant la debacle*, pp. 62–3.
228. Grant, Jonathan A., 'The Sword of the Sultan, Ottoman Arms Imports, 1854–1914', *The Journal of Military History* 66 (2002), p. 24.
229. Birken, *Die Wirtschaftsbeziehungen zwischen Europa und dem Vorderen Orient*, p. 176.
230. BOA, *Y.A.RES.52/4* (08.01.1308/ 24.08.1890); Ortaylı, *İkinci Abdülhamit Döneminde*, p. 41; Önsoy, *Türk-Alman İktisadi Münasebetleri*, p. 36.
231. Grant, 'The Sword of the Sultan', p. 28.
232. İnalcık, Halil and Quataert, Donald (eds), *An Economic and Social History of the Ottoman Empire: 1600–1914*, vol. 2 (Cambridge, 1994), p. 774.
233. Barth, 'The Financial History of the Anatolian and Baghdad Railways', p. 116.
234. See also Geyikdağı, Necla, V., *Foreign Investment in the Ottoman Empire International Trade and Relations 1854–1914* (London 2011), pp. 47–52.
235. See also Beşirli, Mehmet, 'II. Abdulhamid Döneminde Osmanlı Ordusunda Alman Silahları' *Sosyal Bilimler Enstitüsü Dergisi* 1 (2004), pp. 121–39.

Chapter 2   German Military Advisers: Businessmen in Uniform

1. Marriott, *The Eastern Question*, p. 348.
2. Willi, A. Boelcke, *Krupp und die Hohenzollern in Dokumenten. Krupp-Korrespondenz mit Kaisern, Kabinettschefs und Ministern 1850–1918* (Frankfurt am Main, 1970), p. 20.
3. *The New York Times*, 3 March 1884.
4. Grant, *Rulers, Guns, and Money*, p. 5.
5. Epkenhans, 'Military-Industrial Relations in Imperial Germany', p. 20.
6. HA, Krupp: FAH 3B/244.
7. Wolf, Hellmut, *Die wirtschaftliche Entwicklung der Stadt Oberndorf a. Neckar mit besonderer Berücksichtigung der Mauserwerke und der Schwarzwälder Boten* (Tübingen, 1933), p. 51. See also: *Herrn Geheimrat Kommerzienrat Paul Mauser aus Anlass seines 70. Geburtstages gewidmet von der Redaktion des Schwarzwälder Boten* 1908: 19, in: SA, Oberndorf: XIV Ca 1/13.
8. Mauser to the Prussian Minister of War, in February 1908, in: SA, Oberndorf: M-A6.
9. Bülow, *Memoirs*, p. 576: 'Krupp had spread Germany's reputation and the renown of German work and industry over the world'; Kaiser Wilhelm II's speech, on 20 June 1890, in: HA, Krupp FAH 3E/1: '*Die Kruppische Fabrik hat*

dem deutschen Arbeiter, der deutschen Industrie einen Weltruhm verschafft, wie keine andere Firma dies getan hat.'
10. See Figure 2.1 (Chapter 2 p. 82); Figure 2.2 (Chapter 2 p. 99).
11. See also Benz, Wolfgang, 'Die Entstehung der Kruppschen Nachrichtendienstes', *Vierteljahreshefte für Zeitgeschichte* 24 (1976), pp. 199–205; Seel, 'Mauser-Gewehre' (1981a), p. 800.
12. Krupp to Bülow, 18.02.1899, in: PA.AA. R13295.
13. Krupp's response, 20.02.1900, in: HA, Krupp: FAH 3C/205.
14. Barker, *Modern Germany*, p. 30.
15. Projet des conditions d'engagement du personnel composant la mission militaire et civile allemande en Turquie 14.07.1880, in: PA.AA. R13233.
16. Wallach, *Bir Askeri Yardımın Anatomisi*, p. 33.
17. Hatzfeld to Hirschfeld, 03.02.1882, in: PA.AA. R13233.
18. See Alkan, Necmettin, 'II. Abdülhamid Devrinde İstihdam Edilen İlk Alman Askeri Heyetinin Komutanı Otto von Kähler ve İki Tarafın Beklentileri' *İstanbul Üniversitesi Edebiyat Fakültesi Tarih Dergisi* 43 (2007), pp. 135–165.
19. Menshausen to Krupp, 19.09.1891, in: HA, Krupp: FAH 3C/217.
20. BOA, *Y.PRK.BŞK.41/17* (02.11.1312/ 27.04.1895).
21. Cited in Grant, *Rulers, Guns, and Money*, pp. 81–2.
22. Cram's doctoral dissertation is a well-documented and well-explained study of German–Ottoman relations, in particular for the Bismarckian period. He notes the dispatch of the civil and military advisers to the Ottoman Empire and gives detailed correspondence between the German governments regarding the process. Cram, *German Interests*, pp. 124–132.
23. Kähler's Contract signed on 30.05.1882, in: MA, Freiburg: N.65/4.
24. Griffiths, *The Reorganization of the Ottoman Army*, p. 52.
25. MA, Freiburg: N.65/5 (14.06.1882).
26. MA, Freiburg: N.65/4 (30.05.1882); Griffiths, *The Reorganization of the Ottoman Army*, p. 52.
27. MA, Freiburg: N.65/4 (30.05.1882).
28. 'Projet des conditions d'engagement du personnel composant la mission militaire et civile allemande en Turquie' 14.07.1880, in: PA.AA. R13233.
29. 'Projet des conditions d'engagement du personnel composant la mission militaire et civile allemande en Turquie' 14.07.1880, in: PA.AA. R13233.
30. Wallach, *Bir Askeri Yardımın Anatomisi*, p. 32; Cram, *German Interests*, p. 169.
31. Alkan, 'II. Abdülhamid Devrinde İstihdam Edilen', p. 160.
32. MA, Freiburg: N.65/4 (30.05.1882); Wallach, *Bir Askeri Yardımın Anatomisi*, p. 33; Beydilli, Kemal, 'II. Abdulhamid Devrinde Gelen İlk Alman Askeri Heyeti Hakkında' *İstanbul Üniversitesi Edebiyat Fakültesi Tarih Dergisi* 32 (1979), p. 494.
33. BOA, *Y.PRK.HH.10/39* (24.05.1300/02.04.1883).
34. Wallach, *Bir Askeri Yardımın Anatomisi*, pp. 35, 58; Ortaylı, *İkinci Abdülhamit Döneminde*, pp. 73–6; Morawitz, Charles, *Die Türkei im Spiegel ihrer Finanzen* (Berlin, 1903), pp. 140–1.

35. Wallach, *Bir Askeri Yardımın Anatomisi*, pp. 49–51.
36. Cram, *German Interests*, p. 304.
37. Griffiths, *The Reorganization of the Ottoman Army*, p. 54; Cram, *German Interests*, pp. 258–9.
38. BOA, Y.PRK.ASK.14/5 (18.11.1299/01.10.1882).
39. BOA, Y.PRK.KOM.4/2 (13.01.1300/24.11.1882).
40. BOA, Y.PRK.HH.10/22 (06.04.1300/14.02.1883).
41. BOA, Y.PRK.ASK.18/7 (03.07.1300/10.05.1883).
42. Griffiths, *The Reorganization of the Ottoman Army*, pp. 54–5.
43. For Kähler's recommendations mentioned in his report, see Griffiths, *The Reorganization of the Ottoman Army*, pp. 55–6. See also Goltz, Friedrich, Freiherr von der and Förster, Wolfgang (eds), *Generalfeldmarschall Colmar Freiherr von der Goltz: Denkwürdigkeiten* (Berlin, 1929), pp. 109–112.
44. Wallach, *Bir Askeri Yardımın Anatomisi*, pp. 41–2; Uyar, Mesut and Erickson, J. Edward, *A Military History of the Ottomans: from Osman to Atatürk* (Santa Barbara, 2009), p. 205.
45. *The {London} Times*, 13 September 1882.
46. Griffiths, *The Reorganization of the Ottoman Army*, pp. 44–5; *The {London} Times*: 13.09.1882; Akmeşe, *The Birth of Modern Turkey*, p. 20; Uyar and Erickson, *A Military History of the Ottomans*, p. 205.
47. Chermside to St. John, 29.01.1881, in: NA, London: FO 881/4378.
48. For Kähler's report submitted to the German ambassador, see Wallach, *Bir Askeri Yardımın Anatomisi*, p. 42; for Gazi Ahmed Muhtar's approach to the reform projects see: Griffiths, *The Reorganization of the Ottoman Army*, p. 46f.
49. Cram, *German Interests*, p. 298.
50. Grant, *Rulers, Guns, and Money*, p. 80; Milgrim points out that the war indemnity provided Russia with leverage to exert her own influence on Ottoman finance. Milgrim, Michael, R., 'An Overlooked Problem in Turkish–Russian Relations: The 1878 War Indemnity', *International Journal of Middle East Studies* 9 (1978), p. 521.
51. Kössler, *Aktionsfeld Osmanisches Reich*, p. 120.
52. Cited in Griffiths, *The Reorganization of the Ottoman Army*, p. 63.
53. See also McMurray, *Distant Tie*, p. 26.
54. BOA, Y.PRK.NMH.2/47 (11.08.1300/18.05.1883).
55. Griffiths, *The Reorganization of the Ottoman Army*, p. 46f.
56. *The {London} Times*, 13 September 1882.
57. BOA, Y.PRK.NMH.2/47 (11.08.1300/18.05.1883).
58. Memorandum by Colonel Chermside, 25.05.1893, in: NA, London: FO 78/4479.
59. Wallach asserted that in Goltz Pasha was of opinion that his fellow countrymen (Kähler, Kamphövener, and Ristow) were not suitable for Foreign Service. The training methods and other recommendations they offered, as Goltz Pasha pointed out, just copied what was done in Germany. Wallach, *Bir*

Askeri Yardımın Anatomisi, p. 46; see also: Ortaylı, *İkinci Abdülhamit Döneminde*, p. 76.
60. Memorandum by Colonel Chermside, 25.05.1893, in: NA, London: FO 78/4479. Goltz was not only an able military writer, he also wrote on political/ economic issues like the Macedonian question or Baghdad Railway. See Goltz, Colmar Freiherr, von der, 1903, 'Woran es in Makedonien gefehlt hat?', in: MA, Freiburg Nachlass von Von der Goltz (hereafter MA, Freiburg: NL.737/16).The original paper was published in 1903/18 in: *Velhagen und Klasings Monatshefte*: 641–7; Goltz, Colmar Freiherr, von der, 1900/14, 'Die deutsche Bagdadbahn', in: *Velhagen und Klasings Monatshefte:* 697ff. cited in Schöllgen, *Imperialismus und Gleichgewicht*, p. 123.
61. Karabekir, Kâzım, *Türkiye'de ve Türk Ordusunda Almanlar*, edited by Orhan Hülagü and Ömer Hakan Özalp (İstanbul, 2001), p. 279.
62. Ibid., p. 239.
63. Like many others, for instance, Griffiths also says – without giving any documentary proof – that Goltz Pasha was involved in the Mauser transaction. Wallach, who has also pointed to Goltz's statement about the impact of the personal influence on the Ottoman decision making process, says that 'in the obtaining of the arms contracts, Goltz Pasha's influence was enormous.' Griffiths, *The Reorganization of the Ottoman Army*, pp. 69–70; McGarity, *Foreign Influence*, pp. 35–9; Swanson, W. Glen, 'War, Technology and Society in the Ottoman Empire from the reign of Abdulhamid II to 1913: Mahmud Şevket and the German Military Mission', in V. J. Parry and M. E. Yapp (eds), *War and Technology in the Middle East* (London, 1975), pp. 367–85; Kössler, *Aktionsfeld Osmanisches Reich*, pp. 120–3; Wallach, *Bir Askeri Yardımın Anatomisi*, p. 105; Yasamee, 'Colmar Freiherr von der Goltz and the Rebirth', pp. 91–128; Akmeşe, *The Birth of Modern Turkey*, pp. 19–33; Türk, *Die deutsche Rüstungsindustrie*, pp. 61–7 and 183–4; Grant, *Rulers, Guns, and Money*, pp. 81–94.
64. Yasamee, 'Colmar Freiherr von der Goltz and the Rebirth', p. 92; Foley, Robert T., *German Strategy and the Path to Verdun: Erich von Falkenhayn and the Development of Attrition, 1870–1916* (Cambridge, 2005), pp. 25–30; Uyar and Erickson, *A Military History of the Ottomans*, p. 205.
65. *The New York Times*, 19 July 1908.
66. BOA, *Y.PRK.BŞK.8/23* (19.02.1301/20.12.1883).
67. Griffiths, *The Reorganization of the Ottoman Army*, p. 53.
68. See also 'Mekâtib-i 'askeriye için Almanya'dan celb olunan Baron Goltz için mukâvelenâme tanzîmi', in: BOA, *I.DH. 888/70644* (14.08.1300/20.06.1883); Griffiths, *The Reorganization of the Ottoman Army*, p. 60; Beydilli, 'II. Abdulhamid Devrinde', p. 494.
69. Akmeşe, *The Birth of Modern Turkey*, p. 21; McGarity gives the year of Kähler Pasha's death and Goltz's arrival incorrectly as 1883: 'The group was headed initially by a Colonel von Köhler [Kähler] who unfortunately died in 1883. He was replaced that year by Colonel Colmar Freiherr von der Goltz.' McGarity,

Foreign Influence, p. 36, see also Goltz and Förster, *Generalfeldmarschall Colmar Freiherr von der Goltz*, p. 138; Wallach, *Bir Askeri Yardımın Anatomisi*, p. 51.
70. Wallach, *Bir Askeri Yardımın Anatomisi*, p. 70.
71. Giesl von Gieslingen, Wladimir F., *Zwei Jahrzehnte im Nahen Orient: Aufzeichnungen des Generals der Kavallerie Baron Wladimir Giesl*, Ritter von Steinitz (ed.) (Berlin, 1927), p. 48. Goltz's contract was extended three times. See Wallach, *Bir Askeri Yardımın Anatomisi*, pp. 53–68.
72. BOA, *I.ASK.1327.R.23 Vesika No.26* (20.03.1327/11.04.1909); BOA, *MV.127/23* (29.04.1327/ 20.05.1909).
73. Demirhan, Pertev, *Generalfeldmarschall Colmar Freiherr von der Goltz: Das Lebensbild eines großen Soldaten: aus meinen persönlichen Erinnerungen* (Göttingen, 1960), pp. 130–200; Yasamee, 'Colmar Freiherr von der Goltz and the Rebirth', pp. 112–23. Finally, Goltz Pasha died in Baghdad on 19 April 1916, just before the victory of Kut-al-'Amara where the British were surrounded and he was buried in the grounds of the German Consulate in İstanbul, where he had first come in 1883. Ulus, İbrahim, 'Colmar Freiherr Von der Goltz'un Biyografisi', *Askeri Tarih Bülteni* 11/21 (1986), pp. 81–2; Goltz and Förster, *Generalfeldmarschall Colmar Freiherr von der Goltz*, p. 78; Kâzım Karabekir, *Türkiye'de ve Türk Ordusunda Almanlar*, pp. 280–1; Yasamee, 'Colmar Freiherr von der Goltz and the Rebirth', p. 122.
74. Cram, *German Interests*, p. 262.
75. According to the writers of *Denkwürdigkeiten*, Goltz Pasha arrived in İstanbul on 15 June. Goltz and Förster, *Generalfeldmarschall Colmar Freiherr von der Goltz*, p. 108; however Wallach gave another arrival date as 18 June. Besides, Grant claims incorrectly: 'later that same year [1882] Colmar Freiherr von der Goltz joined the mission.' Grant, *Rulers, Guns, and Money*, p. 81. See also Ulus, 'Goltz'un Biyografisi', pp. 81–2.
76. Goltz and Förster, *Generalfeldmarschall Colmar Freiherr von der Goltz*, p. 108.
77. Ibid., p. 108: 'Man gewinnt sehr schnell das Gefühl, einer hochintelligenten Persönlichkeit gegenüberzustehen.'
78. Goltz, Colmar Freiherr, von der, 'Stärke und Schwäche des türkischen Reiches', *Deutsche Rundschau* 93 (1897a), p. 95.
79. BOA, *İ.DH.888/70644* (14.08.1300/20.06.1883).
80. BOA, *Y.PRK.KOM.4/13* (23.09.1300/28.07.1883).
81. *Abschrift*: Goltz to Menshausen, 01.08.1891, in: HA, Krupp: FAH 3B/216.
82. Goltz to Menshausen, 01.08.1891, in: HA, Krupp: FAH 3B/216.
83. Wilhelm II to the German Chancellor, 19.11.1891, in: PA.AA. R13285. See Chapter IV, pp. 186–193.
84. *Unnamed*, 21.12.1891, in: HA, Krupp FAH 3C/217: This document is a letter from one of the members of the German military mission in the Ottoman army. However, if we compare the wording, expressions, and contents of this letter with Goltz Pasha's other handwritten letters, it seems likely that he wrote this letter as well.
85. *Unnamed*, 21.12.1891, in: HA, Krupp FAH 3C/217.

86. *Unnamed*, 21.12.1891, in: HA, Krupp FAH 3C/217.
87. Hohenlohe-Schillingsfürst, *Memoirs of Prince Chlodwig*, vol. 2, p. 268.
88. BOA, *Y.PRK.MYD.6/34* (14.08.1304/08.05.1887): According to Goltz Pasha's report sent from Berlin to the sultan, he met Bismarck in a family dinner and was questioned in detail about the Ottoman Empire.
89. Herwig, H. Helger, *Germany's Vision of Empire in Venezuela 1871–1914* (Princeton, NJ, 1986); Nunn, M. Fredrick, 'Emil Körner and the Prussianization of the Chilean Army: Origins, Process, and Consequences, 1885–1920', *The Hispanic American Historical Review* 50/2 (1970), pp. 300–22.
90. Griffiths, *The Reorganization of the Ottoman Army*, p. 58.
91. Goltz and Förster, *Generalfeldmarschall Colmar Freiherr von der Goltz*, p. 134.
92. The term 'German politicians in uniform' is cited in Akmeşe, *The Birth of Modern Turkey*, p. 10.
93. See Wallach, *Bir Askeri Yardımın Anatomisi*, p. 42; Griffiths, *The Reorganization of the Ottoman Army*, p. 54.
94. Harrison, Austin, *The Pan-Germanic Doctrine: Being a Study of German Political Aims and Aspirations* (London and New York, 1904), p. 225; In one of his letters to Pertev Pasha, Goltz Pasha indicated the importance of the railroad in terms of its military usage: Goltz to Pertev, 18.12.1910, in: MA, Freiburg: NL.737/5. See also Hallgarten, G. Wolfgang, *Imperialismus vor 1914* (2 vols) (München, 1963), p. 406.
95. BOA, *Y.PRK.MYD.6/34* (17.08.1304/11.05.1887).
96. Grant, 'The Sword of the Sultan,' p. 23.
97. The code of 'Robert' was used for Ragıb Bey by the later director of the Krupp Company, Carl Menshausen. See Chapter 5, p. 242.
98. See the MA, Freiburg: NL.737/5–NL.737/11. See also Demirhan, *Generalfeldmarschall Colmar Freiherr von der Goltz*; Yasamee, F. A. K., 'Colmar Freiherr Von der Goltz and the Boer War,' in Keith M. Wilson (ed.), *The International Impact of the Boer War* (London, 2001).
99. Goltz and Förster, *Generalfeldmarschall Colmar Freiherr von der Goltz*, p. 114.
100. *The New York Times*, 8 November 1885.
101. Wallach, *Bir Askeri Yardımın Anatomisi*, p. 90.
102. Memorandum by Colonel Chermside, 25.05.1893, in: NA, London: FO 78/4479.
103. BOA, *Y.PRK.ASK.31/52* (22.04.1303/28.01.1886); Goltz and Förster, *Generalfeldmarschall Colmar Freiherr von der Goltz*, p. 134.
104. Memorandum of Ritter von Manéga, 06.06.1886, in: PA.AA. R13237.
105. Goltz and Förster, *Generalfeldmarschall Colmar Freiherr von der Goltz*, p. 135.
106. Ibid., p. 1935; Rottenburg to Unterstaatssekretär, 06.06.1886, in: PA.AA. R13237.
107. *Abschrift* of Kaiser Wilhelm I, 22.07.1886, in: PA.AA. R13237.
108. Goltz and Förster, *Generalfeldmarschall Colmar Freiherr von der Goltz*, p. 135; Griffiths, *The Reorganization of the Ottoman Army*, p. 70; Wallach, *Bir Askeri Yardımın Anatomisi*, pp. 55–6.

109. BOA, *Y.PRK.ASK.33/62* (20.10.1303/22.07.1886); *Abschrift* of Kaiser Wilhelm I, 22.07.1886, in: PA.AA. R13237; Radowitz to Bismarck, 02.08.1886, in: PA.AA. R13237.
110. Rottenburg to Unterstaatssekretär, 06.06.1886, in: PA.AA. R13237; Prince Reuss to Bismarck, 29.07.1886, in: PA.AA. R13237; for the Austrian interest in Goltz Pasha's contract's extension see also: Wallach, *Bir Askeri Yardımın Anatomisi*, pp. 55–6.
111. Rottenburg to Unterstaatssekretär, 06.06.1886, in: PA.AA. R13237.
112. Demirhan, *Generalfeldmarschall Colmar Freiherr von der Goltz*, p. 255: '*Goltz war nicht nur für uns (The Ottoman Empire), sondern auch für Deutschland unersetzlich.*'
113. Yasamee, *Ottoman Diplomacy*, p. 190.
114. Ibid., pp. 188–95.
115. Prince Reuss to Bismarck, 29.07.1886, in: PA.AA. R13237.
116. See Chapter 3, pp. 108–47.
117. BOA, *Y.PRK.ASK.40/36* (29.09.1304/21.06.1887): '*Avusturya Devleti Avrupa'nın ve belki kendi hey'etinin zân ve kıyâsından ziyâde kuvvetli bir hâldedir.*'
118. Radowitz to Bismarck, 02.08.1886, in: PA.AA. R13237; Goltz and Förster, *Generalfeldmarschall Colmar Freiherr von der Goltz*, p. 138; Griffiths, *The Reorganization of the Ottoman Army*, pp. 70–1; Wallach, *Bir Askeri Yardımın Anatomisi*, p. 57.
119. Griffiths, *The Reorganization of the Ottoman Army*, p. 72; Zürcher, Erik, Jan, 'The Ottoman Conscription System in Theory and Practise 1844–1918', *International Review of Social History* 43/3 (1998), pp. 437–49; Akmeşe, *The Birth of Modern Turkey*, pp. 6, 23.
120. Radowitz to Bismarck, 02.08.1886, in: PA.AA. R13237; Morawitz, *Die Türkei im Spiegel*, p. 138.
121. Griffiths, *The Reorganization of the Ottoman Army*, p. 75; however, the following authors give different information about the time to be spent in each category: Morawitz, *Die Türkei im Spiegel*, p. 139; Shaw and Shaw, *History of the Ottoman Empire*, p. 245; Zürcher, 'Ottoman Conscription System', p. 440; Akmeşe, *The Birth of Modern Turkey*, p. 23.
122. Yasamee, *Ottoman Diplomacy*, p. 194.
123. Akmeşe, *The Birth of Modern Turkey*, p. 22.
124. Ibid., p. 22.
125. Griffiths, *The Reorganization of the Ottoman Army*, p. 79.
126. Goltz to Kiderlen, 22.11.1891, in: PA.AA. R13763.
127. For the mobilization plan and the distribution of the military forces suggested by the commission, see Griffiths, *The Reorganization of the Ottoman Army*, p. 76–83.
128. BOA, *Y.PRK.ASK.59/6* (07.07.1307/27.02.1890).
129. Chermside Memorandum, 05.12.1889, in: NA, London: FO 195/1664 cited in Griffiths, *The Reorganization of the Ottoman Army*, p. 87.
130. BOA, *Y.PRK.ASK.59/6* (07.07.1307/27.02.1890.
131. See also Griffiths, *The Reorganization of the Ottoman Army*, p. 88.

132. The total amount in the list prepared by Serasker Rıza Pasha consisted of the numbers of the following units: the officer corps; the civil service workers; the students; and the regular soldiers (*Efrâd-ı Şâhâne*). Rıza Paşa, *Hülâsa-ı Hâtırâtım* (İstanbul 1325/1909), Mukâyese-Ekler.
133. BOA, Y.PRK.ASK.59/6 (07.07.1307/27.02.1890).
134. BOA, Y.PRK.ASK.52/77 (04.04.1306/06.01.1889).
135. Goltz to Schellendorf, 13.12.1886, in: SA, Oberndorf: M-A8.
136. BOA, Y.PRK.TKM.10/20 (11.06.1304/07.04.1887).
137. See Küntzer, Karl, *Abdul Hamid II und die Reformen in der Türkei* (Dresden and Leipzig, 1897), p. 22.
138. Hohenlohe-Schillingsfürst, *Memoirs of Prince Chlodwig*, vol. 2, p. 268.
139. Goltz to the Kaiser, 28.10.1891, in: PA.AA. R13763.
140. *The New York Times*, 31 December 1916; Mombauer, Annika, *Helmuth von Moltke and the Origins of the First World War* (Cambridge and New York, 2001), p. 120.
141. Lowther to Grey, 30.11.1908, in: NA, London, FO 371/560.
142. Cited in Lorenz, Charlotte, 'Die Frauenfrage im Osmanischen Reiche mit Besonderer Berücksichtigung der Arbeitenden Klasse', *Die Welt des Islams* 6/3–4 (1918), p. 206: 'Seine [Von der Goltz] größten Erfolge hat er hier sicherlich durch sein psychologisches Feingefühl erworben.'

Chapter 3 Arms Orders and Contracts: The First Fruits of Personal Diplomacy

1. BOA, Y.PRK. ASK. 7/74 (20.08.1898/18.07.1881). See also Şakir, Ziya, *Tanzimat Devrinden Sonra Osmanlı Nizam Ordusu Tarihi* (İstanbul, 1957), pp. 60–2.
2. Captain W. Cecil H. Domville, 'Turkish Fleet and Dockyards 1888', in: NA, London: ADM 231/14:12.See also Grant, 'The Sword of the Sultan', p. 25.
3. Captain W. Cecil H. Domville, 'Turkish Fleet and Dockyards 1890', in: NA, London: ADM 231/18:12. See also Grant, 'The Sword of the Sultan', p. 25.
4. Captain G. Le C. Egerton, 'Turkish Fleet and Dockyards 1894', in: NA, London: ADM 231/24:17.
5. Ibid., pp. 16–7: *Tophâne* Arsenal-Gun factory: 'Very little work is going on in the Gun Factory; 200 men are said to be employed, but I doubt it'; Cartridge factory: 'No work in cartridge factory has been done for years'; Powder factory: 'There was no work going on except some blasting powder for commercial purposes'; *Karaağaç*: 'Only 50 men are employed at present, the only work in hand being percussion fuzes and friction tubes.' See also BOA, Y.PRK. ASK. 7/74 (20.08.1898/18.07.1881) and BOA; Y.PRK.ASK. 7/31 (10.07.1298/08.06.1881).

6. Letters and reports sent and received by Otto Dingler and Krupp between 1872 and 1873, in: HA, Krupp: FAH. 2/B 314a. See also 'Entschiedenheit gegenüber der Dinglerschen Taktik in Konstantinopel, 06.03.1881' in: HA, Krupp: FAH 2M 78/19: 'Ich (A. Krupp) glaube Dingler nicht. Ich glaube auch nicht, dass er [sozusagen] die 4000 [Ottoman Lira] Trinkgeld für den Schmuck gegeben hat auch nicht, dass ihm an unserem Interesse was gelegen sondern dass er, mit viel Gewandtheit und Routine für sein Interesse sich auf unsere Kosten durchfrisst.'
7. *Verzeichnis der von der Gußstahlfabrik und vom Grusonwerk von 1847 bis 1912 gefertigten Kanonen*, in: HA, Krupp: 5a VII f. 862: 44–44a.
8. BOA, Y.PRK.KOM 3/18 (20.09.1298/ 10.08.1881).
9. BOA, Y.PRK.ASK.12/52 (15.07.1299/02.06.1882).
10. BOA, Y.EE.106/18 (02.01.1301/03.11.1883).
11. BOA, Y.PRK.KOM 4/32 (27.01.1301/28.11.1883).
12. *Beziehungen zur Türkei*, 25.05. 1916, in: HA, Krupp: WA 7f -886.
13. BOA, Y.PRK.ASK.49/104 (1305/1887).
14. Murphy used this expression for the tactics of Nordenfelt, Garret, and Zaharoff, who were trying to sell to the Ottoman Empire naval materials (torpedoes, submarines etc.) Murphy, William Scanlan, *Father of the Submarine* (London, 1987), p. 116.
15. Erickson, Edward, J., *Defeat in Detail: the Ottoman Army in the Balkans, 1912–1913* (Westport, 2003), pp. 13–14.
16. According to the British ambassador Sir William White, after reading Şakir Pasha's report the Sultan said: 'I was not aware till now that Şakir Pasha had become so Russian in his views.' White to Salisbury, 12.09.1890, in: NA, London: FO 78/4277; see also Yasamee, *Ottoman Diplomacy*, p. 173.
17. Hatzfeld to the German embassy in Vienna, 20.12.1881, in: PA.AA. R13427.
18. BOA, Y.PRK.ASK.40/36 (29.09.1304/21.06.1887).
19. The term given between the inverted commas quoted in Murphy, *Father of the Submarine*, p. 116.
20. Albertini, Luigi, *Origins of the War of 1914*, Vol. 3 (New York, 2005), p. 606.
21. Cram, *German Interests*, p. 331.
22. Dingler to Ali Saib Pasha, 18.02.1885, in: HA, Krupp: WA 2/249.
23. BOA, I.MMS.80/3473 (04.10.1302/17.07.1885).
24. BOA, I.MMS.80/3473 (04.10.1302/17.07.1885).
25. Schedule of the payment for the ordered Krupp guns, in: BOA, I.MMS. 80/3473 (12.10.1302/25.07.1885).
26. BOA, I.MMS.80/3473 (27.07.1885); BOA, I.MMS. 80/3473 (27.08.1302/11.06.1885); BOA, I.MMS. 80/3473 (19.10.1302/01.08.1885).
27. BOA, I.MMS.80/3473 (28.08.1302/11.07.1885).
28. Grant, 'The Sword of the Sultan', p. 23.
29. Kössler, *Aktionsfeld Osmanisches Reich*, p. 121.

NOTES TO PAGES 105–109   285

30. See also Goltz and Förster, *Generalfeldmarschall Colmar Freiherr von der Goltz*, p. 140.
31. Grant, 'The Sword of the Sultan', p. 23.
32. Ali Saib Pasha was the Serasker between 1886 and 1891. Şakir, *Tanzimat Devrinden Sonra*, pp. 93–4.
33. BOA, *I.MMS.82/3533*; BOA, *Y.A.HUS 486/9*: *Mübâya'ât-ı Mühimme Defteri (HH 26363:2)*.
34. BOA, *Y.A.HUS486/9*: *Mübâya'ât-ı Mühimme Defteri (HH 26363:1)*. See also: BOA, *Y.PRK.ML.7/29* (18.11.1304/08.08.1887).
35. BOA, *Y.MTV.29/102* (25.04.1305/10.01.1888); BOA, *Y.A.HUS 486/9*: *Mübâya'ât-ı Mühimme Defteri (HH 26363:2)*. Griffiths gave the total amount paid to the Krupp Company as 1,206,987 OL. Griffiths, *The Reorganization of the Ottoman Army*, p. 69.
36. BOA, *MV. 4/53* (24.10.1302/06.08.1885).
37. BOA, *MV. 5/76* (15.01.1303/24.10.1885); BOA, *A.MKT.MHM 490/6* (19.07.1303/23.04.1886).
38. BOA, *I.DH.1295.5.102347* (11.05.1305/25.01.1888).
39. BOA, *Y.EE.106/18* (02.01.1301/03.11.1883).
40. Grant, 'The Sword of the Sultan', p. 23.
41. Griffiths, *The Reorganization of the Ottoman Army*, p. 68.
42. Demirhan, *Generalfeldmarschall Colmar Freiherr von der Goltz*, p. 17.
43. Goltz and Förster, *Generalfeldmarschall Colmar Freiherr von der Goltz*, p. 124.
44. 'Turkey: Coast Defences & C. in Europe, Asia, and Africa 1889', in: NA, London: ADM 231/14: 30.
45. BOA, *Y.PRK.ASK.31/82* (28.05.1303/04.03.1886).
46. See for the pictures that illustrate the construction and armament of Fort Macarkale, which had been completely remodelled according to design of a former German officer, General Bluhm Pasha, with Krupp guns 'Turkey: Coast Defences &c. in Europe, Asia, and Africa 1889', in: NA, London: ADM 231/14: 46.
47. Goltz and Förster, *Generalfeldmarschall Colmar Freiherr von der Goltz*, pp. 124–40; see also Hallgarten, G. W. F., *Vorkriegs Imperialismus: Die soziologischen Grundlagen der Außenpolitik Europäischer Großmächte bis 1914* (Paris, 1935), pp. 128–9.
48. BOA, *Y.PRK.ASK.35/60* (21.01.1304/20.10.1886).
49. Grant, 'The Sword of the Sultan', p. 28.
50. BOA, *Y.PRK.ASK.35/22* (14.12.1303/13.09.1886).
51. BOA, *Y.PRK.ASK.35/60* (21.01.1304/20.10.1886).
52. BOA, *Y.A.HUS.486/9:Mübâya'ât-ı Mühimme Defteri (HH 26363:6)*; see also BOA, *A.MKT.MHM.492/35* (29.01.1304/28–10–1886); 'Present and Prospective Ship Building of Foreign Nations 1886 (Turkey)', in: NA, London: ADM 231/10: 18.
53. Captain Henry C. Kane, 'Turkish Fleet and Dockyards 1886', in: NA, London: ADM 231/10:10.
54. Ibid.

55. Cited in Seel, 'Mauser-Gewehre' (1981a), p. 800: '[Mahmud] Schefket [Pasha] ist der richtige Mann, die anderen stehen auf Seiten Ihrer Konkurrenten.'
56. Ibid.
57. BOA, Y.PRK.ASK.1/25 (22.04.1294 /24.06.05.1877).
58. In October 1872, the initial order was 200,000 rifles. BOA, I.MMS. 44/1827 (12.08.1289/ 15.10.1872). However, in May 1873 the order was increased to 500,000. BOA, I.DH.667/46434 (23.03.1290/21.05.1873); finally, in August 1873 the Ottoman government had decided to order a further 100,000 rifles and thus, the final amount reached 600,000. BOA, A.MKT. MHM.462/38 (01.07.1290/25.08.1873); According to Colonel Lennox, the British military attaché, 280,000 of the ordered rifles were delivered on 11 January 1877. Colonel Lennox to charge d'affaires/Constantinople, 13.02.1877, in: NA, London: WO 106/2.
59. BOA, Y.PRK KOM.3/18 (20.09.1298/10.08.1881): *Tophâne-i 'Âmire fazlası and Tersâne-i 'Âmire fazlası*. See also Chapter III, pp. 111–4.
60. BOA, Y.A.RES.36/17 (19.04.1304/15.01.1887).
61. *Abschrift von der Versammlung*, 02.05.1886, in: SA, Oberndorf: M-A3.
62. Seel, 'Mauser-Puzzle', pp. 42–7.
63. Paul Mauser's notebook is mentioned in Seel, 'Mauser-Puzzle'.
64. Seel, Wolfgang, *Mauser: Von der Waffenschmiede zum Weltunternehmen* (Zürich, 1986), pp. 37–8.
65. Haßler, Fridrich and Bihl Adolf (eds), *Geschichte der Mauser-Werke* (Berlin, 1938), p. 89.
66. Kaulla to Mauser, 13.11.1886, in: SA, Oberndorf: M-A3.
67. Following the agreement of partnership signed on 1 April 1884, the bank took over the 1,666 shares, while Paul Mauser had the remaining 334. Speed, J. S. Walter, and Herrmann, Reiner, *Mauser Original Oberndorf Sporting Rifles* (Cobourg, 1997), p. 27; Haßler and Bihl, *Geschichte der Mauser-Werke*, p. 89; see also, Seel, 'Mauser-Gewehre' (1981a), p. 802.
68. Loewe to Kaulla, 18.11.1886, in: SA, Oberndorf: M-A8.
69. Kaulla to Mauser, 22.11.1886, in: Oberndorf: M-A3; Seel, 'Mauser-Puzzle', p. 45; Seel, 'Mauser-Gewehre' (1981a), p. 802.
70. *Depeschen Schlüssel für Constantinopel zwischen Aug. Huber & C. Constantinopel einerseits und Ludw. Loewe & Co. Berlin und Waffenfabrik Mauser, Oberndorf anderseits*, [22–23] November 1886, in: SA, Oberndorf: M-A8.
71. See Chapter 5, p. 242.
72. White to Salisbury, 14.01.1891, in: NA. London: FO 78/4342.
73. Seel, 'Mauser-Gewehre' (1981a), p. 800.
74. Seel, 'Mauser-Puzzle', p. 45; see also Haßler and Bihl, *Geschichte der Mauser-Werke*, p. 90.
75. King to Blaine, 24.12.1889, in: NARA-Microfilm, College Park: M46/50; memorandum by Colonel Chermside, 25.05.1893, in: NA, London: FO 78/4479.
76. Cited in Seel, 'Mauser-Gewehre' (1981a), p. 800.
77. Ibid.

78. Seel, 'Mauser-Gewehre' (1981a), p. 800.
79. Goltz to Schellendorf, 13.12.1886, in: SA, Oberndorf: M-A8.
80. Cited in Seel, 'Mauser-Gewehre' (1981a), p. 800.
81. Goltz to Schellendorf, 13.12.1886, in: SA, Oberndorf: M-A8.
82. BOA, Y.MTV.29/19 (13.01.1305/31.10.1887).
83. See Chapter 5, pp. 242–3.
84. Goltz, Colmar Freiherr, von der, 'Erinnerungen an Mahmud Shewket Pascha', *Deutsche Rundschau* 157 (1913), pp. 32–46; see also Swanson, 'War, Technology, and Society', p. 372. For Mahmud Şevket Pasha's contribution and Pro-Mauser acts and speeches during the commission meeting, see Chapter 5, pp. 235–7.
85. *The {London} Times*, 7 February 1887.
86. BOA, Y.A.HUS.486/9: *Mübâya'ât-ı Mühimme Defteri* (HH 26363:7).
87. BOA, Y.A.RES.37/2 (03.06.1304/27.02.1887).
88. Ball, Robert, W. D., *Mauser Military Rifles of the World* (Iola, WI, 2006), p. 359.
89. BOA, Y.A.RES.37/2 (05.05.1304/30.01.1887); Grant gives the unit price of a single Mauser rifle as 362 kuruş. Grant, *Rulers, Guns, and Money*, p. 83.
90. BOA, Y.A.HUS.486/9:*Mübâya'ât-ı Mühimme Defteri* (HH 26363:7): 36,835,425 marks (1 OL = 18.45 marks): 1,815,000 for rifles; OL 181,500 for carbines.
91. BOA, İ.DH.1019/80376 (19.05.1304/13.02.1887).
92. Seel, 'Mauser-Puzzle', p. 45; Seel, 'Mauser-Gewehre' (1981a), p. 802.
93. Grant, *Rulers, Guns, and Money*, p. 83.
94. Seel, 'Mauser-Gewehre' (1981a), p. 801.
95. Olson, Ludwig, *Mauser: Bolt Rifles* (Montezuma, 1976), p. 37; Speed and Reiner, *Mauser Original*, p. 28.
96. Olson, *Mauser*, p. 37.
97. Speed and Reiner, *Mauser Original*, p. 28.
98. See also pp. 159–60 below.
99. Olson, *Mauser*, p. 37.
100. *The {London} Times*, 19 February 1887.
101. BOA, Y.A.RES.37/2 (03.06.1304/27.02.1887).
102. BOA, İ.DH.1019/80376 (19.06.1304/13.02.1887).
103. BOA, MV.18/10 (17.06.1304/13.03.1887).
104. BOA, Y.PRK.MYD.6/21 (18.06.1304/14.03.1887).
105. BOA, Y.A.RES.37/34 (17.07.1304/ 11.04.1887).
106. BOA, Y.A.RES.37/34 (17.07.1304/ 11.04.1887).
107. Seel, Wolfgang, 'Mauser-Gewehre unter dem Halbmond, Türkenmauser', *Deutsche Waffenjournal* 2 (1981b), p. 977.
108. BOA, MV.18/10 (17.06.1304/13.03.1887).
109. BOA, Y.MTV.91/11 (18.08.1311/24.02.1894).
110. BOA, Y.A.RES.39/50 (20.7.1304/14.04.1887).
111. Türk, *Die deutsche Rüstungsindustrie*, p. 107.
112. Kraus, *Für Geld, Kaiser und Vaterland*, p. 64.

113. Seel, 'Mauser-Gewehre' (1981b), pp. 966–77; Türk, *Die deutsche Rüstungsindustrie*, p. 118; Kraus, *Für Geld, Kaiser und Vaterland*, pp. 63–9.
114. Kraus, *Für Geld, Kaiser und Vaterland*, p. 67; see also Türk, *Die deutsche Rüstungsindustrie*, p. 107.
115. BOA, *MV.21/55* (15.10.1304/07.07.1887).
116. BOA, *Y.A.RES.38/23* (19.10.1304/11.07.1887).
117. BOA, *Y.A.HUS.486/9*: *Mübâya'ât-ı Mühimme Defteri* (HH 26363:13).
118. Uyar and Erickson, *A Military History of the Ottomans*, p. 211.
119. BOA, *Y.PRK.ASK.211/40* (01.11.1321/19.01.1904); see Table 3.9c, Chapter 3, p. 145.
120. Goltz to Mauser, 25.11.1887, in: SA, Oberndorf: M-A8.
121. BOA, *Y.PRK.EŞA.6/61* (19.04.1887). See Chapter 1, pp. 35–6.
122. BOA, *Y.PRK.ASK.39/67* (27.07.1304/21.04.1887): 'Berlin'de en ziyâde me'zûniyet ve hükmü hâ'iz olan menâbi'den ahz eylediğim ma'lûmâta nazaran Mavzer usûlünde mükerrer atışlı tüfenklere mahsûs olan fişenklerde isti'mâl olunacak en ekmel barut Rotvayl'daki [Rottweil] Mösyö Duttenhofer' in [Max Duttenhofer] i'mâl etmekde olduğu barut[dur].'
123. BOA, *Y.PRK.MYD.6/34* (14.08.1304/08.05.1887).
124. Goltz to Schellendorf, 13.12.1886, in: SA, Oberndorf: M-A8.
125. BOA, *Y.PRK.MYD.6/34* (14.08.1304/08.05.1887): 'bâ-husus Duttenhofer mühimmât meselelerinde ziyâdesiyle ehil ve erbâbdır.'
126. Menshausen to Richthofen, 18.01.1898, in: PA. AA. R13291.
127. Mauser to Goltz, 30.11.1887, in: SA, Oberndorf: M-A8.
128. Seel, 'Mauser-Gewehre' (1981b), p. 977.
129. Goltz to Mauser, 25.11.1887, in: SA, Oberndorf: M-A8.
130. See also Goltz Pasha's letter sent to Menshausen, Krupp's agent and later director of the company: Goltz to Menshausen, 01.08.1891, in: HA, Krupp: FAH. 3B/216.
131. Goltz to Mauser, 25.11.1887, in: SA, Oberndorf: M-A8.
132. Mauser to Goltz, 30.11.1887, in: SA, Oberndorf: M-A8: 'Ihre Beschreibung über das französische Pulver, stimmt ganz genau mit dem mir inzwischen zu Gesicht gekommenen, und hoffe ich, Ihnen hierüber noch Näheres schreiben zu können.'
133. Goltz to Mauser, 25.11.1887, in: SA, Oberndorf: M-A8: 'Soweit die chemische Untersuchengen dies bis jetzt hat feststellen können ist die Lagerungsfähigkeit des Pulvers als eine günstige zu betrachten'.
134. BOA, *Y.PRK.ASK.52/77* (29.04.1306/02.01.1889): 'Erbâb-ı vukûfdan bir zât tarafından ahz eylediğim ma'lûmat-ı mevsûkaya nazaran evsâf-ı fevka'l-'âdesi kemâl-i mübâlağa ile i'zâm edilen Fransız barutunun matlûb derecede dayanıklı olmadığı sûret-i kat'iyede tebeyyün etmişdir.'
135. Goltz to Mauser, 23.11.1887, in: SA, Oberndorf: M-A8.
136. Mauser to Goltz, 24.11.1887, in: SA, Oberndorf: M-A8: 'Die Waffenfabrik Mauser besteht und wird bestehen wie bisher. Ich bin und bleibe an der Spitze derselben.'

137. Undated: *Abschrift*, Waffenfabrik Mauser, Oberndorf, in: SA, Oberndorf: M-A6; Haßler and Bihl, *Geschichte der Mauser-Werke*, p. 91.
138. BOA, *Y.PRK.BŞK.13/41* (27.10.1305/07.07.1888).
139. Ragıb to Mauser, 17.10.1887, in: SA, Oberndorf: M-A3.
140. Goltz to Mauser, 22.11.1887, in: SA, Oberndorf: M-A8.
141. Goltz to Mauser, 25.11.1887, in: SA, Oberndorf: M-A8.
142. BOA, *Y.PRK.BŞK.13/41* (22.10.1305/02.07.1888).
143. Speed and Reiner, *Mauser Original*, p. 29.
144. BOA, *Y.MTV.34/11* (08.11.1305/17.07.1888).
145. BOA, *Y.A.HUS.486/9*: *Mübâya'ât-ı Mühimme Defteri* (HH 26363:8); see also: BOA, *Y.MTV. 34/11* (08.11.1305/17.07.1888).
146. Goltz to Mauser, 25.11.1887, in: SA, Oberndorf: M-A8; for the outcomes of the test-firing and other experiments for the M/87:8mm; see also Speed and Reiner, *Mauser Original*, p. 30.
147. BOA, *Y.PRK.ASK.52/77* (27.04.1306/31.12.1888); BOA, *Y.PRK.ASK. 52/77* (29.04.1306/02.01.1889); BOA, *Y.PRK.ASK.52/77* (05.05.1306/07.01.1889).
148. BOA, *Y.PRK.ASK.52/77* (29.04.1306/02.01.1889): 'şimdiye kadar dahî bu tüfenge [Mauser rifle cal. 9.5 mm] fâik hiç bir silah mevcûd olmadığını te'minen arz eylerim.'
149. Huber to Mauser, 14.01.1889, in: SA, Oberndorf: M-A8.
150. BOA, *Y.PRK.ASK.52/77* (06.05.1306/08.01.1889); BOA, *Y.PRK.MM.1/37* (19.09.1306/19.05.1889).
151. Olson, *Mauser*, p. 53.
152. Huber to Mauser, 11.11.1889, in: SA, Oberndorf: M-A8.
153. Huber to Mauser, 08.12.1892, in: SA, Oberndorf: M-A8.
154. White to Salisbury, 28.11.1887, in: NA, London: FO 78/4001; see also Grant, 'The Sword of the Sultan', p. 24.
155. Seel, Wolfgang, 'Mauser-Gewehre unter dem Halbmond, Türkenmauser', *Deutsche Waffenjournal* 5 (1981d), p. 1418.
156. BOA, *Y.A.RES.51/29* (03.12.1307/21.07.1890).
157. BOA, *Y.A.HUS.486/9*: *Mübâya'ât-ı Mühimme Defteri* (HH 26363:12): see also BOA, *Y.PRK.ASK.52.93* (10.04.1308/22.12.1890).
158. BOA, *Y.PRK.MYD.16/92* (21.02.1313/13.08.1895).
159. BOA, *Y.A.HUS.486/9*: *Mübâya'ât-ı Mühimme Defteri* (HH 26363:12). Cf. Seel, 'Mauser-Gewehre' (1981b), p. 979.
160. Ball, *Mauser Military Rifles*, p. 237.
161. Olson, *Mauser*, p. 53; Speed and Reiner, *Mauser Original*, p. 31.
162. BOA, *Y.A.RES.51/29* (03.12.1307/21.07.1890).
163. BOA, *Y.PRK.ASK.62/87* (12.12.1307/30.07.1890).
164. Agreement signed by Paul Mauser and Rıza Pasha, the Ottoman Ministry of War 17 July 1893: Article 1, in: SA, Oberndorf: M-A8; see also: BOA, *Y.MTV.240/128* (23.11.1320/21.02.1903).
165. Seel, 'Mauser-Gewehre' (1981d), p. 1423.

166. BOA, *Y.A.RES.51/29* (03.12.1307/21.07.1890); see also Seel, 'Mauser-Gewehre' (1981c), p. 1164.
167. BOA, *Y.MTV.92/113* (27.09.1311/03.04.1894); BOA, *Y.A.RES.51/29* (03.12.1307/21.07.1890).
168. Mauser to Huber, 30.11.1892, in: SA, Oberndorf: M-A8.
169. Huber to Mauser, 08.12.1892, in: SA, Oberndorf: M-A8.
170. See the postscript on p. 3 of the letter in handwriting: 'von Shakir [Şakir] Pasha hörten wir, dass bei den Versuchen dorten mit dem $9\frac{1}{2}$ ein Lauf gesprungen sei, dass scheint weithin, anzudeuten, dass die Sache doch nicht so leicht geht.'
171. Mahmud Şevket Pasha had been in Oberndorf since 1886 and stayed there until 1895.
172. Precise of Colonel Chermside's Despatches No. 19–21 and Memo of 1 July 1890: in: NA, London: FO 78/4276.
173. Huber to Mauser, 08.12.1892, in: SA, Oberndorf: M-A8.
174. Huber to Mauser, 08.12.1892, in: SA, Oberndorf: M-A8: 'Seien Sie also nur sehr vorsichtig in der Sache und berichten Sie uns gelegentlich, was geschehen ist.'
175. In one of his letters sent to Mauser he described an Ottoman officer who was sent to Oberndorf to investigate the production process as follows: 'Genannter ist ein tüchtiger und im Verkehre angenehmer Offizier, deutschen Sprache in Wort und Schrift kundig.' Huber to Mauser, 31.05.1904, in: SA, Oberndorf: M-A5.
176. 'Sehr Vertraulich! Geheim: Der [Huber] hat mir paar Hundert Pfund angeboten, schlug ich zurück und sagte: dass ich draußen edele Freunde habe und was ich getan gilt für Sie. Die übrige überlasse ich Ihnen, lieber Freund. Nach dem Lesen bitte zu vernichten!!!' in: undated/anonymous writer SA, Oberndorf: M-A8.
177. Unnamed/from Berlin (Direction) to Mauser, 04.09.1890, in: SA, Oberndorf, MA-4: 'Zu den nötigen 'Bakschichs' und zu entsprechendem Honorar sind wir natürlich gerne bereit.'
178. Huber to Mauser, 08.12.1892, in: SA, Oberndorf: M-A8. According to Hallgarten, 'despite his revolutionary Young Turk character, Mahmud Şevket [Pasha] was a most corrupt person [*eine höchst korrupte Persönlichkeit*].' Hallgarten, *Vorkriegs Imperialismus*, p. 278.
179. BOA, *Y.PRK.ASK.62/87* (12.12.1307/30.07.1890).
180. Seel, 'Mauser-Gewehre' (1981c).
181. BOA, *Y.MTV.92/113* (27.09.1311/03.04.1894).
182. Speed and Reiner, *Mauser Original*, p. 31; Ball, *Mauser Military Rifles*, p. 363; Seel, *Mauser: Von der Waffenschmiede*, pp. 44–8.
183. Seel, *Mauser: Von der Waffenschmiede*, p. 46.
184. H. Walter Schmid's note, in: SA, Oberndorf, 793.32/13.1 (Mauser Waffen, Abnahme-Kommission/Türkenzeit); See also Seel, 'Mauser-Gewehre' (1981d), p. 1418.

185. Uyar and Erickson, *A Military History of the Ottomans*, p. 211.
186. Nevinson, Henry, Woodd, *Scenes in the Thirty Days War Between Greece and Turkey 1897* (London, 1898), p. 49.
187. *The New York Times*, 4 November 1912.
188. Goltz Pasha stayed in the Ottoman service between June 1883 and November 1895.
189. Radolin to Caprivi, 20.5.1893, in: PA.AA. R13240, cited in Kössler, *Aktionsfeld Osmanisches Reich*, p. 180: 'Für unseren Einfluss auf die türkische Armee und unsere weiteren Waffenlieferungen an dieselbe von unschätzbarem Wert.'
190. BOA, *Y.PRK.MYD.16/92* (21.02.1313/13.08.1895).
191. Mauser to Goltz, 26.11.1893, in: SA, Oberndorf: M-A8.
192. Huber to Mauser, 09.12.1893, in: SA, Oberndorf: M-A8: '[Goltz Pasha] sagte uns aber, dass er Nötiges veranlassen werde'.
193. Huber to Mauser, 04.01.1894, in: SA, Oberndorf: M-A8.
194. Huber to Mauser, 14.11.1893, in: SA, Oberndorf: M-A8: 'energischen Vorstoß im Palais'; Goltz to Pertev Bey, 18.02.1900, in: MA, Freiburg NL.737/8: 'Die Lehren des Boerenkrieges sind recht beherzigenswert und auch für Sie in der Türkei Wichtigkeit. Zunächst bewährt sich das Mausergewehr vorzüglich.'
195. Huber to Mauser, 14.11.1893, in: SA, Oberndorf: M-A8; *Notizen über Türkei*, in: HA, Krupp: FAH 3C/217.
196. Goltz to Pertev, 18.02.1900, cited in Yasamee, 'Colmar Freiherr Von der Goltz and the Boer War', p. 207.
197. BOA,*Y.PRK.ASK.168/127*.
198. Goltz's letter of condolence for Paul Mauser, in: SA, Oberndorf, *Worte am Grabe des Herrn Geheimen Kommerzienrats Dr. Ing. Paul v. Mauser 1914*, p. 13.

Chapter 4 Kaiser Wilhelm II and the Political Economy of Personal Diplomacy (1898–1914)

1. Isaacson, Walter, *Kissinger: A Biography* (New York, NY 2005), p. 13.
2. Henderson, W.O., 'German Economic Penetration in the Middle East 1870–1914', *The Economic History Review* 18 (1948), p. 59. According to the Ottoman official document, dated 8 October 1898, the transport vehicles and animals, which were provided by 'Thomas Cook and Son' for the German bureaucrats and servants who accompanied Kaiser Wilhelm II during his trip, were obtained without paying any customs duty. BOA, *Y.PRK.BŞK. 57/89* (18.05.1316/04.10.1898); BOA, *Y.PRK.BŞK.57/95* (22.05.1316/08.10.1898).
3. *Neue Freie Presse*, 20 October 1898.

4. According to Robolsky, Bismarck said openly in an interview that he was against the Kaiser's visit to İstanbul in 1889. Robolsky, *Drei Jahre auf dem Throne*, p. 29.
5. On 19 October 1898, the Austrian *Neue Freie Presse* pointed out the differences between the first trip and the second one as follows: 'nine years ago Kaiser Wilhelm II was not yet his own chancellor', *Neue Freie Presse*, 20 October 1898.
6. Wilhelm II, *The Kaiser's Memoirs, Emperor of Germany 1888–1918*, translated by Thomas R. Ybarra (New York and London, 1922), p. 90.
7. BOA, *Y.PRK.AZJ.37/91* (01.06.1316/17.10.1898); BOA, *Y.PRK.SGE. 8/61* (02.06.1316/18.10.1898).
8. BOA, *Y.PRK.ASK.145/36* (30.05.1316/16.10.1898): Because of the adverse weather conditions the *SMY Hohenzollern* had to wait at Zante Island.
9. Sabah, Hatıra-i Seyahat: 'Almanya İmparatoru Haşmetlü [Wilhelm] ve İmparatoriçe [Augusto Victoria] Hazerâtının Dersa'âdet'i def'at-i saniye olarak ziyaretleriyle Suriye seyahatlerine bir Hâtıra-i nâciz olmak üzere Sabah gazetesi tarafından kâri'în-i Osmaniyeye hediye edilmiştir', İstanbul 1316 [1898].
10. Richter, Jan Stefan, *Die Orientreise Kaiser Wilhelms II. 1898. Eine Studie zur deutschen Außenpolitik an der Wende zum 20. Jahrhundert* (Hamburg, 1997), pp. 63–8.
11. Angell to William R. Day, 25.07.1898, in: NARA-Microfilm, College Park: M46/65.
12. Angell to William R. Day, 25.07.1898, in: NARA-Microfilm, College Park: M46/65.
13. BOA, *Y.PRK.ZB.22/13* (03.06.1316/19.10.1898); BOA, *Y.PRK.HH.30/69* (03.06.1316/19.10.1898); *The New York Times*, 20 October 1898.
14. *The New York Times*, 20 October 1898.
15. BOA, *Y.PRK.ASK.145/73* (03.06.1316/19.10.1898): On 19 October, the Kaiserin went to the Beylerbeyi Palace and Çamlıca for sightseeing.
16. *The New York Times*, 6 November 1898.
17. Naumann, *Asia: Eine Orientreise*, p. 73: 'Der Sultan der Germanen imponiert dem Morgenländer mächtig'.
18. *The New York Times*, 6 November 1898.
19. BOA, *Y.PRK.UM.44/42* (28.06.1316/13.11.1898).
20. BOA, *Y.MTV.188/146* (29.11.1316/10.04.1899).
21. The Kaiser delivered the following speech on the date of takeover of the Dormition de la Sainte Vierge, on 31 October 1898. Penzler, *Reden Kaiser Wilhelms II*, p. 123–4; See also Kushner, David, 'The District of Jerusalem in the Eyes of Three Ottoman Governors at the End of the Hamidian Period', *Middle Eastern Studies* 35/2 (1999), p. 92; Hürmen, *Bürokrat Tevfik Biren*, pp. 159–67.
22. White to Salisbury, 22.02.1888, in: NA, London: FO 78/4098.
23. *The New York Times*, 6 November 1898. For the correlation between the *Orientreise* and the increasing German influence on the Christian subjects of the

Ottoman Empire see Lepsius et al., *Die große Politik der Europäischen Kabinette*, vol.12-2, pp. 587–638.

24. Wilhelm II, *The Kaiser's Memoirs, Emperor of Germany 1888–1918*, translated by T. R. Ybarra (New York and London, 1922): pp. 215–6. In Haifa, on 26 October 1898, Kaiser Wilhelm, who wanted to improve his influence among the Catholics, especially those who lived in the Ottoman Empire, addressed to the Catholic delegation the following speech, in which he ensured his protection over them: 'In Erwiederung ergreife Ich gern die Gelegenheit, ein für allemal auszusprechen, daß die katholischen Untertanen wo und wann sie desselben bedürfen sollten, Meines Kaiserlichen Schutzes stets sicher sein werden.' Penzler, *Reden Kaiser Wilhelms II*, pp. 117–8.

25. Bülow to Kaiser Wilhelm II, 04.06.1898, Lepsius et al., *Die große Politik der Europäischen Kabinette*, vol. 12–2, p. 611. The Kaiser remarked Bülow's statement with a marginalia 'Ja.' In addition, the idea of support of the German Catholics in the Orient was formulated by Naumann much as Bülow did. In order to support the assertion that Naumann and Bülow and the other pro-expansionists analysed the events from a very similar, almost from the same, perspective, Naumann's following words are telling: 'Je mehr wir den deutschen Katholiken Stützpunkte geben, desto eher werden wir sie der französischen Bevormundung entziehen.' Naumann, *Asia: Eine Orientreise*, p. 73.

26. Ali Vahbi Bey, *Avant la debacle*, pp. 113–4.

27. *The New York Times*, 6 November 1898.

28. According to Menne, Field-Marshall Waldersee was 'the doubtless well-informed friend of the Emperor'. Menne, *Blood and Steel*, p. 194.

29. Waldersee, Alfred Grafen von, *Denkwürdigkeiten des General-Feldmarschalls Alfred Grafen von Waldersee*, Meisner, Heinrich Otto (ed.) (Stuttgart, 1922), p. 420.

30. Hillis, Newell Dwight, *The Blot on the Kaiser's Scutcheon* (New York, 1918), p. 17.

31. Gooch and Temperley, *British Documents*, vol. 5, p. 43.

32. Ibid.

33. BOA, *Y.PRK.UM.44/6* (14.06.1316/30.10.1898).

34. BOA, *Y.PRK.UM.43/129* (10.06.1316/26.10.1898).

35. Bülow to Hatzfeldt, 02.02.1898 in Lepsius et al., *Die große Politik der Europäischen Kabinette*, vol.12-2, p. 476.

36. Bülow's final remarks to the Hatzfeldt's report dated 2 February 1898, in Lepsius et al., *Die große Politik der Europäischen Kabinette*, vol.12-2, p. 477: 'Seine Majestät autorisierten mich endlich, an Hatzfeldt sehr geheim zu telegraphieren, er habe nichts dagegen, daß die Engländer in irgendeiner Form Kreta bzw. die Sudabai nähmen.'

37. Zeidner, F. Robert, 'Britain and the Launching of the Armenian Question', *International Journal of Middle East Studies* 7/4 (1976), pp. 475–6.

38. Gooch and Temperley, *British Documents*, vol. 5, p. 43.

39. Hillis, *The Blot*, p. 17.
40. Harrison, *The Pan-Germanic Doctrine*, p. 221.
41. Baker, Ray Stannard, 'The Sultan of Turkey', *The Outlook*, 6 September 1902, pp. 67–77.
42. *The {London} Times*, 18 October 1898.
43. BOA, *Y.EE 81/3* (06.07.1316/20.11.1898).
44. Benner, Thomas, *Die Strahlen der Krone: Die religiöse Dimension des Kaisertums unter Wilhelm II. vor dem Hintergrund der Orientreise 1898* (Marburg, 2001), p. 274.
45. For a detailed study on German settlement in Ottoman Palestine, see Yazbak, Mahmoud, 'Templars as Proto-Zionists? The "German Colony" in Late Ottoman Haifa', *Journal of Palestine Studies* 28 (1999), pp. 40–54. Yazbak comments that 'Kaiser Wilhelm's trip to the Holy Land at the end of the century was responsible for a brief upsurge, as it sparked enthusiastic reports about the Templars in the German press and a wave of sympathy back home', p. 51. See also Carmel, Alex, *Die Siedlungen der Württembergischen Templer in Palästina* (Stuttgart, 1973).
46. Röhl, *Wilhelm II: The Kaiser's Personal Monarchy*, p. 952.
47. Penzler, *Reden Kaiser Wilhelms II*, p. 118.
48. Richter, *Die Orientreise*, p. 132.
49. Hürmen, *Bürokrat Tevfik Biren*, p. 41.
50. BOA, *Y.PRK.MYD.21/86* (11.06.1316/27.10.1898).
51. *The New York Times*, 27 November 1898; according to a report dated 14 November 1898, the 13 suspects who was charged with planning an assassination against the German Kaiser and were arrested by the local governor, were released from prison just after the Kaiser left the city. BOA, *Y.PRK.ASK.12/10* (29.06.1316/14.11.1898); see also: BOA, *DH.MKT.2122/41* (07.06.1316/23.10.1898). See more detailed security measures in Hürmen, *Bürokrat Tevfik Biren*, pp. 157–69.
52. General Bernhard von Werder, the German ambassador in St Petersburg, sent a letter to Bülow in the spring of 1901 in which he wrote: 'He [the Tsar] could understand why Germany desired economic advantages in Turkey, but Kaiser Wil[helm]'s enthusiasm for the Sublime Porte, the Koran, and the Sultan, irritated the Tsar.' Bülow added that the Tsar remarked in Werder's presence: 'Je n'aime pas le Sultan, je le cède à l'Empereur d'Allemagne.' Most probably, the Tsar was impressed by a letter the Kaiser sent him from Damascus on 9 November 1898, revealing that 'My personal feeling in leaving the holy city was that I felt profoundly ashamed before the Moslems and that if I had come there without any Religion at all I certainly would have turned Mahometan [Muslim]!' Bülow, *Memoirs*, p. 542. See also Goetz, Walter (ed.), *Briefe Wilhelms II. an den Zaren 1894–1914*, translated by Max Theodor Behrmann (Berlin, 1920), p. 65. In addition, according to Röhl, General Bernhard von Werder was on good terms with Tsar Alexander and also a personal friend of the Russian family. Röhl, *Wilhelm II: the Kaiser's Personal Monarch*, p. 587.

NOTES TO PAGES 140–142 295

53. Bülow, *Memoirs*, p. 542.
54. Ibid., pp. 255–6; the telegraphs sent by the Kaiser to the Sultan were translated and submitted to the Sultan. BOA, *Y.PRK.NMH.7/94* (07.06.1316/23.10.1898).
55. Bülow, *Memoirs*, p. 254: 'Möge der Sultan und mögen die 300 Millionen Mohammedaner, die, auf der Erde zersreut lebend, in ihm ihren Khalifen verehren, dessen versichert sein, daß zu allen Zeiten der deutsche Kaiser ihr Freund sein wird. Ich trinke auf das Wohl Seiner Majestät des Sultans Abdülhamid!' See also Penzler, *Reden Kaiser Wilhelms II*, p. 127; Sabah, *Hatirat*, p. 171.
56. BOA, *Y.EE.91/51* (1315/1898); see also Gauss, Christian Frederick, *The German Emperor as Shown in His Public Utterances* (New York, 1915), p. 129: 'At Damascus, [Kaiser Wilhelm II] likewise laid a wreath upon the tomb of Saladin.'
57. Kaiser Wilhelm II had paid a visit to Tangier (Morocco) and delivered a speech there on 31 March 1905 that severely irritated the other European Great Powers. See Penzler, *Reden Kaiser Wilhelms II*, pp. 247–9.
58. Mortimer, Joanne Stafford, 'Commercial Interests and German Diplomacy in the Agadir Crisis', *The Historical Journal* 10 (1967), p. 440: Mortimer gives more detail about the interrelation between the trade and diplomacy in the case of Germany's attitude in the Agadir Crisis (the second Moroccan Crisis) in July 1911.
59. Marschall to Auswärtiges Amt, 22.03.1907, in: PA.AA. R13775. Prince Bülow wrote some more detailed information about the Kaiser's Tangier visit: 'On March 31, 1905, His Majesty the Emperor, in pursuance of my advice, landed at Tangier, where he defended the independence and sovereignty of Morocco in unequivocal language.' Bülow, Prince von, *Imperial Germany*, translated by M. A. Lewenz (New York, 1917), p. 97. Howe made another explanation of the Kaiser's speeches and acts in the Muslim countries. He wrote: 'A successful attack upon the Moorish Government would injure German prestige with the Mohammedans, among whom Germany hoped for the new markets she deems of such vital importance. Loss of influence at Constantinople might mean the wrecking of Germany's Baghdad Railway project. It was for this reason that Germany refused to join Christendom in protecting the Armenians from massacre. Yet she was unable to stop Italy from driving the Turks out of Tripoli.' Howe, Frederic Clemson, *Why War* (New York, 1916), p. 192.
60. Vambéry, Armin, *The Story of my Struggles: The Memoirs of Arminius Vambéry* (New York, 1904), p. 379.
61. In 1898, *The {London} Times* published an informative article about the Kaiser's *Orientreise*. In this article sent from İstanbul on 18 October 1898, the importance of Kaiser's visit was discussed as follows: 'The pacific crusade [the Kaiser's *Orientreise*] will be something more than a picturesque and romantic

incident in modern history; it will mark a new and memorable starting-point in the *Drang nach Osten*', *The {London} Times*, 18 October 1898.
62. Bülow, *Imperial Germany*, p. 69.
63. Lindow, Erich, *Freiherr Marschall von Bieberstein als Botschafter in Konstantinopel 1897–1912* (Danzig, 1934), pp. 45–6.
64. Marschall was right when he wrote in 1898 about the Sultan's closeness to the Kaiser as follows: 'Vor allem hat der Sultan eine warme Freundschaft für Seine Majestät den Kaiser...' Marschall to Hohenlohe, 24.05.1898, in Lepsius et al., *Die große Politik der Europäischen Kabinette*, vol.12–2, pp. 564–5.
65. Bülow, *Imperial Germany*, p. 120.
66. Dunn, Archibald Joseph, *Turkey and Its Future* (London, 1905), p. 54.
67. Barth, 'The Financial History of the Anatolian and Baghdad Railways', pp. 121–2.
68. Ibid., p. 122.
69. Leishman to Hay, 17.06.1903, in: NARA-Microfilm, College Park: M46/71.
70. Kössler gives the following quotation from the French newspaper the 'Le Figaro', which supports the meaning of the expression given above: 'Der Deutsche Kaiser ist der rührigste und gewandteste Geschäftsreisende für das große Haus Deutschland.' Kössler, *Aktionsfeld Osmanisches Reich*, p. 248.
71. Benner, *Die Strahlen der Krone*, p. 255.
72. Bode, *Der Kampf um die Bagdadbahn*, p. 4.
73. *Alldeutsche Blätter*, 16 July 1899.
74. Naumann, *Asia: Eine Orientreise*, pp. 162–3.
75. Angell to Day, 25.07.1898, in: NARA-Microfilm, College Park: M46/65.
76. Naumann, *Asia: Eine Orientreise*, pp. 162–3.
77. Ibid, p. 73.
78. Marschall to Hohenlohe, 23.09.1899, Lepsius et al., *Die große Politik der Europäischen Kabinette*, vol.12–2, p. 583.
79. For some other examples of the application of personal diplomacy in international policy see Larres, Klaus, *Churchill's Cold War: The Politics of Personal Diplomacy* (New Haven and London, 2002); Otte, G. Thomas and Constantine A. Pagedas (eds) *Personalities, War and Diplomacy, Eassys in International History* (London and Portland OR, 1997); Fry, Michael Graham (ed.), *Power, Personalities and Policies: Essays in Honour Donald Cameron Watt* (London ann Portland, OR 1992); Plischke, Elmer, *Summit diplomacy; personal diplomacy of the President of the United States* (Westport, Conn 1974); Isaacson, *Kissinger*.
80. Osman Nuri, *Abdulhamid-i Sâni ve Devr-i Saltanatı. Hayat-ı Husûsiye ve Siyâsiye* (İstanbul, 1327/1911) p. 1052: '{Almanlar} hiçden işe başlayarak şarkdaki ticaretlerini hayli ilerlettiler.'
81. Bode, *Der Kampf um die Bagdadbahn*, p. 4.
82. *The {London} Times*, 18 October 1898.
83. As one of the most discussed topics in German–Ottoman relations, the Baghdad Railway has mostly been studied in the context of German imperialist expansion and the causes of World War I. In fact, there is an

extensive literature on the history of the Baghdad Railway, in which the following are some of the foremost studies: Rohrbach, Paul, *German World Policies*, translated by E. v. Mach (New York, 1915); Earle, *Turkey, The Great Powers*; Holborn, *Deutschland und die Türkei*; Butterfield, Paul R, *The Diplomacy of the Bagdad Railway 1890–1914* (Göttingen, 1932); Bode, *Der Kampf um die Bagdadbahn*; Henderson, 'German Economic Penetration', pp. 54–64; Wolf, B. John, *The Diplomatic History of the Baghdad Railroad* (New York, 1973); Mejcher, Helmut, 'Die Bagdadbahn als Instrument deutschen wirtschaftlichen Einflusses im Osmanischen Reich', *Geschichte und Gesellschaft* 1 (1975), pp. 447–481; Özyüksel, Murat, *Osmanlı-Alman İlişkilerinin Gelişim Sürecinde Anadolu ve Bağdat Demiryolları* (İstanbul, 1988); Barth, 'The Financial History of the Anatolian and Baghdad Railways'; McMurray, *Distant Ties*, p. 32; Gencer, *Imperialismus und die Orientalische Frage*.
84. Luxemburg, *The Crisis in the German Social-Democracy*, p. 48.
85. Scherer, Friedrich, *Adler und Halbmond: Bismarck und der Orient 1878–1890* (Paderborn, 2001), p. 490.
86. Barth, 'Financial History', p. 116.
87. White to Salisbury, 16.08.1887, in: NA, London: FO 78/3999.
88. King to Blaine, 24.12.1889, in: NARA-Microfilm, College Park: M46/50.
89. Wilhelm II to the the German Chancellor, 09.12.1891, in: PA.AA. R13763.
90. Goltz to the Kaiser, 28.10.1891, in: PA.AA. R13763.
91. Goltz to the Kaiser, 28.10.1891, in: PA.AA. R13763.
92. Gencer, *Imperialismus und die Orientalische Frage*, p. 105; additionally Woods mentioned that he was of opinion that the Sultan made a verbal promise to the Kaiser regarding the Baghdad Railway as early as 1898 during Kaiser's *Orientreise*. Woods, 'The Baghdad Railway'p. 38.
93. Cited in Gencer, *Imperialismus und die Orientalische Frage*, p. 105; Pohl, *Philipp Holzmann*, p. 53–4; *The Neue Presse (Morgenblatt)*, 20 October 1898.
94. *The New York Times*, 2 January 1898.
95. *The Neue Presse (Morgenblatt)*, 20 October 1898.
96. McMurray, *Distant Ties*, p. 32; On 16 July 1899, the news of the Baghdad railway concession was published by the German pro-colonialist newspaper *Alldeutsche Blätter* on the first page with the title 'Deutsche Arbeit in der Türkei' in *Alldeutsche Blätter*, 16 June 1899.
97. Woods, 'The Baghdad Railway', p. 38.
98. Barth, 'The Financial History of the Anatolian and Baghdad Railways', p. 122; McMurray, *Distant Ties*, p. 32.
99. Woods, 'The Baghdad Railway', p. 38; Gencer, *Imperialismus und die Orientalische Frage*, p. 106.
100. BOA, Y.EE.62/15 (06.10.1319/ 16.01.1902).
101. Geyikdağı, *Foreign Investment in the Ottoman Empire*, pp. 85–100.
102. McMurray, *Distant Ties*, p. 8.
103. *The Standard*, 23 August 1899 cited in Schöllgen, *Imperialismus und Gleichgewicht*, p. 131.

104. Ali Vahbi Bey, *Avant la debacle*, p. 60.
105. Ibid.
106. Marschall to Bülow, 26.12.1907, in: NA, London: GFM 10/11.
107. An unnamed newspaper cutting dated 24 March 1899, in: NA, London: FO 78/5000.
108. Pohl, *Philipp Holzmann*, p. 104: The board of directors of the Société were: Karl Schrader (Railway Director and the member of the German Reichstag), Arthur von Gwinner (Deutsche Bank), Max Steinthal (Deutsche Bank), Kurt Zander (Anatolian Railway Company) and Eduard Huguenin (Anatolian Railway Company).
109. Richter, *Die Orientreise*, pp. 119–22.
110. O'Conor to Salisbury, 08.02.1899, in: NA, London: FO 78/5000; British ambassador O'Conor paid a visit to the German ambassador on March 11, 1899 and spoke to him on this subject. During the conversation, as O'Conor reported, Marschall assured him positively that the potential rates would be excluded and that no lower or different rates would be accorded to German than to British goods arriving at Haydarpaşa by whatever route they came. O'Conor to Salisbury 11.03.1899, in: NA, London: FO 78/5000.
111. O'Conor to Salisbury, 08.02.1899, in: NA, London: FO 78/5000. See also BOA, *Y.PRK.EŞA.32/27* (01.11.1316/13.03.1899).
112. BOA, *Y.PRK.BŞK.58/8* (14.07.1316/28.11.1898); BOA, *Y.PRK.HR.26/71* (22.07.1316/06.12.1898); BOA, *Y.PRK.HR.26/78* (06.08.1316/28.12.1898); however, according to the document dated June 17 1899, and referred to the Turkish newspaper *Servet*, French ambassador Constans' action had born fruit, and the French Quay Company had succeeded in obtaining favourable modifications in their *cahier de charges* to offset to the privileges acquired by the Anatolian Railway Company. O'Conor to Salisbury, 17.06.1899, in: NA, London: FO 78/5000; for detail study regarding Ernest Constans' acts and doings in the Ottoman Empire see Fulton, L. Bruce, 'France's Extraordinary Ambassador: Ernest Constans and the Ottoman Empire, 1898–1909', *French Historical Studies* 23 (2000), pp. 683–706.
113. *The New York Herald*, 26 October 1908.
114. Siemens to Thielen, 01.07.1893, in: PA.AA. R13451.
115. O'Conor to Salisbury, 08.02.1899, in: NA, London: FO 78/5000.
116. Ibid.
117. Gall, *Die Deutsche Bank*, p. 74.
118. Pohl, *Philipp Holzmann*, p. 104; Özyüksel, *Osmanlı-Alman İlişkilerinin Gelişim Sürecinde*, pp. 129–30.
119. Henderson, 'German Economic Penetration', pp. 59, 62; Quataert, 'Limited Revolution', p. 149.
120. See for detail Pohl, *Philipp Holzmann*, pp. 96–108.
121. Lindow, *Freiherr Marschall von Bieberstein*, p. 48.
122. Richter, *Die Orientreise*, pp. 113–8.

123. BOA, *Y.PRK.BŞK.58/8 (14.07.1316/28.11.1898)*; BOA, *Y.A.HUS.390/88* (16.06.1316/01.11.1898); Osman Nuri, *Abdulhamid-i Sâni*, pp. 1050–1.
124. Riesser, *The German Great Banks*, p. 454; Tschoegl, E. Adrian, 'Financial Integration, Disintegration and Emerging Re-integration in the Eastern Mediterranean, c.1850 to the Present', *Financial Markets, Institutions & Instruments* 13 (2004), p. 252; see also *Die Post*, 16 December 1898, in: PA.AA: R12456.
125. Riesser, *The German Great Banks*, p. 454.
126. Ibid.
127. Tschoegl, 'Financial Integration', 252.
128. Osman Nuri, *Abdulhamid-i Sâni*, pp. 1049–50.
129. Pamuk, *The Ottoman Empire and European Capitalism*, p. 79.
130. Newbold, J. T. Walton, *How Europe Armed for War: 1871–1914* (London, 1916), p. 87; Geyikdağı, *Foreign Investment in the Ottoman Empire*, pp. 119–26.
131. Marschall to the German Chancellor, 05.09.1906, in: PA.AA. R13305.
132. *The Standard*, 7 June 1899, in: PA.AA. R14148.
133. Ibid.
134. Ibid.
135. *Alldeutsche Blätter*, 16 July 1899: 'Sir Ellis Aschmead Bartlett macht seinem Jammer... in seinem Briefe an die 'Pall Mall Gazette' gar in dem Schreckenrufe Luft: Die Deutschen verschlucken einfach die ganze Türkei.' Gemach, Gemach, Herr Bartlett, wir Deutschen sind doch keine – Engländer!'
136. Trumpener, 'Germany and the End of the Ottoman Empire', p. 111; Menne, *Blood and Steel*, p. 240.
137. *The Standard*, 13 July 1899, in: PA.AA. R14148.
138. Kaiser Wilhelm II's speech on 1 December 1898: 'Ich hoffe..., daß meine Reise dazu beigetragen hat, der deutschen Energie und der deutschen Tatkraft neue Absatzgebiete zu eröffnen, und daß es mir gelungen ist mitzuwirken die Beziehungen zwischen unseren beiden Völkern, dem türkischen und dem deutschen, zu befestigen.' Penzler, *Reden Kaiser Wilhelms II*, pp. 127–8. Also, it is interesting to notice that the notion of 'German energy' was earlier conceptualized by *The {London} Times*. In an article sent from İstanbul on 18 October 1898, the special correspondent asserted that 'nowhere has German commercial enterprise and energy gained greater triumphs than in Turkey. In the supply of war material to the Sultan Germany enjoys a practical monopoly; the Ottoman army receives its rifles from Mauser, its cannon from Krupp.' *The {London} Times*, 18 October 1898.
139. Lehmann explains this arguments in a general meaning as follows: 'Je aggressiver die Zielsetzung des erstarkenden deutschen Imperialismus wurde, desto stärker wurden die Positionen der Rüstungsindustrie -und das ist ohne Zweifel nach 1900 der Fall-, um so stärker verwuchsen sie mit dem Staat.' Lehmann, 'Der Funktionswandel', pp. 96–7.
140. Manchester, *The Arms of Krupp*, p. 111.

141. Showalter, E. Dennis, *Railroads and Rifles: Soldiers, Technology, and the Unification of Germany* (Hamden, 1975), p. 169.
142. *The New York Times*, 23 November 1902.
143. Hull, *The Entourage of Kaiser Wilhelm*, p. 158.
144. *The New York Times*, 23 November 1902; Hull puts forward that Wilhelm II saw Krupp almost yearly. Hull, *The Entourage of Kaiser Wilhelm*, p. 159.
145. Owen has cited from HA, Krupp: FAH IV E 782: Wilhelm II to Frl. Bertha Krupp of 12 December 1902. Owen described the Kaiser's letter sent to Bertha Krupp 'a superlative exposition of socio-political nostrum which the twentieth century was fast eroding'. Owen, Richard, 'Military–Industrial Relations: Krupp and the Imperial Navy Office', in Richard J. Evans (ed.), *Society and Politics in Wilhelmine Germany* (London, 1978), p. 81.
146. Pollard and Holmes, *Industrial Power and National Rivalry*, pp. 84–5; see original in German, Boelcke, *Krupp und die Hohenzollern in Dokumenten*, pp. 123–5.
147. Lehmann, 'Der Funktionswandel', pp. 95–6; see also Röhl's work for more information regarding some other crucial disagreements between the Kaiser and Verdy, Röhl, *Wilhelm II: the Kaiser's Personal Monarch*, pp. 373–5.
148. *Ansprache des Kaisers an Krupp'sche Arbeiter gelegentlich seines Besuches in Essen*, 20.06.1890, in: HA, Krupp: FAH 3E/1. The same point about the contribution of Krupp's work to the German reputation was argued by Prince Bülow as well. According to Bülow, 'Krupp's concern had long ago surpassed the Schneider iron and machine works at Creusot, which were the pride of France. Krupp had spread Germany's reputation and the renown of German work and industry over the world.' Bülow, *Memoirs*, p. 576.
149. The term *'Unternehmungsgeist'* was used in the German edition of Helfferich's book. Helfferich, Karl, *Deutschlands Volkswohlstand 1888–1913* (Berlin, 1914), pp. 81–3; cf. Helfferich, *Germany's Economic Progress*, pp. 81–4.
150. Wells, Herbert George, *The War That Will End War* (New York, 1914), p. 8.
151. Kössler, *Aktionsfeld Osmanisches Reich*, p. 254; Türk, *Die deutsche Rüstungsindustrie*, pp. 121–5.
152. Marginalie Wilhelms II, 20.1.1899: 'Nein, die andere Firma muss eins gehörig auf den Deckel kriegen, und Krupp die Bestellung unter allen Umständen zugebilligt werden.' Cited in Kössler, *Aktionsfeld Osmanisches Reich*, p. 254.
153. Director of Vickers, Sons & Maxim Limited to Brackenbury, 17.12.1900; 19.01.1901; and 05.02.1901, in: NA, London: WO 108/323.
154. Benz, 'Die Entstehung der Kruppschen Nachrichtendienstes', pp. 201–2; Howe, *Why War*, p. 119.
155. Burchardt, Lothar, 'Between War Profits and War Costs. Krupp in the First World War', in Hans Pohl and Bernd Rudolph, *German Yearbook on Business History* 1988 (Berlin and Heidelberg, 1990), p. 1.
156. Fa. Krupp to Schoen, 14.02.1908, in: PA.AA. R13306.

157. Lowther to Grey, 28.12.1908, in: NA, London: FO 371/561; Surtees to Lowther, 18.12.1898, in: NA, London: FO 244/721.
158. The agent of Ehrhardt Company requested through a letter sent to the German Chancellor an equal support on the Ottoman war business among the German suppliers: 'Die von mir vertretene Fabrik bittet, dass ihr im Auslande das gleiche Wohlwollen und dieselbe Unparteiligkeit andern Unternehmungen gegenüber gewährt, wie sie dies im Interesse des Kriegsministeriums seitens letzterer Behörde im Inlande genießt.' Rittmeister A.D. Ehrhardt Werke to Bülow, April 1902, in: PA.AA. R13299; see also Forbes, Ian L. D., 'Social Imperialism and Wilhelmine Germany', *The Historical Journal* 22 (1979), p. 343.
159. Cited in Forbes, 'Social Imperialism and Wilhelmine Germany', p. 343. See also for the competition of two German arms makers in China market: Clear (Peking) to Kriegsminister (Berlin), 30.12.1905, in: PA.AA. R13304.
160. The German Arms and Munitions Factories (Deutsche Waffen-und-Munitionsfabriken- DMW) was formed by the leadership of the Ludwig Loewe & Co. on 4 November 1896. Consequenetly, the following factories and companies became a part of DMW: Deutsche Metallpatronenfabrik, Karlsruhe; Ludwig Loewe & Co. AG., Berlin; Rheinisch-Westfälischen Powder Company, Cologne; Rottweil-Hamburg Powder Co., Rottweil. Since the control of more than 50 per cent of the share of the Mauser Company belonged to Ludwig Loewe & Company, the Mauser Company became also a part of DWM. Ball, *Mauser Military Rifles*, p. 8.
161. This contract was obtained, as mentioned before, by Sultan Abdülhamid's personal intervention. See Marschall to Hohenlohe, 24.05.1898, in Lepsius et al., *Die große Politik der Europäischen Kabinette*, vol.12-2, p. 563.
162. *Neue Wiener Journal*, 15 January 1899, in: PA.AA. R13295.
163. *The New York Times*, 4 March 1918.
164. Murray, H. Robertson, *Krupp's and the International Armaments Ring: The Scandal of Modern Civilization* (London, 1915), p. 81.
165. BOA, Y.PRK.ASK.168/128 (1318/1900).
166. BOA, Y.PRK.ASK.168/128 (1318/1900).
167. Goltz to the Kaiser, 28.10.1891, in: PA.AA. R13763.
168. Goltz to the Kaiser, 28.10.1891, in: PA.AA. R13763: 'Auch ist es bedenklich, daß mit dem Schiffe Geschütze nach dem System Canets hier eingeführt werden und somit Krupps Monopol durchlöchert.'
169. Goltz to Kiderlen, 10.11.1891, in: PA.AA.R13763.
170. Wilhelm II to the German Chancellor, 19.11.1891, in: PA.AA. R13285.
171. Menne, *Blood and Steel*, p. 134.
172. Ibid.
173. Wilhelm II to the German Chancellor, 19.11.1891, in: PA.AA. R13285.
174. Gözeller, *Osmanlı-Alman Yakınlaşmasının Basına Yansıması*, p. 45.
175. Marschall to the Kaiser, 03.12.1891, in: PA.AA. R13763.
176. Wilhelm II to the German Chancellor, 09.12.1891, in: PA.AA. R13763.

177. Ibid.
178. Ibid.
179. Howe, *Why War*, p. 119.
180. Menshausen to Geheimrat, 23.12.1891, in: PA.AA. R13763.
181. Kiderlen to Goltz, 10.12.1891, in: PA.AA. R13763.
182. Goltz to Geheimrat, 18.12.1891, in: PA.AA. R13763.
183. Menshausen to Krupp, 20.12.1891, in: PA.AA. R13763.
184. Goltz to Geheimrat, 18.12.1891, in: PA.AA. R13763; Menshausen to Krupp, 20.12.1891, in: PA.AA. R13763.
185. Goltz to Geheimrat, 19.12.1891, in: PA.AA.13763; Goltz to Geheimrat, 22.12.1891, in: PA.AA. R13763.
186. Hirst, *The Political Economy of War*, pp. 93–4.
187. BOA, *Y.A.HUS. 256/52* (12.07.1309/11.02.1892).
188. BOA, *Y.PRK.EŞA.32/52* (07.01.1317/ 17.06.1899).
189. BOA, *Y.PRK.EŞA.32/52* (07.01.1317/ 17.06.1899).
190. BOA, *Y.PRK.EŞA.50/35* (28.03.1325/09.07.1907); See also BOA, *Y.PRK.BŞK.43/14* (21.03.1313/11.09.1895).
191. BOA, *Y.PRK.ASK.166/70* (27.09.1318/18.01.1901).
192. Krupp to Wilhelm II, 02.11.1898, in: PA.AA. R13295.
193. Das Directorium-Krupp to Hohenlohe, 25.01.1899, in: PA.AA. R13295; BOA, *Y.PRK.ASK.148/20* (09.11.1316/21.03.1899).
194. *The New York Times*, 17 January 1899.
195. Kössler, *Aktionsfeld Osmanisches Reich*, p. 251.
196. Goetz, *Briefe Wilhelms II*, pp. 164–5.
197. Krupp to Bülow, 18.02.1899, in: PA.AA. R13295: 'Der Gedanke einer Modernisierung der türkischen Flotte wurde im Mai 1897 zuerst vom Sultan ausgesprochen'; See also Grant, *Rulers, Guns, and Money*, pp. 89–90.
198. BOA, *Y.PRK.ASK.134/105* (05.07.1315/30.11.1897): The investigated ships were: *Hamîdiye, Mesûdiye, Osmâniye, Azîziye, Mahmûdiye, Orhâniye, Âsâr-ı Tevfîk, Feth-i Bülend, Mukaddime-i Hayriye, Avnûllah, Muîn-i Zafer, Cism-i Şevket, Âsâr-ı Şevket, İclâliye, Hıfz-ı Rahmân*.
199. Grant, *Rulers, Guns, and Money*, p. 89.
200. In his 12-page letter to Bülow, Krupp explained the reasons for the abolishing of the *Vereinigung* in a very great detail. F. A. Krupp to Bülow, 18.02.1899, in: PA.AA. R13295. Additionally the letter sent to Admiral Freiherrn v. Senden-Bibran by the Krupp Company gives more detail about earlier stage of the negotiations on 9 November 1897: HA. Krupp: FAH. 3C/205.
201. Krupp to Bülow, 18.02.1899, in: PA.AA. R13295.
202. Krupp to Bülow, 18.02.1899, in: PA.AA. R13295: 'Die bereits ziemlich weit gediehenen Verhandlungen wurden damals auf Grund eines energischen von Eurer Exzellenz in dankenswerter Weise veranlassten Protestes der Botschaft wieder abgebrochen'; Hallgarten, *Imperialismus vor 1914*, vol. 1, p. 481.
203. Grant, 'The Sword of the Sultan', p. 29.
204. *The Daily News*, 21 June 1900, in: PA.AA. R13297.

205. BOA, Y.MTV.235/79 (13.07.1320/16.10.1902): The actual cost was 200, 000 in British pounds (222,222 OL = 4,100,000 marks).
206. Boelcke, *Krupp und die Hohenzollern in Dokumenten*, p. 102.
207. See also Moulton, 'Economic and Trade Position of Germany', p. 1.

Chapter 5   Sultan Abdülhamid II and his Bureaucrats (1876–1909)

1. Foreign Affairs Committees of England, *Proposed Annexation of Turkey: To His Imperial Majesty the Sultan {Abdülhamid II}*. The Address of the Undersigned Foreign Affairs Committees of England; 16.02.1879: Diplomatic fly-sheets Vol. II. No. 87: 84–6, in: University of Birmingham, Special Collection, r DS, 757, 6. Report Nr. 24, page 86.
2. Rose, *The Origins of the War*, p. 99.
3. The son of Sultan Abdulmecid I (1823–61) and the nephew of Sultan Abdülaziz (1830–76), Sultan Abdülhamid II (1842–1918), succeeded his brother Murad V (1840–1904) as the 34th Sultan of the Ottoman Empire, ruling from 31 August 1876 until 27 April 1909.
4. Railways had played a crucial role in deploying the soldiers to the frontiers where the operation occurred. McGarity argued that the Prussian army during the Prussian–Franco war had based their military planning, which was Moltke's concept, upon the utilization of railroads. McGarity, *Foreign Influence*, p. 23. Goltz Pasha indicated the importance of the railroad in 1910 as follows: 'Aber sie wird sich ändern, sobald die türkische Armee schlagfertig ist, das syrische Bahnnetz den schnellen Transport eines starken Heeres nach der ägyptischen Grenze gestattet, und auf der anderen Seite die anatolische Bahn ihre Fortführung bis Bagdad erfahren hat.' in: MA, Freiburg: NL.737/5 (18.12.1910).
5. Shaw and Shaw, *History of the Ottoman Empire*, p. 191; Karal, Enver Ziya, *Osmanlı Tarihi: Birinci Meşrutiyet ve İstibdat Devirleri 1876–1907*, vol. 8 (Ankara, 1988) pp. 76–9; Gencer, *Imperialismus und die Orientalische Frage*, p. 72.
6. İnalcık and Quataert, *An Economic and Social History*, p. 768.
7. The war indemnity was fixed firstly at 1,410,000,000 roubles (OL 300 million). Later on, after long negotiations in 1881, the amount was reduced to OL 34 million with annual payments of 350,000 OL. Griffiths, *The Reorganization of the Ottoman Army*, pp. 37–8; Shaw and Shaw, *History of the Ottoman Empire*, p. 191; Karal, *Osmanlı Tarihi*, pp. 422–4; Akmeşe, *The Birth of Modern Turkey*, p. 19.
8. Griffiths, *The Reorganization of the Ottoman Army*, p. 34.
9. Grant says, 'Moreover the Ottoman import strategy yielded a significant qualitative advantage for the Turks over the Russian in this war... Yet, when

war came in 1877, the Turks undoubtedly held the advantage in quality of arms.' Grant, 'The Sword of the Sultan' p. 16.
10. Henderson, 'German Economic Penetration', p. 58; Yasamee, *Ottoman Diplomacy*, p. 45; Grant, 'The Sword of the Sultan', pp. 9, 16.
11. In 1873, 500 cannons were ordered from Krupp and they arrived at the Ottoman Arsenal in 1876–7. See BOA, *A.MKT.MHM.448/62* (28.11.1289/27.01.1873); BOA, *A.MKT.MHM.460/18* (06.05.1290/02.06.1873); BOA, I.DAH.47883 (23.05.1291/08.07.1874). The cost of this order was 18 million marks. BOA, *Y.EE.29/107* (1294/1877). According to the document, dated 2 October 1876, at the end of the purchasing process, the officers who had engaged in the process were rewarded with some prizes and medals. BOA, *I.DH.720/50255* (13.09.1293/02.10.1876).
12. Savile to Earl of Derby, 11.08.1877, in: NA, London: WO 106/2.
13. Grant, 'The Sword of the Sultan', p. 15. According to Rose, the Ottoman Army had in hand 300,000 American-Winchester rifles, and bought 200,000 more early in the war. See Rose, *The Origins of the War*, p. 191. Türk argues, quoting from Seel's article, that the Ottoman Army was equipped with 310,000 Martini-Peabody arms, 323,000 Snider arms and 39,000 Winchester rifles. Türk, *Die deutsche Rüstungsindustrie*, p. 135. See also Colonel Lennox to chargé d'affaires/Constantinople, 13.02.1877, in: NA, London: WO 106/2.
14. Herbert, Frederick William, *The Defence of Plevna 1877* (London and New York, 1895), pp. 23–4.
15. Shaw and Shaw, *History of the Ottoman Empire*, p. 182; Herbert, *Defence of Plevna*, p. 24.
16. Marriott, *The Eastern Question*, p. 348.
17. Yasamee, *Ottoman Diplomacy*, p. 45; Griffiths, *The Reorganization of the Ottoman Army*, p. 5.
18. Grant claims that after the Crimean War the Empire moved closer to total dependency on Western imports to modernize their forces. Grant, 'The Sword of the Sultan', p. 16. For previous eras of Ottoman military power and warfare see Murphey, Rhoads, 'The Ottoman Attitude towards the Adoption of Western Technology: The Role of the *Efrenci* Technicians in Civil and Military Applications', *Collection Turcica* 3 (1983) pp. 287–98; Özden, Gani, 'Osmanlı İmparatorluğu Silahlı Kuvvetlerinin Harp Sanayii Tesisleri', *Askeri Tarih Bülteni* 12/22 (1987), pp. 59–69; Finkel, Caroline, *The Administration of Warfare: The Ottoman Military Campaigns in Hungary, 1593–1606* (Wien, 1988); Elena, Alberto, 'Models of European Scientific Expansion: The Ottoman Empire as a Source of Evidence,' in P. Pettijean et al. (eds), *Science and Empires: Historical Studies about Scientific Development and European Expansion* (Dordrecht, 1992), pp. 259–67; Murphey, Rhoads, *Ottoman Warfare, 1500–1700* (London, 1999); Agoston, Gabor, *Guns for the Sultan: Military Power and the Weapons Industry in the Ottoman Empire* (Cambridge, 2005); Aksan, Virginia H., *Ottoman Wars 1700–1870: An Empire Besieged* (Harlow, 2007).

19. Rose claimed that the Ottoman Empire was lacking in brainpower among the chief leaders and organizers. Rose, *Origins of the War*, p. 221.
20. The Ottoman Army passed through several stages of modernization where the models were European states. Because of this fact, the modernization was influenced directly by the European advisers and assistance. According to McGarity, direct influence of Europe on the modernization of the Ottoman Army began as early as 1718 following the Treaty of Passarowitz. He argued that the mission under the leadership of Yirmisekiz Çelebi Mehmed was sent to Paris in order to learn western techniques from which the Ottoman Army might profit. McGarity, *Foreign Influence*, p. 10.
21. Schiff, Warren, 'The Influence of the German Armed Forces and War Industry on Argentina, 1880–1914', *The Hispanic American Historical Review*, 52/3 (1972), p. 437.
22. Sater, William F. and Holger H. Herwig, *The Grand Illusion: The Prussianization of the Chilean Army* (Lincoln, 1999), p. 7.
23. See Holborn, *Deutschland und die Türkei*; Ortaylı, *İkinci Abdülhamit Döneminde*; Önsoy, *Türk-Alman İktisadi Münasebetleri*; Wallach, *Bir Askeri Yardımın Anatomisi*; Yasamee, *Ottoman Diplomacy*; Soy, *Almanya'nın Osmanlı Devleti Üzerinde*. The official approach of Germany to the Ottoman territory policy was as the Freiherr von Rotenhan's following statement: 'Weder Deutschland noch Sie [der Botschafter in London Grafen von Hatzfeldt] persönlich dürfen Vorschläge wegen Landverteilung im Mittelmeer machen. Wir wollen dort nichts haben, [...]' Rotenhan to Hatzfeld, 05.08.1895, in Lepsius et al., *Die große Politik der Europäischen Kabinette*, vol. 10, p. 21; Marschall's following statement is also of importance to understand the way the Germans propagandized: 'Deutschland wünscht, daß die Türkei militärisch und auch sonst erstarke, daß seine Unabhängigkeit und Ansehen vor jeder Gefahr sichergestellt werden und daß sie wieder einen Platz unter den Großmächten einnehme. Das ist die Politik, die Deutschland schon seit langem verfolgt und die sie auch weiterverfolgen wird.' MA, Freiburg: NL.737/16.
24. Marschall to Bülow, 04.09.1908, in: PA.AA. R13745.
25. As the following passage from *Alldeutsche Blätter* shows, the importance of the Ottoman Empire and the position of the Sultan for the German interest was mentioned several times in public opinion. 'Uns Deutschen kommt es darauf an, die Herrschaft des Sultans und der Türkei zu kräftigen, weil für Deutschland die Existenz des türkischen Reiches erwünscht ist.' *Alldeutsche Blätter*, 16 July 1899. During the Ottoman bureaucrats' visit to Berlin; Bismarck discussed the German position as follows: 'İmparator hazretlerinin ve hükûmetimizin ve bil-hassa benim aha'ssi emelimiz Devlet-i 'Aliyenin tamamıyle bekâsıdır.' BOA, Y.EE.7/6 (02.02.1299/24.12.1881).
26. For Germany, the Ottoman Empire and her territory appeared both as a profitable market for the German goods, and a source of raw material resources for her rapid growing industry. See Osman Nuri, *Abdulhamid-i Sâni*; Rohrbach, *German World Policies*; Jäckh, Ernst, 'Die Beziehungen der Deutschen Industrie zum türkischen

Reich', *Technik und Wirtschaft* 5 (1916), pp. 189–204; Helfferich, Karl, *Georg von Siemens: Ein Lebensbild aus Deutschlands großer Zeit*, Vol. 3 (Berlin, 1923); Holborn, *Deutschland und die Türkei*; Rathmann, *Berlin–Bagdad*; Wolf, *The Diplomatic History*; Kössler, *Aktionsfeld Osmanisches Reich*; Ortaylı, *İkinci Abdülhamit Döneminde*; Önsoy, *Türk-Alman İktisadi Münasebetleri*.

27. *Alldeutsche Blätter*, 8 December 1895.
28. Pears, Edwin, *Life of Abdul Hamid* (London, 1917), p. 154.
29. Hale, William, M., *Turkish Foreign Policy, 1774–2000* (London, 2002), p. 19; Osmanoğlu, Ayşe, *Babam Sultan Abdulhamid. Hatıralarım* (Ankara, 1984), p. 55; Yasamee, *Ottoman Diplomacy*, p. 43. Referring to Abdülhamid's interest in foreign policy, Ray S. Baker said: 'In his early years he is said to have been a good deal of a reader, and sometimes surprises his foreign visitors by his knowledge of affairs in other lands. Not long ago he talked with an American visitor about President Roosevelt, showing himself informed to an unusual degree as to American politics.' Baker, 'The Sultan of Turkey', p. 76.
30. Marriott, *The Eastern Question*, p. 342.
31. Sater and Herwig, *The Grand Illusion*, p. 7.
32. Ali Vahbi Bey, *Avant la debacle*.
33. For a detail study of Sultan Abdülaziz's visit to Europe in 1867, see Upton-Ward, Judith Mary Ayse, *European attitudes towards the Ottoman Empire a case study Sultan Abdülaziz's visit to Europe in 1867*, Ph.D. Thesis: University of Birmingham (Birmingham, 1999).
34. Goltz to Wilhelm II, 28.10.1891, in: PA.AA. R13763.
35. Hatzfeld to the Botschafter Wien, 20.12.1881, in: PA.AA. R13247.
36. Memorandum by Colonel Chermside, 25.05.1893, in: NA, London: FO 78/4479.
37. Ali Vahbi Bey, *Avant la debacle*, p. 114.
38. Goltz to Wilhelm II, 28.10.1891, in: PA.AA. R13763.
39. Ali Vahbi Bey, *Avant la debacle*, p. 208.
40. Ibid., p. 208.
41. Ibid., p. 207.
42. This type of explanation was used on the eve of World War I in order to manipulate Turkish public opinion. Yusuf Akçuraoğlu, for instance, made such an argument in one of his influential speeches to encourage the Ottoman public to ally with Germany. See Akçuraoğlu, Yusuf, *Türk, Cermen ve Slavların Münâsebât-ı Tarihîleri: 06 Teşrîn-i sâni 1330 da Türk Ocağı'nda Verilen Konferans Metni* (İstanbul, 1330/1914), p. 24. Ali Vahbi Bey, *Avant la debacle*, p. 208.
43. Strempel to the Kriegsministerium, 14.07.1907, in: PA.AA. R13306.
44. Ali Vahbi Bey, *Avant la debacle*, p. 109.
45. Ibid., p. 110.
46. Ibid., p. 154.
47. Ibid., pp. 124–5.
48. Ibid., pp. 147–8.
49. Ibid., p. 128.

NOTES TO PAGES 184–187 307

50. Ibid., p. 117.
51. Ibid., p. 217; see also Osmanoğlu, *Babam Sultan Abdulhamid*, pp. 175–80; Karal, *Osmanlı Tarihi*, p. 420.
52. During my research in the Politisches Archiv des Auswärtigen Amtes (PA. AA), I encountered the following index note: Transferring of the Sultan's deposit from England to America, at the same time as a reserve for the Treasury ('Angebliche Überweisung von Depots des Sultans von England nach Amerika, gleichzeitig als Reserve für die Staatskasse'). Unfortunately, in the file there was no documentation relating to the money deposited in the American banks. See: PA. AA, R13939. Moreover, this transaction was reported in *The New York Times*, on 8 May 1909. The newspaper reported the transaction with the following words: 'The Parliamentary Commission, which is taking an inventory of the contents of the imperial palace at Yıldız [...] has learned that Abdülhamid deposited, during recent months, considerable sums of money in New York banks through a confidential agent. The amounts thus sent to America and the names of the institutions holding them are, however, strictly withheld.' *The New York Times*, 8 May 1909.
53. According to the document, Sultan Abdülhamid placed the following shares in the Reichsbank: on 07.07.1886: 960.000 marks; on 30.09.1886: 48,500 marks; on 06.01.1887: 42,000 marks; on 13.07.1887: 38,500 marks; on 27.09.1887: 51,000 marks; on 30.12.1887: 40,200 marks; on 22.03.1888: 52,700 marks and on 26.06.1886 40,000. See more detail: PA.AA. R13939-R13340.
54. BOA, Y.EE.4/35 (24.10.1304/16.07.1887).
55. Tahsin Paşa, *Sultan Abdulhamid: Tahsin Paşa'nın Yıldız Hatıraları* (İstanbul, 1931), p. 42.
56. Osmanoğlu, *Babam Sultan Abdulhamid*, pp. 159–64.
57. Yasamee indicates that 'in intention at least, Abdülhamid II was a realist in foreign affairs: he judged international relations in terms of power, and assessed power chiefly in military terms.' Yasamee, *Ottoman Diplomacy*, p. 41.
58. Grant, *Rulers, Guns, and Money*, p. 9.
59. Griffiths, *The Reorganization of the Ottoman Army*, p. 17; The British foreign policy makers described Abdülhamid's governance as follows: 'Sultan Abdülhamid II has laboured throughout his long reign to concentrate all authority into his own hands.' Gooch and Temperley, *British Documents*, vol. 5, p. 5.
60. Tahsin Paşa, *Sultan Abdulhamid*, p. 30.
61. Baker, 'The Sultan of Turkey', p. 67.
62. Griffiths, *The Reorganization of the Ottoman Army*, p. 43; Shaw and Shaw, *History of the Ottoman Empire*, p. 245; Erickson, *Defeat in Detail*, p. 11.
63. Erickson, *Defeat in Detail*, p. 11.
64. Huber to DWM (*Auszug aus Hubers Schreiben*), 29.10.1907, in: PA.AA. R13306.
65. Oscar S. Straus stated that the indemnity claim was Ottoman Lira 18,478 or 19,209 which was equal to $90,000: Straus to Hay, 23.09.1899, in: NARA-

Microfilm, College Park: M46/63; See also BOA, *HR.SYS.2833/64* (24.04.1900): The amount for the indemnity for the loss of the houses and properties was according to this document 20,000 OL, whereas according to the document dated 19 December 1900, it was £19,000, in: BOA, *Y.PRK. EŞA.37/18* (12.09.1318/03.01.1901).
66. Olney to Department of State 17.10.1896, in: NARA-Microfilm, College Park: M77/167; See also: BOA, *HR.SYS.2832/80* (08.10.1896); *The New York Times*, 30 March 1896; Erhan stressed that the American College in Merzifon was damaged as well during the Army's intervention however the Ottoman government made the payment (500 OL) for the damaged American College in Merzifon in 1893 to the United States Legation in İstanbul. Erhan, Çağrı, 'Ottoman Official Attitudes toward American Missionaries', *Working Paper: Yale Center for International and Area Studies: The United States & the Middle East: Cultural Encounters* 5, p. 331. See for detail on the political activity of the American missionaries in terms of the indemnity claim in the Ottoman Empire: Reed, James, Eldin, 'American Foreign Policy, The Politics of Missions and Josiah Strong 1890–1900', *Church History* 41 (1972), pp. 230–45.
67. Reed, *American Foreign Policy*, p. 240; additionally according to a document the rumour of sending the American fleet to the Ottoman harbour had been made as early as in 1896. BOA, *Y.A.HUS.343/84* (28.08.1313/ 14.01.1896).
68. Reed, *American Foreign Policy*, p. 240.
69. Straus to Hay, 23.09.1899, in: NARA-Microfilm, College Park: M46/63.
70. Ibid.
71. *Selamlık*: The public procession of the Sultan to the mosque for the congregational prayer on Friday.
72. Straus to Hay, 23.09.1899, in: NARA-Microfilm, College Park: M46/63.
73. Ibid.
74. Ibid.
75. Hill to Straus, 09.10.1899, in: NARA-Microfilm, College Park: M77/168.
76. Akyıldız gives also some examples of the Sultan's tactics playing for time. Akyıldız, Ali, *Osmanlı Bürokrasisi ve Modernleşme* (İstanbul, 2004), pp. 180–1.
77. BOA, *Y.PRK.HR.29/42* (08.08.1318/01.12.1900): 'Amerika tebaası tazminâtı [...] bu gemi bedeline dâhil[dir].'
78. BOA, *Y.PRK.EŞA.37/18* (12.09.1318/03.01.1901).
79. Erhan, *Ottoman Official Attitudes*, p. 331.
80. Grant, *Rulers, Guns, and Money*, p. 90. As Menne pointed out 'political action and business reaction frequently followed each other with suspicious promptness'. Menne, *Blood and Steel*, p. 242.
81. Menne, *Blood and Steel*, p. 242.
82. Goltz to Kiderlen, 22.11.1891, in: PA.AA. R13763: *'Räumung des Landes'*; see also Smith, *The Embassy of Sir William White*, pp. 148–57.
83. Smith, *The Embassy of Sir William White*, p. 149.
84. BOA, Y.EE.106/18 (02.01.1301/03.11.1883).
85. Griffiths, *The Reorganization of the Ottoman Army*, p. 155.

86. Ibid., p. 135.
87. Ottoman arms importation was widely reported by the British, Russian, Bulgarian, and Greek newspapers. For instance the *Times* [BOA, Y.PRK. TKM.12/35 (16.11.1305/25.07.1888)] reported that the state bonds (*Tahvilat*) were held in the state treasury as a reserve for the payment of the ordered Krupp cannons and Mauser rifles, in spite of marketing the state's block of shares on the market. In a Bulgarian newspaper [BOA, Y.A. HUS.523/39 (06.08.1326/03.09.1908)] it was reported that the Ottoman Empire had purchased war materials from the Krupp Company. According to this newspaper, the intent of the Ottoman Empire was to attack Bulgarian territory; and the Russian newspaper [BOA, Y.PRK.TKM.10/20 (11.05.1324/ 03.07.1906)] reported on the Ottomans financial state and her military expenditures and military policy.
88. Terrell to Sherman, 28.05.1897, in: NARA-Microfilm, College Park: M46/63.
89. Goltz, Colmar Freiherr, von der, 'Bilder aus der türkischen Armee', *Militär-Wochenblatt* 38 (1897b), pp. 1151–62.
90. Goltz, Colmar Freiherr, von der, *The Turkish Army, its Characteristics and Capabilities: A Series of Letters by Von der Goltz*, translated by W. E. Fairholme (London, 1898), p. 26.
91. Yasamee, F. A. K., 'Abdulhamid II and the Ottoman Defence Problem', *Diplomacy and Statecraft* 4/1 (1993), p. 21.
92. Memorandum of Colonel Ponsonby 07.07.1898, in: NA London: FO 195/2016 cited in Griffiths, *The Reorganization of the Ottoman Army*, p. 143.
93. Kiderlen to Bülow, 02.08.1907, in: PA.AA. R13306: The Italian bid to be awarded with an order for a cruiser became a matter of diplomatic debate.
94. Marschall to Hohenlohe, 06.08.1898, in Lepsius et al., *Die große Politik der Europäischen Kabinette*, vol.12–2, pp. 566–7.
95. The military reform of Sultan Mahmud II (1785–1839) was based on the French influence. The young officers were mostly sent to France for military training, and French was the second language for students in the military schools. The dominance of the French language and system remained in place until Abdülhamid II established the new friendship with Germany. See Shaw, J. Stanford, 'The Origins of Ottoman Military Reform: The Nizam-ı Cedid Army of Sultan Selim III', *Journal of Modern History* 37 (1965), pp. 291–305; Griffiths, *The Reorganization of the Ottoman Army*, pp. 14–7; McGarity, *Foreign Influence*, pp. 10–14.
96. Ali Vahbi Bey: *Avant la debacle*, pp. 126–8. However, later on, according to The New York Times, Abdülhamid had mentioned his regret about the displacement of the French by the Germans. The article noted: 'in what purported to be a translation of Abdülhamid's private memoirs, published in Germany in 1913, the monarch ascribed to 'Fate, which drives men to do things in the wrong way', the responsibility for his displacement of the French by the Germans.' *The New York Times*, 12 February 1918.

97. Fulton, L. Bruce, 'France and the End of the Ottoman Empire' in Marian Kent (ed.), *The Great Powers and the End of the Ottoman Empire* (London, 1996), p. 141.
98. Marschall to Hohenlohe, 24.05.1898, in Lepsius et al., *Die große Politik der Europäischen Kabinette*, vol. 12–2, p. 564: 'In Paris ist man längst nervös über unsere hiesige Stellung'.
99. Holborn, *Deutschland und die Türkei*, p. 76; see also Kraus, Jacob, *Deutsch-türkische Handelsbeziehungen. Seit dem Berliner Vertrag unter besonderer Berücksichtigung der Handelswege* (Jena, 1901); Aybar, Celal, *Osmanlı İmparatorluğu'nun Ticaret Muvazenesi 1878–1913* (Ankara, 1939); Henderson, 'German Economic Penetration'; Önsoy, *Türk-Alman İktisadi Münasebetleri*; Pamuk, *The Ottoman Empire and European Capitalism.*
100. See also Eldem, Vedat, *Osmanlı İmparatorluğunun İktisadi Şartları Hakkında Bir Tetkik* (Ankara, 1970); Birken, *Die Wirtschaftsbeziehungen zwischen Europa und dem Vorderen Orient*; Pamuk, *The Ottoman Empire*; Pamuk, Şevket (ed.), *19. Yüzyılda Osmanlı Dış Ticareti, Tarihi İstatistikler 1* (Ankara, 1995).
101. Marschall von Bieberstein preferred being called as he wrote in the following report as 'Freiherr von Marschall': '*Er nennt mich fortwährend: "Freiherr von Bieberstein" oder "Baron Bieberstein", während kein Deutscher mich anders nennt als 'Freiherr von Marschall'.* Marschall to Bülow, 26.07.1907, in: PA.AA. R13745.
102. Marschall to Hohenlohe, 06.08.1898, in Lepsius et al., *Die große Politik der Europäischen Kabinette*, vol. 12–2, p. 567: 'Als ich dann im entscheidenden Moment den Sultan bitten ließ, der deutschen Industrie sein Vertrauen zu erhalten, ließ er mir umgehend sagen: 'es sei feststehendes Prinzip bei ihm [Sultan Abdülhamid], Kriegsmaterial in Deutschland zu bestellen, und er werde davon nicht abgehen.'
103. Terrell to Gresham, 20.10.1894, in: NARA-Microfilm, College Park: M46/56, cited in Sander, O. and K. Fişek, *ABD Dışişleri Belgeleriyle Türk-ABD Silah Ticaretinin İç Yüzü, 1828–1925* (Ankara and Istanbul, 2007), pp. 125–6.
104. Mauser to Einem, 16.12.1907, in: SA, Oberndorf: M-A6.
105. See Chapter 3, p. 139.
106. BOA, *Y.MTV.281/21* (07.10.1323/05.12.1905).
107. BOA, *Y.PRK.BŞK.43/14* (21.03.1313/11.09.1895).
108. Marschall to Auswärtiges Amt, 06.04.1907, in: PA. AA. R13775. Quotation mark is in original.
109. Paul Horn was the consultant and under-secretary of the Minister of Public Works (*Nafıa Nezareti Müsteşarı*). He entered Ottoman service in April 1885 and stayed in the Ottoman Empire for ten years. See: BOA, *I.DH.938/74290* (09.07.1302/24.04.1885); BOA, *Y.PRK.NMH.6/53* (05.11.1312/ 30.04.1895); see also Kırmızı, Abdulhamit, *II. Abdülhamid Dönemi (1876–1908) Osmanlı Bürokrasisinde Gayrimüslimler*, MA Thesis, Hacettepe Üniversitesi (Ankara, 1998), pp. 43–4.
110. King to the Secretary of State, 24.12.1889, in: NARA-Microfilm, College Park: M46/50.

111. Horn to Krupp, 09.08.1891, in: HA. FAH 3B/216.
112. BOA, *Y.A.RES.36/17* (14.05.1304/08.02.1887): The Sultan tried to learn both the Mauser rifle's real price (*fiyat-ı hakîkîlerini*) and also the price offered to the other governments; in the other documents we see that the Sultan found the price offered by Mauser very high and ordered the Ottoman ambassador to Berlin to renegotiate the terms. BOA, *Y.A.RES.51/29* (03.12.1307/21.07.1890).
113. BOA, *Y.PRK.BŞK.12/14* (28.04.1304/24.01.1887).
114. BOA, *Y.PRK.EŞA.50/35* (25.03.1325/08.05.1907); see also: BOA, *Y.A. HUS.498/60* (17.11.1323/13.01.1906).
115. Marschall to Hohenlohe, 24.05.1898, in Lepsius et al., *Die große Politik der Europäischen Kabinette*, vol. 12–2, p. 563.
116. Fulton, 'France and the End', p. 155; Howe pointed out that the German embassy also used the same method to secure some Ottoman armaments order. Howe, *Why War*, p. 104.
117. BOA, *Y.MRZ.D.12578* (26.09.1322/04.12.1904).
118. Fulton, 'France and the End', p. 155.
119. Langensiepen, Bernd and Güleryüz, Ahmet, *1828–1923 Osmanlı Donanması* (İstanbul, 2000), p. 181.
120. BOA, *Y.MRZ.D.13014* (14.02.1323/20.04.1905).
121. Huber to Mauser, 27.05.1905, in: SA, Oberndorf: M-A5; Huber to Mauser, 03.06.1905, in: SA, Oberndorf: M-A5.
122. See also Fulton, 'France's Extraordinary Ambassador: Ernest Constans'.
123. *Aufzeichnung des Botschafters in London Grafen von Metternich*, 14.08.1908, in Lepsius, Mendelssohn-Bartholdy, and Thimme, *Die große Politik der Europäischen Kabinette*, Vol. 25, pp. 606–7.
124. See also McMeekin, *Berlin-Bagdad Express*, p. 67.
125. Bülow, *Imperial Germany*, p. 69.
126. *Deutsche Zeitung*, 09.07.1907, in: PA.AA. R13745.
127. Ibid. Deutsche Zeitung, 09.07.1907, in: PA.AA. R13745: 'Hier also, insbesondere bei den Jung Türken, die nach erfolgtem Thronwechsel höchst wahrscheinlich die maßgebende Partei bilden werden, muss eine weitschauende Diplomatie sowie die von ihr geleitete Presse die Überzeugung stärken, daß das deutsche Volk der natürliche Verbündete und Freund des Osmanenreichs ist.'
128. Hirst, *The Political Economy of War*, pp. 92–3.
129. See Fig. 2.1: Chapter 2, p. 82.
130. See Chapter 3, pp. 114–7.
131. Hirst, *The Political Economy of War*, p. 94.
132. BOA, Y.PRK.BŞK.12/14 (20.01.1304/19.10.1886).
133. BOA, *Y.A.RES.36/17* (01.05.1304/26.01.1887); BOA, *Y.PRK.BŞK.13/41* (23.01.1305/11.10.1887); BOA, *Y.PRK.BŞK.13/41* (06.04.1305/22.12.1887); BOA, *Y.PRK.MYD.7/34* (20.11.1305/29.07.1888); BOA, *Y.PRK.MYD.7/137* (29.12.1305/06.09.1888); BOA, *Y.A.RES.41/42* (28.06.1308/ 12.03.1888).

134. BOA, Y.A.RES.37/2 (05.05.1304/30.01.1887); See also BOA, Y.PRK. TKM.13/44 (14.01.1306/20.09.1888).
135. Cited in Werner, Max, *The Military Strength of the Powers*, translated by Edward Fitzgerald (London, 1939), p. 16.
136. BOA, Y.MTV.89/67 (08.07.1311/15.01.1894); BOA,Y.PRK.ASK.62/87 (13.11.1307/01.07.1890); see also: BOA, Y.A.HUS.498/83 (22.11.1323/ 18.01.1906).
137. *Abschrift*, 21.03.1895, in: HA, Krupp: FAH 3C/71.
138. BOA, *HR.SYS.218/121* (02.06.1312/02.12.1894).
139. *Abschrift*, 20.01.1898, in: HA, Krupp: FAH 3C/224.
140. BOA, Y.MTV.295/159 (29.01.1325/14.03.1907).
141. *The New York Times*, 25 August 1903.
142. BOA, Y.MTV.253/82 (11.09.1321/01.12.1903).
143. Hirst, *The Political Economy of War*, p. 96.
144. BOA, Y.A.HUS.484/11 (02.12.1322/07.02.1905).
145. Report on Changes in Foreign Armies during 1905, in: NA, London: WO/106–6182: 11.
146. Ibid., p. 21.
147. *The {London} Times*, 21 December 1904.
148. BOA, Y.PRK.ASK.227/135 (30.01.1323/06.04.1905); see also for table for the installment payment: BOA, Y.PRK.ASK.207/4 (04.01.1324/28.02.1906).
149. BOA, Y.MTV.281/21 (07.10.1323/05.12.1905): The commission described the Krupp quick-firing guns as follows: '*Krupp fabrikasından celbi mukarrer bulunan ve Avrupada en müterakkî hükûmet-i 'askeriyeden ekseriyesinin bile henüz elde etmeye muvaffık olamadıkları efvâh-ı nâriyeden serî atışlı toplar...*'
150. BOA, Y.MTV.295/159 (29.01.1325/14.03.1907).
151. Werner, *Military Strength*, p. 16.
152. See Erickson, *Defeat in Detail*.
153. BOA, Y.PRK.TKM.10/38 (26.07.1304/20.04.1887).
154. McGarity, *Foreign Influence*, p. 24.
155. BOA, Y.A.RES.36/17 (01.05.1304/26.01.1887).
156. BOA, Y.PRK.OMZ.2/43 (03.08.1317/ 07.12.1899).
157. Trained in the British Royal Navy, Halil İbrahim Pasha was appointed to the Ministry of Navy on 12 January 1910. Çoker, Fahri, *Deniz Harp Okulumuz: 1773* (Ankara 1994), part III, p. 37; See also Bal, Nurcan, *Süleyman Nutki Bey'in Hatıraları* (İstanbul, 2003), p. 145.
158. BOA, Y.PRK.OMZ.2/43 (03.08.1317/ 07.12.1899): '*Âsâr-ı Tevfîk Fırkateyn-i Hümâyûnlarının Krupp toplarıyla techîzini emr u fermân-ı kerâmet-beyân-ı zillu'l-lahîlerinin şeref-sünûh ve südûr buyurulmasındaki hikmetin sırf ilhâm-ı rabbânîden münba'is olduğu sâbit olup...*'
159. See also Strempel to the Kriegsministerium, 14.07.1907, in: PA.AA. R13306.
160. BOA, Y.PRK.ASK.52/77 (06.05.1306/08.01.1889).
161. BOA, Y.EE.106/18 (02.01.1301/03.11.1883).
162. Lowther to Grey, 31.05.1910, in: NA, London: FO 78/371–1000.

163. According to Sir G. Lowther, the reasons for his resignation were not clear, but it seemed probable that his fall was occasioned by intrigues of the German and American competitors, combined with those of the rival English firms of Palmer and Fairfield. Lowther to Grey, 31.05.1910, in: NA, London: FO 78/371–1000; see also Çoker, *Deniz Harp Okulumuz*, p. 37; Grant, *Rulers, Guns, and Money*, pp. 176–7; Beşirli, Mehmet, 'Sultan Abdülaziz'den Birinci Dünya Savaşı'na Osmanlı Donanması', *Atatürk Üniversitesi Türkiyat Araştırmaları Enstitüsü Dergisi* 11/25 (2004), pp. 262–6.
164. Ali Vahbi Bey, *Avant la debacle*, pp. 21–3; 74–5.
165. Grant, *Rulers, Guns, and Money*, p. 14; Hallgarten, *Imperialismus vor 1914*, vol. 1, p. 137.
166. Ali Vahbi Bey, *Avant la debacle*, p. 75.
167. Fay, Sidney B., 'The Baghdad Railway: A German Defense of the Financial Arrangements', *The Journal of Modern History* 4/2 (1932), p. 240.
168. Cited in Fay, 'The Baghdad Railway', pp. 240–1.
169. *Leipziger Neuesten Nachrichten*, 14 September 1906, in: PA.AA. R13305: 'Daß man in Konstantinopel mit 'Bakschisch' kräftig arbeitet, ist eine bekannte Tatsache.'
170. Leishman to Hay, 17.07.1903, in: NARA-Microfilm, College Park: M46/72.
171. Scott, John Dick, *Vickers: A History* (London, 1962), p. 81. Cited in Sampson, *The Arms Bazaar*, p. 52.
172. Sampson, *The Arms Bazaar*, p. 53.
173. Lindow, *Freiherr Marschall von Bieberstein*, p. 26.
174. Osman Nizami Pasha was the Ottoman ambassador in Berlin between 1908 and 1915.
175. The very interesting point is here the expression 'being more German than Turks'. The American adviser Bucknam Pasha used the same justification for Rauf Pasha as follows: 'Rauf [...] is far more an American in his idea than a Turk.' *The New York Times*, 11 May 1913. It seems that some of the Ottoman officers who occupied very important positions in the Ottoman Army were in their ideas far more others than Turk.
176. Marschall to Bülow, 25.10.1908, in: PA.AA. R13746.
177. *Deutsche Zeitung*, 9 July 1907, in: PA.AA. R13745; However, Giesl described Halil Rıfat Pasha as an uneducated and inferior man. 'Der Sultan hatte den 80 jährigen Großvezier Halil Rıfat Pascha, einen ganz ungebildeten und inferioren Mann, [...] zu diesem Amte berufen.' Giesl, Zwei Jahrzehnte im Nahen Orient, p. 25. Nevertheless, Giesl was wrong about Halil Pasha's age. Halil Pasha was not at his eighties when he became Grand Vizier, he was 68 years old and, when he died in 1901, he was 74. See Birol, Nurettin, 'Halil Rıfat Paşa' *C.Ü. Sosyal Bilimler Dergisi* 27/2 (2003), pp. 278–80.
178. Ahmed Rıfat Bey's letter, 11.08.1907, in: PA.AA. R13745.
179. Kiderlen to the Foreign Office, 15.07.1907, in: PA.AA. R.13306; See also Strempel to the Kriegsministerium, 14.07.1907, in: PA.AA. R13306.
180. Yasamee, 'Colmar Freiherr von der Goltz and the Rebirth', pp. 94–5.

181. Marschall to Bülow, 03.09.1908, in Lepsius et al., *Die große Politik der Europäischen Kabinette*, vol.25, pp. 614–5.
182. Yasamee, 'Colmar Freiherr von der Goltz and the Rebirth', pp. 109–10.
183. Wangenheim to Hollweg, 28.08.1912 cited in Türk, *Die deutsche Rüstungsindustrie*, p. 82.
184. For more insightful approach regarding the influence of the Amry in the late Ottoman political life see Turfan, Naim M., *Rise of the Young Turks: Politics, the Military and Ottoman Collapse* (London, 2000).
185. Wangenheim to Hollweg, 28.08.1912 cited in Türk, *Die deutsche Rüstungsindustrie*, p. 82.
186. Akmeşe, *Birth of Modern Turkey*, p. 25.
187. Brose, Eric Dom, *The Kaiser's Army: The Politics of Military Technology in Germany during the Machine Age, 1870–1918* (New York, 2001), pp. 13, 41.
188. Menne, *Blood and Steel*, p. 194.
189. BOA, Y.PRK.MYD.21/15 (21.12.1315/11.05.1898).
190. Swanson, 'War, Technology, and Society', p. 374.
191. See also Chapter 3, pp. 140–1.
192. Goltz, 'Erinnerungen an Mahmud Shewket Pascha', p. 34.
193. Swanson, 'War, Technology, and Society', p. 372.
194. Goltz, 'Erinnerungen an Mahmud Shewket Pascha', p. 34.
195. Ibid., p. 35.
196. Goltz to Mahmud Şevket Pasha, 30.09.1911, in: MA, Freiburg: NL.737/10.
197. Cemal Paşa, *Hatırat*, Martı Metin (ed.) (İstanbul, 1996), p. 73.
198. BOA, Y.PRK.ASK.227/13 (30.01.1323/06.04.1905): '93 Batarya sahra topu esmânı olarak'.
199. Grant, 'The Sword of the Sultan', p. 26.
200. BOA, Y.MTV.285/100 (27.01.1324/23.03.1906).
201. BOA, Y.MTV.285/100 (27.01.1324/23.03.1906).
202. Cemal Paşa, *Hatırat*, p. 73.
203. For more information about the *Mâbeyn* see Hürmen *Bürokrat Tevfik Biren*; Shaw and Shaw, *History of the Ottoman Empire*, pp. 213–4: The chief scribes of the Sultan were Küçük Sait Pasha (1876–78); Ali Fuat Bey (1878–81); Süreyya Pasha (1881–94); Tahsin Pasha (1894–1909).
204. See for more information about the importance of *Mâbeyn* and Yıldız administration during the reign of Sultan Abdülhamid: Akyıldız, *Osmanlı Bürokrasisi*, pp. 167–73.
205. Goltz, *The Turkish Army, its Characteristics and Capabilities*, p. 14; see also Akyıldız, *Osmanlı Bürokrasisi*, p. 180.
206. White to Salisbury, 28.06.1887, in: NA, London: FO 78/3998.
207. *The Times of India*, 10 August 1908, in: PA.AA. R13745.
208. İzzet Bey was one of the most influential figures during the reign of Abdülhamid II. With the declaration of the constitution, İzzet escaped from İstanbul to Europe. See Farah, Caesar E., 'Arab Supporters of Sultan Abdulhamid II: Izzet al-Abid', *Archivum Ottomanicum* 15 (1997), pp. 189–219.

209. Gooch and Temperley, *British Documents*, vol. 5, p. 8; Kamphövener Pasha, who also held an office at *Mâbeyn*, described İzzet Bey as follows: 'Der Sultan sei in den Händen eines verworfenen Menschen, des İzzet Bey, der ihn ganz leite, und durch den alle Geschäfte gehen.' Lepsius et al., *Die große Politik der Europäischen Kabinette*, vol. 12–1, p. 17.
210. *The New York Times* called him the 'Machiavelli of Turkey' and gave the following interpretation in 1915, seven years after his escape from İstanbul: 'In 1908, on the eve of the revolution he became a Sheik–to save his soul, he said. Then he joined the Young Turks to save his body. He finally escaped from the country in order, as he again declared, to keep body and soul together. He is reported to be very wealthy with money on deposit in London and New York. He undoubtedly visited London incognito half a dozen years ago and is said also to have been seen in New York.' *The New York Times*, 6 January 1915.
211. Currie to Salisbury, 16.04.1896, in: NA, London: FO 78/4706.
212. Farah, 'Arab Supporters', p. 194.
213. Shaw and Shaw, *History of the Ottoman Empire*, p. 214.
214. Farah, 'Arab Supporters', p. 198; Kössler, *Aktionsfeld Osmanisches Reich*, p. 272.
215. Cited in Boelcke, *Krupp und die Hohenzollern in Dokumenten*, pp. 147–8.
216. Marschall to the Auswärtiges Amt, 11.10.1902, in Lepsius et al., *Die große Politik der Europäischen Kabinette*, vol. 14, p. 421.
217. BOA, *Y.PRK.ASK.168/128* (1318/1900).
218. Kössler, *Aktionsfeld Osmanisches Reich*, p. 274–5.
219. Mutluçağ, Hayri, 'Dost Bildiğimiz ve Ordumuzu Islah için İçimizde Bulundurduklarımızın Marifetleri', *Belgelerle Türk Tarihi Dergisi* 12 (1968), pp. 34–41; Ortaylı, *İkinci Abdülhamit Döneminde*, pp. 64–6; Türk, *Die deutsche Rüstungsindustrie*, p. 73. Mutluçağ and Ortaylı both referred to the same documents, which accuse Goltz Pasha of direct involvement in the *Baksheesh* traffic. BOA, *Y.EE.15/212* (28.08.1307/20.03.1890). However, these documents that were produced and submitted to Artin [Dadyan] Pasha by a well-known French novelist Théodore Cahu (also known as Theo Critt), who had claimed that he captured some secret letters/reports of Goltz Pasha sent to Bismarck and General Walderseee, appear to be fabricated. According to one of these quasi-captured documents, Goltz Pasha had paid (bribed) three Ottoman officers based on a direction given by Bismarck. Mutluçağ gave the following transcription, which was also quoted by Türk, 'Bu paşaları sizde [Bismarck] tanırsınız, emirleriniz üzere şimdiye değin kararlaştırılan paraları kendilerne iki defa vermiş olduğumu biliyorsunuz. İşte bu ödemeler tekrarlandığı takdirde, yukarıda adlarını açıkladığım kişilerin geniş ve önemli yardımlarını göreceğimize eminim.' In fact these documents were among those reports of the Sultan's informers (*Jurnaller*), some of which were saved and submitted later to the Prime Minister Ottoman Archives-State Archive by Asaf Tuğay. See Tuğay, Asaf, *İbret: Abdülhamid'e verilen Jurnaller ve Jurnalciler* (İstanbul, 1962); and Tuğay, Asaf, '*Saray dedikoduları ve bazı mâruzat*'

(Istanbul, 1963). It is important, also, to mention here that–as it was also pointed out by Artin Pasha–Théodore Cahu was expecting some gift made by Sultan Abdülhamid on these reports and secret information that was submitted by him (... *kendilerinin de {Théodore Cahu} ihsan-ı celil tacdarilerine nail olacağı ümidinde bulunuduğunu ima etti*). BOA, *Y.EE.15/212* (28.08.1307/20.03.1890).
220. Sater and Herwig, *The Grand Illusion*, pp. 134–6.
221. See Chapter 3, pp. 121–47.
222. BOA, *HR.TO.30/11* (02.08.1285/18.11.1868); BOA, *HR.TO.30/9* (11.06.1285//29.09.1868).
223. BOA, *Y.A.RES.36/17* (19.04.1304/15.01.1887).
224. See Chapter 2, pp. 102–5.
225. BOA, *Y.A.RES.36/17* (19.04.1304/15.01.1887).
226. BOA, *Y.A.RES.36/17* (19.04.1304/15.01.1887).
227. See Chapter 3, pp. 123–4.
228. BOA, *Y.A.RES.36/17* (19.04.1304/15.01.1887).
229. Grant, *Rulers, Guns, and Money*, p. 83.
230. See also Chapter 3, p. 128.
231. Menshausen to Krupp, 20.12.1891, in: PA.AA. R13763.
232. BOA, *Y.EE.14/195* (29.11.1318/20.03.1901): 'Bugüne kadar ben efendimizden [Sultan Abdülhamid] başka kimseye hizmet etmedim ve inşallah şimdiden sonrada hizmet etmek namussuzluğuna irtikâb etmem.'
233. White to Salisbury, 28.06.1887, in: NA, London: FO 78/3998; BOA, *Y. EE.136/119* (02.11.1316/14.03.1899), see also Ali Vahbi Bey, *Avant la debacle* p. 55: 'des minerais sont amenés sur les marchés mondiaux, tels par exemple les minerais de chromite de mon chambellan Raghib Bey.'
234. Ali Vahbi Bey, *Avant la debacle*, pp. 79–80: 'Le secrétaire de ma cassette Raghib-Bey a fait pour moi des spéculations extraordinairement heureuses et le produit récent de nos spéculations sur les mines d'or Sud-Africaines a été fort considérable.'
235. Memorandum of Ritter von Manéga, 06.06.1886, in: PA.AA. R13237.
236. White to Salisbury, 24.06.1887, in: NA, London: FO 78/3998.
237. White to Salisbury, 28.06.1887, in: NA, London: FO 78/3998.
238. Ragıb to Mauser, 17.10.1887, in: SA, Oberndorf: M-A3: 'Entschuldigen Sie mich, bitte, daß ich Ihnen bis jetzt nicht geschrieben habe. Aber seien Sie versichert, daß ich stets Ihrer gedenke. Es ist überflüssig Ihnen zu schreiben, daß ich die größte Hochachtung für Sie hege.- Ihr Herz hat mich Ihnen verbunden und ich hoffe Sie glauben dem Wort eines Mannes mit dem Sie monatelang verkehrt haben.'
239. White to Salisbury, 28.06.1887, in: NA, London: FO 78/3998.
240. Most probably, Menshausen meant the three prominent German arms factories: The Mauser AG., Oberndorf; Ludwig Loewe & Co., Berlin; and Deutsche Metallpatronenfabrik, Karlsruhe.
241. *Notizen über Türkei*, undated document, in: HA, Krupp: FAH 3C/2/217.

242. Cf. Goltz to Menshausen, 01.08.1891, in: HA, Krupp: FAH 3B/216; *Abschrift*: 21.12.1891, in: HA, Krupp FAH 3C/217; Goltz to Geheimrat, 10.11.1891, in: PA.AA. R13763; *Notizen über Türkei*, undated document, in: HA, Krupp: FAH 3C/217.
243. Cf. Marschall's statements about Osman Nizami Pasha: Chapter 5, pp. 231–2.
244. Menshausen to Geheimrath, 23.12.1891, in: PA.AA. R13763.
245. *Notizen über Türkei*, undated Document, in: HA, Krupp: FAH 3C/217.
246. Menshausen to Krupp, 20.12.1891, in: PA.AA. R13763.
247. Menshausen to Krupp, 20.12.1891, in: PA.AA. R13763.
248. Goltz to Geheimrat, 10.11.1891, in: PA.AA. R13763.
249. Goltz to Geheimrat, 23.12.1891, in: PA.AA. R13763.
250. According to Baker, Sultan Abdülhamid's spy system worked as follows: 'When an official is appointed, it is matter of course that a spy is appointed to watch him, and it is more than likely that if the place be one of especial importance a second spy is there to watch the first, and perhaps a third and fourth to report on the doings of all others.' Baker, 'The Sultan of Turkey', p. 68.
251. Menshausen to Krupp, 20.12.1891, in: PA.AA. R13763.
252. Lowther to Grey, 08.12.1908, in: NA, London: FO 371/560.
253. *Schwarzwälder Bote*, 13 March 1887:414, in: SA, Oberndorf: Z59: Tevfik Pasha; İzzet Pasha; Mahmud Şevket [Pasha]; Hasan Sabri Bey; Tahir Bey; Ahmed Effendi.
254. *Schwarzwälder Bote*, 13 March 1887: 414, in: SA, Oberndorf: Z59.
255. *Schwarzwälder Bote*, 14 September 1887: 1606, in: SA, Oberndorf: Z60.
256. Undated note, in: SA, Oberndorf: 793.32/13.1 (Mauser Waffen, Abnahme-Kommission/Türkenzeit).
257. Grant, *Rulers, Guns, and Money*, p. 83; see also Chapter 3, pp. 128–30.
258. During their stay in Oberndorf, the Brazilian commission also used the *Türkenbau* as their residence.
259. H. Walter Schmid's note, in: SA, Oberndorf: 793.32/13.1 (Mauser Waffen, Abnahme-Kommission/Türkenzeit.)
260. H. Walter Schmid's note, in: SA, Oberndorf: 793.32/13.1 (Mauser Waffen, Abnahme-Kommission/Türkenzeit.)
261. Hüseyin Hüsnü Bey married an Oberndorfer woman and they had children. One of them (Leyla) died of lung and intestinal catarrh at age three and was buried in Oberndorfer cemetery. 'The Registry of Death dated on 18 February 1889', in: SA, Oberndorf.
262. During my research stay in Oberndorf I visited the cemetery and saw a gravestone on which the following epitaph was engraved: 'Allah is the eternal creator. Dying in a foreign country is without a doubt the greatest misfortune.' See also 'The Registry of Death dated 3 September 1888', in: SA, Oberndorf.
263. Seel, 'Mauser-Gewehre' (1981d), p. 1423.
264. Ibid.
265. Seel, 'Mauser-Gewehre' (1981e), p. 1722.
266. BOA, *Y.PRK.MYD.15/50* (10.04.1312/11.10.1894).

267. BOA, *DH.MKT.2057/51* (13.08.1310/02.03.1893).
268. Gözeller, *Osmanlı-Alman Yakınlaşmasının Basına Yansıması*, p. 59; see also: Sater and Herwig, *The Grand Illusion*, p. 134.
269. Sater and Herwig, *The Grand Illusion*, p. 134.
270. The Iranian Shah, for example, paid a visit to the Krupp factory in Essen after his Berlin tour. BOA, *Y.A.HUS.226/34* (15.10.1306/14.06.1889). See also for the Moroccon delegation's visit to the Krupp factory in Essen: *Schwarzwälder Bote*, 21 February 1889.
271. The following are some selected scholarly works on the German military/economic influence on Latin American countries: Rippy, J. Fred, 'German investments in Guatemala', *The Journal of Business of the University of Chicago* 20/4 (1947), pp. 212–9; Rippy, J. Fred, 'German investments in Argentina', *The Journal of Business of the University of Chicago* 21/1 (1948), pp. 50–4; Brunn, Gerhard, 'Deutscher Einfluss und Deutsche Interessen in der Professionalisierung einiger Lateinamerikanischer Staaten vor dem 1. Weltkrieg (1885–1914)', *Jahrbuch für Geschichte von Staat, Wirtschaft und Gesellschaft Lateinamerikas* 6 (1969), pp. 281–5; Forbes, Ian, L. D., 'German informal imperialism in South America before 1914,' *The Economic History Review*, New Series 31 (1978), pp. 384–98; Schaefer, Jürgen, *Deutsche Militärhilfe an Südamerika: Militär- und Rüstungsinteressen in Argentinien, Bolivien, Chile vor 1914* (Düsseldorf, 1974); Schiff, Warren, 'German Military Penetration into Mexico during the late Díaz period', *The Hispanic American Historical Review* 39/4 (1959), pp. 568–79; Schiff, Warren, 'The Germans in Mexican Trade and Industry During the Díaz Period', *The Americas* 23/3 (1967), pp. 279–96; Herwig, *Germany's Vision of Empire;* Sater and Herwig, *The Grand Illusion*.
272. Sater and Herwig, *The Grand Illusion*, p. 134. See also Kössler, *Aktionsfeld Osmanisches Reich*.
273. BOA, Y.MTV.35/44 (17.01.1306/23.09.1888); BOA, Y.PRK.ASK.70/37 (27.11.1308/04.07.1891). In 1885, Krupp's representative Otto Dingler sent a telegraph reporting the Sabit Pasha's visit to Essen. 'Ali Saib Pascha mir eben mitgetheilt dass Sabit Pascha in wenigen tagen nach Essen reisen wird.' Dingler to Krupp, 26.09.1885, in: HA Krupp: WA-2/248.
274. Sabit Pasha to Krupp, 21.05.1889, HA Krupp: FAH-3-B/227. Additionally, in the Krupp Family Archive I have seen an interesting index-remark for a letter sent from İstanbul to Herr Krupp, which makes Sabit Pasha's position in Krupp family more remarkable. According to the index Sadi Bey sent F. A. Krupp a gift of a real Turkistan carpet. Interestingly it was noted in the index that this little issue should not come to the Sabit Pasha's attention (*Teilt mit, daß einige Turkistan-Teppiche an F.A.K. von Sadi Bey gesandt wurden. Diese kleine Angelegenheit soll nicht zur Kenntnis Sabit Pashas gelangen.*) Otto Reil to A. Krupp, 27.02.1886, in: HA, Krupp: WA 4/2277.
275. Sabit Pasha to Krupp, 27.12.1885, in: HA, Krupp: FAH 3B/227.
276. BOA, *Y.PRK.ASK.70/37* (27.07.1308/08.03.1891).
277. Sabit Pasha to A. Krupp, 27.11.1889, in: HA, Krupp: FAH 3 B/227.

278. Goltz to Menshausen, 01.08.1891, in: HA, Krupp: FAH 3 B/216.
279. *The New York Times*, 27 October 1889.
280. Ibid.
281. BOA, *DH.MKT.2578/36* (11.10.1319/21.01.1902); BOA, *DH.MKT.2587/30* (03.11.1319/11.02.1902).
282. BOA, *DH.MKT.854/61* (09.03.1322/24.05.1904): According to these documents, the Ottoman Government paid back to Krupp the cost of his entire treatment, which had been earlier covered by the Krupp Company.

Chapter 6   The Power Shift and its Consequences (1908–14)

1. *The {London} Times*, 23 July 1909, in: PA.AA. R13564: Talat Pasha's speech at the luncheon at the House of Commons on 22 July 1909.
2. For more detail see Ahmad, Feroz, *The Young Turks, the Committee of Union and Progress in Turkish Politics 1908–1914* (Oxford, 1969); Quataert, Donald, 'The Economic Climate of the "Young Turk Revolution" in 1908', *Journal of Modern History* 51/3 (1979), pp. 1147–61; Hanioğlu, M. Şükrü, *The Young Turks in Opposition* (New York and Oxford, 1995); Kansu, Aykut, *The Revolution of 1908 in Turkey* (Leiden, 1997); Kayalı, Hasan, *Arabs and Young Turks: Ottomanism, Arabism, and Islamism in the Ottoman Empire, 1908–1918* (Berkeley, Los Angeles, and London, 1997); Hanioğlu, M. Şükrü, *Preparation for a Revolution: The Young Turks 1902–1908* (Oxford, 2001); Turfan, *Rise of the Young Turks*.
3. See Chapter 1, p. 26.
4. See also McMurray, *Distant Ties*, pp. 69–74.
5. Gooch and Temperley, *British Documents*, vol.6, p. 38.
6. *The Amrita Bazar Patrika*, 16 August 1907, in: PA.AA. R13745. According to the report sent by Keller to Bülow, a very similar statement was also published in the *Indian Daily Telegraph*. See Keller to Bülow, 22.08.1907, in: PA.AA. R13745.
7. Beyens, Eugene-Napoleon, *Germany before the War*, translated by Paul V. Cohn (London, Edinburgh, and New York, 1916), p. 242.
8. Kiderlen to Bülow, 20.08.1908, in: PA.AA. R13745.
9. Cited in Okyar, Osman, 'Turco-British Relations in the Inter-War Period: Fethi Okyar's Mission to London', in W. Hale and A. İ. Bağış (eds), *Four Centuries of Turco-British Relations: Studies in Diplomatic Economic and Cultural Affairs* (Walkington, 1983), p. 68.
10. Akmeşe, *Birth of Modern Turkey*; Hanioğlu, *Preparation for a Revolution*; Ahmad, *The Young Turks*.
11. Cited in McMurray, *Distant Ties*, p. 75.
12. Cited in Türk, *Die deutsche Rüstungsindustrie*, p. 82.

13. Pears, Edwin, 'The Baghdad Railway', *The Contemporary Review* 94 (1908), p. 591.
14. *The Times of India*, 10 August 1908, in: PA.AA. R13745.
15. Lowther to Grey, 30.07.1910, in: Gooch and Temperley, *British Documents*, vol. 9, pp. 180–3.
16. Lowther to Grey, 08.12.1908, in: NA, London: FO 371/560.
17. Marschall to Bülow, 03.09.1908, in Lepsius et al., *Die große Politik der Europäischen Kabinette*, vol.25, p. 615.
18. Cemal Paşa, *Hatırat*, p. 73.
19. Cited in Akmeşe, *Birth of Modern Turkey*, p. 92.
20. Using a German idiom 'Hals über Kopf' (in a mad hurry), German ambassador Marschall von Bieberstein narrated this incidence as follows: 'er ist am Tage seiner Thronentsetzung Hals über Kopf nach Salonik geschickt worden'. Marschall to Stemrich, 19.09.1909, PA.AA. 13940.
21. Marschall to Stemrich, 19.09.1909, PA.AA. 13940.
22. Lowther to Grey, 08.12.1908, in: NA, London: FO 371/560.
23. McGarity, *Foreign Influence*, p. 57.
24. Marschall to Stattsskretär, 21.08.1909, PA.AA. 13940.
25. Marschall to Stattsskretär, 21.08.1909, PA.AA. 13940.
26. Marschall to Stattsskretär, 21.08.1909, PA.AA. 13940: 'Unter dem alten Regime konzentrierte sich die ganze Staatsgewalt in einem Manne, der in seiner nervösen und ängstlichen Eigenart jedem Fingerdruck von Aussen nachgab. Jetzt dagegen haben wir es mit einer ganzen Menge von Leuten zu tun, die Jung und unerfahren, aber meist doch recht klare Köpfe sind und dabei infolge der fortgesetzten Schmeicheleien des Auslandes von einem unglaublichen Hochmute und einem krankhaft gesteigerten Nationalgefühle besessen sind. Diese Leute müssen zunächst pathologisch behandelt werden.'
27. Wallach, *Bir Askeri Yardımın Anatomisi*, p. 81; Akmeşe, *Birth of Modern Turkey*, p. 108.
28. Wallach, *Bir Askeri Yardımın Anatomisi*, p. 81; Akmeşe, *Birth of Modern Turkey*, pp. 108–9; Aksakal, Mustafa, *The Ottoman Road to War in 1914, The Ottoman Empire and the First World War* (Cambridge, 2011), p. 69.
29. Akmeşe, *Birth of Modern Turkey*, p. 109.
30. Huber to Mauser, 10.11.1909, in: SA, Oberndorf: M-A6.
31. *Schwarzwälder Bote*, 26 April 1903: in: SA, Oberndorf: Z73; See also Seel, 'Mauser-Gewehre' (1981e), pp. 1722–5.
32. Mahmoud Fethi to Mauser, 26.07.1910, in: SA, Oberndorf: M-A6: 'Mit hiesigen Vertretern möchte Ich kein Geschäft machen'.
33. Huber to Mauser, 09.08.1910, in: SA, Oberndorf: M-A6.
34. Huber to Mauser, 13.08.1910, in: SA, Oberndorf: M-A6.
35. Grant, *The Sword of the Sultan*, pp. 31–2.
36. Türk, *Die deutsche Rüstungsindustrie*, p. 121.
37. Surtees to Lowther, 18.12.1908, in: NA, London: FO 244/721.
38. See also: *The Daily News*, 21 June 1900, in: PA.AA. R13297.

39. Grey to J. M. Falkner, 16.12.1908, in: NA, London: FO 371/560.
40. Einstein to Knox: 23.08.1909, in: NARA-Microfilm, College Park: M862/1093.
41. According to the Krupp's records the company did not receive any order from the Ottoman Empire in 1908 and 1909. The last orders before 1910 were only for four machine-guns (3.7 cm cal.) for each year in 1906 and 1907. *Verzeichnis der von der Gußstahlfabrik und vom Grusonwerk von 1847 bis 1912 gefertigten Kanonen*, in: HA, Krupp: 5a VII f. 862: 44–44a.
42. *Verzeichnis der von der Gußstahlfabrik und vom Grusonwerk von 1847 bis 1912 gefertigten Kanonen*, in: HA, Krupp: 5a VII f. 862: 44–44a.
43. BOA, BEO. 3996/299685 (10.01.1329/10.02.1911).
44. Beehler, William H., *The History of the Italian–Turkish War, September 29, 1911, to October 18, 1912* (Annapolis, MD, 1913). p. 16; see also Childs, Timothy, Winston, *Italo-Turkish Diplomacy and the War over Libya: 1911–1912* (Leiden and New York, 1990).
45. Beehler, *The History of the Italian–Turkish War*, pp. 22, 51–8; Langensiepen, Bernd and Güleryüz, Ahmet, *The Ottoman Steam Navy, 1828–1923* (Annapolis, MD, 1995), pp. 15–6.
46. Beehler, *The History of the Italian–Turkish War, September 29, 1911, to October 18, 1912*, p. 82.
47. For more information see Erickson, *Defeat in Detail*; Hall, C. Richard, *The Balkan Wars, 1912–1913: Prelude to the First World War* (Routledge, 2000).
48. Erickson, *Defeat in Detail*, p. 331.
49. Menne, *Blood and Steel*, pp. 302–4; See also Türk, *Die deutsche Rüstungsindustrie*, pp. 193–4.
50. Wallach, *Bir Askeri Yardımın Anatomisi*, p. 113.
51. *The New York Times*, 9 November 1912.
52. Ball, *Mauser Military Rifles*, p. 148; Epkenhans, 'Military–Industrial Relations in Imperial Germany', p. 22; Hall, *The Balkan Wars*, pp. 15–7; Grant, *Rulers, Guns, and Money*, pp. 78–115; The Imperial War Museum, *Armies of the Balkan States*. *The New York Times*, 24 February 1913; Yorulmaz, 'Krupps weitreichende Kanonen', pp. 206–7.
53. Jäckh, Ernst, *Deutschland im Orient nach dem Balkankrieg* (München, 1913), p. 69.
54. Jäckh, *Deutschland im Orient*, p. 70.
55. Imperial War Museum, *Armies of the Balkan States*, p. 30.
56. BOA, MV. 231/380, 11.12.1331/11.11.1913.
57. Langensiepen and Güleryüz, *The Ottoman Steam Navy*, pp. 18–27.
58. Aksakal, *The Ottoman Road to War in 1914*, p. 79.
59. Cited in Menne, *Blood and Steel*, p. 310.
60. Mutius to the German Foreign Office, 08.02.1914, in: PA.AA. 13319.
61. Mutius to the German Foreign Office, 10.02.1914, in: PA.AA. 13319.
62. Mutius to the German Foreign Office, 11.02.1914, in: PA.AA. 13319.
63. Grant, *The Sword of the Sultan*, p. 32.
64. Grant, *The Sword of the Sultan*, p. 32.

65. Grant, *The Sword of the Sultan*, pp. 32–3.
66. Nottelmann, Dirk, *Die Brandenburg-Klasse: Höhepunkt des deutschen Panzerschiffbaus* (Hamburg, Berlin, Bonn, 2002), p. 84; Langensiepen and Güleryüz, *The Ottoman Steam Navy*, p. 17.
67. Mutius to the German Foreign Office, 09.02.1914, in: PA.AA. 13319.
68. For more information about this organization see Özçelik, Selahattin, *Donanma-yı Osmanî Muavenet-i Milliye Cemiyeti* (Ankara, 2000). See also Beşikçi, Mehmet, *The Ottoman Mobilization of Manpower in the First World War: Between Voluntarism and Resistance* (Leiden, 2012), pp. 43–8.
69. Lowther to Grey, 31.05.1910, in: NA, London: FO 78/371–1000.
70. Lowther to Grey, 31.05.1910, in: NA, London: FO 78/371–1000; Grant, *Rulers, Guns, and Money*, pp. 176–7.
71. Lowther to Grey, 15.06.1910, in: NA, London: FO 78/371–1000.
72. Cited in Türk, *Die deutsche Rüstungsindustrie*, p. 74.
73. Marling to Grey, 16.11.1910, in: NA, London: FO 78/371–1000.
74. Marling to Grey, 16.11.1910, in: NA, London: FO 78/371–1000.
75. Yasamee, 'Colmar Freiherr von der Goltz and the Rebirth', p. 110; see also Akmeşe, *Birth of Modern Turkey*, pp. 29–30.
76. Wangenheim to German Foreign Office, 01.05.1914, in: PA.AA. R13319.
77. BOA, HR.SYS. 22/28 (07.01.1910); for more information about the Brandenburg-Class warships and its history see Nottelmann, *Die Brandenburg-Klasse*, pp. 82–98.
78. BOA, BEO, 3793-284440 (01.01.1328/19.01.1910).
79. Reinhard Koch, 'Militärpolitischer Bericht über die Überführung Euerer Majestät Schiffe "Kurfürst Friedrich Wilhelm" und "Weißenburg" und Übergabe an die Kaiserlich Ottomanische Regierung', 21.09.1910, in: PA.AA. R13313.
80. *The New York Times*, 8 October 1911.
81. Decypher Sir G. Lowther, Constantinople, 10. 01. 1910, in: NA, London: FO 78/372–1000.
82. *Daily Mail*, 16 August 1910, in: PA.AA.13312.
83. *The {London} Times*, 22 August 1910, in: PA.AA. 13312.
84. Miquel to the Foreign Office, 31.08.1910, PA.AA. 13312.
85. *L'Egypte*, 20 August 1910, in: PA.AA. 13312.
86. *Karagöz*, 17 August 1910, in: PA.AA.13312.
87. Miquel to Hollweg, 10.08.1910, in: PA.AA. 13312.
88. Miquel to Hollweg, 23.08.1910, in: PA.AA. 13312.
89. Miquel to Hollweg, 02.09.1910, in: PA.AA. 13312.
90. Miquel to Hollweg, 03.09.1910, in: PA.AA. 13312.
91. Miquel to Hollweg, 01.09.1910, in: PA.AA. 13312.
92. Miquel to Hollweg, 07.09.1910, in: PA.AA. 13312; See also Miquel to Hollweg, 03.09.1910, in: PA.AA. 13312.
93. Reinhard Koch, 'Militärpolitischer Bericht über die Überführung Euerer Majestät Schiffe "Kurfürst Friedrich Wilhelm" und "Weißenburg" und

NOTES TO PAGES 248–255   323

Übergabe an die Kaiserlich Ottomanische Regierung', 21.09.1910, in: PA. AA. R13313.
94. Miquel to Hollweg, 08.09.1910, in: PA.AA. 13312.
95. Deutsche Bank to Anatolische Eisenbahn-Gesellschaft, 01.10.1910, in: PA. AA. 13313.
96. Cited in Komatsu Kaori, 'Financial Problems of the Navy during the Reign of Abdülhamid II' *Oriente Moderno, 20* (2001), p. 209.
97. cf. Komatsu, 'Financial Problems of the Navy', p. 209.
98. Strempel to German Foreign Office, 17.12.1910, in: PA.AA. R13255, cited in Beşirli, 'Sultan Abdülaziz'den Birinci Dünya Savaşı'na', pp. 266–7.
99. BOA, MV. 156/47 (27.09.1329/21.09.1911).
100. Childs, *Italo-Turkish Diplomacy and the War*, p. 24.
101. Cited in Aksakal, *The Ottoman Road to War in 1914*, p. 179.
102. See Chapter I, pp. 22–3; pp. 45–6; see also Smith, 'Military Strategy versus Diplomacy', p. 48; Kössler, *Aktionsfeld Osmanisches Reich*, p. 122; BOA, Y.PRK. BŞK.13/41 (06.04.1305/22.12.1887).
103. BOA, Y.EE.115/6 (24.08.1887). See also Yasamee, *Ottoman Diplomacy*, pp. 245–50.
104. Yasamee, *Ottoman Diplomacy*, pp. 188–95; Prince Reuss to Bismarck, 29.07.1886, in: PA.AA. R13237; see also Chapter 1, pp. 45–6.
105. See Chapter 2, pp. 105, 114, 116–9.
106. *The New York Times*, 31 December 1916; Annika Mombauer, *Helmuth von Moltke and the Origins of the First World War*, p. 120.
107. Cited in Aksakal, *The Ottoman Road to War*, p. 17. English translation of Goltz's remarks belongs to Aksakal.
108. Corrigan, H. S. W., 'German-Turkish Relations and the Outbreak of War in 1914: A Re-Assessment', *Past and Present* 36 (1967), p. 144.
109. See Aksakal, *The Ottoman Road to War*.
110. BOA. Y.EE. 7/6 (02.02.1299/24.12.1881); see Chapter 1, pp. 25–7.

Conclusion

1. Pamuk, Şevket, 'The Ottoman Economy in World War I', in S. Broadberry and M. Harrison (eds), *The Economics of World War I* (Cambridge, 2005), p. 112.
2. Reichsministerium des Innern, *Deutsches Handels-Archiv; Zeitschrift für Handel und Gewerbe*, vol. 2 (Berlin, 1898), p. 512.
3. Howe, *Why War*, p. 94.
4. *The Daily News*, 21 June 1900, in: PA.AA. R13297.
5. Bülow, *Imperial Germany*, p. 69: 'These relations were not of a sentimental nature, for the continued existence of Turkey served our interests from the industrial, military and political points of view.'
6. Boelcke, *Krupp und die Hohenzollern in Dokumenten*, p. 19.

7. According to Quataert, the net profit of the German-dominated Anatolian Railway Company disappointed its investors. Quataert points out that 'the financial performance of the Anatolian Railway Company was poor'. He further adds, 'for the German financier, investor and government, however, the less than spectacular profits were a disappointment'. Quataert, 'Limited Revolution', p. 158.
8. Howerth, W. Ira, 'War and Social Economy' *International Journal of Ethics*, 17/1 (1906), pp. 71.
9. Chirol, Valentine, *The Middle Eastern Question or some Political Problems of Indian Defence* (London, 1903), p. 186.

BIBLIOGRAPHY

I. UNPUBLISHED SOURCES

TURKEY

Başbakanlık Osmanlı Arşivi İstanbul/The Prime Ministry Ottoman Archives-State Archive: BOA

BOA, A. MKT. MHM.
BOA, DH. MKT.
BOA, HR. SYS.
BOA, HR. TO.
BOA, İ. ASK.
BOA, İ. DH.
BOA, İ. MMS.
BOA, MV.
BOA, Y. A. HUS.
BOA, Y. A. RES.
BOA, Y. EE.
BOA, Y. MRZ. D.
BOA, Y. MTV.
BOA, Y. PRK. ASK.
BOA, Y. PRK. AZJ.
BOA, Y. PRK. BŞK.
BOA, Y. PRK. EŞA.
BOA, Y. PRK. HH.
BOA, Y. PRK. HR.
BOA, Y. PRK. KOM.
BOA, Y. PRK. ML.
BOA, Y. PRK. MM.
BOA, Y. PRK. MYD.
BOA, Y. PRK. NMH.
BOA, Y. PRK. OMZ.
BOA, Y. PRK. PT.
BOA, Y. PRK. SGE.
BOA, Y. PRK. SRN.
BOA, Y. PRK. TKM.
BOA, Y. PRK. UM.
BOA, Y. PRK. ZB.

GERMANY
Politisches Archiv des Auswärtigen Amtes (Berlin): PA. AA.

R12456	R13286
R13233	R13291
R13237	R13295
R13240	R13296
R13247	R13297
R13285	R13299
R13304	R13745
R13305	R13746
R13306	R13763
R13340	R13775
R13427	R13939
R13451	R14148

GERMANY
Historisches Archiv Krupp: HA, Krupp

5a VII f/862	FAH 3E/1
FAH 2B/314a	FAH 2M 78/19
FAH 2M 78/15	WA 2/248
FAH 3B/216	WA 2/249
FAH 3B/227	WA 4/2277
FAH 3B/244	WA 4/749
FAH 3C/205	WA 4/757
FAH 3C/217	WA 7f/886
FAH 3C/224	

GERMANY
Stadt- und Zeitungsarchiv (Oberndorf am Neckar): SA, Oberndorf

M-A3
M-A4
M-A5
M-A6
M-A7
M-A8

M-A9
M-A12
XIV. CA 1/13
Z59
Z60

793. 32/13. 1 (Mauser Waffen Abnahme- Kommission: Türkenzeit)
793. 32/13. 1 (Mauser Werke: Verschiedene Abnahmekommission)

GERMANY
Bundesarchiv- Militärarchiv (Freiburg): MA, Freiburg

N. 65/4
N. 65/5
N. 65/16
NL. 737/5
NL. 737/8

NL. 737/9
NL. 737/10
NL. 737/11
NL. 737/16

GERMANY
Landesarchiv Schleswig-Holstein
Nachlass Kamphövener, Abt. 399.26 Nr.8.

GREAT BRITAIN
The National Archives (London): NA, London

ADM 231/10
ADM 231/14
ADM 231/18
ADM 231/24
FO 78/371–1000
FO 78/3998
FO 78/3999
FO 78/4001
FO 78/4002
FO 78/4022

FO 78/4277
FO 78/4342
FO 78/4479
FO 78/4706
FO 78/5000
FO 881/4378
FO 195/1664
FO 195/2016
FO 244/721
FO 371/560

FO 78/4095
FO 78/4098
FO 78/4207
FO 78/4276
WO 108/323

FO 371/561
GFM 10/11
WO 106/2
WO 106/6182

UNITED STATES OF AMERICA
The National Archives and Records Administration (College Park, Maryland): NARA-Microfilm, College Park

M46/50
M46/63
M46/65
M46/71
M46/72

M46/56
M77/165
M77/167
M77/168

II. NEWSPAPERS AND PERIODICAL ARTICLES

Alldeutsche Blätter
Deutsche Rundschau
Militär Wochenblatt
Neue Freie Presse
Schwarzwälder Bote
The Century: Illustrated Monthly Magazine
The {London} Times
The Neue Presse (Morgenblatt)
The New York Times
The Outlook
The Standard

BIBLIOGRAPHY 329

III. PUBLISHED SOURCES

(Official documents, memoirs, correspondence, speeches)

Akçuraoğlu, Yusuf, *Türk, Cermen ve Slavların Münâsebât-ı Tarihîleri: 06 Teşrîn-i sâni 1330 da Türk Ocağı'nda Verilen Konferans Metni* (İstanbul, 1330/1914).

Ali Vahbi Bey (ed.), *Avant la debacle de la Turquie: Pensées et Souvenirs de l'ex-Sultan Abdul-Hamid* (Paris, 1913).

Bey, Ismail Kemal, *The Memoirs of Ismail Kemal Bey*, Sommerville Story (ed.) (London, 1920).

Blowitz, Henri G.S. de, *Memoirs of M. de Blowitz* (New York, 1903).

Boelcke, Willi. A., *Krupp und die Hohenzollern in Dokumenten. Krupp-Korrespondenz mit Kaisern, Kabinettschefs und Ministern 1850–1918* (Frankfurt am Main, 1970).

Bolayır, Ali Ekrem, *Hatıralar*, Özgül, Metin, Kayahan (ed.), (Ankara, 2007).

Burchardt, Lothar, 'Between War Profits and War Costs. Krupp in the First World War', in Hans Pohl, and Bernd Rudolph (eds) *German Yearbook on Business History 1988* (Berlin and Heidelberg, 1990).

Bülow, Prince von, *Imperial Germany*, translated by M. A. Lewenz (New York, 1917).

—— *Memoirs of Prince Von Bülow*, 2 vols, translated by F. A. Voigt (London and New York, 1931).

Busch, Moritz, *Bismarck: Some Secret Pages of His History* (Vol. 2) (London, 1898).

Cemal, Paşa, *Hatırat*, Martı Metin (ed.), (İstanbul, 1996).

Demirhan, Pertev, *Generalfeldmarschall Colmar Freiherr von der Goltz: Das Lebensbild eines großen Soldaten: aus meinen persönlichen Erinnerungen* (Göttingen, 1960).

Foreign Affairs Committees of England, *Proposed Annexation of Turkey: To his Imperial Majesty the Sultan {Abdulhamid II}*. The Address of the Undersigned Foreign Affairs Committees of England; 16.02.1879: Diplomatic fly-sheets Vol. II. No. 87: 84–86, in: University of Birmingham, Special Collection, r DS, 757, 6. Report Nr. 24.

Giesl von Gieslingen, Wladimir F., *Zwei Jahrzehnte im Nahen Orient: Aufzeichnungen des Generals der Kavallerie Baron Wladimir Giesl*, Ritter von Steinitz (ed.) (Berlin, 1927).

Goetz, Walter (ed.), *Briefe Wilhelms II. an den Zaren 1894–1914*, translated by Max Theodor Behrmann (Berlin, 1920).

Goltz, Colmar Freiherr, von der, 'Stärke und Schwäche des türkischen Reiches', *Deutsche Rundschau* 93 (1897a), pp. 95–119.

—— 'Bilder aus der türkischen Armee', *Militär-Wochenblatt* 38 (1897b), pp. 1151–62.

—— 'Erinnerungen an Mahmud Shewket Pascha', *Deutsche Rundschau* 157 (1913), pp. 32–46.

—— *The Turkish Army, its Characteristics and Capabilities: A Series of Letters by Von der Goltz*, translated by W.E. Fairholme (London, 1898).

—— and Förster, Wolfgang (eds), *Generalfeldmarschall Colmar Freiherr von der Goltz: Denkwürdigkeiten* (Berlin, 1929).

Gooch, P. George and Harold W.V. Temperley (eds), *British Documents on the Origins of the War 1898–1914*, 11 vols (London, 1927–36).

Helfferich, Karl, *Georg von Siemens: Ein Lebensbild aus Deutschlands großer Zeit*, 3 vols, (Berlin, 1923).

Hohenlohe-Schillingsfürst, Chlodwig K.V., *Memoirs of Prince Chlodwig of Hohenlohe Schillingsfürst*, edited by Fridrich Curtius, translated by George. W. Chrystal, 2 vols (London, 1907).
Imperial War Museum, *Armies of the Balkan States, 1914–1918: The Military Forces of Bulgaria, Greece, Montenegro, Rumania, and Servia* (London and Nashville, TN., 1996).
Karabekir, Kâzım, *Türkiye'de ve Türk Ordusunda Almanlar*, Orhan Hülagü and Ömer Hakan Özalp (eds) (İstanbul, 2001).
Lepsius, Johannes, Mendelssohn-Bartholdy, Albrecht, and Thimme, Friedrich W.K., (eds), *Die große Politik der Europäischen Kabinette 1871–1914: Sammlung der Diplomatischen Akten des Auswärtigen Amtes*, 40 vols (Berlin, 1922–6).
Osmanoğlu, Ayşe, *Babam Sultan Abdulhamid. Hatıralarım* (Ankara, 1984).
Penzler, Johannes (ed.), *Die Reden Kaiser Wilhelms II in den Jahren 1896–190*, vol. 2, (Leipzig, 1904).
———— (ed.), *Fürst Bülows Reden nebst Urkundlichen Beiträgen zu seiner Politik: 1897– 1903*, vol. 1 (Berlin, 1907).
Peters, Carl, *Lebenserinnerungen* (Hamburg, 1918).
Reichsministerium des Innern, *Deutsches Handels-Archiv; Zeitschrift für Handel und Gewerbe*, vol. 2 (Berlin, 1898).
Rıza, Paşa, *Hülâsa-ı Hâtırâtım* (İstanbul 1325/1909).
Sabah, *Hatırâ-i Seyâhat* (İstanbul 1316/1898).
Sander, Oral and Kurthan Fişek, *ABD Dışişleri Belgeleriyle Türk-ABD Silah Ticaretinin İç Yüzü, 1828–1925* (Ankara and Istanbul, 2007).
Tahsin, Paşa, *Sultan Abdulhamid: Tahsin Paşa'nın Yıldız Hatıraları* (İstanbul, 1931).
Vambéry, Armin, *The Story of my Struggles: The Memoirs of Arminuis Vambe´ry* (New York, 1904).
Waldersee, Alfred Grafen von, *Denkwürdigkeiten des General-Feldmarschalls Alfred Grafen von Waldersee*. Meisner, Heinrich Otto (ed.) (Stuttgart, 1922).
Warner, Charles Dudley (ed.), *Library of the World's Best Literature, Ancient and Modern* Vol. 5 (first published in 1896) (New York, 2008).
Wilhelm II, Kaiser, *The Kaiser's Memoirs, Emperor of Germany 1888–1918*, translated by Thomas R. Ybarra (New York and London, 1922).
Yetimzade, M. Tevfik Hamdi, *Bürokrat Tevfik Biren'in II. Abdulhamid, Meşrutiyet ve Mütareke Hatıraları*, 2 vols, Fatma R. Hürmen (ed.) (İstanbul, 2006).

IV. SECONDARY SOURCES

Agoston, Gabor, *Guns for the Sultan: Military Power and the Weapons Industry in the Ottoman Empire* (Cambridge, 2005).
Ahmad, Feroz, *The Young Turks, the Committee of Union and Progress in Turkish Politics 1908–1914* (Oxford, 1969).
Akmeşe, Handan Nezir, *The Birth of Modern Turkey: The Ottoman Military and the March to World War I* (London and New York, 2005).
Aksakal, Mustafa, *The Ottoman Road to War in 1914, The Ottoman Empire and the First World War* (Cambridge, 2011).
Aksan, Virginia. H., *Ottoman Wars 1700–1870: An Empire Besieged* (Harlow 2007).
Akyıldız, Ali, *Osmanlı Bürokrasisi ve Modernleşme* (İstanbul, 2004).

BIBLIOGRAPHY

Albertini, Luigi, *Origins of the War of 1914* (3 vols) (New York, 2005).
Alkan, Necmettin, 'II. Abdülhamid Devrinde İstihdam Edilen İlk Alman Askeri Heyetinin Komutanı Otto von Kähler ve iki Tarafın Beklentileri', *İstanbul Üniversitesi Edebiyat Fakültesi Tarih Dergisi* 43 (2007), pp. 135–65.
Aybar, Celal, *Osmanlı İmparatorluğu'nun Ticaret Muvazenesi 1878–1913* (Ankara, 1939).
Baker, Ray Stannard, 'The Sultan of Turkey', *The Outlook*, 6 September 1902, pp. 67–77.
Bal, Nurcan, *Süleyman Nutki Bey'in Hatıraları* (İstanbul, 2003).
Ball, Robert W.D., *Mauser Military Rifles of the World* (Iola, WI, 2006).
Barker, J. Ellis, *Modern Germany: Her Political and Economic Problems, Her Foreign and Domestic Policy, Her Ambitions, and the Causes of Her Success* (London, 1909).
Barth, B., 'The Financial History of the Anatolian and Baghdad Railways, 1889–1914', translated by J. C. Whitehouse, *Financial History Review* 5 (1998), pp. 115–37.
Baykal, Bekir Sıtkı, 'Bismarck'ın Osmanlı İmparatorluğu'nu Taksim Fikri', *Ankara Üniversitesi Dil ve Tarih-Coğrafya Fakültesi Dergisi* 5 (1943), pp. 3–12.
Benner, Thomas, *Die Strahlen der Krone: Die religiöse Dimension des Kaisertums unter Wilhelm II. vor dem Hintergrund der Orientreise 1898* (Marburg, 2001).
Benz, Wolfgang, 'Die Entstehung der Kruppschen Nachrichtendienstes', *Vierteljahreshefte für Zeitgeschichte* 24 (1976), pp. 199–205.
Beşikçi, Mehmet, *The Ottoman Mobilization of Manpower in the First World War: Between Voluntarism and Resistance* (Leiden, 2012).
Beşirli, Mehmet, 'II. Abdulhamid Döneminde Osmanlı Ordusunda Alman Silahları', *Sosyal Bilimler Enstitüsü Dergisi* 1 (2004), pp. 121–39.
――― 'Sultan Abdülaziz'den Birinci Dünya Savaşı'na Osmanlı Donanması', *Atatürk Üniversitesi Türkiyat Araştırmaları Enstitüsü Dergisi*, 11/25 (2004), pp. 243–74.
Beydilli, Kemal, 'II. Abdulhamid Devrinde Gelen İlk Alman Askeri Heyeti Hakkında', *İstanbul Üniversitesi Edebiyat Fakültesi Tarih Dergisi* 32 (1979), pp. 481–94.
Beyens, Eugene-Napoleon, *Germany before the War*, translated by Paul V. Cohn (London, Edinburgh, and New York, 1916).
Birinci, Ali, 'Sultan Abdülhamid'in Hâtıra Defteri Meselesi', *Divan İlmî Araştırmalar* 19 /2 (2005), pp. 177–94.
Birken, Andreas, *Die Wirtschaftsbeziehungen zwischen Europa und dem Vorderen Orient im ausgehenden 19. Jahrhundert* (Wiesbaden, 1980).
Birol, Nurettin, 'Halil Rıfat Paşa', *C.Ü. Sosyal Bilimler Dergisi* 27/2 (2003), pp. 267–88.
Blaisdell, Donald C., *European Financial Control in the Ottoman Empire* (New York, 1929).
Bode, Friedrich Heinz, *Der Kampf um die Bagdadbahn 1903–1914: Ein Beitrag zur Geschichte der deutsch-englischen Beziehungen* (Breslau, 1941).
Bontrup, Heinz-Josef and Norbert Zdrowomslaw, *Die deutsche Rüstungsindustrie, vom Kaiserreich bis zur Bundesrepublik* (Heilbron, 1988).
Brandenburg, Erich, *From Bismarck to the World War*, translated by Annie Elizabeth Adams (London, 1933).

Brose, Eric Dorn, *The Kaiser's Army: The Politics of Military Technology in Germany during the Machine Age, 1870–1918* (New York, 2001).

Brown, David, *Palmerston and the Politics of Foreign Policy, 1846–1855* (Manchester, 2002).

Brunn, Gerhard, 'Deutscher Einfluss und Deutsche Interessen in der Professionalisierung einiger Lateinamerikanischer Staaten vor dem 1. Weltkrieg (1885–1914)', *Jahrbuch für Geschichte von Staat, Wirtschaft und Gesellschaft Lateinamerikas* 6 (1969), pp. 281–5.

Butterfield, Paul. R., *The Diplomacy of the Bagdad Railway 1890–1914* (Göttingen, 1932).

Carmel, Alex, *Die Siedlungen der Württembergischen Templer in Palästina* (Stuttgart, 1973).

Childs, Timothy Winston, *Italo-Turkish Diplomacy and the War over Libya: 1911–1912* (Leiden and New York, 1990).

Chirol, Valentine, *The Middle Eastern Question or some Political Problems of Indian Defence* (London, 1903).

Çoker, Fahri, *Deniz Harp Okulumuz: 1773* (Ankara, 1994).

Corrigan, H.S.W., 'German-Turkish Relations and the Outbreak of War in 1914: A Re-Assessment', *Past and Present* 36 (1967), pp. 144–52.

Cram, Robert Gordon, *German interests in the Ottoman Empire, 1878–1885* (Ph.D. Thesis: University of London (London, 1999).

Dunn, Archibald Joseph, *Turkey and Its Future* (London, 1905).

Earle, Edward Mead, 'The Importance of the Near East in Problems of Raw Materials and Foodstuffs', *Annals of the American Academy of Political and Social Science* 112 (1924), pp. 183–6.

—— *Turkey, The Great Powers, and The Baghdad Railway A Study in Imperialism* (New York, 1924).

Eldem, Vedat, *Osmanlı İmparatorluğunun İktisadi Şartları Hakkında Bir Tetkik* (Ankara, 1970).

Elena, Alberto, 'Models of European Scientific Expansion: The Ottoman Empire as a Source of Evidence', in Patrick Pettijean et al. (eds) *Science and Empires: Historical Studies about Scientific Development and European Expansion* (Dordrecht, 1992).

Epkenhans, Michael, 'Krupp and the Imperial German Navy 1898–1914: A Reassessment', *The Journal of Military History* 64 (2000), pp. 335–70.

—— 'Military–Industrial Relations in Imperial Germany, 1870–1914', *War in History* 10/1 (2003), pp. 1–26.

Erhan, Çağrı, 'Ottoman Official Attitudes toward American Missionaries', *Working Paper: Yale Center for International and Area Studies: The United States & the Middle East: Cultural Encounters 5. http://opus.macmillan.yale.edu/workpaper/pdfs/MESV5-11.pdf*.

Erickson, Edward J., *Defeat in Detail: the Ottoman Army in the Balkans, 1912–1913* (Westport, 2003).

Farah, Caesar E., 'Arab Supporters of Sultan Abdulhamid II: Izzet al-Abid', *Archivum Ottomanicum* 15 (1997), pp. 189–219.

Fay, Sidney B., 'The Baghdad Railway: A German Defense of the Financial Arrangements', *The Journal of Modern History* 4/2 (1932), pp. 240–1.

Feis, Herbert, *Europe the World's Banker, 1870–1914: An Account of European Foreign Investment and the Connection of World Finance with Diplomacy before the War* (New Haven, 1930).

BIBLIOGRAPHY

Finkel, Caroline, *The Administration of Warfare: The Ottoman Military Campaigns in Hungary, 1593–1606* (Wien, 1988).
Foley, Robert T., *German Strategy and the Path to Verdun: Erich von Falkenhayn and the Development of Attrition, 1870–1916* (Cambridge, 2005).
Forbes, Ian L. D., 'German Informal Imperialism in South America before 1914', *The Economic History Review*, New Series 31 (1978), pp. 384–98.
―――― 'Social Imperialism and Wilhelmine Germany', *The Historical Journal* 22 (1979), pp. 331–49.
Fortna, Benjamin C., 'The Reign of Abdülhamid II', in Reşat Kasaba (ed.), *The Cambridge History of Turkey. Turkey in the Modern World*, Vol. 4 (Cambridge, 2008).
Franzke, Jurgen (ed.), *Bagdadbahn und Hedjazbahn. Deutsche Eisenbahngeschichte im Vorderen Orient* (Nürnberg, 2003).
Fry, Michael Graham (ed.), *Power, Personalities and Policies: Essays in Honour Donald Cameron Watt* (London and Portland, OR, 1992).
Fuller, Joseph V., *Bismarck's Diplomacy at its Zenith* (Cambridge, MA, 1922).
Fulton, L. Bruce, 'France and the End of the Ottoman Empire' in Marian Kent (ed.), *The Great Powers and the End of the Ottoman Empire* (London, 1996).
―――― 'France's Extraordinary Ambassador: Ernest Constans and the Ottoman Empire, 1898–1909', *French Historical Studies* 23 (2000), pp. 683–706.
Gall, Lothar, *Die Deutsche Bank, 1870–1995* (München, 1995).
Gauss, Christian Frederick, *The German Emperor as Shown in His Public Utterances* (New York, 1915).
Gencer, Mustafa, *Imperialismus und die Orientalische Frage. Deutsch-Türkische Beziehungen 1871–1908* (Ankara, 2006).
Geyikdağı, Necla, *Foreign Investment in the Ottoman Empire International Trade and Relations 1854–1914* (London, 2011).
Gillis, R. John, (ed.), *The Militarization of the Western World* (New Brunswick, 1989).
Gözeller, Ali, *Osmanlı-Alman Yakınlaşmasının Basına Yansıması: Sabah Gazetesi Örneği (1889–1895)*, M. A. Thesis: Marmara University (Istanbul, 2005).
Grant, A. Jonathan, 'The Sword of the Sultan, Ottoman Arms Imports, 1854–1914', *The Journal of Military History* 66 (2002), pp. 9–36.
―――― *Rulers, Guns, and Money: the Global Arms Trade in the Age of Imperialism* (Cambridge, MA. 2007).
Graudenz, Karlheinz and Hanns-Michael Schindler, (eds), *Die Deutschen Kolonien: 100 Jahre Geschichte in Wort, Bild und Karte* (Augsburg, 1988).
Griffiths, Merwin Albert, *The Reorganization of the Ottoman Army under Abdulhamid II. 1880 -1897*, Ph.D. Thesis: University of California (Los Angeles, 1966).
Hacker, C. Barton, 'Military Institutions, Weapons, and Social Change: Toward a New History of Military Technology', *Technology and Culture* 35/4 (1994), pp. 768–834.
―――― 'Military Technology and World History: A Reconnaissance', *The History Teacher* 30/47 (1997), pp. 461–87.
Hale, M. William, *Turkish Foreign Policy, 1774–2000* (London, 2002).
Hall, C. Richard, *The Balkan Wars, 1912–1913: Prelude to the First World War* (Routledge, 2000).
Hallgarten, G. Wolfgang, *Vorkriegs Imperialismus: Die soziologischen Grundlagen der Außenpolitik Europäischer Großmächte bis 1914* (Paris, 1935).
―――― *Imperialismus vor 1914* (2 Vols) (München, 1963).

Hanioğlu, M. Şükrü, *The Young Turks in Opposition* (New York and Oxford, 1995).
— *Preparation for a Revolution: The Young Turks 1902–1908* (Oxford, 2001).
Harrison, Austin, *The Pan-Germanic Doctrine: Being a Study of German Political Aims and Aspirations* (London and New York, 1904).
Haßler, Fridrich and Adolf Bihl (eds), *Geschichte der Mauser-Werke* (Berlin, 1938).
Headrick, R. Daniel, 'The Tools of Imperialism: Technology and the Expansion of European Colonial Empires in the Nineteenth Century', *The Journal of Modern History* 51 (1979), pp. 231–63.
Helfferich, Karl, *Germany's Economic Progress and National Wealth 1888–1913* (Berlin, 1913).
— *Deutschlands Volkswohlstand 1888–1913* (Berlin, 1914).
— *Die deutsche Türkenpolitik* (Berlin, 1921).
— *Georg von Siemens, Ein Lebensbild aus Deutschlands großer Zeit*, vol. 3 (Berlin, 1923).
Henderson, W.O., 'German Economic Penetration in the Middle East 1870–1914', *The Economic History Review* 18 (1948), pp. 54–64.
Herbert, Frederick William, *The Defence of Plevna 1877* (London and New York, 1895).
Herwig, H. Helger, *Germany's Vision of Empire in Venezuela 1871–1914* (Princeton, NJ, 1986).
Hill, David Jayne, 'Economic Imperialism: Germany's Self-revelation of Guilt', *The Century: Illustrated Monthly Magazine* 44 (1917), pp. 356–63.
Hillis, Newell Dwight, *The Blot on the Kaiser's Scutcheon* (New York, 1918).
Hirst, Francis Wrigley, *The Political Economy of War* (London, 1916).
Holborn, Hajo, *Deutschland und die Türkei 1878–1890* (Berlin, 1926).
Howe, Frederic Clemson, *Why War* (New York, 1916).
— *The Only Possible Peace* (New York, 1919).
Howerth, W. Ira, 'War and Social Economy', *International Journal of Ethics*, 17/1, (1906), pp. 70–8.
Hull, V. Isabel, *The Entourage of Kaiser Wilhelm II 1888–1918* (Cambridge, 1982).
Illich, Niles Stefan, *German Imperialism in the Ottoman Empire: A Comparative Study*, Ph.D. Thesis: Texas A & M University (College Station, TX, 2007).
İnalcık, Halil and Quataert, Donald (eds), *An Economic and Social History of the Ottoman Empire:1600–1914* (Vol. 2) (Cambridge, 1994).
Jäckh, Ernst, *Deutschland im Orient nach dem Balkankrieg* (München, 1913).
— 'Die Beziehungen der Deutschen Industrie zum türkischen Reich', *Technik und Wirtschaft* 5 (1916), pp. 189–204.
Jastrow, Morris, *The War and the Bagdad Railway the Story of Asia Minor and its Relation to the Present Conflict* (Philadelphia and London, 1917).
Jerusalimski, A.S., *Die Außenpolitik und die Diplomatie des deutschen Imperialismus Ende des 19. Jahrhunderts* (Berlin, 1954).
Kampen, v. Wilhelm, *Studien zur deutschen Türkeipolitik in der Zeit Wilhelm II* (Kiel, 1968).
Kansu, Aykut, *The Revolution of 1908 in Turkey* (Leiden, 1997).
Karal, Enver Ziya, *Osmanlı Tarihi: Birinci Meşrutiyet ve İstibdat Devirleri 1876–1907* (Vol. 8) (Ankara, 1988).
Karpat, Kemal, *The Politicization of Islam: Reconstructing Identity, State, Faith, and Community in the late Ottoman State* (New York, 2001).

Kayalı, Hasan, *Arabs and Young Turks: Ottomanism, Arabism, and Islamism in the Ottoman Empire, 1908–1918* (Berkeley, Los Angeles, and London, 1997).
Kent, Marian (ed.), *The Great Powers and the End of the Ottoman Empire* (London, 1996).
Kerner, Robert Joseph, 'The Mission of Liman von Sanders', *The Slavonic Review*, Vol. 6/16 (1927), pp. 12–27.
Kırmızı, Abdülhamit, *II. Abdülhamid Dönemi (1876–1908) Osmanlı Bürokrasisinde Gayrimüslimler*, M. A. Thesis, Hacettepe Üniversitesi (Ankara, 1998).
Klass, v. Gert, *Die Drei Ringe* (Tübingen and Stuttgart, 1953).
Kohut, A. Thomas, *Wilhelm II and the Germans: A Study of Leadership* (New York, 1991).
Komatsu, Kaori, 'Financial Problems of the Navy during the Reign of Abdülhamid II' *Oriente Moderno*, 20 (2001), pp. 209–19.
Kössler, Armin, *Aktionsfeld Osmanisches Reich. Die Wirtschaftsinteressen des Deutschen Kaiserreiches in der Türkei 1871–1908* (New York, 1981).
Kraus, Jacob, *Deutsch-türkische Handelsbeziehungen. Seit dem Berliner Vertrag unter besonderer Berücksichtigung der Handelswege* (Jena, 1901).
Kraus, Jörg, *Für Geld, Kaiser und Vaterland: Max Duttenhofer, Gründer der Rottweiler Pulverfabrik und erster Vorsitzender der Daimler-Motoren-Gesellschaft* (Bielefeld, 2001).
Küntzer, Karl, *Abdul Hamid II. und die Reformen in der Türkei* (Dresden and Leipzig, 1897).
Kushner, David, 'The District of Jerusalem in the Eyes of Three Ottoman Governors at the End of the Hamidian Period', *Middle Eastern Studies* 35/2 (1999), pp. 83–102.
Langensiepen, Bernd and Ahmet Güleryüz, *The Ottoman Steam Navy, 1828–1923* (Annapolis, MD, 1995).
——— *1828–1923 Osmanlı Donanması* (İstanbul, 2000).
Larres, Klaus, *Churchill's Cold War: The Politics of Personal Diplomacy* (New Haven and London, 2002).
Lehmann, Karin, 'Der Funktionswandel der öffentlichen Haushalte im Deutschen Reich vor dem Ersten Weltkrieg', in L. Zumpe (ed.), *Wirtschaft und Staat im Imperialismus* (Berlin, 1976).
Lerman, Katharina A., 'Wilhelmine Germany', in Mary Fulbrook (ed.), *German History since 1800* (London and New York, 1997).
Lindow, Erich, *Freiherr Marschall von Bieberstein als Botschafter in Konstantinopel 1897–1912* (Danzig, 1934).
Lorenz, Charlotte, 'Die Frauenfrage im Osmanischen Reiche mit Besonderer Berücksichtigung der Arbeitenden Klasse', *Die Welt des Islams* 6/3–4 (1918), pp. 72–214.
Luxemburg, Rosa, *The Crisis in the German Social-Democracy, The "Junius" Pamphlet* (New York, 1919).
Macfie, A.L., *The Eastern Question 1774–1923* (London and New York, 1989).
Maddison, Angus, 'Historical Statistics of the World Economy: 1–2008 AD', http://www.ggdc.net/MADDISON/oriindex.htm (accessed in March 2010)
Manchester, William, *The Arms of Krupp 1587–1968* (London, 1969).
Marriott, John Arthur Ransome, *The Eastern Question: An Historical Study in European Diplomacy* (Oxford, 1917).

McCarthy, Justin, *The Arab World, Turkey and the Balkans (1878–1914): A Handbook of Historical Statistic* (Boston, MA, 1982).
McGarity, James Madison, *Foreign Influence on the Ottoman Army*, Ph.D. Thesis: American University (Washington DC, 1968).
McMeekin, Sean, *The Berlin–Baghdad Express: The Ottoman Empire and Germany's Bid for World Power, 1898–1918* (London, 2010).
——— 'Benevolent Contempt: Bismarck's Ottoman Policy', in M. Hakan Yavuz and Peter Sluglett (eds), *War and Diplomacy, The Russo–Turkisch War of 1877– 1878 and the Treaty of Berlin* (Salt Lake City, 2011).
McMurray, S. Jonathan, *Distant Ties: Germany, the Ottoman Empire, and the Construction of the Baghdad Railway* (Westport, 2001).
Mejcher, Helmut, 'Die Bagdadbahn als Instrument deutschen wirtschaftlichen Einflusses im Osmanischen Reich', *Geschichte und Gesellschaft* 1 (1975), pp. 447–81.
Menne, Bernhard, *Blood and Steel: The Rise of the House of Krupp* (New York, 1938).
Milgrim, R. Michael, 'An Overlooked Problem in Turkish-Russian Relations: The 1878 War Indemnity', *International Journal of Middle East Studies* 9 (1978), pp. 519–37.
Mitchell, Nancy, *The Danger of Dreams: Germany and American Imperialism in Latin America* (Chapel Hill, NC, 1999).
Mombauer, Annika, *Helmuth von Moltke and the Origins of the First World War* (Cambridge and New York, 2001).
Morawitz, Charles, *Die Türkei im Spiegel ihrer Finanzen* (Berlin, 1903).
Mortimer, Joanne Stafford, 'Commercial Interests and German Diplomacy in the Agadir Crisis', *The Historical Journal* 10 (1967), pp. 440–56.
Moulton, H.G., 'Economic and Trade Position of Germany', in *Annals of the American Academy of Political and Social Science* 114 (1924), pp. 1–6.
Murphey, Rhoads, 'The Ottoman Attitude towards the Adoption of Western Technology: The Role of the *Efrenci* Technicians in Civil and Military Applications', *Collection Turcica* 3 (1983), pp. 287–98.
——— *Ottoman Warfare, 1500–1700* (London, 1999).
Murphy, William Scanlan, *Father of the Submarine* (London, 1987).
Murray, H. Robertson, *Krupp's and the International Armaments Ring: The Scandal of Modern Civilization* (London, 1915).
Mutluçağ, Hayri, 'Dost Bildiğimiz ve Ordumuzu Islah için İçimizde Bulundurduklarımızın Marifetleri', *Belgelerle Türk Tarihi Dergisi* 12 (1968), pp. 34–41.
Naumann, Friedrich, *Asia: Eine Orientreise über Athen, Konstantinopel, Baalbek, Nazareth, Jerusalem, Kairo, Neapel* (Berlin, 1913).
Nevinson, Henry Woodd, *Scenes in the Thirty Days War Between Greece and Turkey, 1897* (London, 1898).
Newbold, J. T. Walton, *How Europe Armed for War: 1871–1914* (London, 1916).
Nottelmann, Dirk, *Die Brandenburg-Klasse: Höhepunkt des deutschen Panzerschiffbaus* (Hamburg, Berlin, Bonn, 2002).
Nunn, M. Fredrick, 'Emil Körner and the Prussianization of the Chilean Army: Origins, Process, and Consequences, 1885–1920', *The Hispanic American Historical Review* 50/2 (1970), pp. 300–22.
——— 'Military Professionalism and Professional Militarism in Brazil, 1870–1970: Historical Perspectives and Political Implications', *Journal of Latin American Studies* 4/1 (1972), pp. 29–54.

BIBLIOGRAPHY 337

Okyar, Osman, 'Turco-British Relations in the Inter-War Period: Fethi Okyar's Mission to London', in W. Hale and A. İ. Bağış (eds), *Four Centuries of Turco-British Relations: Studies in Diplomatic Economic and Cultural Affairs* (Walkington, 1983), pp. 62–80.
Olson, Ludwig, *Mauser: Bolt Rifles* (Montezuma, IA, 1976).
Önsoy, Rifat, *Türk-Alman İktisadi Münasebetleri 1871–1914* (İstanbul, 1982).
Ortaylı, İlber, *İkinci Abdülhamit Döneminde Osmanlı İmparatorluğunda Alman Nüfuzu* (Ankara, 1981).
Ortenburg, Georg, *Waffen der Millionenheere 1871–1914* (Augsburg, 2005).
Osman, Nuri, *Abdulhamid-i Sâni ve Devr-i Saltanatı. Hayat-ı Husûsiye ve Siyâsiye* (İstanbul, 1327/1911).
Otte, G. Thomas and Constantine A. Pagedas (eds), *Personalities, War and Diplomacy, Essays in International History* (London and Portland, OR, 1997).
Owen, Richard, 'Military–Industrial Relations: Krupp and The Imperial Navy Office', in Richard J. Evans (ed.), *Society and Politics in Wilhelmine Germany*, pp. 71–90 (London, 1978).
Özçelik, Selahattin, *Donanma-yı Osmanî Muavenet-i Milliye Cemiyeti* (Ankara, 2000).
Özden, Gani, 'Osmanlı İmparatorluğu Silahlı Kuvetlerinin Harp Sanayii Tesisleri', *Askeri Tarih Bülteni* 12/22 (1987), pp. 59–69.
Özyüksel, Murat, *Osmanlı-Alman İlişkilerinin Gelişim Sürecinde Anadolu ve Bağdat Demiryolları* (İstanbul, 1988).
Pamuk, Şevket, *The Ottoman Empire and European Capitalism 1820–1913* (Cambridge, 1987).
——— (ed.), *Yüzyılda Osmanlı Dış Ticareti, Tarihi İstatistikler 1* (Ankara, 1995).
——— 'The Ottoman Economy in World War I', in S. Broadberry and M. Harrison (eds), *The Economics of World War I* (Cambridge, 2005), pp. 112–137.
Passant, Ernest James, *A Short History of Germany 1815–1945* (Cambridge, 1959).
Pears, Edwin, 'The Baghdad Railway', *The Contemporary Review* 94 (1908), pp. 570–91.
——— *Life of Abdul Hamid* (London, 1917).
Peters, Carl, *Zur Weltpolitik* (Berlin, 1912).
Pflanze, Otto, *Bismarck and the Development of Germany* (Princeton, 1990).
——— *Bismarck: Der Reichsgründer* (München, 1998).
Plischke, Elmer, *Summit Diplomacy; Personal Diplomacy of the President of the United States* (Westport, Conn. 1974).
Pohl, Manfred, *Philipp Holzmann: Geschichte eines Bauunternehmens 1849–1999* (München, 1999).
Pollard, Sidney and Colin Holmes, *Industrial Power and National Rivalry 1870–1914* (London, 1972).
Quataert, Donald, 'Limited Revolution: The Impact of the Anatolian Railway on Turkish Transportation and the Provisioning of Istanbul, 1890–1908', *The Business History Review* 51/2 (1977), pp. 139–60.
——— 'The Economic Climate of the "Young Turk Revolution" in 1908', *Journal of Modern History* 51/3 (1979), pp. 1147–61.
Rathmann, Lothar, *Berlin–Bagdad, Die imperialistische Nahostpolitik des kaiserlichen Deutschland* (Berlin, 1962).
Redhouse, James William, *Turkish/Ottoman-English Dictionary* (first published in 1890) (İstanbul, 1999).

Reed, James Eldin, 'American Foreign Policy, The Politics of Missions and Josiah Strong 1890–1900', *Church History* 41 (1972), pp. 230–45.
Richter, Jan Stefan, *Die Orientreise Kaiser Wilhelms II. 1898. Eine Studie zur deutschen Außenpolitik an der Wende zum 20. Jahrhundert* (Hamburg, 1997).
Riesser, Jacob, *The German Great Banks and Their Concentration in Connection with the Economic Development of Germany* (Washington, D.C., 1911).
Ripley, Z. William, 'The Commercial Policy of Europe', *Political Science Quarterly* 7 (1982), pp. 633–55.
Rippy, J. Fred, 'German Investments in Guatemala', *The Journal of Business of the University of Chicago* 20/4 (1947), pp. 212–9.
——— 'German Investments in Argentina', *The Journal of Business of the University of Chicago* 21/1 (1948), pp. 50–4.
Robolsky, Hermann, *Drei Jahre auf dem Throne 1888–1891* (Leipzig, 1891).
Röhl, C.G. John, *Wilhelm II: the Kaiser's Personal Monarchy 1888–1900* (London, 2004).
Rohrbach, Paul, *German World Policies*, translated by E.v. Mach (New York, 1915).
Rose, John Holland, *The Origins of the War* (Cambridge, 1915).
Şakir, Ziya, *Tanzimat Devrinden Sonra Osmanlı Nizam Ordusu Tarihi* (İstanbul, 1957).
Sampson, Anthony, *The Arms Bazaar in the Nineties: From Krupp to Saddam* (London, 1991).
Sater, William, F. and H. Holger Herwig, *The Grand Illusion: The Prussianization of the Chilean Army* (Lincoln, 1999).
Schaefer, Jürgen, *Deutsche Militärhilfe an Südamerika: Militär- und Rüstungsinteressen in Argentinien, Bolivien, Chile vor 1914* (Düsseldorf, 1974).
Scherer, Friedrich, *Adler und Halbmond: Bismarck und der Orient 1878–1890* (Paderborn, 2001).
Schiff, Warren, 'German Military Penetration into Mexico during the Late Díaz Period', *The Hispanic American Historical Review* 39/4 (1959), pp. 568–79.
——— 'The Germans in Mexican Trade and Industry during the Díaz Period', *The Americas* 23/3 (1967), pp. 279–96.
——— 'The Influence of the German Armed Forces and War Industry on Argentina, 1880–1914', *The Hispanic American Historical Review*, 52/3 (1972), pp. 436–55.
Schmidt-Richberg, Wigand, 'Die Regierungszeit Wilhelms II', in Militärgeschichtliches Forschungsamt (ed.), *Handbuch zur deutschen Militärgeschichte 1648–1939: Von der Entlassung Bismarcks bis zum Ende des Ersten Weltkrieges (1890–1918)* (Frankfurt am Main, 1968).
Schölch, Alexander, 'Wirtschaftliche Durchdringung und politische Kontrolle durch die europäischen Mächte im Osmanischen Reich' (Konstantinopel, Kairo, Tunis), *Geschichte und Gesellschaft*, 1/4 (1975), pp. 404–46.
Schöllgen, Gregor, *Das Zeitalter des Imperialismus* (München, 1986).
——— *Imperialismus und Gleichgewicht, Deutschland, England und die orientalische Frage 1871–1914* (München, 2000).
Scott, John Dick, *Vickers: A History* (London, 1962).
Seel, Wolfgang, 'Mauser-Gewehre unter dem Halbmond, Türkenmauser', *Deutsche Waffenjournal* 1 (1981a), pp. 796–803.
——— 'Mauser-Gewehre unter dem Halbmond, Türkenmauser', *Deutsche Waffenjournal* 2 (1981b), pp. 976–81.

―――― 'Mauser-Gewehre unter dem Halbmond, Türkenmauser', *Deutsche Waffenjournal* 3 (1981c), pp. 1160–4.
―――― 'Mauser-Gewehre unter dem Halbmond, Türkenmauser', *Deutsche Waffenjournal* 5 (1981d), pp. 1418–23.
―――― 'Mauser-Gewehre unter dem Halbmond, Türkenmauser', *Deutsche Waffenjournal* 7 (1981e), pp. 1722–27.
―――― *Mauser: Von der Waffenschmiede zum Weltunternehmen* (Zürich, 1986).
―――― 'Mauser-Puzzle', *Deutsche Waffenjournal* 1 (1993), pp. 42–7.
Seymour, Charles, *The Diplomatic Background of the War 1870–1914* (New Haven, 1916).
Shaw, J. Stanford, 'The Origins of Ottoman Military Reform: The Nizam-ı Cedid Army of Sultan Selim III', *Journal of Modern History* 37 (1965), pp. 291–305.
―――― and K. Shaw Ezel, *History of the Ottoman Empire and Modern Turkey: Reform, Revolution and Republic Vol. 2: The Rise of Modern Turkey 1808–1975*, (Cambridge, 1977).
Showalter, E. Dennis, *Railroads and Rifles: Soldiers, Technology, and the Unification of Germany* (Hamden, 1975).
Smith, D. Woodruff, 'Friedrich Ratzel and the Origins of Lebensraum', *German Studies Review* 3 (1980), pp. 51–68.
―――― *The Ideological Origins of Nazi Imperialism* (New York, 1986).
Smith, L. Colin, *The Embassy of Sir William White at Constantinople 1886–1891* (Oxford, 1957).
Smith, Munroe, 'Military Strategy versus Diplomacy', *Political Science Quarterly* 30 (1915), pp. 37–81.
Soy, H. Bayram, *Almanya'nın Osmanlı Devleti Üzerinde İngiltere ile Nüfuz Mücadelesi 1890–1914* (Ankara, 2004).
Speed, J. S. Walter, and Reiner Herrmann, *Mauser Original Oberndorf Sporting Rifles* (Cobourg, 1997).
Stern, Fritz, *Gold and Iron: Bismarck, Bleichröder and the Building of the German Empire* (London, 1980).
Swanson, W. Glen, 'War, Technology, and Society in the Ottoman Empire from the reign of Abdulhamid II to 1913: Mahmud Şevket and the German Military Mission', in V. J. Parry and M. E. Yapp (eds), *War and Technology in the Middle East*, pp. 367–85 (London, (1975).
Trebilcock, Clive, 'Spin-Off in British Economic History: Armaments and Industry, 1760–1914', *The Economic History Review* 22/3 (1969), pp. 474–90.
―――― 'Legends of the British Armament Industry 1890–1914: A Revision', *Journal of Contemporary History* 5/4 (1970), pp. 3–19.
Trumpener, Ulrich, 'Germany and the End of the Ottoman Empire', in M. Kent (ed.), *The Great Powers and the End of the Ottoman Empire* (Oxford and New York, 1996).
Tschoegl, E. Adrian, 'Financial Integration, Disintegration and Emerging Reintegration in the Eastern Mediterranean, c.1850 to the Present', *Financial Markets, Institutions & Instruments* 13 (2004), pp. 245–85.
Tuğay, Asaf, *İbret: Abdülhamid'e verilen Jurnaller ve Jurnalciler* (İstanbul, 1962).
―――― *Saray Dedikoduları ve Bazı Marûzât* (İstanbul, 1963).
Turfan, Naim M., *Rise of the Young Turks: Politics, the Military and Ottoman Collapse* (London, 2000).

Türk, Fahri, *Die deutsche Rüstungsindustrie in ihren Türkeigeschäften zwischen 1871 und 1914: Die Firma Krupp, die Waffenfabrik Mauser und die Deutschen Waffen- und Munitionsfabriken* (Berlin, 2006).

Ulus, İbrahim, 'Colmar Freiherr Von der Goltz'un Biyografisi', *Askeri Tarih Bülteni* 11/21 (1986), pp. 73–82.

Upton-Ward, Judith Mary Ayse, *European Attitudes Towards the Ottoman Empire a Case Study Sultan Abdülaziz's Visit to Europe in 1867*, Ph.D. Thesis: University of Birmingham (Birmingham, 1999).

Uyar, Mesut and J. Edward Erickson, *A Military History of the Ottomans: from Osman to Atatürk* (Santa Barbara, 2009).

Vagts, Alfred, 'Bismarck's Fortune', *Central European History* 1 (1968), pp. 203–32.

Wallace, William Kay, *The Trend of History: Origins of Twentieth Century Problems* (New York, 1922).

Wallach, Jahuda Luther, 'Bismarck and the "Eastern Question"–A Re-Assessment', in *Germany and the Middle East 1835–1939* (Tel Aviv, 1975), pp. 23–30.

——— *Anatomie einer Militärhilfe. Die preußisch-deutschen Militärmissionen in der Türkei 1835–1919* (Düsseldorf, 1976).

——— *Bir Askeri Yardımın Anatomisi*, translated by Fahri Çeliker (Ankara, 1985).

Walter, Isaacson, *Kissinger: A Biography* (New York, 2005).

Wehler, Hans Ulrich, 'Bismarck's Imperialism 1862–1890', *Past and Present* 48 (1970), pp. 119–55.

——— *The German Empire 1871–1918*, translated by K. Traynor (Oxford, 1991).

Wells, Herbert George, *The War That Will End War* (New York, 1914).

Werner, Max, *The Military Strength of the Powers*, translated by Edward Fitzgerald (London, 1939).

Willis, F. Edward, *Prince Lichnowsky, Ambassador of Peace: A Study of Prewar Diplomacy 1912–1914* (Berkeley and Los Angeles, 1942).

Windelband, Wolfgang, *Bismarck und die Europäischen Großmächte 1879–1885* (Essen, 1942).

Wolf, B. John, *The Diplomatic History of the Baghdad Railroad* (New York, 1973).

Wolf, Hellmut, *Die wirtschaftliche Entwicklung der Stadt Oberndorf a. Neckar mit besonderer Berücksichtigung der Mauserwerke und der Schwarzwälder Boten* (Tübingen, 1933).

Woods, H. Charles, 'The Baghdad Railway and Its Tributaries', *The Geographical Journal* 50/1 (1917), pp. 32–56.

Yapp, M.E., 'The Modernisation of Middle Eastern Armies in the Nineteenth Century: A Comparative View', in V. J. Parry and M. E. Yapp (eds), *War and Technology in the Middle East* (London, 1975).

Yasamee, F. A. K., 'Abdulhamid II and the Ottoman Defence Problem', *Diplomacy and Statecraft* 4/1 (1993), pp. 20–36.

——— 'Colmar Freiherr von der Goltz and the Rebirth of the Ottoman Empire', *Diplomacy and Statecraft* 9/2 (1998), pp. 91–128.

——— *Ottoman Diplomacy: Abdulhamid II and the Great Powers, 1878–1888* (İstanbul, 1996).

——— 'Colmar Freiherr Von der Goltz and the Boer War,' in Keith M. Wilson (ed.), *The International Impact of the Boer War* (London, 2001).

Yazbak, Mahmoud, 'Templars as Proto-Zionists? The "German Colony" in Late Ottoman Haifa', *Journal of Palestine Studies* 28 (1999), pp. 40–54.

Yorulmaz, Naci, 'Krupps weitreichende Kanonen. Bewertung der Quellen im Osmanischen Archiv zu den Aktivitäten der Fa. Krupp im Osmanischen Reich', in Claus Schönig, Ramazan Çalik, and H. Bayraktar (eds), *Türkisch-Deutsche Beziehungen: Perspektiven aus Vergangenheit und Gegenwart* (Berlin, 2012).

Zeidner, F. Robert, 'Britain and the Launching of the Armenian Question', *International Journal of Middle East Studies* 7/4 (1976), pp. 465–83.

Zimmermann, Moshe, 'A Road Not Taken–Friedrich Naumann's Attempt at a Modern German Nationalism', *Journal of Contemporary History*, 17/4 (1982), pp. 689–708.

Zucker, D. Richard, 'Germany's Industrial Position', *Ind. Eng. Chem.* 11 (1919), pp. 777–80.

Zürcher, Erik-Jan, 'The Ottoman Conscription System in Theory and Practise 1844–1918', *International Review of Social History* 43/3 (1998), pp. 437–49.

INDEX

Abdülaziz (Sultan), 27, 100, 116, 183, 195
Abdülhamid II (Sultan), 2–5, 7–9, 13, 17, 18, 20, 21, 23–5, 36, 41, 44, 54, 59, 75, 76, 80–2, 86, 87, 107, 108, 117, 124, 125, 136–8, 149, 150, 154, 164, 165, 168, 170, 174, 176, 178, 180, 182–6, 189–92, 194–6, 204, 205, 209, 213, 217, 219, 224, 230, 232, 234–7, 240, 241, 244, 248–50, 253, 256, 259, 260
Abdülmecid I (Sultan), 195, 303
Action Army (*Hareket Ordusu*), 232
Ahmed İzzet Pasha, 210
Ahmed Rıfat Bey, 208
Ahmed Tevfik Pasha, 32, 40, 115, 168–73
Ali Nizami Pasha, 5, 20, 23, 257
Ali Saib Pasha, 105, 106, 114, 118, 119, 124, 211, 226
Alldeutsche Blätter, 144, 159, 181
Alpagot (Warship), 240
Anatolian Railways, 5, 38, 59–62, 149, 152–5
Angell, James B., 46, 134, 145, 187
Ankara (City), 59–61, 150
Ankara (Warship), 240
Ansaldo, 175, 240

Argentina, 224
Armenian Question, 6, 14, 137, 138, 187, 191
Armstrong Company, 205, 238, 239
Armstrong Guns, 100, 102, 204, 205
Âsâr-ı Tevfik (Warship), 101, 174–6, 204, 205
Asia Minor, 17, 59, 147, 149, 155, 181
Atatürk (Kemal, Mustafa), 76, 77
Austria–Hungary, 18, 40, 67, 102, 103, 157, 178, 180, 181, 195, 203, 231, 245
Avnillah (Warship), 101, 240
Azarian, 112, 217

Baghdad, 57, 139, 149, 150, 155, 181
Baghdad Railway, 10, 12, 38, 87, 92, 95, 134, 138, 139, 143, 148–50, 152, 153, 155, 169, 171, 206, 213, 252
Baksheesh (*see also* Bribery and Corruption), 35, 109, 127, 205, 206, 214
Balance of Power, 27, 182, 231
Balkan Cities, 230, 232
Balkan States, 180, 200, 201, 240–2, 250
Balkan Wars, 129, 203, 240, 241
Bankhaus von der Heydt & Co., 156

INDEX

Banque Ottomane, 39
Baruthâne-i 'Amire (Imperial Powder Factory), 97
Bayard, Thomas F., 35
Berlin, 5, 11, 20, 21, 25, 27, 29, 30, 36, 37, 41, 47, 48, 50, 53, 56, 59, 66, 67, 73, 81, 83, 98, 101–3, 110, 119, 127, 128, 131, 135, 136, 143, 154, 167, 172, 184, 187, 188, 197, 211, 223, 225, 226, 241, 248, 261
Bethlehem, 144
Bieberstein, Adolf Marschall von (Marschall), 3, 16, 84, 154, 155, 158, 162, 177, 197, 207, 214, 218, 233, 235, 236
Birmingham, 35
Bismarck, Otto von, 1–6, 8, 10, 16–38, 40–7, 55–9, 74–6, 86, 87, 90, 95, 103, 112, 113, 115, 120, 133, 136, 162, 231, 249, 250, 254, 256, 257, 259
Black Sea, 57, 250
Bleichröder, Gerson von Bleichröder, 42, 43, 112, 171
Boer War, 132
Bolayır, Ali Ekrem, 20
Bosnia-Herzegovina 1878, 178, 180
Brazil, 37
Bribery (*see also* Corruption and Baksheesh), 3, 35, 199, 206, 220
Britain (*see* Great Britain)
British Government, 21, 154, 216, 242, 243
British Influence, 30, 136, 141, 167, 194
British Interest, 58, 136, 154, 157, 167, 170, 197, 198
Browning Pistol, 237
Bulgaria, 25, 180, 201–3, 241, 242, 250
Bülow, Prens Bernhard von, 45, 71, 135, 136, 138, 140, 142, 143, 148, 232

Cambon, Pierre Paul, 168
Canet System (*see also* Schneider-Le Creusot), 167, 212, 226
Caprivi, Chancellor, 47
Cavid, Bey, 243
Chile, 86
China, 3
Church of the Redeemer (Erlöserkirche), 58
Committee of Union and Progress (CUP), 181, 232, 233
Constantine, Crown Prince, 54
Constitution of 1876, 5, 230, 231, 233
Corrupt (*see* Corruption)
Corruption (*see also* Bribery and Baksheesh), 3, 80, 113, 205, 206, 214, 218, 236, 259
Cramp Shipbuilding, 189, 190
Crete Question, 6, 137, 138
Cyprus, 178, 180

Damascus, 6, 7, 138, 139, 141, 142, 156
Danube Steam Shipping Company (Donau-Dampfschiffahrts-Gesellschaft), 201
Dardanelles, 59, 105, 108
Darmstaedter Bank, 157
Dar-ül 'aceze (Poorhouse), 224
Dethronement of the Sultan, 5, 7, 235
Deutsche Bank, 5, 39, 59, 62, 66, 112, 143, 150, 152, 153, 157
Deutsche Levante Linie, 62
Deutsche Metallpatronenfabrik Lorenz of Karlsruhe (*see* Lorenz Company)
Deutsche Orient Bank, 157
Deutsche Palästina und Orient Gesellschaft, 156
Deutsche Vereinsbank, 59
Deutsche Waffen-und Munitionsfabrik, 243
Dingler, Otto, 100, 101, 104
Disconto Gesellschaft, 157
Donanma-yı Osmanî Muavenet-I Millîye Cemiyeti, 244

Dormition La Dormition de la Sainte Vierge, 135–7
Drang nach Osten, 142
Duttenhofer, Carl, 32, 33
Duttenhofer, Max, 32, 33, 118–20

East Rumelia (*see* Eastern Rumelia)
Eastern Question, 5, 16, 17, 256
Eastern Rumelia, 40, 41, 103, 180
Egypt, 2, 3, 22, 26, 95, 178, 180, 191
Ehrhardt, Heinrich, 162, 238
Einstein, Lewis D., 240
Ellis, Ashmead-Bartlett, 158, 159
Encrypted Codes, 112
England (*see also* Great Britain), 3, 43, 164, 184, 203, 230, 232
Eskişehir, 60
Essen, 11, 30, 102, 108, 161, 162, 168, 173, 174, 214, 225, 226, 228, 259

Fairfax, L. Cartwright, 231
Falkner, J. M., 238
Ferdinand from Bulgaria, Prince, 40
Ferguson Rifle, 195
First Balkan War, 203, 240, 241
First World War (*see* World War I)
Foreign Debt/Loan, 4, 39, 40, 42, 66, 67, 81, 117, 129, 157, 178, 189, 192, 195, 197, 202, 213, 242, 243
France, 2, 3, 25, 26, 30, 38, 41, 49, 50, 51, 67, 90, 136, 149, 151, 157, 159, 164, 167–9, 171, 172, 178, 180, 181, 184, 185, 191, 194, 195, 197, 203, 204, 216, 226–8, 230, 233, 238, 242, 243, 253
Franco–Prussian War (1870–1), 2, 26, 27, 74, 180, 194, 203
Frankfurt am Main, 110, 155
Frederick III, Crown Prince, 18
French Government, 21, 154, 216, 242, 243
French Influence, 30, 136, 141, 167, 194

French Interest, 58, 136, 154, 157, 167, 170, 197, 198

Gazi Ahmed Muhtar Pasha, 80, 100, 102
Gazi Osman Pasha, 77, 179
German Armament Firms (GAFs), 1–3, 6–9, 12, 38, 40, 66, 68, 70, 73–5, 87–9, 95, 98, 101, 107, 120, 132, 164, 166, 172, 173, 176, 191, 196, 197, 200, 206, 212, 214, 217, 220, 224, 231, 252–7, 259
German Arms and Munitions Factories (*Deutsche Waffen-und Munitionsfabriken*- DWM), 165
German Arms Companies (*see also* German Armament Firms), 4, 8, 11, 25, 28–30, 32, 37, 40, 41, 43, 62, 64, 69, 71, 74, 75, 81, 84, 90, 94, 112, 121, 160, 165, 171, 174, 176, 180, 182, 192, 194, 198, 199, 204, 207, 209, 210, 224, 234, 238, 242, 255–7, 260
German Banks, 4, 39, 40, 42, 156, 157, 184, 185, 244, 253
German Diplomacy, 4, 60, 143, 175
German Dreadnought Programme, 245
German Expansionism, 3, 5–8, 13, 24, 26, 28, 29, 43, 45, 46, 48–50, 52–4, 56, 67, 69, 73, 143, 145, 146, 148, 153, 160, 162, 166, 169, 184, 241, 249, 254–7, 260, 261
German Financiers, 45, 68, 143, 152, 154, 253, 257
German Foreign Office, 12, 13, 36, 37, 39, 42, 53, 69, 78, 85, 87, 88, 103, 112, 113, 145, 153, 168, 171, 196, 209, 242, 255
German Government, 3, 4, 19, 20, 36, 38, 53, 71, 86, 89, 96, 120, 136, 143, 144, 153, 176, 198, 232, 248, 254, 255

INDEX

German Influence, 16, 42, 46, 58, 67, 160, 198, 200, 208–10, 232, 233, 235, 242, 260
German Interests, 23, 43, 92, 132, 136, 170, 181, 211, 219, 220, 225, 253, 260
German Method (Deutsche Methode)
German strategy, 3, 7, 145, 146, 152, 212, 225, 232
German Military Advisers (GMAs), 2, 4–12, 17–19, 24–6, 38, 40, 56, 67–9, 71, 73–5, 81, 86, 95, 107, 180, 199, 200, 210, 214, 224, 232, 242, 249, 255–9
German Military Diplomacy, 2, 6, 74, 75
German Reichsbank, 185
German Style of War Business, 13, 112
Germania-Work, 39, 40, 64, 66, 108, 109, 174–6, 191, 201
Germanism, 134
German–Palestine Bank, 156
Germany, 1–3, 5, 9, 15–19, 24, 25, 27, 31, 36, 37, 40, 43, 45, 47, 48, 49–53, 57, 59, 62, 63, 65–7, 71, 74, 81, 82, 86, 102, 103, 109, 120, 136, 138, 142, 144–6, 149, 155–7, 159, 161, 162, 164, 165, 169, 172, 174, 175, 177, 181–5, 194, 195, 197, 198, 204, 207–10, 216, 219, 220, 225, 228, 231–4, 243–5, 247–50, 252, 253, 256, 259, 260, 261
Golden Horn, 91, 108, 220, 248
Goltz Pasha, Colmar Freiherr von der, 2, 4, 8, 10, 12, 13, 24, 34, 37, 43, 65, 75, 76, 82–96, 100, 103, 105, 107–10, 112–16, 119–24, 126, 131, 132, 150, 151, 166, 167, 171, 183, 191, 193, 209–13, 215, 217–19, 226, 229, 235, 236, 250, 254–6, 258
Great Britain (see also England), 25, 35, 51, 67, 149, 157, 159, 178, 180, 233, 248, 253

Greco–Turkish War of 1897, 129, 191
Greece, 55, 108, 191, 200, 240
Greek, 184, 201
Grey, Edward, 162, 238, 244
Gwinner, Arthur von Gwinner, 152, 205, 206

Haifa, 6, 139, 140, 156
Halil Ibrahim Pasha (1862–1917) (see also Halil Pasha), 204, 205, 244
Halil Rıfat Pasha, 208
Hamidian Regime, 213, 234
Hamidiye (Warship), 240
Hamidiye Cavalry, 130
Hannoversche Maschienenbau-Actien Gesellschaft, 62
Harpoot School, 188
Harput, 187
Hasan Pasha, 108
Hatzfeld, Graf von, 138, 183
Hay, John, 187
Haydarpaşa, 59, 149, 154, 155
Henry-Martini (see Martini-Henry)
Hobe Pasha, 8, 76, 78, 79, 112
Hohenlohe, Prince von, 18–20, 25, 133, 134, 197
Hohenlohe-Schillingsfürst, Prince of (see Prince Hohenlohe)
Holzmann, Philipp, 155
Horn, Paul, 196
House of Hohenzollern, 160
House of Krupp, 171, 174
Howaldtswerke, A.G., 109
Huber Brothers, 13, 97, 110–13, 123, 124, 126–8, 132, 166, 187, 214, 234, 237, 238, 242, 258
Huber, August, 112, 124, 126, 187, 242, 258
Huber, Joseph, 13

İbrahim Hakkı Pasha, 244
India, 3
Industrial Espionage, 3, 8, 121
Ismail Kemal Bey, 16, 17, 18

İstanbul, 3, 6, 9, 12, 14, 19, 21, 24, 33,
34, 36, 37, 39, 40, 45, 46, 48, 53,
54, 56–9, 62–4, 67, 76, 80, 81,
84–6, 90, 91, 95–8, 100, 101,
103, 104, 110–19, 122, 123, 125,
126, 129, 133, 134, 136, 137,
139, 145, 147, 150, 151, 154,
156, 158, 163, 164, 168, 171,
174, 175, 179, 183–5, 187, 195,
197, 198, 203, 206, 207, 209,
210, 213, 214, 216, 217, 223,
224, 231–3, 236–8, 240, 242,
253, 255, 257, 258
Italy, 50, 67, 157, 174, 175, 181, 240, 250
İzzet, Arap (İzzet Bey), 166, 213, 214

Jäckh, Ernst, 241, 242
Jaffa, 6, 139, 140, 156
Jerusalem, 6, 58, 134–6, 139–41, 145, 151, 156

Kähler Pasha, 43, 76, 77–80, 82–4, 101
Kaiser, The (*see also* Wilhelm II), 1, 5–7, 9, 13, 20, 43–8, 54–9, 62, 63, 67, 85, 90, 133–48, 150, 151, 153, 154, 156, 158, 160–76, 183, 184, 219, 231, 233, 235, 258, 259
Kálnoky, Count Gustav, 91
Kamphövener Pasha, 8, 34, 76–9, 113–15, 118, 132
Karagöz, 246
Kaulla, Alfred von, 37, 111, 112, 118
Kiderlen-Wächter, Alfred von, 84, 88, 167, 171, 209, 232
Kiel, 40, 64, 174, 175, 191
King, Pendleton, 35, 58, 150, 196
Kırkağaç Fişenkhânesi (Cartridge Factory), 97
Köln–Rottweiler powder, 32, 33, 118–21, 241, 243
Konya, 60
Körner, Emil, 86

Krupp Company, 6, 29–31, 63, 68, 71, 76, 84, 99–102, 104–9, 120, 131, 161–4, 166–9, 171, 174–6, 187, 191, 197, 201, 202, 204, 206, 212, 214, 215, 218, 219, 224, 225, 228, 234, 235, 237–40, 243, 253
Krupp Family, 3, 160–3, 165, 176, 225, 259
Krupp Guns, 2, 8, 95, 97, 100, 102, 104, 105, 132, 166, 172, 173, 179, 180, 192, 203–5, 210, 212, 241, 242, 253
Krupp, Alfred, 30, 31, 107, 160, 162, 163, 225, 253
Krupp, F. A. (*see* Krupp, Friedrich Alfred)
Krupp, Friedrich Alfred, 161, 162, 167–9, 171, 174, 175, 218, 219, 225, 228, 254, 259
Krupp-Germania (*see* Germania-Work)
Kurfürst Friedrich Wilhelm (*see* Barbaros Hayreddin-Warship), 245

Latin America, 224
Lebensinteresse, 162, 202
Lebensraum, 47, 51
Loewe Company, Ludwig Loewe & Co., 31, 37, 64, 111, 113, 116, 120, 121, 125
Loewe, Isidor, 37, 110–12, 118, 119, 122
Loewe, Ludwig, 37, 110, 119
London, 11–13, 57, 111, 198, 232
Lorenz Company of Karlsruhe, 117–19, 121
Lorenz, Wilhelm, 117–19
Lowther, Gerald, 96, 163, 233, 234, 244, 245
Luxemburg, Rosa, 10

Maffei, J. A., 62
Mahmud II (Sultan), 92, 186
Mahmud Muhtar Pasha, 220, 234, 244

INDEX

Mahmud Şevket Pasha (Colonel Mahmud Bey), 97, 109, 114–16, 125–9, 205, 209–12, 221, 234, 236, 238, 244, 248
Mannlicher Rifles, 113, 114, 116, 124, 128, 165, 211
Maraş, 187
Martini-Henry, 34, 98, 110, 113, 129, 215
Martini-Peabody (*see* Peabody-Martini)
Maschienenfabrik Esslingen, 62
Mauser Rifle Company, 2, 6, 8, 12, 13, 31–5, 38–40, 71, 95, 111, 113, 114, 116, 117, 122, 123, 125, 129, 131, 132, 204, 211, 214, 217, 218, 220, 221, 224, 258, 260
Mauser Rifles, 8, 13, 32, 34, 35, 65, 71, 94, 113, 115, 116, 120, 123, 124, 128–132, 193, 195, 210, 211, 214, 216, 221, 241
Mauser, Paul, 6, 13, 37, 71, 88, 97, 109–12, 114, 116–19, 121–4, 126–9, 131, 133, 196, 218, 220, 221, 223, 237, 254, 258, 259
Mauthner, Max, 165
Mediterranean, 57, 90
Mehmed Ferid Pasha, 181
Mehmed Reşad (Sultan Mehmed V.), 236, 247
Menshausen, Carl, 41, 76, 85, 104, 112, 120, 167, 168, 171, 217–20, 226
Merzifon, 187
Mesopotamia, 3
Mesudiye (Warship), 101, 191
Mexico, 224
Mezahib-i Sa'ire Efradı, 257
Midilli (Warship), 249
Military Diplomacy, 2, 4, 6, 74, 75
Military Mission, 8, 19, 25, 34, 40, 64, 74, 75, 77, 78, 81–3, 85, 86, 97, 100, 101, 107, 110, 133, 184, 200, 207, 214, 221, 236, 242, 255, 257

Moltke, Helmuth von, 86
Montenegro, 240

Naumann, Friedrich, 1, 48, 49, 51, 135, 144, 145
Norddeutscher, Lyod, 248

Oberndorf, 13, 31, 72, 111, 112, 118, 124, 126, 127, 129, 214, 220–5, 237, 259
Orientreise, Kaiser Wilhelm II's second, 5–7, 10, 42, 45, 48, 54, 58, 133–5, 139, 140, 142–8, 151, 154, 156, 160, 164, 173–5
Osman Nizami Pasha, 177, 207, 218
Ottoman Bureaucrats, 6, 9, 39, 95, 187, 203
Ottoman Converted Debt, 66, 67, 129, 157
Ottoman Public Debt Administration, 42

Paris, 195, 197, 233, 243
Peabody-Martini, 110, 179
Peaceful Penetration, 7, 8, 17, 23, 26, 38, 39, 42, 44, 53, 56, 58, 71, 74, 86, 95, 142, 151, 160, 209, 255, 256
Persian Gulf, 139, 149–51, 155, 184
Personal Trust, 9, 195, 196, 198
Pertev Pasha (Demirhan), 88, 132
Peters, Carl, 26, 46, 143
Pomeranian Grenadier, 5, 16, 17, 156, 256
Providence Tool Company, 110

Radolin, Prince von, 131
Radowitz, Josef Maria von, 81, 84–6, 104, 117, 120, 168, 185, 218, 219
Ragıb Bey, 13, 87, 89, 115, 122, 217–20
Ratzel, Friedrich, 47

Reşid Bey, 5, 18, 20–22, 36, 56, 67, 250, 257
Rheinische Metallwaaren-und Maschinenfabrik of Heinrich Ehrhardt, 162, 238
Ristow Pasha, 8, 76, 78, 79
Rıza Pasha, Serasker, 241
Rumania, 200
Russia, 2, 17, 20–22, 28, 40, 41, 56, 57, 81, 87, 90, 91, 102, 103, 107, 108, 143, 149, 151, 173, 174, 178–81, 200, 245, 247, 249, 250

Sabit Pasha, 225, 226, 228
Said Pasha, 77
Şakir Pasha, 103, 118, 126, 139, 224
Salonika, 158, 185, 235, 236
Sanders, Liman von, 242
Schellendorf, Prussian Minister of War, 115, 120
Schichau, 64, 66, 109, 170, 175
Schneider-Le Creusot, 27, 162, 197, 202, 239, 241
Schoen (Staatssekretär des Auswärtigen Amts), 163
Second Balkan War, 241
Serbia, 93, 128
Sevastopol, 249
Sherman, John, 193
Siemens, Georg von, 37, 152
'Sick Man', The, 181, 193
SMS Breslau (*see* Midilli)
SMS Goeben (*see* Yavuz)
Snider, 98, 110, 129, 215, 216
Spain, 86, 203
Sublime Port, 4, 36, 40, 41, 78, 84, 89, 100, 101, 107, 118, 140, 159, 169, 198, 202, 203
Sultan, The (*see also* Abdülhamid II), 2, 5, 7–9, 12, 17, 22, 24, 46, 54, 57–60, 62, 73, 79, 80, 82, 84, 85, 89, 91–3, 101–3, 105, 107, 108, 116, 117, 122–6, 128, 132, 134, 135, 140, 142, 144, 146, 150–4,
156, 158, 159, 164–74, 180, 182–92, 194–200, 204, 205, 207, 209, 212–20, 226, 230–2, 235, 247, 250, 256–9
Süreyya Pasha, 107, 115, 215–17
Surtees, Colonel, 163, 164, 238
Syria, 34

Tahsin Pasha, 76, 185, 186, 190
Talat Bey (Pasha), 230, 243
Terrell, Alexander W., 193, 195
Therapia, 58
Thomas Cook and Son, 133, 291
Tomb of Saladin, 141, 295
Tophâne-i 'Âmire Nezâreti (Imperial Gun Factory), 97
Treaty of Berlin, 1
Triple Alliance, 18, 56, 57, 245
Tüfenkhâne-i 'Âmire (Imperial Small Arms Factory), 97
Tunis, 22, 157, 178, 180
Turgut Reis (Warship), 245
Türkenbau, 221, 222
Turkey, 17, 20, 55, 134, 135, 159, 164, 177, 193, 206, 208, 220, 232, 233, 242, 250, 259
Turkification, 4

United States of America, 36, 188, 191, 216

Vickers, Sons & Maxim Limited, 27, 163
Vulcan, 109, 170, 175

Waffenbrüderschaft (Brothers in Arms), 25, 252
Waldersee, Count Alfred von, 136, 210
Wangenheim, 209, 233, 242
Washington, D.C., 13, 35, 187
Weißenburg (*see* Turgut Reis)
Weltmacht (World Power), 1, 28, 46, 53, 181, 250
Weltmarkt, 49, 50, 162

INDEX

White, William, 34–6, 56, 57, 136, 150, 213, 217, 218
Wilhelm I, Kaiser, 20, 30, 31, 86, 89, 90, 103, 120, 160, 163
Wilhelm II (*see also* Kaiser, The), 1–3, 5, 6, 10, 16, 24, 26, 28, 29, 42–9, 53, 54, 56, 58, 71, 82, 88, 133, 134–8, 141, 142, 144, 146, 147, 150–3, 160–3, 166, 167, 169, 170, 172–5, 208, 236, 246, 254–6, 259
Winchester (Rifles), 35, 98, 110, 179, 215, 216
World Reich, 47
World War I, 1, 4, 8, 25, 84, 137, 212, 231, 232, 243, 252, 261

Württembergische Vereinsbank, 59, 111

Yavuz (Warship), 249
Yıldız Kiosk (*see* Yıldız Palace)
Yıldız Palace, 8, 87, 93, 114, 115, 120, 125, 132, 135, 139, 150, 159, 171, 186, 187, 195, 202, 212, 213, 217–19, 231, 235
Young Turk Revolution, 5, 7, 181, 198, 199, 205, 209, 234, 235
Young Turks, 232–5, 238, 240, 243, 244, 248, 250, 251

Zeytinburnu Fabrikâyi Humâyun (Imperial Foundry), 97

www.ingramcontent.com/pod-product-compliance
Lightning Source LLC
Chambersburg PA
CBHW070010010526
44117CB00011B/1497